Walk in the Light Series

The Messiah

A Scriptural and Historical Examination
of the Purpose and Identity
of the Messiah

Todd D. Bennett

Shema Yisrael Publications, LLC

The Messiah
A Scriptural and Historical Examination of the Purpose and
Identity of the Messiah

First printing 2010
Second printing 2012

For information write:
Shema Yisrael Publications, LLC
123 Court Street,
Herkimer, New York 13350

ISBN: 0-9768659-6-3
Library of Congress Number: 2009913448

Printed in the United States of America.

Please visit our website for other titles:
www.shemayisrael.net

For information regarding publicity for author interviews call
(315) 939-7940

The Messiah

A Scriptural and Historical Examination
of the Purpose and Identity
of the Messiah

"For to us a Child is born, to us a Son is given,
and the government will be on His shoulders.
And He will be called Wonderful Counselor, Mighty God,
Everlasting Father, Prince of Peace.
Of the increase of His government and peace there will
be no end. He will reign on David's throne and over his
kingdom, establishing and upholding it with justice and
righteousness from that time on and forever. The zeal of
YHWH Almighty will accomplish this."
Isaiah (Yeshayahu) 9:6-7

Table of Contents

Acknowledgments

I must first and foremost acknowledge my Creator, Redeemer and Savior who opened my eyes and showed me the Light. He never gave up on me even when, at times, it seemed that I gave up on Him. He is ever patient and truly awesome. His blessings, mercies and love endure forever and my gratitude and thanksgiving cannot be fully expressed in words.

Were it not for the patience, prayers, love and support of my beautiful wife Janet, and my extraordinary children Morgan and Shemuel, I would never have been able to accomplish this work. They gave me the freedom to pursue the vision and dreams that my Heavenly Father placed within me, and for that I am so very grateful. I love them all more than they will ever know.

Loving thanks to my father for his faithfulness along with his helpful comments and editing. He tirelessly watched and held things together at the office while I was away traveling, researching, speaking and writing.

Many thanks to my good friend Eliyahu David ben Yissachar for all of the time spent in discussions and editing. He took time away from his own research to make this a better book, and I am extremely grateful for his efforts.

Introduction

This book is part of a larger body of educational work called the "Walk in the Light" series. This book and the entire series were written as a result of my search for the truth. Having grown up in a major protestant denomination since I was a small child I had been steeped in doctrine which often times seemed to contradict the very words contained within the Scriptures. I always considered myself to be a Christian although I never took the time to research the origins of Christianity or to understand exactly what the term Christian meant. I simply grew up believing that Christianity was right and every other religion was wrong or deficient.

Now my beliefs were founded on more than simply blind faith. I had experienced a "living God", my life had been transformed by a loving Redeemer and I had been filled with a powerful Spirit. I knew that I was on the right track, regrettably I always felt something was lacking. I was certain that there was something more to this religion called Christianity; not in terms of a different God, but what composed this belief system which I subscribed to, and this label which I wore like a badge.

Throughout my Christian walk I experienced many highs and some lows, but along the way I never felt like I fully understood what my faith was all about. Sure, I knew that "Jesus died on the cross for my sins" and that I needed to believe in my heart and confess with my mouth in order to "be saved". I "asked Jesus into my heart" when I was a child and sincerely believed in what I had done but something always felt like it was missing. As I grew older, I found myself progressing through different denominations, each time learning and growing, always adding some pieces to the puzzle, but never seeing the entire picture.

College ministry brought me into contact with the baptism of the Holy Spirit and more charismatic assemblies yet, while these people seemed to practice a more complete faith than those in my previous denominations, many of my original questions remained

unanswered and even more questions arose. It seemed that at each new step in my faith I added a new adjective to the already ambiguous label "Christian". I went from being a mere Christian to a Full Gospel, New Testament, Charismatic, Spirit Filled, Born Again Christian; although I could never get away from the lingering uneasiness that something was still missing.

For instance, when I read Matthew 7:21-23 I always felt uncomfortable. In that Scripture most English Bibles indicate that Jesus says: *"Not everyone who says to Me, Lord, Lord, will enter the kingdom of heaven, but he who does the will of My Father Who is in heaven. Many will say to Me on that day, Lord, Lord, have we not prophesied in Your name and driven out demons in Your name and done many mighty works in Your name? And then I will say to them openly (publicly), I never knew you; depart from Me, you who act wickedly [disregarding My commands]."* The Amplified Bible.

This passage of Scripture always bothered me because it sounded an awful lot like the modern day Christian Church, in particular, the charismatic churches which I had been attending where the gifts of the Spirit were operating. According to the Scripture passage it was not the people who **believed** in the spiritual manifestations that were being rejected, it was those who were **actually doing** them. I would think that this would give every Christian pause for concern.

First of all "in that day" there are **many** people who will be calling Him "Lord". They will also be performing incredible spiritual acts in His Name. Ultimately though, the Messiah will openly and publicly tell them to depart from Him. He will tell them that He never knew them and specifically He defines them by their actions, which is the reason for their rejection; they acted wickedly or lawlessly. In short, they disobeyed His commandments. Also, it seems very possible that while they thought they were doing these things in His Name, they were not, because they may have never known His Name. In essence, they did not know Him and He did not know them.

I think that many Christians are haunted by this Scripture because they do not understand who it applies to or what it means and if they were truly honest they must admit that there is no other group on the face of the planet that it can refer to except for the "Christian Church." This series provides the answer to that question and should provide resolution for any who have suffered anxiety over this verse.

Ultimately, my search for answers brought me right back to the starting point of my faith. I was left with the question: "What is the origin and substance of this religion called Christianity?" I was forced to examine the very foundations of my faith and to examine many of the beliefs which I subscribed to and test them against the truth of the Scriptures.

What I found out was nothing short of earth shattering. I experienced a parapettio which is a moment in Greek tragedies where the hero realizes that everything he knew was wrong. I discovered that many of the foundations of my faith were not rocks of truth, but rather the sands of lies, deception, corruption and paganism. I saw the Scripture in Jeremiah come true right before my eyes. In many translations, this passage reads: *"O LORD, my strength and my fortress, My refuge in the day of affliction, The Gentiles shall come to You from the ends of the earth and say, "Surely our fathers have inherited lies, worthlessness and unprofitable things. Will a man make gods for himself, which are not gods?"* Jeremiah 16:19-20 NKJV

I discovered that I had inherited lies and false doctrines from the fathers of my faith. I discovered that the faith which I had been steeped in had made gods which were not gods and I saw very clearly how many could say "Lord, Lord" and not really know the Messiah. I discovered that these lies were not just minor discrepancies but critical errors which could possibly have the effect of keeping me out of the New Jerusalem if I continued to practice them. (Revelation 21:27; 22:15).

While part of the problem stemmed from false doctrines which have crept into the Christian religion, it also had to do with anti-Semitism imbedded throughout the centuries and even translation errors in the very Scriptures that I was basing may beliefs upon. A good example is the next verse from the Prophet Jeremiah (Yirmeyahu) where most translations provide: *"Therefore behold, I will this once cause them to know, I will cause them to know My hand and My might; and they shall know that My Name is the LORD."* Yirmeyahu 16:21 NKJV.

Could our Heavenly Father really be telling us that His Name is "The LORD"? This is a title, not a name and by the way, won't many people be crying out "Lord, Lord" and be told that He never knew them? It is obvious that you should know someone's name in order to have a relationship with them. How could you possibly say that you know someone if you do not even know their name. So then we must ask: "What is the Name of our Heavenly Father?" The answer to this seeming mystery lies just beneath the surface of the translated text. In fact, if most people took the time to read the translators notes in the front of their "Bible" they would easily discover the problem.

You see the Name of our Creator is found in the Scriptures almost 7,000 times. Long ago a false doctrine was perpetrated regarding

speaking the Name. It was determined that the Name either could not, or should not, be pronounced and therefore it was replaced. Thus, over the centuries the Name of the Creator which was given to us so that we could know Him and be, not only His children, but also His friends, (Isaiah 41:8, James 2:23, John 15:15) was suppressed and altered. You will now find people using descriptions, titles and variations to replace the Name such as: God, Lord, Adonai, Jehovah and Ha Shem ("The Name") in place of the actual Name which was given in Scriptures. What a tragedy and what a mistake!

One of the Ten Commandments, also known as the Ten Words, specifically instructs us not to take the Name of the Creator "in vain" and "He will not hold him guiltless who takes His Name in vain." (Exodus 20:7). Most Christians have been taught that this simply warns of using the Name lightly or in the context of swearing or in some other disrespectful manner. This certainly is one aspect of the commandment, but if we look further into the Hebrew word for vain - שוא (pronounced shav) we find that it has a deeper meaning in the sense of desolating, uselessness or naught.

Therefore, we have been warned not only to avoid using the Name lightly or disrespectfully, but also not to bring it to naught, which is exactly what has been done over the centuries. The Name of our Creator which we have the privilege of calling on and praising has been suppressed to the point where most Believers do not even know the Name, let alone use it.

This sounds like a conspiracy of cosmic proportions and it is. Anyone who believes in the Scriptures must understand that there is a battle between good and evil. There is an enemy, Ha Shatan, who understands very well the battle which has been raging since the creation of time. He will do anything to distract or destroy those searching for the truth and he is very good at what he does. He is the Master of Deception and the Father of Lies and he does not want the truth to be revealed. His goal is to steal, kill and destroy. (John 10:10). The enemy has operated openly and behind the scenes over the centuries to infect, deceive, distract and destroy Believers with false doctrine. He truly is a wolf in sheep's clothing and his desire is to rob the Believer of blessings and life.

As you read this book I hope that you will see how people have been deceived regarding the Messiah of Yisrael. History details numerous individuals who claimed to be the Messiah yet all pale in scope and stature to the one Christians claim to be the Messiah, namely Jesus Christ. Regardless, most Jews refuse to acknowledge that Jesus

Christ was or is the Messiah. This book will examine their objections and will discern the proper Scriptural basis for the Messiah. The true identity and function of the Messiah will also be revealed so that there should be no doubt remaining with respect to this most important issue.

My hope is that every reader has an eye opening experience and is forever changed. I sincerely believe that the truths which are contained in this book and the "Walk in the Light Series" are essential to avoid the great deception which is being perpetrated upon those who profess to believe in, and follow the Holy One of Yisrael.

This book, and the entire series, is intended to be read by anyone who is searching for the truth. Depending upon your particular religion, customs and traditions, you may find some of the information offensive, difficult to believe or contrary to the doctrines and teachings which you have read or heard throughout your life. This is to be expected and is perfectly understandable, but please realize that none of the information is meant to criticize anyone or any faith, but merely to reveal truth.

The information contained in this book had better stir up some things or else there would be no reason to write it in the first place. The ultimate question is whether the contents align with the Scriptures and the will of the Creator. My goal is to strip away the layers of tradition which many of us have inherited and get to the core of the faith which is described in the Scriptures.

This book should challenge your thinking and your beliefs and hopefully aid you on your search for truth. May you be blessed in your journey of faith as you endeavor to Walk in the Light.

I

In the Beginning

The world is filled with many different religions and belief systems, all of which attempt to explain the origins of mankind and the nature of the Creator of the Universe. Clement of Alexandria is noted for stating: "There is one river of truth which receives tributaries from every side." In other words, there are many different paths that all lead to the one Truth.

This is the traditional mantra of the ecumenicist who believes that all religions ultimately lead to the same destination. As a result, they believe that everyone should simply tolerate one another and live in peace. We are all merely on different courses, but our journeys eventually end at the same destination.

While this has a nice ring to those who desire harmony, it certainly does not withstand any degree of scrutiny. If you take the time to examine what the various religions teach and the glaring contradictions that exist between them, it is plain to see that the universalist ideal is not plausible.

The diverse religions that exist with their varying accounts of creation cannot all be true at once. The religions of Christianity and Judaism are two particular religions that leave no room for tolerance. They both share the same Scriptures which describe the Creator of the Universe as One. (Deuteronomy 6:4).

Science, and particularly evolutionists, offer an explanation for the existence of our material world. They supposedly do this outside of any religious framework, although I would argue that evolution is actually a religion. In essence, these proponents deny that the physical universe had anything to do with a Creator, but they utterly fail to offer an explanation as to the undeniably spiritual dimension of life.

As a result, evolution and its diverse theories are deficient in their quest to explain the origins of the Universe, despite the artillery

of mathematical equations, technology and equipment which appear to support this "godless" form of religion.

This "anti-religion" believes that there was no powerful Creator, but rather that the beauty and order that exists in this seemingly endless Universe was all formed by chance through the chaos of an explosion. No one can seem to describe how this cosmic detonation occurred. Nor can they explain how matter came into existence in the first place.

I find it ironic when I hear a typical "scientific" explanation for the origin of our solar system. It is first explained that our sun was "born" 4.6 billion years ago – not 4.5 billion and not 4.7 billion. This gives the impression that evolutionists have the knowledge and ability to look back into the past with pinpoint accuracy.

In reality they cannot even explain how the sun came into existence - it just happened. After this mysterious birth, the sun then apparently "created" the planets from the cosmic "dust" that circled this newborn celestial body. This occurred with assistance of the invisible and unexplainable appearance of gravity.

Clearly, those who follow this "religion" are exercising blind faith which, in its arrogant attempt to disprove the existence of a Creator, actually fails to prove anything at all. In fact, while science feigns disassociation with religion, it resembles a "redesigned and technically advanced" system of sun worship originating from Babylon, a subject that will be discussed further in this text.

The scientific methodology, by its accepted protocol, cannot prove an occurrence in the past unless it can be replicated in the present. Thus evolutionists may continue to conjecture how the Universe and man came into existence, but they will never be able to prove their speculations.

The Bible, on the other hand, provides a clear description of how this world came into existence and, with some digging, it even provides the time when it was created.[1] According to the English translation of the Bible, *"In the Beginning God created the Heavens and the Earth."* Genesis 1:1.

The Hebrew Scriptures describe that Creation occurred "In the Beginning." The Hebrew word Beresheet (בראשית) literally means "in beginning" and it is also the name of the entire text commonly called Genesis in English Bibles.[2] Beresheet describes the creation of the universe and clearly reveals that "God" existed prior to that time, so we see a distinction between physical and spiritual existence.

The first ten words in the English translation of Beresheet 1:1 amount to 7 words in Hebrew, only 6 of which are ever translated. Here

is what we read in the Hebrew text:

בראשית ברא אלהים אֵת השמים וְאֵת הארץ

Now it is important to recognize that the Hebrew language reads from right to left which is the opposite of the English language which reads from left to right. This is a striking example of the difference between eastern thought and western thought. In many respects this linguistic difference aptly demonstrates how two cultures can look at things from very different perspectives.

Anyone who studies eastern and western civilizations will agree that westerners often think, speak and act differently than easterners. It appears that our differing cultures result in our wiring being different and this can lead to tension, frustration, conflict, confusion and even wars as two cultures fail to understand and effectively communicate with one another.

This anomaly has been amplified with the passage of time to the point where it is often very difficult to understand the mindset and thinking of those who lived centuries and millennia before us in different cultural settings. For example, it is challenging for someone raised in the 20th Century to understand how a person 2,000 years ago viewed their existence without automobiles, telephones, radios, televisions, computers, plumbing, electricity etc.

These individuals in the past woke up every day as we do, but they lived their lives entirely different than most of us in this modern age – life was a lot simpler and quieter in the past. Things were difficult, for sure, but while they did not have the same technological advances, they excelled on a spiritual level in a way that we find difficult to do in the midst of our technological haze.

Our technology has deceived us into thinking that we are somehow smarter than our predecessors. While technological advances have certainly resulted in more luxuries, gadgets and an "easier" life, they have also pushed us farther from our "beginnings." Our predecessors would likely marvel at our achievements, but grieve at how we have foolishly allowed our technology to dominate our existence. Modern society is, in many ways, diametrically opposed to that of our ancestors, which often places us in opposition to that which was and should be common and acceptable cultural norms.

This cultural clash is probably no more apparent and significant than in the Bible, a book that divides itself in two portions: 1) The Hebrew Scriptures - which were written in an Eastern language often

called the "Old" Testament, and 2) The Greek Scriptures - which were written in a western language and called the "New" Testament.[3] This is a critical point to understand as we study concepts such as the Messiah and I will continue to point out these differences when at all possible.

Now back to Genesis (Beresheet) 1:1. The word "resheet" means "beginning," but not necessarily in the linear sense - more in a circular sense. Western readers filter the Scriptures through their linear mindset, but it is important to grasp the concept of cycles because that is how the Creator operates. In fact, it is these cycles of righteousness which are described in the Scriptures.[4]

Now if we transliterate the passage from Hebrew into English, the Hebrew text reads as follows:

Beresheet bara Elohim et hashamayim v'et ha'erets

Go ahead and read it out loud and you will actually be reading one of the most important verses in the Bible as it sounds in the original Hebrew. Those seven words make a powerful and profound statement and only in the Hebrew can we see some of the important messages contained therein.

For instance, you may have noticed that the first Hebrew character bet (ב) was larger than the other characters. The Hebrew character bet (ב) stands for "house," so at the very beginning the reader is shown that the Creator is building a house, which is the central theme of the rest of the text. You will not see this in any translation, only in the Hebrew text

Another important inclusion in the Hebrew text is the existence of words which are not translated. In Beresheet 1:1, the one word which is not translated into English is the fourth word et (את). The word et consists of two Hebrew characters - the aleph (א) which is the first character in the Hebrew alphabet, and the taw (ת) which is the last letter in the Hebrew alphabet. "This word את is used over 11,000 times (and never translated into English as there is no equivalent) to point to the direct object of the verb."[5]

It is embedded throughout the Hebrew Scriptures, and while it has a known grammatical function the Sages have long understood that it has a much deeper and mysterious function – many believe that it is a direct reference to the Messiah – the subject of this book. There are deep mysteries associated with the ancient Hebrew alphabet, or rather aleph-bet (אב).

The aleph-bet consists of 22 characters and it is through these

characters, the spoken word, that the Universe and all that is in it was created. (Psalms 33:6-9). This notion stands in stark contrast to the thinking of an evolutionist who has allowed technology to overtake his spiritual nature. In this discussion we will attempt to return to our spiritual origins which clearly precede our physical existence.

Since everything that we know is encapsulated within the span of this aleph (א) and this taw (ת) the sages have looked to the center of this span and discovered that when you insert the letter mem (מ) in between you have the Hebrew word emet (אמת) which is "truth." The mem represents water and it also represents the womb, the source of life.

All Hebrew characters also have a numeric value which can provide even deeper insights and messages than the words themselves. For instance, the numerical equivalent for the letter mem (מ) is forty (40). As we explore the Scriptures we will see the number forty (40) associated with water in very interesting ways. We can also discern that the source of the living waters of truth is found within the Aleph Taw (את).

Throughout this book we will explore many intriguing examples of the word et (את) as we search the Hebrew Scriptures. Interestingly, there are actually two instances of the untranslated Aleph Taw (את) in the first passage of Beresheet – they were underlined so that you can easily identify them.

The untranslated Aleph Taw (את) is the fourth word, and there is also an Aleph Taw (את) in the sixth word - v'et (ואת) which is simply translated as "and." The vav (ו) typically attaches two concepts, which is aptly demonstrated by the fact that its ancient pictographic representation is a nail or a stake. We can see that in the Ancient Hebrew pictographic script (𐤅) as well as the more modern Babylonian Hebrew Script (ו).

The implications of these two instances of the Aleph Taw (את) are quite profound. If we agree with the Sages and recognize it as representing the Messiah, then in a very basic sense one could infer that the Messiah would be revealed two times within creation. The first occurrence of the Aleph Taw (את) in the text is found at the fourth word. Interestingly, the fourth letter of the aleph-bet (אב) is the dalet (ד) which represents the "door." The fourth lamp in the seven light menorah is the location of the servant light. Known as the "shamash" light it is the source of all the rest of the lights.

Since the third word is "God" (Elohim) it is easy to see that the Aleph Taw (את) is the door between "God" (Elohim) and the fifth word "The Heavens." The second instance of the Aleph Taw (את) connects "the heavens" (השמים) and "the earth" (הארץ) which reveals that the Messiah brings "God" (Elohim) and man together.

Even more profound is the fact that the second Aleph Taw (את) is the sixth word and the number six (6) is always related to man. Also, the sixth letter in the aleph-bet is the vav (ו). Thus, one could interpret this Hebrew text to mean that the Aleph Taw (את) would come from Elohim, and be the door from the heavens to the earth in the form of a man and he would bring the two together - by a nail.

This ancient mystery led many to believe that there would be two Messiahs, but it could be that there is one Messiah functioning in two different roles, possibly at two different times. In fact, some consider that the first seven (7) Hebrew words in Beresheet encapsulate all of time and represent a 7,000 year period. As such, the location of each Aleph Taw (את) could give us a clue as to when, in time, we would see the Messiah

The Hebrew text also informs us that the Aleph Taw (את) was involved in Creation as it stands next to the word "God." It is important to recognize that you will not find God in the Hebrew text. The Hebrew Scriptures describe that in the beginning of time and physical existence, it was Elohim (אלהים) that Created everything – not God. Now most modern Bibles simply translate Elohim into English as "God," but as a person begins to examine the subject of translating texts from one language to another it is clear that often times concepts are lost or diminished through the translation process.[6]

In the case of Elohim, there is a plurality to the word which I believe better describes the One that stated *"Let us make man in our image."* Genesis (Beresheet) 1:26.[7] The word "God" arguably has pagan origins. Therefore, I will use the proper title "Elohim" when referring to the Creator of the Universe throughout this book, because that is what He was originally called.[8]

So now we know that the Creator of the Universe was referred to as Elohim and there is likely a Messianic reference - Aleph Taw (את) - within the first passage of the Scriptures which implies that the Messiah had something to do with Creation.

This understanding perfectly ties in with the words of the Book of John (Yahanan),[9] found in the New Testament, which declares: *"[1] In the beginning was the Word, and the Word was with Elohim, and the Word was Elohim. [2] He was with Elohim in the beginning. [3] Through Him all things*

were made; without Him nothing was made that has been made. ⁴ In Him was life, and that life was the light of men. ⁵ The light shines in the darkness, but the darkness has not understood it." Yahanan 1:1-5.

Notice that this verse begins with the same words as the passage in Beresheet - "In the beginning." The similarity is not a coincidence. In fact, it was intentional and it turns out that this portion of Yahanan is actually a midrash, which is a study, commentary or explanation of the passage in Beresheet 1:1. The writer specifically tied the two passages together with the intention of showing that "The Word" was there from the beginning which is exactly what we see in the Hebrew text through the untranslated Aleph Taw (את).¹⁰

So the writer of Yahanan was clearly revealing that "The Word" and the Aleph Taw (את) were one and the same. The revelation provided through this text was that the Aleph Taw (את) was the Messiah. While most Christians would likely agree with this conclusion, most would be hard pressed to explain why. This is because most Christians lack a proper foundation in the Hebrew language and the Hebrew Scriptures.

Notice also the reference that Yahanan makes to the light. The text is revealing another mystery which is embedded in the Creation account. In Beresheet 1:3-5 we read the words "³ Then Elohim said, 'Let there be light' and there was light. ⁴ And Elohim saw את the light, that it was good; and Elohim divided the light from the darkness. ⁵ Elohim called the light Day, and the darkness He called Night. So the evening and the morning were the first day."

The average reader will never notice the Aleph Taw (את) in the text because they are not reading it in the Hebrew, and the Aleph Taw (את) is not translated into English. Also in the Hebrew text the Aleph Taw (את) bridges the word Elohim (אלהים) and Light (אור) so we see אלהים את אור.

The word for light is owr (אור) in Hebrew and one might assume that this is referring to the sun. Interestingly, we are told later in the text that the sun, the moon and the stars were actually created on the fourth day. "¹⁴ Then Elohim said, 'Let there be lights in the firmament of the heavens to divide the day from the night; and let them be for signs and seasons, and for days and years; ¹⁵ and let them be for lights in the firmament of the heavens to give light on the earth'; and it was so. ¹⁶ Then Elohim made two great lights: the greater light to rule the day, and the lesser light to rule the night. He made the stars also. ¹⁷ Elohim set them in the firmament of the heavens to give light on the earth, ¹⁸ and to rule over the day and over the night, and to divide the light from the darkness. And Elohim saw that it was good. ¹⁹ So the evening and the morning were the fourth day." Beresheet 1:14-19.

So then, the Light on the first day must be different from the lights of the fourth day. What was this Light? According to the text in Yahanan, it was the Word that was the Light from the beginning and that Light was the source of life. This brings us back to the concept of the truth – emet (אמת) – with the womb being surrounded by the Aleph Taw (את).

"The Yalkut, a rabbinic medieval anthology, says: 'And [Elohim] saw the light, that it was good.' This is the light of Messiah ... to teach you that [Elohim] was the generation of Messiah and His works before He created the universe, and He hid the Messiah ... under His throne of Glory. Satan asked [Elohim], Master of the Universe: 'For whom is this Light under your Throne of Glory?' [Elohim] answered him, 'It is for ... [the Messiah] who is to turn you backward and who will put you to scorn with shamefacedness.'"[11]

It is interesting to see that both Christianity and Judaism recognize this Light of the first day as the Messiah. This Light was separated from darkness, and from that point on we have the reckoning of time as we begin to discern days as the passage from evening to morning. It is important to understand that the world began in darkness – the evening. The Light was then brought forth and there was morning – the dawning of the day.

As a result, every day should remind us of creation as we begin the evening in darkness which is when we sleep. Sleep in Hebrew thought often represents death. As the light appears at the dawning of the day we awake from our sleep and begin to live our lives. As long as we have the light we stay awake and we remain alive. As the light fades into dusk and darkness we go to sleep. Therefore the "dawning of the day" should remind us of the Messiah – The Light which brings life.

This daily cycle is a pattern for the cycle of our lives. Each day is divided into two parts: 1) Evening which is typified by darkness which proceeds into the night, and 2) Morning which is typified by light and proceeds into the day. The light of the dawning of the day is linked with the Messiah and as you study the Scriptures with this understanding it will become evident that the time of day when things occur is often just as important as the day of the month, the year or the geographic location.

This is a concept which is often lost to those in western society because they lack the experience or familiarity of eastern thought. While Christians are certainly familiar with the Messianic references and titles such as "The Light" and "The Word" - the Hebrew Aleph Taw (את) is not so familiar. Interestingly, Christianity places significance on the

Greek title "The Alpha and the Omega" (AΩ) which is mentioned three times in the English translations of the Revelation given to Yahanan.[12]

Sadly, what they typically fail to recognize is that this particular title is taken from a Greek manuscript and presented in the Greek language, which would not be attributed to a Messiah coming from a Creator Who designated Hebrew as His chosen language. The Alpha (A) is the first letter and the Omega (Ω) is the last letter in the Greek Alphabet.

Thus, a Hebrew Messiah would have referred to Himself as the Hebrew Aleph and Taw (את), the first and last letters of the Hebrew Alph-Bet, not the Greek Alpha and Omega (AΩ) which has no significance in the Hebrew texts. When you understand this difference it has profound implications as it unlocks certain mysteries in the Hebrew Scriptures which have puzzled some Sages and scholars for centuries.[13]

This is a vivid example of the conflict which exists between the two portions of the Bible. The "New Testament" translated from the Greek language proposes to shed light on the "Old Testament" written in the Hebrew language, but because of translation issues and traditions, the two often oppose each other rather than compliment one another.

If we can resolve these conflicts we can gain a better understanding of the texts and ultimately the subject of the Messiah. Armed with this knowledge we now have a clear picture from the first words in the Scriptures that there is One Who was there in the Beginning and that One is associated with the Messiah, although not necessarily the one that Christianity has promoted for centuries.

As the title implies, this book is about the Messiah, a subject which carries much debate depending upon your cultural or religious background. Those in the Christian religion believe that Jesus was and is that Messiah, although they call him by a variation of a Greek name which is not a Hebrew Name attributed to a Hebrew Messiah.

The typical path that a Christian convert follows as they enter into their faith is to first recognize that they are sinners in need of forgiveness. They often then "accept" Jesus as their "personal Savior" and "believe" in their hearts that they are "saved." They usually make their decision without much knowledge of ancient history or the Hebrew Scriptures, known collectively as the Tanak.[14]

In fact, most Christian evangelistic outreaches do not require any rigorous training, study or instruction before a person is invited to make a confession of faith. That process is usually reserved for when a person desires to become a member of a church. I have found that the major thrust of Christian evangelism is to get a decision, and have the person say what is commonly called "The Sinner's Prayer" which includes the so-called "Four Spiritual Laws." This formula has become the accepted path to salvation, and getting people saved is a primary focus of the Christian religion.[15]

Therefore, a Christian convert's "decision" to accept Jesus Christ as their personal savior is often based more on faith than it is on their knowledge of the Scriptures and the Prophetic expectations of the coming Messiah.[16] Sometimes this decision could be described as "blind faith," because it rests solely upon certain representations and promises made by the religious proponent which are not necessarily supported by the Scriptures. I make this statement having spent most of my life in the Christian religion with many years in Christian lay ministry. During that time I have witnessed many preachers and evangelists espouse promises of eternal life upon the utterance of a simple prayer.

This is an important observation because the present focus in Christian evangelism differs greatly from that of the Israelites who originally followed the One described in the "New Testament," and who are often erroneously considered to be the first Christians. Interestingly most, if not all of them, likely had a significant understanding of the Hebrew Scriptures, and were living lives according to those Scriptures while actively anticipating and seeking the Messiah.[17]

Tradition often tries to categorize them as simple working class illiterate individuals with little to no education or knowledge of the Scriptures. To the contrary these Israelites, often referred to as "disciples" but more accurately called "talmidim," were quite different from the typical Christian convert. The talmidim were what we might loosely classify as Orthodox Israelites. Many lived in the northwest region of the Sea of Galilee in close knit villages such as Capernaum, Bethsaida and Korazim. All of these villages had synagogues where the community would meet to fellowship, commune, pray, worship and study the Scriptures.

They were considered "religious" or "observant" because they lived strict lives according to the Torah. The Torah was the instructions found in the first five books of the Scriptures, often incorrectly referred to as "The Law."[18] Essentially, they knew the Scriptures and were

diligent to obey the commandments.[19]

These individuals were not Christians, and never became Christians. Rather, they were Israelites who had certain expectations of the Messiah, some correct, some incorrect. They certainly knew the Scriptures, which consisted of the Torah, the Prophets and the Writings, and they knew what those texts said about the Messiah. It was because of their knowledge of the Scriptures that many believed and followed a Rabbi that they considered to be the promised Messiah.

In contrast, many modern Christians express faith in a Messiah without a solid foundation concerning the prophecies and purpose of this long anticipated Messiah. They often take the step of faith without knowing or being able to express the basis for their belief that Jesus is the Messiah according to the Scriptures. They tend to approach the entire subject from the complete opposite direction than the original talmidim described in the "New Testament."

Modern Christians have inherited a western tradition concerning the Messiah, and they fail to comprehend His function from an eastern perspective. In fact, they have so westernized the Hebrew Messiah that most "Jews"[20] vehemently reject the Christian Jesus as Messiah, because he simply does not qualify in their eyes. Christians continue to wonder why so many people of Hebrew descent do not accept their messiah when, in fact, there is no reason that a person knowledgeable in the Scriptures would accept the Jesus Christ presented by Christianity who, as presented, actually does not meet the requirements of the Messiah.

As a result, most modern day adherents to the religion of Judaism reject Jesus as their Messiah and continue to wait for a Messiah that they believe fully comports with the Scriptures. Over the centuries, "Jews" have recognized numerous Messianic figures to varying degrees – some place the number at over fifty different individuals.[21]

Throughout the centuries those in Judaism have been looking for a Messiah, but they do not appear to have found one that they can agree upon. Interestingly, it seems that there is one that they can all agree is not the Messiah – namely the Christian Jesus. Because of their failure to agree upon and recognize a Messiah, most in Judaism have modified, and even diminished their definition and expectations of the Messiah to fit within their understanding of history, and their belief that the Messiah has not yet come. They are forced to do this because, as we shall see in this discussion, the prophetic window for the appearance of the Messiah has long since passed.

Therefore, Judaism must either adapt or concede. Adaptation is nothing new to Judaism which developed as a hybrid religion by certain descendants of the tribes of Judah, Benjamin and Levi - descendants of the Pharisees from the Southern Kingdom collectively known as the House of Judah. In fact, Judaism developed the artificial hierarchy of the Rabbinic order and through the various teachings of the Rabbis their religion has progressed and changed throughout the centuries.[22] Judaism is by no means the same faith that we read about in the "Old Testament" in the same fashion that Christianity is not the same faith that we read about in the "New Testament."

Thus we see these two religions: Christianity and Judaism which share a common text, but they fail to agree on many issues contained therein, particularly the issue of the Messiah. The Christians call the Hebrew Scriptures the "Old Testament" which accurately reflects their view of these texts - "old." Interestingly, those texts were the primary Scriptures that the original talmidim read and studied.[23]

How odd that the descendents of those who originally were the exclusive followers of the Messiah presented in the "New Testament" are currently those who are least likely to profess Him as the Messiah. What has happened in the past two thousand years to cause such a shift? Much indeed. But before we examine those issues it is important to lay a proper foundation.

When a person reads a book, rarely do they start with the last sentence, paragraph or chapter. They do not start at the end and read backwards to the beginning. Rather they start at the beginning, and work their way toward the end, which allows the necessary foundation to be laid so that the story can be built up to the climactic end.

This is the way we are supposed to read the Scriptures. We are supposed to start in the Beginning - Beresheet. Regrettably, most Christians start with the "New Testament," believing that it has the information most relevant to their faith. They often look back at the "Old Testament" as if it is filled with good historical information, but not necessarily as applicable or relevant as the "New."

In contrast, most in Judaism look upon the New Testament as possibly historical, but definitely involving a pagan religion which worships a pagan christ. As a result, they discount those texts and certainly do not use them as part of their religious texts.

The way that Christianity has handled the Scriptures has resulted in some erroneous doctrine which often skews the very teaching and understanding of their messiah. As previously mentioned, the goal of evangelical Christianity is typically to get a person "saved" at a revival meeting or crusade. After this, the new convert may be

given a New Testament, or the Book of Yahanan, which we already determined begins as a midrash of the Hebrew Book of Beresheet. How on earth are these converts expected to fully understand what they are reading without the proper foundation being laid by the original Hebrew Scriptures – The Torah, The Prophets and the Writings (Tanak).

As a result, many new converts to the Christian faith have no idea what the Scriptures actually say about the Messiah from the beginning - they only know what they have been taught. Often times what they have been taught is error which simply gets perpetuated over time.

Throughout this book one of the goals is to relate the fact that while historically, some of the things in the Old Testament happened prior to those in the New Testament, there is nothing "Old" about those Scriptures in terms of relevance. In fact, it is absolutely vital that one understands these Scriptures in order to fully comprehend what the "New" Testament texts are relating. As a result, I like to refer to the "New Testament" as the Messianic writings because that is what they are supposed to be about, the fulfillment of the Messianic promises found in the Tanak.

If you read the Scriptures backwards, you will end up with an inaccurate understanding of the Messiah, as well as many other issues of faith and doctrine. I say this from experience because this is exactly what happened to me as I was raised and taught in a mainline Protestant denomination.

It was only when I started discovering that I had inherited lies and false traditions that I experienced a paradigm shift, and began to see and understand the Scriptures in their proper order and context. I realized that instead of starting at the end I needed to go back to where it all started – "In the Beginning."

2

The Garden

After the creation account provided in Beresheet we read about a special garden in a place called Eden. This continues the theme of Elohim building a house, and we all know that every house needs a family: "*Now YHWH Elohim had planted a garden in the east, in Eden; and there He put the man He had formed.*" Beresheet 2:8. In most English Bibles you would read that: "The LORD God had planted a garden . . . " but this is not an accurate rendering from the Hebrew text.

As we already discussed the title Elohim has been replaced with the word "God" in most English Bibles. Aside from Elohim, which is a title, the Name of Elohim has also been replaced with another title - The LORD. The Name of Elohim is not "The LORD" although this is what appears in most English translations whenever the Name of Elohim is found in the Hebrew text.

As a result, if you simply examine an English translation of the Scriptures you will rarely ever read, recognize or speak the actual Name of the Creator of the Universe[24] which is rendered as ꓱꓱꓱꓱ in Ancient Hebrew. The Name is written יהוה in modern Hebrew and often depicted as YHWH or YHVH in English.[25]

Therefore, it was YHWH Elohim that created man, planted the Garden and placed man within that Garden. The Garden of Eden represented paradise, it was not some ethereal place called "heaven" where winged creatures with halos float about the clouds and strum on harps - paradise was a tangible, real physical place.

It was the perfect environment where the Creator of the Universe could dwell with His Creation. It was a place where the spiritual and the physical came together. Man was connected with the Creator and with Creation - there was no separation between them. The Hebrew word for garden is gan (גן) which reveals that it was an enclosed or protected space. Within this paradise man was to obey the

commandments and if he was obedient, he would remain in fellowship with YHWH.

Adam (אדם) was the name of the man who was placed in the Garden. His name actually means "man" or even more inclusively "earthling." He was a unique creation and he was intimately related with the entire created world. In fact, his name is directly linked with the word "ground" - adamah (אדמה) - from which he was derived. Adam was unique though because he also received the "Breath of Life" - nishmat chayim (נשמת חיים) from Elohim.

He was the special link between the Creator and the Creation. He was a bridge, so to speak, between the two. This should make us think of the Aleph Taw (את), which was a door and connection between Elohim and Creation. The Scriptures record that Adam was made *"in the image of Elohim"* and as long as he remained obedient he could remain in the garden and partake of the Tree of Life.

Just exactly what it meant to be made "in the image of Elohim" is not entirely clear. It has been the subject of great religious and philosophical inquiry throughout the ages. There is no doubt that a unique and divine connection existed between the Creator, Adam and the rest of creation. Just how we describe that connection remains elusive, although it is clear that Elohim is spirit and therefore there is more to man than just flesh.

Adam was instructed to fill the earth and subdue it and rule over the creatures of the earth. (Beresheet 1:28). We read that Adam was given a "bride" who was taken from his side. She was not created from the ground as he was, nor was the breath of life breathed directly into her, as was the case with Adam. She was literally birthed from the man.

We are told that during this "birthing process" Adam was placed in a "deep sleep." The Hebrew word used here is tardemah (תרדמה) - which means more than just deep sleep. In fact, it means: "trance or stunned - like death." So what we see is a picture of Adam dying so that his bride could live. Adam was then "brought back to life," or "resurrected" so that he and his bride could dwell together in paradise. This was a pattern established at the very beginning which would have profound implications in the future.

The word for man is aish (איש) in Hebrew and the word for woman is aishah (אשה). Aishah means "taken out of man." Notice that there is a Hebrew letter hey (ה) added to the word. The hey (ה) has changed over the centuries and in ancient Hebrew script it symbolizes a man standing with arms raised (⹁) and means: "behold." It is meant

to announce something and can also mean: "to reveal." The hey (ה) also represents breath, which is life - the Spirit of Elohim. Interestingly, the passage of Scripture detailing this event includes the untranslated Aleph Taw (את) in the Hebrew which is drawing our attention to a deeper meaning hidden in the text involving the Messiah.

This entire birthing process is an important event that we are meant to learn from. YHWH could have merely created a woman from scratch. Instead, He chose to create a new being, similar, but very different from Adam. Both the man and the woman were unique in their beings and the fashion which they were created. Now along with man, the woman was chosen to dwell in a special place and to perform a specific purpose. The woman is often described as a "help mate" for the man, but she was really much more. The Hebrew Scriptures describe that no ezer k'negedow (עזר כנגדו) could be found so woman was created. Adam needed an intelligent, capable, equal partner so Elohim created woman. This begs the question why he needed a partner. Quite simply, he had work to do and he needed help.

While in the Garden man was commanded "*to tend and keep it.*" Beresheet 2:15. The Hebrew word for "tend" is abad (עבד) and the Hebrew word for "keep" is shamar (שמר). Both of these words are verbs and they involve action. These concepts are very important as we shall see throughout our discussion and another way of describing Adam's mission is "*to work and to watch*" or "*to do and to guard.*"

After we are told what Adam was to <u>do</u> in the Garden we are then told of one specific commandment which he was given. The Scriptures record: "*¹⁶ And YHWH Elohim commanded the man, saying, 'Of every tree of the garden you may freely eat; ¹⁷ but of the tree of the knowledge of good and evil you shall not eat, for in the day that you eat of it you shall surely die.'*" Beresheet 2:16-17.

Now this was by no means the only command given to man, but it happened to be the first one that was transgressed - that is why we are provided the specific details of this particular command. Adam was surely given instructions concerning his duties and what was expected of him as he and his Creator walked and fellowshipped together in the Garden.

The Scriptures record an incident when the woman was deceived by a serpent that had entered the Garden. Adam and the woman both transgressed a command – they partook of the fruit of the tree of knowledge of good and evil - better known as the tree of all knowledge.

It has been suggested that "the phrase [tov v'ra] טוב ורע

translated *good and evil*, is a merism. This is a figure of speech whereby a pair of opposites are used together to create the meaning *all* or *everything*, as in the English phrase, 'they came, great and small', meaning just that they all came. So the *Tree of Knowledge of Good and Evil* they take to mean the *Tree of All Knowledge*. This meaning can be brought out by the alternative translations *Tree of Knowledge of Good and of Evil* (the word *of* not being expressed in the Hebrew) or *Tree of Knowledge, both Good and Evil*."[26]

Prior to the incident involving the Tree of All Knowledge, the Scriptures provide that "*they were both naked, the man and his wife, and they were not ashamed.*" Beresheet 2:25. When Adam and the woman partook of this forbidden fruit, their eyes were suddenly opened to their "nakedness" which is arom (ערום) in Hebrew. They were suddenly afraid and made for themselves coverings of leaves, likely leaves from the very tree from which they partook the fruit.[27]

Most people who read this account will ask: "What could have possibly happened to cause such a sudden change in their perception and how could eating a piece of fruit do such a thing?" While the fruit of that particular tree may have had special "powers" there is likely more to the story than meets the eye. This episode was a sensual event and we read in the text the emphasis placed upon the senses of touching, tasting and seeing.

The act of eating, drinking and tasting is at times used in the Scriptures in a metaphorical fashion to describe intimacy. For example in Song of Solomon we read "*Like an apple tree among the trees of the woods, so is my beloved among the sons. I sat down in his shade with great delight, and his fruit was sweet to my taste.*" Song of Solomon 2:3 NKJV. The Proverbs speak about a man drinking water from his own cisterns and not being enraptured by an immoral woman. Proverbs 5:15. We are encouraged to: "*Taste and see that YHWH is good.*" Psalms 34:8

The key is that they now "knew" that they were naked. The fact that they were naked had not changed, rather the fact that they "knew," which is yada (ידע) in Hebrew. Interestingly, the man and the woman were not the only ones who were naked during this event. The Scriptures record that the serpent was also arom (ערום), which was the same word to describe the man and woman as naked. Relative to the serpent, the word arom (ערום) is usually translated as "cunning."

The word translated "the serpent" is hanachash (הנחש) in Hebrew. The noun nachash (נחש) can mean a "snake, serpent or one who practices divination." The adjective nachash (נחש) means: "bright or brazen." So was it actually a snake or was it some bright, serpentine

being? It is possible that the text is a word play that will have greater significance as we proceed with this discussion.

No matter how you describe this "serpent" something happened here which should draw our attention to the prohibitions found within Leviticus 18-20. The fact that a serpent is unique from most other creatures because of the hemipenes, which are two sex organs, makes this incident even more profound. Most commentators allude to the fact that something graphic occurred, but typically shy away from the details.

It appears that something sordid likely occurred which was offensive to the Creator. The man and the woman, who thought they would be like YHWH, were suddenly ashamed because they had done something wrong. They had become defiled. This prompted them to cover themselves and hide. They had not only eaten from the Tree of All Knowledge, they had participated in evil – through their disobedience they had sinned.

As Job aptly stated, "Naked I came from my mother's womb, and naked shall I return there." Job 1:21. It is in a state of nakedness that we are all delivered into this world by our Creator, and in that same state we will depart. We should all endeavor to return to that condition where man once was - standing before the Creator naked and not ashamed. The only way that this can occur is if the issue of the sin in our lives is dealt with by the Creator. That problem began in the Garden, and most recognize that the Messiah is needed to resolve the problem.

When confronted concerning their newly donned apparel they both participated in the blame game. The man blamed the woman, and the woman blamed the serpent. Various punishments were meted out and the following was directed to the serpent by YHWH: "I will put enmity between you and the woman, and between your seed and her Seed. He will crush your head and you shall crush His heel." Beresheet 3:15.

This is considered by many to constitute a direct reference to the Messiah. In other words, there would be One that would come from the woman Who would crush the head of the one that deceived mankind and helped bring sin into the world. Some who take a strictly literal interpretation of the Hebrew text proclaim that there is no such promise and this verse could simply be translated as a curse without the hope that many read into the text.

The interesting part of the passage is that there are also seed from the serpent that will be in opposition to the Seed from the woman. This begs the question why it was the Seed of the woman, and not the Seed of the man. Since it is the male that has the seed and not the

woman, what could possibly be meant by this statement?

The easy answer is that this verse simply refers to offspring. Another view proposes that the woman represents the Bride of YHWH that will consist of both men and women, thus the existence of seed. The Messianic interpretation hints of a virgin birth. In any case, the timing of the promise is critical to understanding the verse.

A critical shift had just occurred in the relationship between Elohim and mankind made in His image. Man and woman had violated His commands which necessitated punishment. They would be subjected to separation and death which would be the end of these marvelous creatures unless there was some sort of atonement made on their behalf.

Clearly, by distributing individual punishments to all of the perpetrators, YHWH was revealing that He was not pleased. He was also providing hope by revealing the avenue through which He would provide restoration for mankind. How, when, where and by Whom were all questions left unanswered – that would become clearer in the future. For the time being mankind would have to be satisfied with this promise – the promise of a Seed from a woman.

The Aramaic Targum specifically connects this portion with the Messiah when it speaks of the enmity between the two and concludes "they are to make peace in the end, in the days of King Messiah."[28]

Despite this hope of a future fix, their transgression resulted in immediate punishment followed by atonement, which bought mankind some time. Just how much time would be revealed during the life of a man named Noah. YHWH told man that he would die in the day he ate the forbidden fruit, and Adam died at 930 years of age in the first millennial day, just as YHWH said. However, Adam and Hawah did not immediately experience physical death because there was no atonement for them.

This atonement consisted of blood being shed on their behalf, and they were then each clothed with the skin of the dead animal that was killed. They were literally and symbolically clothed with death because of their transgression. While they chose fig leaves to cover their nakedness, YHWH chose skins. This is a powerful picture provided for us to learn and understand.

It vividly demonstrates the model of atonement through the shedding of blood – which is the essence of the life of the sacrifice. It also demonstrates substitution – one life taken on behalf of another. Both of these concepts are intimately involved in the eventual restoration of mankind through the promised Seed – the Messiah.

Therefore, what occurred in the Garden is not just a story from days gone by, it is filled with images and concepts that we must learn and understand. It not only shows us the problem created by the sin of the first man and woman, but also the path to a solution.

It was only after the transgression that we are told how Adam named the woman Hawah (חוה) which means: "life-giver."[29] Man was originally created to dwell in paradise, communing with Elohim for eternity. After the transgression in the Garden, Adam and Hawah were expelled and denied access to the Tree of Life. This resulted in the introduction of death to mankind, which again, was directly linked to the rest of creation. The impact was immediate, although the process of both physical and spiritual death took their own unique courses.

Prior to the fall, Adam was "plugged in to Elohim" spiritually. Adam could commune directly with Elohim in an intimate fashion which no created being was able to do after the fall. Once he was expelled from the Garden and from the presence of Elohim, he experienced spiritual death.

Death began to take hold of his physical body as well as the rest of creation. Those things that were made to last forever began to die. While mankind was originally created in the image of Elohim, the offspring of Adam, beginning with Seth, were born in the image of Adam, not in the image of YHWH. (Beresheet 5:3). Adam contained the "breath of Life" which cannot be killed, although he existed in a body which was once eternal, but now subject to death. As a result, his offspring were born in this same state.

The problem is evident, although the solution was not so clear. Adam was expelled from paradise, which essentially was the same as being kicked out of the House of Elohim. Adam chose not to live according to the rules of the House so he was evicted. As a result, all of his offspring were also excluded from the House, which is the source of eternal life.

To solve their problem, mankind needed to somehow regain entrance to the House and receive life. The breach in the relationship between man and the Creator needed to be restored. This is the rest of the story that we read about in the Scriptures. The underlying theme is the restoration of mankind to the Garden, and it is generally understood that this would be accomplished through One known as the Messiah. It would turn out to be a long journey, as we shall see, and mankind ultimately became divided between the few who followed the ways of YHWH and the many who chose to rebel against their Creator.

3

Noah

Following the expulsion from paradise Hawah bore both Cain (Qayin)[30] and Abel (Hebel)[31] although we do not know exactly where and when they were conceived. Whether it was before or after the fall is unclear. The Scriptures describe the births of Qayin and Hebel and a mechanical translation of Beresheet 4:1 reads *"the Man (Adam) had known את Hawah his woman and she conceived and she brought forth את Qayin and she said I purchased a man with את YHWH."*[32]

Notice the three instances of the Aleph Taw (את) in this passage and that each Aleph Taw (את) is immediately next to a name: Qayin, Hawah and YHWH. They are clearly pointing to something important. Was Qayin intended to be the Seed of woman that would restore mankind or is this simply showing us a shadow picture of how the Messiah will enter Creation – we shall see.

There is ancient and intriguing speculation concerning the origin of both Qayin and Hebel. We do not have the space to fully investigate that subject, but I will simply point out that the text only records Adam as "knowing" Hawah once but it describes two births.[33] When a person studies the Torah over time it becomes apparent that nothing is by chance – neither omissions, inclusions or repetitions – every word has a purpose.

Some speculate whether Qayin and Hebel were twins or whether only one of them was from Adam. No doubt these two brothers both came from the womb of Hawah, and they were unique beings. We are told of an incident when they both presented offerings to YHWH *"at the end of days"* or *"in the process of time."*

"2 Now Hebel was a keeper of sheep, but Qayin was a tiller of the ground. 3 And at the end of days (in the process of time) it came to pass that Qayin brought an offering of the fruit of the ground to YHWH. 4 Hebel also brought of the firstborn of his flock and of their fat. And YHWH respected

Hebel and his offering, ⁵ but He did not respect Qayin and his offering. And Qayin was very angry, and his countenance fell." Beresheet 4:2-5.³⁴

It is important to recognize that this was not any day, it was an Appointed Time,³⁵ also known as "moadi" in Hebrew. The brothers knew that they were supposed to bring offerings to YHWH at this particular time, but the offering of Qayin was not looked upon favorably by YHWH. This passage reveals that there was an established time and method of worship which was known from the beginning. There was a right way and a wrong way to worship YHWH – Hebel did it right and Qayin did it wrong.

Instead of repenting and changing his ways, Qayin decided to kill his brother Hebel. This homicide had a great impact upon the earth as the blood of Hebel cried out and Qayin was punished by YHWH.

Hebel was later replaced by another son, a son of Adam, named Seth. *"²⁵ Adam lay with his wife אֵת again, and she gave birth to a son and named אֵת him Seth, saying, 'Elohim has granted me another seed (zera) in place of Hebel, since Qayin killed him. ²⁶ Seth also had a son, and he named אֵת him Enosh. At that time men began to call on the Name of YHWH."* Beresheet 4:25-26. Notice in this account of Seth there are three instances of the Aleph Taw (אֵת). So it appears that the righteous line of Hebel was cut off, but then reestablished through the Son of Adam – Seth.

There is significant tradition that it was during the generation of Enosh when mankind began to fall into idolatry, and thereby profane the Name of YHWH through their idolatry. From that generation onward, Creation clearly continued on a downward spiral away from the Creator. With the passage of centuries, the effects of sin originating from Adam, Hawah and Qayin had firmly taken root.

After the passage of many generations we read an interesting account: *"⁴ There were giants on the earth in those days, and also afterward, when the sons of Elohim came in to the daughters of men and they bore children to them. Those were the mighty men who were of old, men of renown."* Beresheet 6:4.

The "giants" being referred to are actually Nephilim. It is important to remember, this text was written by Moses centuries after the fact. He is talking about mighty men of old, men of renown. He is speaking of things that were probably familiar to him. Some believe that the giants and men of renown were the result of fallen angels copulating with mankind. Just who were these "sons of Elohim" is not clear and has been debated for centuries.

The Targums state the following: "Shamhazai and Azael fell from Heaven and were on earth in those days, and also after the sons of the great ones had gone into the daughters of men, who bore them

children, these are called the heroes of old, the men of renown."³⁶

These men of renown were likely the source of the mythological heroes that we read about to this day that have been romanticized and even incorporated into pagan worship. In any event, it appears that there was a variety of cross-breeding going on between different beings and species which corrupted all creation and the original design of the Creator.³⁷

Because of what was happening on the planet YHWH made an interesting declaration. He stated: *"My Spirit shall not strive with man forever, for he is indeed flesh; yet his days shall be one hundred and twenty years."* Many interpret this to mean that men would only live to be 120 years old after that time, but this is not what YHWH is saying. First, he is talking about mankind in general, not the individual lifespans of men. Second, He is saying that He will not strive with mankind forever – He put a limit on His Creation.

Remember that eastern thought and the Hebrew language work in cycles, and this was how YHWH chose to present His Ways. With that understanding we should then be looking for 120 cycles of years as the limit for mankind.

As previously seen from the seven words in Beresheet 1:1, the Scriptures reveal that creation is divided into seven one thousand year periods. (See also Psalm 90:4). That the creator divided time into millennia has been well understood historically, but many fail to understand that each one thousand year cycle consists of twenty Jubilee cycles. The Jubilee cycle is a period of 50 years when everything is restored at the end of the cycle.

The Jubilee cycle provides the pattern for restoration so it only makes sense that the restoration of mankind and all of creation would involve the Jubilee cycle. With this knowledge we can discern that YHWH was referring to 120 Jubilee years or 6,000 years until everything would be restored.

The Scriptures record that the Creation was in a terrible state: *"¹¹ The earth also was corrupt before Elohim, and the earth was filled with violence. ¹² So Elohim looked upon the earth, and indeed it was corrupt; for all flesh had corrupted their way on the earth."* Beresheet 6:11-12. Despite the condition  of the planet, we know of one man, named Noah, who was different. We read that: *"⁵ YHWH saw that the wickedness of man was great in the earth, and that every intent of the thoughts of his heart was only evil continually. ⁶ And YHWH was sorry that He had made man on the earth, and He was grieved in His heart. ⁷ So YHWH said,*

I will destroy man whom I have created from the face of the earth, both man and beast, creeping thing and birds of the air, for I am sorry that I have made them. ⁸ But Noah found favour in the eyes of YHWH." Beresheet 6:5-8.

The account of Noah continues by stating: *"Noah was a just man, perfect in his generations. Noah walked with Elohim."* Beresheet 6:9. The Hebrew word translated as "just" is tzedek (צדיק) which means: *"straight or righteous."* The Hebrew word translated as "perfect" is tamiyim (תמים) which means: *"clean or unblemished."* The Hebrew word translated as "walked" is halak (הלך) which is where we get halakah - a word used to describe our walk with the Almighty. Our halakah is the way we live in a manner which is pleasing to Him - according to His instructions found within the Scriptures.

Therefore, Noah walked with the Almighty and was righteous. This meant he followed the instructions of YHWH and was obedient. Because of his walk, he found favour in the eyes of YHWH and he and his family were spared from the flood. Noah obviously knew the distinctions between right and wrong, righteousness and unrighteousness, clean and unclean - he was actually described as "clean" and "righteous."

There came a time when YHWH commanded Noah to build an Ark. According to the Dead Sea Scrolls, Noah was told by an angel that a flood would occur after a certain number of Shemitah cycles. Each Jubilee cycle contains seven Shemitah cycles each consisting of seven years. The seven Shemitah cycles totaling 49 years are followed by one Jubilee Year. These 50 years form a Jubilee cycle. According to the Dead Sea Scrolls 1 QapGen Col. 6, the flood was to occur in the year that followed a Shemitah cycle.[38] This would have either been Year 1 of a new Shemitah cycle or a Jubilee Year. The point is, YHWH had Noah counting Shemitah cycles. The importance of the Shemitah count will be seen further on in this discussion as we look at information concerning the appearance of the Messiah.

Seven is not the only significant number in the account of Noah. For instance, the flood account is couched within two different forty (40) day periods. We will continue to see that the number forty (40) is very significant when examining the subject of the Messiah.

Noah was six hundred (600) when the floodwaters came. The number six (6) is closely tied with man and we know that six thousand (6,000) is the number of years given to man. It is striking to note that Noah lived the equivalent of twelve (12) Jubilee cycles before the flood. We already saw that the Jubilee is intimately connected with restoration as is the number twelve (12). This will become even more significant

when we examine the role of Yisrael in the restoration of Creation. Noah is a type of savior for mankind and creation so we would expect these patterns and numbers to be linked with The Messiah.

There is another number that stands out in the story of Noah. The Scriptures record that Noah obeyed YHWH and, as a result, he and his wife along with their three sons and their wives were saved from a flood that wiped out the inhabitants of the Earth. The number of people on board the ark was eight. This number is significant because eight means: "new beginnings." This was to be a new beginning for mankind. They carried with them in the Ark remnants of the creatures of the Earth along with all of the preceding history of mankind. The number eight is also closely linked with covenants and following the flood we are told of a Covenant established by Elohim.

"⁸ Then Elohim spoke to Noah and to his sons with him, saying: ⁹ 'And as for Me, behold, I establish My Covenant with you and with your descendants after you, ¹⁰ and with every living creature that is with you: the birds, the cattle, and every beast of the earth with you, of all that go out of the ark, every beast of the earth. ¹¹ Thus I establish My Covenant with you: Never again shall all flesh be cut off by the waters of the flood; never again shall there be a flood to destroy the earth.' ¹² And Elohim said: 'This is the sign of the Covenant which I make between Me and you, and every living creature that is with you, for perpetual generations: ¹³ I set My rainbow in the cloud, and it shall be for the sign of the covenant between Me and the earth. ¹⁴ It shall be, when I bring a cloud over the earth, that the rainbow shall be seen in the cloud; ¹⁵ and I will remember My Covenant which is between Me and you and every living creature of all flesh; the waters shall never again become a flood to destroy all flesh. ¹⁶ The rainbow shall be in the cloud, and I will look on it to remember the everlasting Covenant between Elohim and every living creature of all flesh that is on the earth.' ¹⁷ And Elohim said to Noah, 'This is the sign of the Covenant which I have established between Me and all flesh that is on the earth.'" Beresheet 9:8-17.

Part of this covenant process involved the shedding of blood. The Scriptures record that: "²⁰ Noah built an altar to YHWH, and took of every clean animal and of every clean bird, and offered burnt offerings on the altar. ²¹ And YHWH smelled a soothing aroma. Then YHWH said in His heart, 'I will never again curse the ground for man's sake, although the imagination of man's heart is evil from his youth; nor will I again destroy every living thing as I have done.'" Beresheet 8:20-21.

Now many think of a covenant as a contract or an agreement, but it has a much deeper meaning. In Hebrew the word for covenant is brit (ברית) and it literally means "cutting." This is why we see

sacrifices as part of covenants. Typically, when making an ancient blood covenant, the parties to the covenant would cut the sacrifice in two and then pass between the pieces – literally walking in the blood of the covenant.

This was intended to symbolize the consequences to anyone who broke the covenant: "may they be as the slaughtered animal" (Jeremiah 34:18). If you break a contract in most societies it is deemed a civil matter, and there are usually monetary damages assessed for the breach. When you break a blood covenant, someone is supposed to die - just as the sacrifice died when the covenant was formed.

If we look at the Ancient Hebrew Script we can see that this word also provides us with a story. The bet (ב) in Ancient Hebrew is ⊔ which represents a house or a tent. The resh (ר) is a head 𝕽. The yod (י) is an arm – ⊐ and the taw (ת) is a cross – †, which actually means: "covenant."

So the word picture for "brit" provided by the pictographs tells us that a house will be established through covenant, and the arm of YHWH will be the head. As we shall see further in this discussion, the Arm of YHWH is a common Messianic reference. In fact, the entire covenant process, as it turns out, is really about the Messiah.

To emphasize this point, there are three instances of the untranslated Aleph Taw (את) in Beresheet 8:21 when the burnt offerings were being made to YHWH. There are also three instances of the Aleph Taw (את) when YHWH declares that He will make a covenant. (Beresheet 9:9-10).

If we look at the Aleph Taw את in ancient Hebrew pictographs we see the following: †𝕭. The aleph (א) is depicted as the head of an ox (𝕭), symbolizing strength. The taw (ת) is the sign of a cross (†) which means "covenant." Therefore the את actually means: "strength of the covenant."

We know that covenants are the way that YHWH plans to restore Creation, and it is now clear that the Messiah is an integral part of the covenant process. The very fact that YHWH offers restoration through a covenant is a wonderful example of the favour of YHWH - which is often mislabeled as grace. He did not have to enter into any covenants with man, but He did so as a gesture of His kindness and mercy and as part of His Plan to restore His creation.

When Adam and Hawah disobeyed YHWH in the garden of Eden, it did not destroy the plan YHWH had for creation. He knew that sin would enter the universe through Adam. Although Adam and Hawah were sentenced to die in the first millenial day, they had a destiny and a purpose before the physical was created, just like every child of Elohim. The first death is not the final judgment on a child of Elohim as a Covenant existed with every child of Elohim from before the physical universe was created, satan's rebellion caused the earth to become chaotic and desolate in Beresheet 1:2 before YHWH ever created the physical universe. Creation was corrupted in the garden and that continued in the days of Noah, but this did not in any way thwart the plan of YHWH. Instead, He continued to work with Noah to bring about restoration. And after Noah, there was Shem, and after Shem there was Abraham, Yitshaq and Yaakob.

All of the Covenants detailed in the Scriptures are specifically designed to bring about the restoration of all things, and YHWH always preserves a righteous line through which He operates His Covenant promises. Thanks to the mercy of the Almighty and the obedience of Noah, Shem, Abraham, Yitshaq and Yaakob, we are all here today to participate in this process.

After the flood, mankind began to reproduce, and we are told about an incident involving Noah and Canaan, the son of Ham. Here is the account as provided in the Scriptures:

"*20 And Noah began to be a farmer, and he planted a vineyard. 21 Then he drank of the wine and was drunk, and became uncovered in his tent. 22 And Ham, the father of Canaan, saw the nakedness of his father, and told his two brothers outside. 23 But Shem and Japheth took a garment, laid it on both their shoulders, and went backward and covered the nakedness of their father. Their faces were turned away, and they did not see their father's nakedness. 24 So Noah awoke from his wine, and knew what his younger son had done to him. 25 Then he said: 'Cursed be Canaan; a servant of servants he shall be to his brethren.'*" Beresheet 9:20-25.

Now many fail to recognize what occurred here. They think that Ham did something wrong, and then his son Canaan was unfairly cursed. What they fail to understand is that the focus of this story was always on Canaan. Notice that the text refers to all of the sons of Noah but specifically describes Ham as "the father of Canaan."

Also, when Noah woke up and saw what "his younger son had done" he was not referring to Ham. Ham was not Noah's younger son, but Canaan was Ham's younger son. Therefore "his younger son" was not Noah's younger son, but rather, Ham's younger son. Ham was apparently not completely innocent though - he "saw" something, but did not do anything except "tell" his two brothers. It was his two brothers Shem and Yapheth who "acted" and resolved the problem.

This passage begins with the righteous Noah being called a

farmer, and ends with Canaan being cursed to be a servant. The story is couched in a time period from when Noah became drunk with wine to when he awoke from his wine. The meat of the story occurs during this period while he was under the influence of wine, and it alludes to an incident described as ervah (ערוה) which is translated - "nakedness."

As with the nakedness in the Garden, the same holds true with this event - there seems to have been more than just nudity. The Scriptures detail various incidents referred to as ervah (ערוה) in Leviticus 18, the first of which is: "*None of you shall approach anyone who is near of kin to him, to uncover his nakedness: I am YHWH.*" Leviticus 18:6.

Amazingly, the earth had just been cleansed by a flood. This was supposed to be a fresh start, but it obviously did not last very long. Certainly, some time elapsed from the flood to this incident since Canaan was not even born at the time of the flood, but nevertheless, it should have been fresh in everyone's minds. Surely the children were told the story repeatedly as they grew up.

The fact that Canaan was the perpetrator seems to be reinforced by the fact that the instructions in the Scriptures concerning sexual sins are prefaced by the warning not to do: "*according to the doings of the land of Canaan.*" Leviticus 18:3. Apparently, those living in Canaan, the descendents of Canaan, continued the sins of their father.

This incident is clearly intended to draw our attention back to the Garden - back to the incident when mankind first sinned. Noah was, after all, a type of Adam. Just as there were three participants in the Garden involved in an incident of sin surrounding the fruit of a tree, here we have Noah, Canaan and Ham involved in an incident stemming from the fruit of the vine. Interestingly the Targums state that Noah found the vine which was brought in a river from the Garden of Eden.

Within this period of time, when Noah was under the influence of the wine, there are three instances of the untranslated Aleph Taw (את). There are also three sons described and three separate events involving the sons and the Aleph Taw (את). The first instance occurs when Ham saw the nakedness of his father. The second occurs when Yapheth and Shem took a garment, and the third occurred when they covered the nakedness of their father.

As we think back to the Garden we see the problem of our nakedness. We now can see the sin of man passed through this son of Adam, the father of mankind - Noah. We then see two sons taking a mantle between their "shoulders," which is the word shechem (שכם) in Hebrew. These two sons covered the nakedness (ערות) just as YHWH

covered the sins of Adam and Hawah. We later see blessings and curses meted out by Noah. This is a shadow picture of an event that will occur centuries later at a place, "between the shoulders" of two mountains – a place called Shechem.[39]

It is important to recognize these connections, because the Scriptures are not just a collection of random stories that make for interesting reading. Everything contained in the Scriptures fits together and only when we can see and appreciate this perfect design will we begin to fully comprehend the plan of the Creator.

From the seed of Ham came the Canaanites who later populated the land of Canaan, including Sodom and Gomorah. These descendents of Ham were reknowned for their sexual deviancy. Also from Ham came the Cushites who became the founders of Babylon.

4

Babylon

We read a very brief but telling portion of history in the Scriptures when it describes Babylon. *"¹ Now the whole earth had one language and one speech. ² And it came to pass, as they journeyed from the east, that they found a plain in the land of Shinar, and they dwelt there. ³ Then they said to one another, 'Come, let us make bricks and bake them thoroughly.' They had brick for stone, and they had asphalt for mortar. ⁴ And they said, 'Come, let us build ourselves a city, and a tower whose top is in the heavens; let us make a name for ourselves, lest we be scattered abroad over the face of the whole earth."* Beresheet 11:1-4 NKJV.

The inhabitants of Babylon had established their own political and religious system. They were going to build a city *for themselves* and make a name *for themselves*. Contrast this city with Eden and Jerusalem – both locations where YHWH would place His Name and dwell with His people.[40]

Babylon stood in direct contrast with the desire of the Creator for His Creation and it continues to be used as an example and symbol of that attitude. Mankind had become haughty and arrogant - they reveled in their own intelligence and abilities rather than giving the honor and esteem to YHWH. We see that much of modern civilization shares the same attitude as mankind once had in Babylon as they built a Tower *"to the heavens."* (Beresheet 11:1-9).

Today we share more with Babylon than mere attitude or architectural accomplishments. In fact, what many fail to recognize is that it was the false religious system, established by men, that was at the heart of the Babel incident. While many popular renderings show a round tower reaching to the heavens, the tower was more likely an ancient ziggurat which served as the centerpiece to the sun god worship established through Nimrod and his mother Semiramis.[41]

It was at Babylon that we see the man Nimrod being worshipped as a god. There are various traditions which describe a violent fate met by Nimrod. Despite his death, he became deified through a Trinitarian religious system. From Babylon we can trace the roots of a counterfeit system which is commonly called sun god worship.

History reveals a very ancient struggle between the worship of the Creator of the Universe and that of the sun or some pagan deity which can be traced directly back to Babylon. What we see happening in Babylon was a religious and political system that was challenging the authority and government of Elohim. Babylon does not worship the Elohim of the Scriptures called YHWH, it always represents a false system of worship.

Beresheet 10:6 tell us that Noah's son Ham had a son named Cush. Pagan tradition indicates that Cush married Semiramis and that their son was the "Nimrod" of Scripture. Nimrod *"began to be a mighty one in the earth. He was a mighty hunter before YHWH: wherefore it is said, even as Nimrod the mighty hunter before YHWH. And the beginning of his kingdom was Babel, and Erech, and Accad, and Calneh, in the land of Shinar."* Beresheet 10:8-10.

Most people do not quite grasp the meaning of this passage and think that maybe Nimrod was simply good with the bow and arrow. There are many different legends associated with Nimrod. Some claim that "mighty hunter" should actually be interpreted as "giant hunter"

because he slew giants and conquered lands. Others claim that his great success in hunting was due to the fact that he wore the coats of skin which Elohim made for Adam and Hawah. These coats were handed down from father to son, and thus came into the possession of Noah, who took them with him into the ark, whence they were stolen by Ham. The latter gave them to his son Cush, who in turn gave them to **Nimrod**, and when the animals saw the latter clad in them, they crouched before him so that he had no difficulty in catching them. The people, however, thought that these feats were due to his extraordinary strength, so that they made him their king.[42]

There is one thing which is clear - at some point Nimrod became opposed to YHWH. "Until Nimrod, mankind was governed by the

patriarchal system where the heads of families heard from [Elohim] and guided their individual tribes. Nimrod, more accurately a 'mighty hunter against YHWH,' usurped patriarchal rule, and crowned himself the first king in all of history. Now man ruled instead of [Elohim]."[43]

As common tradition has it - Nimrod became a god-man to the people and Semiramis, his wife and mother, became the Queen of ancient Babylon. Nimrod was eventually killed by an enemy - some traditions state that it was Shem, the son of Noah. His body was apparently cut into pieces and sent to various parts of his kingdom to demonstrate that he was a man and he was dead. This was supposed to put an end to his being worshipped as a god, but here is where Semiramis stepped in - she apparently had all of Nimrod's body parts gathered, except for one part that could not be found - his phallus.

Semiramis claimed that Nimrod could not come back to life without it and told the people of Babylon that Nimrod had ascended to the sun and was now to be called "Baal," the sun god. She was creating a mystery religion. Claiming to be immaculately conceived she established herself as a goddess named Ishtar, also known as Easter. She claimed that she descended from the moon in a giant moon egg that fell into the Euphrates River at the time of the first full moon after the spring equinox. Ishtar soon became pregnant and declared that it was the rays of the sun-god Baal that caused her to conceive.

The son that she brought forth on the winter solstice, was named Tammuz.[44] This child was believed to be the son of the sun-god, Baal. Tammuz, like his supposed father, became a hunter. When Tammuz was forty (40) he was killed during a freak accident by a wild pig. Ishtar proclaimed that Tammuz was now ascended to his father, Baal, and that the two of them would be with the worshippers in the sacred candle or lamp flame as Father, Son and Spirit. Ishtar, who was now worshipped as the 'Mother of God and Queen of Heaven,' continued to build her mystery religion.

She also proclaimed a forty day period of time of sorrow each year prior to the anniversary of the death of Tammuz. It was called "Weeping for Tammuz" and it lasted for forty (forty) days – one day for each year that Tammuz was alive. The concept was to deprive oneself of an earthly pleasure. During this time, no meat was to be eaten. Worshippers were to meditate upon the sacred mysteries of Baal and Tammuz, and to make the sign of the cross in front of their hearts as they worshipped. The cross represented the "t" of Tammuz.

This is where the act of making the sign of the cross originated as well as Lent, which is simply a modified version of "Weeping for Tammuz." Those involved in this sun god worship also ate sacred cakes with the marking of a "+" or cross on the top. This ancient rite is the origin of the wafers marked with the Tammuz "+" which Catholics use during their Eucharist service.

Tammuz, "the son of god," was known as a Sumerian god of fertility and of new life. He was called a shepherd and he was also called a "healer" and regarded as a savior. His death and resurrection were celebrated yearly and the cycles of the sun and the growing season were intimately connected and part of this religious cycle. This is where we derive such holidays as Christmas and Easter. They originated in Babylonian sun worship and were later adopted by Christianity, which is a derivative of the Babylonian system of sun worship.[45]

YHWH was obviously not pleased with what He observed in Babylon. Read what happened: "[5] *But YHWH came down to see the city and the tower which the sons of men had built.* [6] *And YHWH said, 'Indeed the people are one and they all have one language, and this is what they begin to do; now nothing that they propose to do will be withheld from them.* [7] *Come, let Us go down and there confuse their language, that they may not understand one another's speech.'* [8] *So YHWH scattered them abroad from there over the face of all the earth, and they ceased building the city.* [9] *Therefore its name is called Babel, because there YHWH confused the language of all the earth; and from there YHWH scattered them abroad over the face of all the earth.*" Beresheet 11:5-9.

This Babylonian religious tradition was directly linked to sun worship and stood in opposition to the worship of YHWH. The people were worshipping creation instead of the Creator, and as a result, they were scattered throughout the Earth.

Imagine for a moment what this meant. People who once lived in the land of Shinar were transplanted all over the earth. Not only were they moved, but they also spoke different languages – quite a change. Regardless, of their different languages and different locations, they continued with their Babylonian mystery religion, only now they had different names and structures involved in their sun worship.

From Babylon we see the pattern for a false system of worship that would repeat, perpetuate and morph throughout the centuries. This system and its varied progeny which worship a trinity "godhead" are in competition to steal worship from the true Creator described in the Scriptures.

One city in the region of Babylon that is of particular interest to this discussion is the City of Ur. It was located in southern Mesopotamia and it was an important metropolis of the ancient world situated on the Euphrates River. Ur was the capital of Sumer for two centuries until the Elamites captured the city. The city came to be known as "Ur of the Chaldees" or "Ur of the Kashdim" (אור כשדים) after the Chaldeans entered southern Babylonia after 1000 B.C.E.

The city was a prosperous center of religion and industry. Thousands of recovered clay documents attest to thriving business activity. . . The Babylonians worshiped many gods, but the moon god Sin was supreme. Accordingly, the city of Ur was a kind of theocracy

centered around the moon deity. Ur-Nammu, the founder of the strong Third Dynasty of Ur [1900 1793 BCE]*, built the famous Ziggurats, a system of terraced platforms on which temples were erected.[46]

Because Ur was a center of worshipping the moon god it is apparent that astrology would have been widely known and practiced. The Chaldeans, who later conquered this region, were highly acclaimed for their astrology.

"The 'wisdom' personified by the moon-god is likewise an expression of the science of astrology, in which the observation of the moon's phases is so important a factor. The tendency to centralize the powers of the universe leads to the establishment of the doctrine of a triad consisting of Sin, Shamash, and Ishtar, respectively personifying the moon, the sun, and the planet Venus.

[The moon god] was named Sin in Babylonia and Assyria, and was also worshipped in Harran. Sin had a beard made of lapis lazuli and rode on a winged bull. His wife was Ningal ("Great Lady"), who bore him Utu ("Sun") and Inanna (Inanna is recognized as being the Sumerian name for Ishtar). His symbols are the crescent moon, the bull (through his father, Enlil, "Bull of Heaven"), and the tripod (which may be a lamp-stand)."[47]

Interestingly, the Hebrew spelling of this city named Ur (אור) is exactly the same as the spelling for the Hebrew word "light" (אור)

as in: On the first day Elohim said "*Let there be light* (אור) *and there was light* (אור)." Beresheet 1:3.[48] For some reason, out of this place called "light" where people worshipped the moon, YHWH called a man who would be a light, and eventually bring forth the Light of the World to all flesh – a man who would be called Abraham.

5

Abraham

The Scriptures describe a man named Abram who dwelled in the city called Ur of the Chaldees. This man, who lived in the midst of a pagan society, was called out by YHWH Who told him to leave his father's household and travel to the Land of Canaan.

YHWH promised the following to Abram:

> *"I will make you into a great nation*
> *and I will bless you;*
> *I will make your name great,*
> *and you will be a blessing.*
> *I will bless those who bless you,*
> *and whoever curses you I will curse;*
> *and all peoples on earth*
> *will be blessed through you."*
> Beresheet 12:2-3 NIV

Leaving his home was surely no small thing. It meant leaving the life that he knew and had labored to build. It meant leaving the security of the position that he held in his society. It meant traveling through unknown lands and dwelling in those lands as a stranger.

We do not know if Abram struggled with this decision, all we know is that he obeyed by going to the land of Canaan. Prior to travelling to the land of Canaan, his father Terah moved the family to Haran, where they lived until his death. Interestingly, Haran was also the name of Abram's brother who predeceased Terah.

The Scriptures record the following: "⁴ *So Abram departed as YHWH had spoken to him, and Lot went with him. And Abram was seventy-five years old when he departed from Haran.* ⁵ *Then Abram took* אֵת *Sarai his wife and* אֵת *Lot his brother's son, and* אֵת *all their possessions that they*

had gathered, and את the people whom they had acquired in Haran, and they departed to go to the land of Canaan. So they came to the land of Canaan. ⁶ Abram passed through the land to the place of Shechem, as far as the terebinth tree of Moreh. And the Canaanites were then in the land. ⁷ Then YHWH appeared to Abram and said, 'To your seed I will give את this Land.' And there he built an altar to YHWH, Who had appeared to him." Beresheet 12:4-7.

The above Scripture passage that details Abram's departure includes the Aleph Taw (את). Notice that the text describes how he left with "the people they had acquired." The household of Abram included more than just his wife and his nephew. There were many others who travelled with him. The first location where Abram built an Altar is in Shechem. This is also the location where YHWH appeared to Abram – obviously a special place of great significance. After his experience with YHWH at Shechem, he then moved near Beth El, built another altar and proceeded further south.

Abram was on the move much of his life after leaving Haran and his travels and experiences provide a pattern for future events. He went to Egypt when there was famine and returned to the land of Canaan when instructed. He paid tithes to Melchizedek, the Priest of the Most High in Jerusalem. He lived a life exemplified by obedience. In Beresheet 26:5 YHWH declares that he "obeyed My voice and kept My charge, My commandments, My statutes, and My Torah."

The word shamar (שמר) is found in this passage as he kept and guarded the charge, the commandments, statutes and Torah of YHWH- just as Adam was to keep and guard the Ways of YHWH. He was obeying the Torah because that was part of the Covenant he made with YHWH. Unlike other covenants made between men, this Covenant was different because of the fact that it was between the Creator and a man. Besides the parties, it was also unique because only YHWH became liable for either party breaking the Covenant.

Here is the account of the Covenant process: "¹² Now when the sun was going down, a deep sleep fell upon Abram, and behold, dread and great darkness fell upon him. ¹³ Then He said to Abram know certainly that your descendants will be strangers in a land that is not theirs, and will serve them, and they will afflict them four hundred years. ¹⁴ And also the nation whom they serve I will judge, afterward they will come out with great possessions. ¹⁵ Now as for you, you shall go to your fathers in peace, you shall be buried at a good old age. ¹⁶ But in the fourth generation they shall return here, for the iniquity of the Amorites is not yet complete. ¹⁷ And it came to pass – then the sun went down and it was dark, that behold there appeared a smoking firepot and a flaming torch that passed between those pieces. ¹⁸ On the same day YHWH made a

Covenant with Abram saying: '*To your descendants I have given this Land, from the river of Egypt to the great river, the River Euphrates -* ¹⁹ *the Kenites, the Kennizites, the Kadmonites,* ²⁰ *the Hittites, the Perrizites, the Rephaim,* ²¹ *the Amorites, the Canaanites, the Girgashites, and the Jebusites.*" Beresheet 15:12-21.

We read that YHWH put Abram into what is described as a "deep sleep." Notice also that horror and great darkness fell upon him. This is a picture of death and the Hebrew word used here is tardemah (תרדמה). This was the same word used in Beresheet 2:21 when Hawah was taken from the side of Adam. These events parallel one another and something very important is going on in each instance.

Amazingly, in the portion which describes the Covenant that YHWH made with Abram there are twelve (12) instances of the untranslated Aleph Taw (את). Because of this we see a picture of the Messiah passing through the pieces. Therefore, the message is clear that the Messiah would carry the punishment for either party breaking the Covenant. The fact that there are twelve (12) instances of the Aleph Taw (את) appears to reveal that the punishment inflicted upon the Messiah will save the seed of Abraham – the twelve (12) tribes of Israel which eventually inherit this Covenant from Abraham.

After YHWH entered into Covenant with Abram, he later confirmed the covenant when Abram was 99 years old. YHWH changed his name to Abraham by adding a hey (ה) to his name. (Beresheet 17:5). YHWH then detailed the Covenant of circumcision (Beresheet 17:10 - 14).

The Covenant involved cutting his flesh and shedding his blood - not just the flesh and blood of the animals previously sacrificed. The fact that it was cut in the male organ is extremely significant since this Covenant was made with Abraham and his seed. In this Scripture passage there are three (3) instances of the untranslated Aleph Taw (את).

YHWH also changed the name of Abraham's wife from Sarai to Sarah. He added a hey (ה) to her name also. (Beresheet 17:15). This reveals that the Covenant would pass from the seed of Abraham through the cutting - brit - into the womb of Sarah. Just as Hawah was a bride for Adam - YHWH is showing us that through Abraham and Sarah - He was preparing a Bride for Himself. Interestingly, we see two heys (ה) added to this union and we find the hey (ה) two times in the Name of YHWH (יהוה).⁵⁰

An important part of the original execution of this Covenant is the fact that Abraham <u>did not</u> pass through the cuttings. Remember, both of the participants of a covenant would literally walk between the pieces of the covenant, which was drenched with the blood of the slaughtered animal. The parties to the covenant would both have the blood of the covenant upon them. This entire process symbolized the severity of breaking the covenant – bloodshed and death.

At Beresheet 15:17 we are told to "behold," which is hineh (הנה) in Hebrew or (𐤄𐤍𐤄) in ancient Hebrew. The ancient language is particularly interesting in this instance because the character surrounded by each hey (𐤄) is a nun (𐤍) which means: "continue" or "perpetuate." It is specifically pointing to the "seed" continuing through this Covenant which is made while one of the participants is virtually "dead."

A smoking firepot and a burning torch passed through the cuttings as a demonstration that YHWH would bear the responsibility for both of the parties. All Abraham was responsible to do was carry the sign of the Covenant in his flesh through circumcision. Abraham was instructed to circumcise himself and <u>every male in his household</u> - not just his physical seed.

This is a very critical point to understand - Abraham had a very large household that traveled with him. They were not all his physical seed, but they were part of his household and they dwelled within his tents. Therefore, the Covenant was made with him and included all of his household - just as the rainbow was the sign of the Covenant made previously with Noah and all of his household in perpetuity.

The significance of the circumcision was that Abraham's seed would pass through the cutting of the Covenant, and then the promises of the Covenant would pass through with the seed. The male child would then be circumcised on the eighth day and when that child grew up to become a man - his seed would in turn pass through the cutting of the Covenant and so on - it was an everlasting Covenant.

There is a distinct connection between the eight pieces of flesh involved in the Covenant and the eighth day circumcision when the flesh of the male child is cut. The number eight typically signifies a "new beginning" after the completion of the Scriptural cycle of seven that began on the first day of creation and continues to this day. The number eight is the same as the letter het (ח) in Hebrew which means: "a fence" or "separation." This can be plainly seen in the ancient Hebrew script - "𐤇".

Therefore, from this Covenant we can see that the physical descendants of Abraham and those in his household who were circumcised were to be set apart. They were to be surrounded by the

hedge of the Torah – just as we saw in the Garden. This is very clear in the Scriptures. In fact, here is what YHWH said about Abraham in Beresheet 18:19: *"For I have known him, in order that he may command his children and his household after him, that they **keep** the Way of YHWH, to do righteousness and justice, that YHWH may bring to Abraham what He has spoken to him."*

Once again, we read in the Hebrew text the word "shamar" (שמר) which has been translated as "keep." Abraham watched and kept the hedge around his children and his entire household - all those who dwelled with him. He instructed them all in the Way - which is the Torah. Abraham had joined with YHWH and his household represented the House of YHWH – a people in Covenant with their Creator.

The purpose of this Covenant with Abraham was to prepare a people who could be restored to their Creator. They needed to know and obey the ways of YHWH and their faith demonstrated by their conduct would be counted toward righteousness.

This is an important point to understand. While YHWH demonstrates that He alone will suffer the penalty for the Covenant being broken, those in the Covenant must be obedient. Had Abram not gone from Ur as instructed, he never would have seen the Land and he would not have then entered into covenant with YHWH. His obedience was important to get him to the place where he could be in Covenant with YHWH.

There was still a problem that haunted all of mankind since the garden – death. All the good works in the world would not overcome this barrier. That is where the Messiah comes in, and we are given a vivid description of His work through the pattern of the son. The promised son was specifically to come from the union of Abraham and Sarah through the child named Isaac, more correctly Yitshaq (יצחק). (Beresheet 17:19).

It was not until Abraham was 99 years old, and Sarah was 89, that YHWH indicated He would fulfill His promise of a child, next year at *"the Appointed Time."* Beresheet 18:14.[51] This is quite significant because these words were spoken immediately prior to the judgment that was about to befall Sodom and Gomorrah.

Since we are provided some hints that Lot was eating unleavened bread (Beresheet 19:3) this event likely occurred at the time of Passover. Just as the righteous were delivered from Egypt hundreds of years later, Lot and his family were delivered from judgment during Passover thus, *"the Appointed Time next year"* in which Yitshaq was born would have likely been Passover.[52]

This is important because we can see the life of Yitshaq as a pattern for the Son of Elohim. We know this through his fulfillment of the Appointed Times. We can also see this from direct references to Yitshaq as the "only son" of Abraham. This was specifically stated three times when Abraham was instructed to sacrifice Yitshaq at Moriah.

After Yitshaq was born and grown Elohim said to Abraham: *"Take your son, your only son, Yitshaq, whom you love, and go to the region of Moriah. Sacrifice him there as a burnt offering on one of the mountains I will tell you about."* Beresheet 22:2.

Imagine that! This promised son, a miracle child that was given to Abraham and Sarah in their old age, was now to be sacrificed. I doubt that Abraham told Sarah. Instead, early the next morning he arose and took Yitshaq and two servants. On the third day[53] they arrived in the land of Moriah and Abraham placed the wood of the sacrifice on the shoulders of Yitshaq.

Yitshaq must have known that something was amiss. Abraham was probably not himself as he struggled to obey this difficult command. They typically would have brought their sacrifice with them, leading Yitshaq to ask the question: *"Where is the lamb?"* Abraham's response was: *"Elohim Himself will provide the lamb for the burnt offering, my son."* Beresheet 22:8. A direct translation from the Hebrew reads: *"Elohim will provide Himself a lamb."*

Abraham then bound Yitshaq and laid him on the altar to sacrifice him. It is important to note that there is nothing to indicate that Yitshaq struggled or protested. He was a grown man while Abraham was very old. According to the Book of Yasher he was 37 years old so he likely could have escaped, but it appears that he willingly laid down his life. (Yasher 22:41,53).[54]

As Abraham was about to kill his son he was stopped by the Messenger of YHWH and was told not to touch his son. The Messenger then went on to state: *"Now I know that you fear Elohim, because you have not withheld from me your son, your only son."* Beresheet 22:12. *"15 Then the Messenger of YHWH called to Abraham a second time out of heaven, 16 and said: 'By Myself*

I have sworn, says YHWH, because you have done this thing, and have not withheld your son, your only son - [17] blessing I will bless you, and multiplying I will multiply your seed as the stars of the heaven and as the sand which is on the seashore; and your seed shall possess the gate of their enemies. [18] _In your seed all the nations of the earth shall be blessed_, because you have obeyed My voice." Beresheet 22:15-18.

There is so much more going on in this passage than we can possibly imagine by just reading the English. On the surface we see a great promise that "the seed" of Abraham will be incredibly numerous and powerful and all the nations of the earth would be blessed because of the seed.

As with many Scripture passages we can only understand the profound depth of the text by reading and studying the original Hebrew. For instance, this entire passage is filled with the untranslated Aleph Taw (את) which is a clear indication that it is a Messianic reference.

There are three times that Yitshaq is referred to Abraham as "your son, your only son." In each of those three references there are three occurrences of the untranslated Aleph Taw (את). In Beresheet 22:9, the passage where it describes Abraham as laying the wood on the altar and binding Yitshaq, there are three occurrences of the untranslated Aleph Taw (את). Also in the following passage when Abraham was prepared to slay Yitshaq there are three occurrences of the untranslated Aleph Taw (את).

It could not be any clearer that this incident, often referred to as "the Akeda," was a shadow picture of the fact that Elohim would provide a Lamb, His only Son. It is equally clear that Abraham must have believed that his "only son" would be resurrected, since the Covenant was promised to pass through the son. The Lamb of Elohim would be slain and the promise to Abraham that "all nations would be blessed" would extend through this Lamb. This is powerful information and it can only fully be seen in the Hebrew text.[55]

Many fail to recognize the Messianic significance of this "second" Covenant made with Abraham immediately after he offered his son. In this passage of Scripture the word "son" is couched between two instances of the untranslated Aleph Taw (את). Likewise, when the Messenger refers to the seed, there are two occasions when the untranslated Aleph Taw (את) is right next to the word "seed."

This is a clear Messianic reference and it is interesting to note that the word "seed" is a singular subject noun, it is not plural. While the seed of Abraham is often interpreted to mean his descendants, the text can also refer to one Seed. This is the same Seed described

in Beresheet 3:15 as the promised Seed of Hawah that would crush the head of the serpent.[56]

So we see from this example in the life of Abraham that YHWH would offer up the Lamb of Elohim - His only Son. This offering would be specifically related to the Covenant made with Abraham. Abraham called the place where this occurred YHWH Yireh because "*On the mountain of YHWH it will be provided.*" Beresheet 22:14.

Therefore, on this mountain in Moriah the Lamb of Elohim would be provided. While tradition holds that this is the same location that the House of YHWH was later constructed by Solomon, it is also very possible that this was on the Mount of Olives where the Red Heifer was sacrificed on what is called the Miphkad Altar.[57]

It is also important to point out that the Scriptures only describe Abraham coming down from the mountain. We read the following: "*Then Abraham returned to his servants, and they set off together for Beersheva. And Abraham stayed in Beersheva.*" Beresheet 22:19. This begs the question: "Where was Yitshaq?"

Some use this passage to assert the position that Yitshaq actually was sacrificed and was later resurrected, but the text simply does not support such a theory. Rather, he may have stayed on the mountain. What we see is a pattern that is later repeated by Moses and Joshua. They both go up, but when Moses goes down there is no mention of Joshua going down. It is from these simple, consistent underlying messages and patterns that we can begin to understand great mysteries.

Yitshaq was likely alive, but the absence of him returning with Abraham, and then his sudden appearance years later when Abraham decides to find him a bride, makes an interesting metaphorical death and resurrection. This, of course, is consistent with the pattern provided by the event, and the faith demonstrated by Abraham that his "only son" would be resurrected. The theme of the promised son, born at the Appointed Time, dying and later being resurrected is repeated in the incident involving the Shunammite woman and Elisha. (2 Melakim 4:1-37).

We will discuss how the bride of Yitshaq was selected further in this discussion. For now it is important to point out when Yitshaq comes "back to life" in the text, it is for the purpose of joining with his bride. At that time we find Yitshaq in a field "meditating" in the evening.

A literal reading of the Hebrew is much more intriguing than the English translation. The Hebrew text in Beresheet 24:63 indicates that "*Yitshaq lifted up his eyes and saw and behold the camels coming.*" The

text goes on to state that "*Rivkah lifted up* את *her eyes and when she saw* את *she fell off her camel.*" (Beresheet 24:64). Abraham's servant then tells Rivkah that this man is his master whereupon she covers herself with a veil. The servant told Yisthaq את all that he had done. (Beresheet 24:65-66).

There are three instances of the Aleph Taw (את) in the passage involving Yitshaq meeting his bride. They once again point us to the Messiah and the life of "the only son" of Abraham provides great insight into "the only Son of YHWH" - the Messiah.

6

Moshiach

Thus far we have established the fact that the Scriptures provide information concerning a Messiah without giving a specific definition concerning the word "messiah." This was done intentionally to lay the necessary foundation and to show some of the early patterns and promises related to the Messiah. It is imperative to comprehend the need for a messiah in order to understand the purpose and function of the Messiah.

Most people probably have some belief or understanding of the Messiah – the real question is whether it is accurate. Having grown up in the 20th century, the concept of a Messiah was nothing new to me, although it was based upon presumptions and inherited traditions which skewed my understanding.

Anyone that ascribes to one of the mainstream world religions such as Christianity, Judaism or Islam likely believes that the world needs a savior or messiah. While their beliefs and expectations concerning a messiah will no doubt differ from each other, their beliefs may also be far removed from the patterns and prophecies provided in the Scriptures. In fact, there are many messianic traditions in existence today that derive from Babylonian sun worship rather than the Scriptures. Some of the Babylonian concepts have even infiltrated their way into these mainstream religions.

Christians refer to their savior as "Christ," those in Islam refer to this individual as "al-Mahdi," while Judaism and those who study the Hebrew Scriptures refer to Moshiach, also pronounced Mashiach. Interestingly, all of these religions share a common set of sacred texts, namely the Hebrew Scriptures. Despite these shared texts their understanding of the Messiah is very different.

Some come to their understanding of messiah with the hindsight afforded to them by thousands of years of history while others simply

believe in a messiah because that is what they have been taught. As a result of the different religions, traditions and sources of knowledge, there are diverse opinions regarding the anticipated messiah. Is the messiah a man? Is he God? Is there one messiah or are there many? Does the messiah save from sin, death, both or does he save at all?

There are many different beliefs concerning messiah because there are few direct references to The Messiah in the Scriptures. So far, we have largely seen patterns that have attracted our attention because of the presence of the Aleph Taw (את). We have not read anything which specifically states that it has anything to do with the Messiah. In fact, we have not seen anything that unequivocally provides that there would even be a Messiah.

Traditionally, the very word moshiach in Hebrew was simply used to refer to one who was "anointed" – specifically anointed with oil. There are many in the Scriptures who were anointed, but they were simply individuals assigned or appointed to function in a particular role such as a priest or a king.

Moses anointed Aaron and his sons to act as priests. Thus, they were individuals who were anointed to perform a specific role (Exodus 28:41). Saul and David were anointed by Samuel to be Kings of Israel. Even certain things were anointed, such as the Tabernacle and everything in it, the Altar, the Laver and items used in the service of Elohim.

Thus we see examples of prophets anointing things, as well as other individuals such as priests and kings. There is a distinction made between prophets, and anointed ones, as it was the prophets who did the anointing. This is aptly demonstrated in the passage which states: *"Do not touch My anointed ones, and do My prophets no harm."* Psalms (Tehillim) 105:15.[58]

The priests and kings of Israel are examples of "anointed ones," but somehow we understand that there was a difference between these men being anointed and The Anointed One - Messiah. In fact, while King Saul was attempting to kill David, he was still considered to be YHWH's anointed or moshiach (1 Shemuel 24:10). Therefore, a person can be moshiach, or "anointed" without being the One who is understood to be The Moshiach. While there are many who are referred to as anointed in the Scriptures, there is a constant theme regarding The Anointed.

Christians believe that Jesus was The Messiah although they typically refer to "The Christ" rather than to HaMoshiach, which means: "The Messiah" in Hebrew. Thus a Christian is someone who

follows a christ, which is not necessarily the same as The Messiah. While these terms are often used interchangeably, their origins and history are quite different.

The use of the word "christ" in place of the word "moshiach" is demonstrative of a problem which exists in the Christian religion involving the influence and adoption of pagan concepts. Over the centuries Christianity adopted certain pagan notions, festivals and beliefs through a process known as syncretism. One such influence is the use of the term "christ."

While moshiach is a Hebrew word and can only refer to the anointed or messiah revealed in the Hebrew Scriptures – the word "christ" is not so specific. The English word "christ" derives from the Greek word "christos." "Christos" is typically defined as meaning "anointed" but it does not originate with the Christian religion or the Christian Savior. It literally means: "to smear, to rub or to contact."

Christos was originally "applied in the Greek Mysteries to a candidate who had passed the last degree and become a full initiate. Also the immanent individual god in a person, equivalent in some respects to Dionysus, Krishna, etc. What we know as Christianity is a syncretism of borrowings from Neoplatonism, neo-Pythogoreanism, Greek Gnosticism, and Hebrew religion. Christos was commonly used in the Greek translation of the Bible as a title of the Jewish Kings, those who had been anointed for reigning . . ."[59]

Concerning the word Christos: "there is little doubt that the pagans and the Christian authors of the first two centuries [CE] used the word synonymously with Christus, Chrestus, Christiani, and Chrestiani. According to *Realencyclopaedie*, the inscription "Chrestos" is to be seen on a Mithras relief in the Vatican. Osiris, the sun-god of Egypt, was revered as Chrestos - as was Mithra. In the Synagogue of the Marcionites on Mount Hermon, built

in the 3rd century [CE], Jesus' title is spelled Chrestos, this name was used by the common people of that time. The Gnostics used the name "Christos" as the 3rd person in their godhead - Father, Spirit (the first woman), and Son, completing the "Divine Family" - a concept adopted by "Christianity."[60]

"The syncretism between Christos and Chrestos (the Sun-deity Osiris), is further elucidated by the fact of emperor Hadrian's report, who wrote, 'There are there (in Egypt) Christians who worship

Serapis; and devoted to Serapis, are those who call themselves Bishops of Christ." Serapis was another Sundeity who superceded Osiris in Alexandria.[61] Thus it can be seen that "christ" was a term applied to many pagan gods before it was ever attached as a sort of surname to the name Jesus – thus Jesus Christ.

This is one of the primary reasons why Jews do not believe that the Christian Christ named Jesus is the Hebrew Moshiach. The term "Christ" has pagan origins and they argue that a pagan title would never be attributed to The Messiah. This is certainly a valid point and it is not the only pagan element attributed to the Messiah through the religion of Christianity.

In response to this allegation, a Christian that uses an English translation of the Scriptures would typically retort that there cannot be anything wrong with the title "Christ" because it is used in their Bible. Sadly, this is an example the problems resulting from translation errors - particularly in the English "New Testament" texts which derive from various Hellenized Greek manuscripts.

Read the following statement found in the New King James Version of the Bible which deals with the popular story of the Samaritan woman at the well. *"[25] The woman said to Him, 'I know that Messiah is coming' (who is called Christ). 'When He comes, He will tell us all things.' [26] Jesus said to her, 'I who speak to you am He.'"* Yahanan 4:25-26 NKJV.

Besides using the Hellenized Greek Name Jesus, which will be discussed in a later chapter, the parenthesis in this passage denotes a translator's insertion. This means that somewhere in history somebody tampered with the manuscript and altered the essence of the interchange which is taking place in this account.

In reality, there was never mention of a "Christ" in that conversation. This was a Samaritan woman and it may be helpful to understand the relationship between the Jews and the Samaritans to put this passage into context.

According to Mathew Henry's Commentary: "The Samaritans, both in blood and religion, were mongrel Jews, the posterity of those colonies which the king of Assyria planted there after the captivity of the ten tribes, with whom the poor of the land that were left behind, and many other Jews afterwards, incorporated themselves. They worshipped the [Elohim] of Israel only, to whom they erected a temple on mount Gerizim, in competition with that at Jerusalem."[62]

There is a dispute whether any native Israelites were left in the Land after the Assyrian captivity. The Scriptures record that YHWH rejected all of Yisrael and only Yahudah was left after the Assyrian conquest (see 2 Kings 17:1-24). Therefore, many believe that the Samaritans were all foreigners transplanted into the Land who adopted a hybrid form of the worship of YHWH (see 2 Kings 17:24-41).

The woman would have spoken Hebrew or Aramaic. In fact, to this day, the Samaritans continue to maintain their Scriptures in Paleo-Hebrew Script which is quite ancient. Jews currently use the much more modern Babylonian Hebrew Script.

As a result, her religious background would have made her very familiar with the Hebrew faith and the expectation of Moshiach. The "Jews" never did, nor will they ever, expect a "Christ." Likewise, the woman would not have spoken that term which was alien to her belief system. So then we see that those who rely exclusively on an English Bible will get a skewed perspective of this exchange.

That having been said, most Christians will still proclaim that Jesus was and is the Messiah of Israel - the long awaited Savior. The interesting thing is that they often make this leap of faith without really knowing where to find the promises of the Messiah in Scriptures.

When I became a Christian by professing a faith in Jesus, I was only a child, and I made this profession without knowing the Hebrew Scripures. I did not think that I needed them because, after all, I had the "New Testament" which told me that Jesus was the Messiah. I made a true confession of faith which had everything to do with my heart and nothing to do with my head. I really did not know very much about various world religions, denominations or doctrines. It was a very simple matter - I was told that I was a sinner and that I needed a Savior. I was then told that the Savior was Jesus Christ.

I did not actually know what the definition of sin was, because I was told that I was no longer under "the Law." Since "the Law" is how Christianity describes much of the Hebrew Scriptures, I did not see them as having much relevance to me. Their value was more in providing a history lesson than anything else. With that foundation having been laid early in my life, my concept of the Messiah was learned more from tradition than it was from the Scriptures.

This is quite similar to most Christian conversions, no matter what the age. It usually does not involve a person studying the Scriptures, discovering that YHWH promised to send a Messiah to Israel, and then searching out all of the promises until they finally discover One

that actually fits the description. This may indeed happen, but I would guess that it is rare.

As stated previously, Christian converts generally put the cart before the horse. They take the leap of faith by believing in a christ without having much of an understanding about what the Scriptures say about the Messiah.

Most people of Jewish descent, on the other hand, are typically born into a religion called Judaism. It is important to understand that there is not one unified religion of Judaism. As with Christianity, there are various sects and denominations ranging from ultra Orthodox to liberal. In fact, some use the term "Jewish" so loosely that even if a person is an atheist, they are considered to be Jewish as long as they come from Jewish descent.

The religion of Judaism was developed and controlled by Rabbis and has its roots in the Pharisaic Sect of Israel which is often referenced in the New Testament. It developed as a unique religion after the Temple was destroyed in 70 CE and it is very different from the Way established by YHWH in the Torah. As a result, while those in Judaism generally have an expectation of Messiah, their belief in who or what will constitute the Messiah differs. In fact, over the centuries there have been numerous people who were thought to be the Messiah by various groups of Jews.[63]

Currently there is a sect of Hasidic Jews called Lubavitchers who believe that Rabbi Menachem Mendel Schneerson is the Messiah. Rabbi Schneerson, who died on June 12, 1994 at the age of 92, is buried in the Old Montefiore Cemetary in Cambria Heights, Queens and the movement is based in Crown Heights, Brooklyn.

Despite the fact that the Rabbi has not resurrected in the years since his death, these Hasidic Jews and even non-adherents continue to visit his grave and many consider it to be a holy pilgrimage site. If you travel to the modern State of Israel you will likely see pictures of Rabbi Schneerson posted all over the country indicating that he is moshiach. This is just one example of the expectation that the Jews have for a messiah.

An interesting point in this regard is that the majority of Judaism does not believe that Rabbi Schneerson is the Messiah. Regardless, Lubavitchers are all still considered to be Jews and no one is claiming that because they may be wrong in their belief in the Messiah that they can no longer be a part of Judaism.

In fact, throughout history, people have believed in various messiahs who turned out not to be the Messiah, but they still were considered to be Jews. Rabbi Akiva, one of the most famous rabbis in Judaism wrongly thought that Bar Kokhba was the Messiah, yet Jews continue to adhere to his teachings and esteem him as a great rabbi.[64]

There is only one exception that I can see in history and that is in the case of Jesus. I have been told by Orthodox Rabbis and Orthodox Jews that if you want to convert to Judaism, you cannot believe that Jesus was the Messiah. Currently, the modern State of Israel strongly discriminates against those who try to believe in Jesus while attempting to make "aliyah."

This is really quite profound, ironic and hypocritical, and should certainly raise some red flags concerning this particular messianic figure. It is especially interesting since most Jews will agree that he was a great Rabbi. So then, why would the followers of this particular Rabbi be denied citizenship in Israel or be precluded from the religion of Judaism?

A person can be a Jew or convert to Judaism professing that Rabbi Schneerson is the Messiah, but it is not permissible to convert if a person believes that Jesus is the Messiah. Also, a Jew can obtain citizenship in the modern State of Israel if they believe that Rabbi Schneerson is the Messiah, but they will have a terrible, if not impossible time, if they believe that Jesus is the Messiah. Again, this begs the question: What is the difference?

As we continue our investigation the answer will become clear, but first we still need to examine what the Scriptures say about Moshiach before we can determine who, if anyone at all, fits the description.

When I refer to the Scriptures, I will primarily be referring to the texts that the religions of Judaism and Christianity hold in common. Christians refer to them as the "Old Testament" which really does them a disservice because they are every bit as relevant, and important as those Scriptures which are called the "New Testament." In fact, the "New Testament" is really not so new at all, following the oldest text in the "Old Testament" by only about five centuries.

So when I refer to the Hebrew Scriptures or the "Old Testament" I will use the term commonly used which is "Tanak." Tanak is actually an acronym which stands for the Torah, the Prophets (Nebi'im) and the Writings (Kethubim) - T-N-K. We will now examine each portion of the Tanak to determine what, if anything, these texts have to say about Moshiach. We have already looked at various references found in the Torah so it only makes sense that we continue our discussion there.

7

The Torah

The Torah is the first, and arguably most important component of the Tanak. We have already examined Beresheet and some of the Messianic clues and references found within that text. The Torah actually consists of one scroll but it has been divided into five different sections or books.

In a very general sense, the word Torah is used to refer to the first five books of the Scriptures which some call the Pentateuch, or the five books of Moses. Torah may sound like a strange word to anyone who reads an English translation of the Scriptures, but it is found throughout the Hebrew text. The reason is because it is a Hebrew word which translators have chosen to replace with "the Law." Whenever the word "Torah" is found in the Hebrew, it has been translated as "the Law" in English Bibles.

Therefore, if you grew up reading an English Bible then you would never have come across this word. On the other hand, if you read the Hebrew Scriptures the word Torah is found throughout the text. The word Torah (תורה) in Hebrew means: *"utterance, teaching, instruction or revelation from Elohim."* It comes from horah (הורה) which means **to direct**, **to teach** and derives from the stem yara (ירה) which means to **shoot** or **throw**. Therefore there are two aspects to the word Torah: 1) aiming or pointing in the right direction, and 2) movement in that direction.

When showing the spelling of certain Hebrew words thus far I have used modern Hebrew characters although it is important to point out that the modern Hebrew language consists of a character set which is vastly different from the original language. The current Hebrew language uses characters which were developed around the 6th century B.C.E. and was adopted during the Babylonian exile of the House of Yahudah after the Kingdom of Israel was divided in two.

The language which was originally written by the Hebrews is now referred to as Ancient Hebrew or Paleo-Hebrew. Although it went through a number of changes over the centuries we are able to discern the original symbols and unlike modern Hebrew, these early Semitic languages used pictographs which actually resemble their meanings.

In modern Hebrew the word Torah is spelled תורה and in Ancient Hebrew it would look something like this: 𐤉𐤅𐤓𐤕. When these pictographs were joined together they became words with meanings that derived from the individual symbols. I find it particularly interesting in my research and studies to look at the original symbols of a word to derive its meaning.

The word Torah is a combination of four symbols:

† - a cross which means "mark, seal, monument or covenant."

Y - a nail or peg which means "to add or secure."

𐤓 - a head which means "a person, the head or the highest."

𐤔 - a person with hands raised which means "to reveal or behold or what comes from."

Combining the meanings of these symbols gives us a profound definition of the word "Torah" as "what comes from the man nailed to the cross" or "behold the man who secures the covenant." So then, from the very word associated with the Scriptures given through Moses, we have a clear understanding that there is a message concerning the Messiah found within them. In fact, one could argue that the Torah is all about the Messiah.

If you read and study the Torah you will no doubt walk away with the understanding that there is a promised Messiah, but you will never read one particular passage that provides you with a point by point checklist detailing the identity and purpose of the Messiah. What you will find are patterns and pictures provided through the Torah. We then glean more information from the prophets and the writings and when you put it all together you can properly identify the True Messiah.

One of the predominate features found within the Torah is that of the first-born and the promised son. Undoubtedly the most quoted text used by Christians to promote their faith comes from Yahanan 3:16 which states: *"For Elohim so loved the world that He gave His only begotten Son, that whosoever believes on Him should not perish but have everlasting life."*

This text unequivocally presupposes that Elohim has a Son. Now this is not a difficult concept for a Christian to grasp if they have

grown up being taught that fact, nor should it be difficult for a Jew, raised in the teachings of the Torah. The patterns appear to be clear from the Torah although Judaism currently rejects this notion.

There is never any direct statement made in the Torah that YHWH had a Son and that His Son would be the Messiah. In fact, the Shema, a most important prayer in Judaism specifically states: *"Hear O Yisrael YHWH your Elohim, YHWH is One."* Devarim 6:4.

Strictly looking at this passage in the English, it seems to squarely oppose the notion of Elohim having a Son, as well as the Christian concept of the Trinity. In fact, it was the belief in one Elohim which was the primary factor that separated Yisrael from the heathens[65] who believed in many gods.

In pagan religions the concept of the gods having children is quite common and there have been many savior gods throughout the millennia that have been considered to be sons of gods. Pictured here is one of those gods named Dionysus as he dies on the cross. Interestingly, this relic predates Christianity by hundreds of years.

Christianity has acquired many pagan doctrines over the centuries which will be discussed further in this book. As a result, to a Jew, Christianity appears to be just another pagan religion. This is primarily based upon its many adopted pagan holidays[66] and doctrines as well as the fact that it considers Jesus Christ to be the Son of God. Having made these observations, most Jews quickly dismiss the Christian Messiah.

Those who currently adhere to Judaism find this to be an unacceptable concept that Elohim could become flesh. They base this belief, not so much on a Scriptural prohibition, but rather one of their principles of faith established by a Rabbi.[67] In fact, their refutation of this notion appears to be based more on their rejection of Christianity than it is on any Scriptural prohibition.

Since Christianity is supposed to be founded upon the Hebrew Scriptures, it would seem vital that those Scriptures provide some basis for all of their doctrine, including the belief that Elohim has a Son. If not, how could the Christian religion cope with such a glaring discrepancy. After all, their Scriptures also state that *"YHWH is One."*

Interestingly, the Hebrew word for "one" in the Shema is echad (אחד). The word echad does not necessarily mean the number one (1). In fact, the word Elohim is actually the plural form of the singular word El. There are various times when Elohim is referenced in the plural

sense as in *"Let Us make man in Our image."* Beresheet 1:26.

Quite often the Scriptures do not specifically state things which only become apparent through prayer and study. This is why one text proclaims: *"Oh the depth of the riches both of the wisdom and knowledge of Elohim. How unsearchable are His judgments and His ways beyond tracing out."*[68] In other words, His ways run deep and there are treasures to be found as we explore the Scriptures.

Now this is something a Jew would certainly agree with, and Judaism has developed a form of exegesis known as PaRDeS. PaRDes is an acronym which stands for Peshat, Remez, Derash and Sod. Each of these is a level of meaning of Scriptures beginning with Peshat which is the "plain, simple or direct meaning of a verse." Remez provides hints or the deeper meaning beyond just the literal while Derash means to inquire or seek. Derash seeks to penetrate into the inner meaning of the words of a passage and concepts as they appear throughout the Scriptures. Finally, Sod is the "secret" or "mystery" meaning of a passage.

I will not spend a great deal of time explaining this concept, suffice to say that this model recognizes the fact that there are many layers of meaning within the Scriptures from the plain and obvious to the hidden gems which can only be discerned from much digging, study and prayer. While I may not necessarily subscribe to this specific approach of Scriptural exegesis, the important thing to note is the recognition that there are layers of truth hidden within the Scriptures, and as we mine deeper and deeper we can unearth great treasures. If we never dig, then we should not expect to discover certain truths.

Often times we can only see these treasures in the Hebrew text. For instance, you should have noticed that the dalet (ד) in the word echad (אחד) was larger than the other characters. This only occurs in the text found in the Shema and it is meant to draw our attention to something. Dalet (ד) is the fourth letter in the Hebrew alphabet and has the numerical equivalent of four.

Dalet (ד) means: "door" and there are many who understand that the enlarged dalet has Messianic implications. The dalet is the "door" to a four sided house or tent and therefore we can see how this could reveal that the Messiah would be the door back into the Garden – the House of YHWH.

There are many instances in the Hebrew text when we see things such as the Aleph Taw (את) and the enlarged dalet, which stand out and make us dig deeper for their meaning. We can also derive much truth from the patterns provided within the Scriptures. The patterns

often describe a literal and physical event on the surface, but they also have deeper meaning.

A very important pattern already mentioned is that of "the son" or "the seed." One of the very first things that we see in the Scriptures is the concept of planting and perpetuation of species – both plant and animal. All that is living derives from and is involved in the process of continuing life. When Elohim spoke, He started a creative process which continues to this day. That is why our Universe is expanding, the word spoken by the Creator continues on throughout time.

In the process of life passing through the seed, we see the powerful pattern of the father and the son. The father contains the seed, which then is planted in the womb, leading to the son who then carries the seed and passes his seed on.

Now we know from the creation account that Elohim created Adam. Adam was not born of a woman and he had no earthling father - his father was Elohim. He was not born as an infant, but created as a fully grown being. The same can be said about Hawah, although she was taken out of Adam. Adam, however, was not taken from another person.

Even though Adam was cast out of Eden, that by no means diminished his stature amongst all of creation. He was still created in the image of Elohim and had the privilege of walking and fellowshipping with the Creator of the Universe for a time. This, after all, is the desire of the Creator - to walk (halakah) with His creation. We can only walk with the Creator if we are on the same path that He is on – the righteous path.

Adam was the first of all creation, and while he walked in obedience, he was on the righteous path. Righteousness, after all, involves living according to the ways established by the Creator - not some esoteric conception of holiness that exists in the ethereal realm. It simply involves living a life in accordance with the instructions of YHWH - the Torah.

Adam disobeyed and as a result he was no longer privileged to live in the Garden. Due to his unique standing, Adam was the patriarch of the Earth and his seed was actually named after him ie. - mankind. He was given dominion over creation - a sort of King and High Priest of the Earth. This is where we derive the mysterious Melchizedek that we read about in Beresheet 14:18 who was not only the King of Jerusalem, but also the *"priest of Elohim Most High."*

Many who read the Scriptures are puzzled by the seemingly first appearance of Melchizedek when Abram tithed to him (Beresheet

14:19), because they fail to understand the Melchizedek line. While the Levitic priesthood included the Tribe of Levi and the progeny of Aaron (Aharon),[69] it was finite in time and space and limited by lineage. The Melchizedek priesthood has none of those restrictions.

What exactly made Adam unique so that he could function in that role? Adam was different from all of creation because Elohim deposited His Spirit within him who was without sin "in the beginning." Thus, if the Messiah were to be the Son of Elohim, He would likely be another Adam. As Adam was originally, so this Last Adam should also be sinless, "in the beginning," which would place Him in a position to restore what was lost due to the fall of the First Adam.

The Last Adam would therefore finish what the First Adam did not. Looking at creation from that perspective, it is not so difficult to imagine Elohim having a Son "In His Image" in the same fashion that He made Adam "In His Image." A pattern was established in the beginning which would prove critical for the restoration of mankind. With this understanding of the significance of patterns within the Scriptures it is likewise helpful to look at the physical sons of Adam – Qayin and Hebel.

Adam failed to watch and guard the Garden, and allowed the serpent to enter and deceive the woman and ultimately himself. Hawah later bore a son, Qayin who was the first born of all creation. Qayin also holds the prestige of being the first murderer. Not a very good start for mankind made in the image of Elohim. The son, as the seed of the father, is supposed to represent the father and continue his line and his character.

Adam's actions brought death and destruction into the world and likewise, Qayin, as the first born son, sadly perpetuated that conduct. This was not the intended purpose of Adam or his son and we can see right back from the beginning, mistakes needed to be corrected in order for mankind to be restored back into fellowship with the Creator.

We know from the Scriptures that Qayin killed Hebel and he was thereafter banished. It appeared that the righteous line from Adam and Hawah was cut off, but not completely. The Scriptures provide that: "25 Adam knew his wife את again, and she bore a son and named את him Seth, 'For Elohim has appointed another seed for me instead of Hebel, whom Qayin killed.' 26 And as for Seth, to him also a son was born; and he named him Enosh. Then men began to call on the Name of YHWH." Bereshett 4:25-26.

Notice that Hawah uses the term "another seed" in this passage which is particularly important since the Messianic Aleph Taw (את) is imbedded twice in this verse. It implies that the Messiah will come

from the seed of a woman, just as was provided earlier in the Messianic prophecy given in Beresheet 3:15.

In other words, the righteous line - which began with Hebel, but was cut off - would conquer the enemy of mankind, only now it would be through Seth instead of Hebel. The righteous son would be "cut off," as Hebel was killed, but the seed would continue.

How will this be accomplished? By the very pattern of atonement which was provided to Adam and Hawah – the shedding of innocent blood to cover the sin of mankind. All of creation provides us with tangible patterns that can help us to learn about the Creator and His ways, which begs the question: Was the Creator surprised by the sin of Adam and Hawah? The answer is: Absolutely not. Did He have a plan to restore mankind to His favor? Absolutely.

He could have protected Adam and Hawah from the serpent. He established the ground rules and allowed them to be tested. It was His way of teaching men what He desired – obedience from the heart. He then revealed His great mercy by providing the solution for their transgression. His plan for restoration was revealed through patterns, such as the sacrifice which was made for Adam and Hawah.

The Scriptures do not provide much detail concerning this sacrifice – it is one of those gems that you need to see as you read into the text. All that we read in the Scriptures is *"for Adam and his wife YHWH Elohim made tunics of skin, and clothed them."* Beresheet 3:21.

Understand that Adam and Hawah now wore the skin of dead animals. These animals did nothing wrong, but nevertheless they died so that Adam and Hawah could live. As a result, blood was shed which, literally and metaphorically, provided a covering for their sins. While this sacrifice allowed them to live, it did not restore them into the relationship that they once had with YHWH – this is the pattern of atonement that we see repeated throughout the Scriptures.

While the shedding of the blood of animals provides a covering for the sin which requires immediate judgment, it does not provide forgiveness which delivers mankind from the death sentence that ultimately awaits every person.

This was the condition which man was in, and as the world spiraled into chaos and corruption, from generation to generation, YHWH preserved his righteous line. In 1 Chronicles 1 we are provided with a list of ten generations from Adam to Noah as follows: *"¹ Adam, Seth, Enosh, ²Kenan, Mahalalel, Jared, ³ Enoch, Methuselah, Lamech, Noah."* 1 Chronicles 1:1-3.

While there were many other genealogical lines stemming from

Adam, it was this line which was unique. That line later progressed through ten more generations as follows: "²⁴ *Shem, Arphaxad, Shelah,* ²⁵ *Eber, Peleg, Reu,* ²⁶ *Serug, Nahor, Terah,* ²⁷ *and Abram, who is Abraham.*" I Chronicles 1:24-27.

It is in the Torah that we read and follow this line through which YHWH would establish His Covenant, in order to bring about the restoration of all creation.

8

Covenants

Adam was cast out of the Garden because of his disobedience, but he was still allowed to live. His life was spared – he and all of mankind were given a second chance. This is an excellent example of the mercy of YHWH, and that mercy is expressly demonstrated by the fact that He makes covenants with men.

While Adam should have immediately died for his transgression, he actually lived to see the birth of his children. He knew eight generations of his descendants and eight of the nine antidiluvian patriarchs who followed him in the righteous line – all except Noah. Interestingly, it was after the death of Adam and during the life of Noah that we are told how horribly wrong things were on the planet. The event in Eden came full circle and most of mankind was now living in opposition to the righteous conduct required by YHWH.

Noah was not a religious man - he was a righteous man. He obeyed the instructions of YHWH and he and his entire family lived as a result. It was the rest of mankind, choosing not to obey, that fell under judgment. The entire family of Noah was covered because of his conduct - not just Noah. While the entire planet was being judged by water, Noah and his family were protected in an ark. Noah had to obey the instructions of YHWH and build the Ark, otherwise he would have presumably been drowned along with everyone else.

After the flood we read that a Covenant was made with Noah that extended through his offspring – the future generations of the planet. The Covenant made with him included his seed. Thus mankind was once again given a second chance through the seed of Noah. The rest of mankind was blessed because of one man.

We see this as a common pattern in the Covenants made between YHWH and man. A mediator is often chosen to represent those in his "household" who would then benefit from the promises of

the Covenant.

This was the case with the Covenant made with Abraham as was already detailed. From the Covenant made with Abraham we can get a clear picture of a promised Son Messiah that will come from the line of Abraham and Yitshaq.

Remember that Yitshaq was considered to be "the only son of Abraham despite the fact that Abraham had an older son Yishmael. Yishmael was not the promised son because he did not pass through the cutting of the Covenant and he did not come from Sarah. The Promised son is a son of the Covenant and that seed must come from the proper womb. Through Yitshaq we see not only how the son would pass through the Covenant, but also how the son would be offered up as the Lamb of Elohim.

These are all powerful Messianic references and we see another through the life of Yitshaq when a bride is chosen for him. We read in the Scriptures how Yitshaq married a virgin bride named Rivkah, who was the daughter of Bethuel. Interestingly the Hebrew word for virgin is Bethula (בתולא) while her mother's name is Bethuel (בתואל), almost the identical word only it means "desolate." It turns out that this apparent Hebrew word play is quite significant.

It was very important to Abraham that Yitshaq not intermarry with those who dwelled in the Land of Canaan. Even though this was the Land that his seed would eventually inherit, the people of the Land were polluted and it was important that his son marry from within his clan.

It is also important to note that Yitshaq did not leave the Land to seek out a bride, rather the servant went out and found a bride and brought her back to the Land. Rivkah is brought to Yitshaq from a far off land by Abraham's servant Eliezer, the same Eliezer that Abraham thought might be his heir. Eliezer means: "El is my helper" or "El is my protector." He left the Promised Land to search out a bride for Yitshaq after swearing an oath to Abraham not to take Yitshaq with him back to Haran.

Many Scriptures record that he made the oath by placing his hand "under the thigh" of Abraham, but it was much more explicit. Eliezer actually placed his hand on the circumcision of Abraham while swearing this oath because this act of finding a bride for Yitshaq was an integral part of the Covenant which, in turn, was linked with the Promised Land.

That circumcision represented all of the promises made by YHWH and it was through the cutting that the promised son was given.

It was therefore imperative that Yitshaq and his Bride be married <u>in the</u> <u>Promised Land</u> as his life was a pattern established for the Messiah

When Yitshaq first meets Rivkah, after she fell off her camel, we read that he took her into his mother's tent and "married" her. The Hebrew is more to the point as it states: *"he took Rivkah and she became his wife, and he loved her."* Beresheet 24:67. This was no ordinary "church wedding" as Yitshaq apparently skipped the nuptials and consummated their relationship without delay.

In this passage we have a clear Messianic reference as can plainly be seen in the Hebrew text. Between the words "took" and "Rivkah" is an untranslated Aleph Taw (את) which represents the Messiah consummating His marriage with His virgin Bride.

Rivkah, was indeed barren as we saw through the word play between her mother's name and the word virgin. Through prayer she eventually conceived what would become two nations. Her older son was named Esau and her younger son was named Jacob.

The life of Jacob is filled with much deception and intrigue. He was a twin who wrestled with life, even inside the womb. We read from the account of his birth how he struggled to be the firstborn and came out of the womb grasping his brother Esau's heel. Thus the name Jacob, which is Yaakov (יעקב) in Hebrew, means "supplanter."

From his birth it appears that he desired the firstborn status and he was reminded daily, through his name, just how close he was to having it. After he was grown we read how his brother Esau sold his birthright for a bowl of stew.

The desperation of Yaakov is compounded later when he actually deceived his elderly father by pretending to be his brother Esau. As a result of this deception Yitshaq, almost reluctantly, blessed Yaakov with the blessing of the firstborn - an act which apparently could not be undone.

Only after he had actually lost the blessing was Esau filled with anguish and rage. This prompted Yaakov to flee the Land that his fathers were promised, and find safe haven with his Uncle Laban. His departure was also based upon the concern of his father and mother that he not marry *"the daughters of the land."* Beresheet 27:46.

This was the same concern expressed by Abraham for Yitshaq. Therefore, Yaakov was sent to the family of Rivkah to find a bride. So while Yitshaq remained in the Land while a bride was brought to him, Yaakov fled the Land in search of his bride.

Before Yaakov left, his father spoke a blessing over him and charged him as follows: *"¹ You shall not take a wife from the daughters of Canaan. ² Arise, go to Padan Aram, to the house of Bethuel your mother's father; and take yourself a wife from there of the daughters of Laban your mother's brother. ³ May Elohim Almighty bless you, and make you fruitful and multiply you, that you may be an assembly of peoples; ⁴ And give you the blessing of Abraham, to you and your descendants with you, that you may inherit the Land in which you are a stranger which Elohim gave to Abraham. ⁵ So Yitshaq sent Yaakov away, and he went to Padan Aram, to Laban the son of Bethuel the Syrian, the brother of Rivkah, the mother of Yaakov and Esau."* Beresheet 28:1-5. In this passage there are three instances of the Aleph Taw (את).

On his way to Paddan-Aram in Mesopotamia Yaakov stopped to rest and experienced a great vision at a place called Bethel or rather

Beit El. Beit means: "house" and El is the short form of Elohim. Thus the place was called "House of El." It was at that place where he set up the stone that he had used to rest his head and poured oil over it. He then made a vow to Elohim saying: *"²⁰ If Elohim will be with me and will watch over me on this journey I am taking and will give me food to eat and clothes to wear ²¹ so that I return safely to my father's house, then YHWH will be my Elohim ²² and this stone that I have set up as a pillar will be Elohim's house, and of all that you give me I will give you a tenth."* Beresheet 28:20-22.

He went on to prosper in the household of Laban although just as he had deceived his father, he too was deceived into marrying Laban's oldest daughter Leah when he thought it was Rachel. While outside the Land he had eleven sons by his two wives, Leah and Rachel, and two concubines, Bilhah and Zilpah. His sons were Reuben, Simeon, Levi, Judah, Dan, Naphtali, Gad, Asher, Issachar, Zebulun and Joseph.

After the birth of Joseph, and 20 years after he began working for Laban, Yaakov departed from the household of Laban and returned to the Land of his fathers. Yaakov then turned his attention to confronting his brother Esau, who he thought might want to kill him after the deception concerning the birthright.

On his way he saw two messengers and called the place "mahanaim" which means "two camps" in Hebrew. This is significant because it explains what Yaakov does next. When he was informed that Esau was coming to meet him, he divided his family – his tribe

- into two camps or two households. (Beresheet 32:8). He did this to protect them in the event that Esau attacked - believing that if one were attacked the other could escape.

In preparation of the impending conflict Yaakov sent gifts ahead of him. He sent his family and possessions to the other side of the ford of Yabbok until he was alone. It is here, when he was alone, that he wrestled with a man until the break of day. Remember, the dawning of the day has great Messianic significance.

The man touched the socket of his hip which was wrenched. Regardless of this inflicted injury, Yaakov would not let go until he received a blessing. The man told him: "*Your name will no longer be Yaakov, but Israel, because you have struggled with Elohim and with men and have overcome.*" Beresheet 32:28. He then blessed Yaakov but he would not tell him his name. When this blessing occurs in the text we see the Aleph Taw (את).

This change of name is quite significant. Yaakov had to get cleaned up and go back to where his journey began - Beit El - the House of Elohim. He had fled the Land promised to his fathers and lived in exile - a veritable slave to his father-in-law. He returned a different man - a man with direction and purpose - a man in Covenant with YHWH. This "new man" was to be named Yisrael (ישראל), signifying that he was not the same person as the last time he was there.

9

Egypt

As the sons of Yisrael grew up in the Land the Scriptures record a conflict which arose between Joseph and his older brothers. Joseph was the favored son of Yisrael who had made him a special robe. Joseph was treated as the firstborn son due to the sins of his brothers, who became extremely jealous. Joseph even had dreams of his entire family bowing down to him which only exacerbated the situation when he revealed the dreams to his family.

As a result of their deep seeded jealousy his brothers conspired to kill him, but ended up throwing him into a pit and determined to sell him into slavery. When a caravan of Midianite merchants came along his brothers, without the knowledge of Rueven, pulled him out of the pit and sold him to Ishmaelites for 20 pieces of silver.[70] It is interesting to note that the passage in the Scriptures describing that event includes three instances of the Aleph Taw (את).

Joseph was then brought to Egypt where he became a slave. This was not the first encounter that the Hebrews had with Egypt. We know from the Scriptures that Abraham had spent time in Egypt and knew Pharaoh. There is even a tradition that Sarah's concubine, Hagar, was an Egyptian princess.[71]

As a matter of fact, a portion of Egypt is included in the Land promised to Abraham. The Nile River is the western border of the Land and the Euphrates River is the eastern border. (Beresheet 15:18). Therefore, land in Egypt which is east of the Nile River would technically be part of the promised inheritance.

How interesting it is to observe in Egypt the clear distinction made between the eastern side of the Nile and the western side. The east is where the sun rises and this side is associated with life. The western side is where the sun sets and it is associated with death. Therefore, the various tombs and pyramids associated with ancient Egypt are almost

always found on the western side of the Nile which is not part of the Promised Land.

Abraham was likely well known in the region as well as his relationship with YHWH. As a result, the Covenant and promises, such as the Lamb of Elohim, were likely no secret. He had access to, and relationships with, the kings of the region and tradition holds that Abraham was a sort of "evangelist." He surely shared the promises and patterns provided by YHWH with the cultures in the region as he lived and journeyed throughout the Land that he was promised.

After Joseph was sent to Egypt, His brothers then killed a goat and put the blood of the goat on his garment. They showed their father the garment and he assumed Joseph had been killed. For all intents and purposes, Joseph was dead. We are told of this event in Beresheet 37:31-32 and interestingly enough, there are three instances of the Aleph Taw (את) in that passage.

Thus we should look for significance in the pattern of Joseph, the great grandson of Abraham. Although he was not the firstborn, he was given the first born status by his father who loved him. His status was shown by his garment, which was later taken from him, torn and dipped in blood. He was betrayed by his own brothers and thrown in a pit – symbolizing death. He was then sold by his brothers.

This was not the end of the story though. He was brought as a slave to the Land that was promised to Abraham. This was his inheritance, yet he was purchased by the Egyptian Potiphera who is refered to as one of Pharaoh's officials, the captain of the guard. Some texts refer to him as "the Eunuch of Pharaoh" and "the Chief of the executioners." The story of Joseph does not end there, but the Scriptures interrupt the narration of Joseph with what would seem like a very odd and even bizarre story about his brother Judah.

Whenever this occurs in the Scriptures it is important to take notice. Apparently, Judah, better known as Yahudah, left his brothers after selling his brother. Interestingly, it was his idea to sell his brother. (Beresheet 37:26). We do not know why he left his family, but it was possibly related to the incident involving Joseph. He apparently went to the region of Adullam, a city south and east of Bethlehem. There he married an unnamed Canaanite woman known only as the daughter of Shua.

They had three sons together: Er, Onan and Shelah. Yahudah found a bride for Er named Tamar. Er was put to death by YHWH because of his wickedness, leaving Tamar a widow and childless. Under these circumstances, it was obligatory for a brother to take the widowed

wife and marry her. Any children would be attributed to the deceased brother so that his line could continue.

Therefore, the responsibility to perpetuate the line of Er rested on Onan. Onan intentionally shirked his responsibility and was also killed by YHWH due to his wickedness. This left one final son who would be obligated to take Tamar so that she could bear children. In an effort to preserve his youngest son, Yahudah delayed allowing Shelah to marry Tamar.

Tamar, being frustrated by Yahudah's delay, took matters into her own hands. Dressing as a prostitute, she waited for Yahudah to pass by. Interestingly, she apparently knew that he would utilize the services of a temple prostitute. This was not something that a follower of YHWH should be doing because temple prosit/tutes were intimately involved in pagan worship. Nonetheless, Yahudah was clearly operating outside of the ways of YHWH during this period of his life. He was living with pagans, rather than his family. He married into the pagan culture and was apparently living like a pagan.

As a result, Yahudah ended up sleeping with her for the price of a goat. Recall that it was the blood of a goat that was placed on the coat of Joseph. As a pledge, Yahudah gave her his seal and its cord along with staff. The seal was known as a "hotemet" (חתמת), the cord was known as a "pathiyl" (פתיל) and the staff or rod was known as a "matteh" (מטה). This word is also translated as "branch" or "scepter."

This is significant because these items were both his individual and corporate identity so to speak. These were his implements used to conduct trade and without them he could be placed in a very difficult position. He left these items with this alleged temple prostitute as a pledge for the payment of the goat.

When Yahudah tried to complete the transaction by having the goat delivered, neither the woman nor his personal items could be located. As a result, he had literally lost his identity and his authority. He had lost his scepter and the Messianic implications of this event will become more evident as we continue.

Only later when Tamar was obviously pregnant did Yahudah become aware of what happened. This was after the passage of around three months when Tamar finally revealed that Yahudah was the father. She ended up bearing twins named Peretz and Zerah. During the birth, Zerah thrust his hand out first and a scarlet thread was tied to his wrist. His brother Peretz then came out, followed by Zerah.

After this event, the story of Joseph continues on as if this story was simply an intermission. The average reader should immediately

ask: What does this have to do with Joseph and why was it inserted in the middle of the story of Joseph. The answer is that it has everything to do with a future struggle between Yahudah and Joseph, and the Messiah would be at the heart of this conflict and resolution.

Also, you might wonder why Tamar sought out Yahudah instead of his son Shelah. According to Yahudah, his son Shelah was next in line. Apparently, Tamar was following a Hittite law which stipulated that when a widow married her late husband's brother and he died, she would marry his father.[72]

Regardless of what motivated her, Tamar's actions were deemed more righteous than Yahudah's. We later learn that the kingly line that would come out of the Tribe of Yahudah would derive from the twin Peretz, the one technically the youngest, but who "broke forth" and came out before his brother.[73]

So even when Yahudah was operating outside of the commandments of YHWH, he was still used to accomplish the will of YHWH. While Joseph did nothing wrong but reveal the promises given to him by YHWH, he was a slave in Egypt. During this process, his brother Yahudah was living like a heathen with heathens, apparently doing everything wrong, but YHWH was still accomplishing His plans.

The placement of this story was intended to stand out, and we therefore see a Messianic reference involving Yahudah in the midst of the suffering of Joseph. Through both of these parallel lives we see Messianic threads, one of a king coming from the most unlikely circumstances, and one of a suffering servant who would eventually be elevated to a great ruler in a pagan society according to the promises given by YHWH.

Before we get ahead of ourselves let us turn back to the story of Joseph who was finding favour in the house of Potiphera, an important man in Pharaoh's court, a man who may have been a eunuch. Interestingly, Potiphera was married. Although it was not common for eunuchs to be married, it was certainly not unheard of. This might explain the aggressive nature of Potiphera's wife as the Scriptures record that she tried to seduce Joseph while he was serving in their home.

Joseph wisely resisted, after all, it is not a good idea to get involved with the wife of the Chief of the executioners. When Joseph resisted her advances, she grabbed hold of his garment which he left with her as he fled the premises. Once again, we see Joseph having his garments taken from him - in a condition of "nakedness." She later

falsely accused him of wrongdoing and he was then thrown into prison.

Joseph went from a slave to a prisoner, but he never lost the favour of YHWH. While in prison Joseph excelled, and had an encounter with two fellow prisoners: 1) Pharaoh's Chief Baker, and 2) Pharaoh's Chief Cupbearer. Each of these men had a dream and Joseph accurately interpreted their dreams. Joseph predicted that the Chief Cup Bearer would be restored to his position within three (3) days, and the Chief Baker would be hung on a tree within three (3) days.

Both of these interpretations came to pass and one cannot ignore the repetiton of the number three (3) in this incident involving three (3) prisoners. The reader is clearly directed to look at the Cup Bearer – The Wine, and the Baker – The Bread. The wine and the bread should direct us to Abraham and the Melchizedek. There are profound patterns here that have deep Messianic implications and provide important patterns. 74

Based upon his accurate interpretations, Joseph eventually was brought before Pharaoh to interpret his dreams. Pharaoh also had two different dreams, although both of his dreams involved the number seven (7). Joseph was able to interpret those dreams also, and through those interpretations he was responsible for saving Egypt and the surrounding nations from famine and starvation.

Joseph was elevated to the level of viceroy in the Egyptian kingdom, second only to Pharaoh. A slave, then a prisoner had become a powerful ruler of Egypt This great event occurred when he was thirty (30) years of age. He then spent seven (7) years preparing so that the people could live through the coming famine. Since we recognize Joseph as a Messianic figure it is important to note the existence of the numbers three (3) and seven (7), as well as the age of thirty (30).

While in Egypt he married Asenath, the daughter of a Poti-Pherah, priest of On. (Beresheet 41:45; 46:20). There is speculation as to whether this is the same Potipher who put Joseph in prison. Some tradition suggests that it is the same person, and that Joseph actually met his wife when he was a slave in his house. The city of On, also known as Heliopolis, was a religious center dedicated to sun god worship. As with most major Egyptian cities, Heliopolis, had its own unique myth concerning the Creation of the Universe.

In essence, it was believed that before anything existed or was created there was chaos, darkness and endless, lifeless water, divinely personified as Nun. From the water a mound of fertile earth emerged and Atum, the solar creator god appeared on the mound and "spit out" the deities Shu (air) and Tefnut (water). This pair of dieties procreated resulting in Geb (the earth) and Nut (the sky). Heliopolis is famous for worshipping the "group of nine" known as the *pesedjet* in Egyptian including the dieties mentioned above as well as the offspring of Geb and Nut – Osiris, Isis, Seth and Nephthys.[75]

The myth of Osiris and Isis is particularily interesting. The brother Osiris and his sister-consort had a son named Horus. This father, mother, son trinity strongly resembles the trinity from Babylon. The fact that different cultures have shared concepts with different names for their gods is actually a common occurence. History is filled with the imitation, duplication and blending of various myths. This is the objection that some outside of Christianity raise regarding Jesus. In fact, many believe that Jesus is simply an updated and modified version of Horus.[76] This will be looked at in further detail throughout this text.

Interestingly, there are even variances of mythologies within cultures – Horus "the son of god" being a good example. In Egyptian culture it was also believed that the fertility goddess Hathor was the

mother of Horus. In fact, Hathor actually means "House of Horus" indicating that Horus was "housed" in her womb. Hathor was often depicted in the form of a cow and while Horus was often depicted as a falcon, he was also shown as a lamb and a calf, particulary in astronomical mythology.[77]

This was the environment into which Joseph married. All three times when the Scriptures mention Asenath, they refer to her as "the daughter of Poti-Pherah priest of On." Surely, the fact that his father-in-law was a pagan priest was a major factor in Joseph's family life. Asenath gave birth to two children, Manasheh and Ephraim. She grew up in this culture and you can easily imagine the influence that this had on the two boys who were born and raised in the midst of this pagan culture.

When the Scriptures refer to the birth of Manasheh and Ephraim in Beresheet 41:51-51 there are three instances of the untranslated Aleph Taw (את). This is significant because they were later adopted by their grandfather Yisrael. During the adoption process Ephraim, the youngest son, was elevated to first born status among the children of

Yisrael.

Joseph was a great leader in this pagan culture and he actually looked just like an Egyptian. He dressed like a pagan, he was married to a pagan and he spoke a pagan language. By all accounts, on the surface, he was a pagan. When the predicted famine came, his estranged brothers were sent to Egypt for relief at the behest of their father, Yisrael. His brothers came to Egypt during a time of famine, just as Abram had done in the past. As a result of their need for food, they were reunited and restored with Joseph who they did not recognize at first until he was revealed from behind his pagan exterior.

To his father Yisrael, it was as if Joseph had come back from the dead. The symbolism found in the life of Joseph is profound and it is full of Messianic patterns from which there is much to learn. After reuniting with his family, Joseph provided them with food and a place to live. As a result, Yisrael and his family moved to Egypt.

Before his death, Yaakov pronounced blessings over his sons. When he spoke of Yahudah he proclaimed the following: "*10 The scepter shall not depart from Yahudah, nor a lawgiver from between his feet, until Shiloh comes; and to Him shall be the obedience of the people. 11 Binding his donkey to the vine, and his donkey's colt to the choice vine, He washed his garments in wine, and his clothes in the blood of grapes. 12 His eyes are darker than wine, and his teeth whiter than milk.*" Beresheet 49:10-12

The first thing that should come to mind was when Yahudah previously gave away his scepter to Tamar. He had lost his scepter in the interlude described within the story of Joseph. Yahudah regained his scepter when he received the revelation of the twins who would eventually lead to King David. That incident involving the scepter had Messianic implications, and this prophetic word also has Messianic implications.

"Until Shiloh comes" turns out to be one of the most significant and well recognized statements in the Torah concerning the Messiah. While we know that Shiloh is a place, in this passage it is personified as the Messiah. The meaning is so obvious that the Targums actually use the phrase "King Messiah" instead of Shiloh.

The Targum Pseudo-Jonathan reads: "*10 Kings and rulers shall not cease from those of the house of Judah, nor scribes teaching the Law from his descendants until the time the King Messiah comes, the youngest of his sons, because of whom the people will pine away. 11 How beautiful is the King Messiah who is to arise from among those of the house of Judah. He girds his loins and comes down arranging battle lines against his enemies and slaying kings together with their*

rulers; and there is no king or ruler who can withstand him. He makes the mountain red with the blood of the slain; his garments are rolled in blood; he is like a presser of grapes. [12] How beautiful are the eyes of the King Messiah, like pure wine, for they have not seen the uncovering of nakedness or the shedding of innocent blood. His teeth are whiter than milk because he has not eaten what has been robbed or taken by force. His mountains and his press will be red from wine, and his hills white from the harvest and from the flocks."

Now the Targums are not meant to replace the Torah, they are Aramaic translations and they are especially helpful to discern how various portions of the Torah were understood at the time they were written. Yaakov's prophecy over Yahudah concerning "Shiloh" has always been understood to refer to the Messiah coming from Yahudah.

"The word "scepter" has been understood by the Rabbis to mean the "tribal staff" or "tribal identity" of the twelve tribes of Israel. This "tribal identity" was linked, in the minds of the Jews, to their right to apply and enforce Mosaic law upon the people, including the right to adjudicate capital cases and administer capital punishment, or *jus gladii* (The *jus gladii* is a legal term which refers to the legal authority to adjudicate capital cases and impose capital punishment.) . . . Therefore, according to this prophecy, the tribal identity or scepter of the tribe of Judah would not cease until the Messiah came. Judah was not only the name of the son of [Yaakov], but it was also the name of the southern kingdom of the divided nation of Israel. With these definitions in place we can restate the prophecy as follows: "The [National identity of Judah, which includes the right to enforce Mosaic law, including the right to administer capital punishment upon the people, as called for in the Torah] shall not depart from [the southern kingdom (Judah)], nor a lawgiver from between his feet, until Shiloh [the Messiah] comes; and to him shall be the obedience of the people."[78] This will become even more significant as we discuss the history of the Kingdom of Yisrael

Judah and his brothers all died in Egypt and there are various and scant records relating to their embalming and burials. After generations of Yisraelites lived in Egypt they eventually became slaves. The word for Egypt is actually "Mitsrayim" in Hebrew because it was settled by the descendents of Mitzrayim, son of Ham. To many Hebrews the word "mitzrayim" has become likened with the word "bondage."

So we see that the children of Yisrael, in order to escape famine, ended up living in the land of Goshen in Egypt where they became slaves. While they were given Goshen because it was good for raising their herds, the Scriptures record that they ended up in the

construction business. They spent a great deal of time making bricks, no doubt to construct pagan temples and related structures for Pharaoh. Coincidentally, this is what the Babylonians were doing when they decided to build the Tower of Babel. (Beresheet 11:3).

This period was foretold to Abraham when he entered into the Covenant with YHWH. "*13 Then YHWH said to him, 'Know for certain that your seed will be strangers in a country not their own, and they will be enslaved and mistreated four hundred years. 14 But I will punish the nation they serve as slaves, and afterward they will come out with great possessions. 15 You, however, will go to your fathers in peace and be buried at a good old age. 16 In the fourth generation your descendants will come back here, for the sin of the Amorites has not yet reached its full measure.'"* Beresheet 15:13-16. Remember that the number four (4) is associated with the Messiah and this passage speaks of the fourth generation as well as a period of four hundred years.

The Yisraelites had become enslaved as foretold and they needed to be delivered. YHWH provided a man whose life would become an important model for the Messiah.

10

Mosheh

When the time of the Yisraelite enslavement was near completion YHWH brought forth a deliverer in the tradition of Noah. The Scriptures describe a time when the Pharaoh of Egypt instructed two Hebrew midwives to kill males that were born to Hebrew women.

The midwives refused to obey and the Yisraelites prospered. Later the Scriptures record: "*So Pharaoh commanded all his people, saying, 'Every son who is born you shall cast into the river, and every daughter you shall save alive.'*" Shemot 1:22. Why would Pharaoh do such a thing? Maybe he was cognizant of the fact that someone important was about to be born. Was he aware of the promise made to Abraham or was there some sign in the sky? We cannot discern from the text, but it is clear that there is more going on than meets the eye.

There was a reason that Pharaoh had the children thrown into the Nile River. These children were an offering to the river god. It has been supposed that Osiris was probably in pre-dynastic times a river-god, or a water-god, and that in course of time he became identified with Hap, or Hapi, the god of the Nile.

Therefore, it was by no coincidence that YHWH sent a deliverer from those very waters. Here is the account from the Scriptures. "*1 And a man of the house of Levi went and took* את *a daughter of Levi.* *2 So the woman conceived and bore a son. And when she saw* את *that he was a beautiful child, she hid him three months.* *3 But when she could no longer hide him, she took an ark of bulrushes for him, daubed it with asphalt and pitch, put therein* את *the child, and laid it in the reeds by the river's bank.*" Shemot 2:1-3.

Interestingly, in this passage which first describes the baby, there are three instances of the untranslated Aleph Taw (את). The Scriptures proceed to describe how this child was spared from the death sentence issued by Pharaoh. "*5 Then the daughter of Pharaoh came down to bathe at the river. And her maidens walked along the riverside; and when she*

saw אֵת the ark among the reeds, she sent אֵת her maid to get it. [6] *And when she opened it, she saw* אֵת *the child, and behold, the baby wept. So she had compassion on him, and said, 'This is one of the Hebrews' children.'"* Shemot 2:5-6.

This passage also includes three instances of the untranslated Aleph Taw (אֵת) so by now a person reading the Hebrew text would begin to realize that this baby was quite special. There are many others that follow in the subsequent text as it describes how Pharaoh's daughter proceeds to adopt the child and name him Mosheh.[79] It was truly a miracle that this child was saved and adopted by the same family that was set to kill him.

There are two important questions that anyone would reasonably ask. First, Why did the mother of Mosheh choose this method of getting her child into the hands of Egyptian royalty? The second is: Why would the daughter of Pharaoh adopt a slave baby that was supposed to be killed? The answer to both questions is better understood when you realize why Pharaoh's daughter was likely bathing in the Nile. We are talking about a River that is generally heavy laden with silt and filled with crocodiles. Not a very inviting place to take a bath. The princess could surely have had a nice, clean relaxing bath in the safety and security of the palace.

Some speculate that she was not taking a bath, rather she was immersing herself in the sacred River because she was barren. She was immersing herself in the hope that Hapi, the fertility god, would give her a child. Under these circumstances, you can imagine that the baby would have been considered to be an answer to prayer – a miracle child straight from the gods. This would account for his name, which in Egyptian means: "from the gods."

It is possible that Mosheh's mother was hoping for just that response. Any other way would have likely led to Mosheh being killed, along with the other slave children. How ironic since the method of disposing of the Hebrew children was to throw them into the Nile as an offering. Mosheh's mother surely knew the story of Noah being protected from the waters in an ark. Therefore, she made an ark for her son.

So we see this child Mosheh who was born to a Yisraelite slave and then placed into an ark. He was put into the Nile River, the very place where the other Hebrew children were being thrown to their death. He survived and was adopted into the Royal family of Egypt. In fact, the name Mosheh is actually an Egyptian name which refers to his miraculous appearance from water.

Mosheh was grafted into the Egyptian culture and power structure for a purpose. Just as Joseph had been grafted into Egypt to bring Yisrael into Egypt, now Mosheh was grafted in to lead them out.

Mosheh was adopted into Pharaoh's family and was actually a prince of Egypt. He began his life as a veritable orphan under a death sentence and then lived a life of royalty until around the age of eighteen according to the Book of Yasher 71:1.

Mosheh was apparently adopted by Sobekhotep IV Khaneferre, of the 13th Dynasty, whose wife was named 'Merris' according to ancient Jewish historian Artaponus.[80] Other texts describe the daughter of Pharaoh as Bathia or Bithia. (Book of Yasher 68:17).

We know that Mosheh grew up in the royal family of Egypt and the Scriptures record an event that entirely changed the course of Mosheh's life. *"[11] Now it came to pass in those days, when Mosheh was grown, that he went out to his brethren and looked at their burdens. And he saw an Egyptian beating a Hebrew, one of his brethren. [12] So he looked this way and that way, and when he saw no one, he killed the Egyptian and hid him in the sand. [13] And when he went out the second day, behold, two Hebrew men were fighting, and he said to the one who did the wrong, 'Why are you striking your companion?' [14] Then he said, 'Who made you a prince and a judge over us? Do you intend to kill me as you killed the Egyptian?' So Mosheh feared and said, "Surely this thing is known! [15] When Pharaoh heard of this matter, he sought to kill Mosheh. But Mosheh fled from the face of Pharaoh and dwelt in the land of Midian; and he sat down by a well."* Shemot 2:11-15.

After murdering an Egyptian at eighteen, Mosheh went to live with the Cushites for nine years according to the Book of Yasher 72:25. After nine years with the Cushites, Mosheh was made King of the Cushites at the age of twenty seven (Yasher 72:37). He remained their King for forty years and at the age of sixty seven he fled to Midian where he met Zipporah at the well. (Yasher 76:3-5 and Shemot 2:16-20).[81]

Zipporah's father Jethro (Yithro) was described as the priest of Midian. He imprisoned Mosheh for a period of ten years. (Yasher 76:23). However, at the end of ten years Mosheh was released and married Zipporah when he was seventy six years old. (Yasher 77:51 and Shemot 2:21). Mosheh had two sons with Zipporah when he was between seventy six and seventy eight, two years before the Exodus.

Like Joseph, Mosheh married into a pagan culture. "[T]he Midianites are described as worshipping a multitude of gods, including Baal-peor and the Asherah. An Egyptian temple of Hathor at Timna continued to be used during the Midianite occupation of the site."[82]

Where there is Hathor you will also likely find her son Horus.

So even while Mosheh was in Midian, he was likely surrounded by pagan religions although there is evidence that, at some point, the Midianites were engaged in the worship of YHWH.[83]

While in Midian he returned to the heritage of his ancestors and became a shepherd of flocks. This life in Midian was quite different than in Egypt. It must have been a humbling experience since shepherding was a lowly profession in Egyptian society. This was important training as he was preparing to lead the flock of Yisrael.

Many believe that around the age of eighty, Mosheh saw a bush that burned with fire but was not consumed – this was fire from Heaven. He then proclaimed: *"I will turn aside now and see* את *this great appearance (phenomenon)."* Shemot 3:3. The implication is that Mosheh actually met with the Messiah.

The Scriptures record that YHWH saw him turn aside and Elohim called from the bush. He is told to take off his sandals for where he stood was holy – set apart – because the presence of YHWH was manifested in that space.

Mosheh was told that YHWH saw the suffering of the Yisraelites. In that passage we see three instances of the Aleph Taw (את). YHWH then charged him to return to Egypt and deliver His people and gather His sheep out of bondage. During the discourse between Mosheh and YHWH there are numerous instances of the Aleph Taw (את).

Mosheh then begged YHWH not to make him speak as he was instructed. He indicated that he was slow of speech and tongue. Amazingly, this son of Pharaoh who was now personally commissioned by YHWH was shy and afraid. This once strong and bold man was now unsure of himself and his ability to speak so YHWH instructed Mosheh to use his brother Aaron (Aharon) as his mouthpiece.

Mosheh and Aharon attempted to obtain the permission of Pharaoh to let the Yisraelites go into the desert for three days to hold a Festival to YHWH. Pharaoh resisted and YHWH decimated this powerful nation through a series of plagues and eventually killed all of the firstborn of Egypt during the Passover, known as Pesach (פסח).

"3 Speak to all the congregation of Yisrael, saying: 'On the tenth of this month every man shall take for himself a lamb, according to the house of his father, a lamb for a household. 4 And if the household is too small for the lamb, let him and his neighbor next to his house take it according to the number of the persons; according to each man's need you shall make your count for the lamb. 5 Your lamb shall be without blemish, a male of the first year. You may take it from the sheep or from the goats. 6 Now you shall keep it until the fourteenth

day of the same month. Then the whole assembly of the congregation of Yisrael shall kill it at twilight. ⁷ And they shall take some of the blood and put it on the two doorposts and on the lintel of the houses where they eat it. ⁸ Then they shall eat the flesh on that night; roasted in fire, with unleavened bread and with bitter herbs they shall eat it. ⁹ Do not eat it raw, nor boiled at all with water, but roasted in fire - its head with its legs and its entrails. ¹⁰ You shall let none of it remain until morning, and what remains of it until morning you shall burn with fire. ¹¹ And thus you shall eat it: with a belt on your waist, your sandals on your feet, and your staff in your hand. So you shall eat it in haste. It is YHWH's Passover." Shemot 12:3-11.

There are three instances of the Aleph Taw (תא) in this passage. Clearly the message behind Passover is the protective covering of the blood of the Lamb and the Passover is intimately related to the Messiah. From Abraham we saw that YHWH would provide His Lamb and it would be His "only Son." From the Passover we see that the Lamb of YHWH must be killed and His blood would provide a covering for those households, in particular the firstborn, that had His blood on their doorposts.

The door represents ownership. Many people place their names and street numbers on or near the entrance to their home to identify their ownership. The blood on the doorposts symbolizes that YHWH lays claim to those inside.[84] Those inside are His redeemed.

Only those who diligently obeyed this commandment of YHWH were spared. The Passover was a meal eaten in haste. You were to wear your outer garments with your sandals on your feet and your walking stick or rod in your hand. The picture that we see in this age is that they had their bags packed and the keys were in the ignition. They were ready to leave. This particular Feast is all about leaving slavery and going to freedom, which is life with YHWH.[85]

The directive to have their staff in their hand not only implies that they would be travelling, but it was also an allusion to the Messiah. The word for staff is maqqel (מקל) in the Hebrew, which can also mean a "rod, a branch or a shoot." We continuously see the connection between the branch and the Messiah and it will become increasingly clear that the Passover is all about the work of the Messiah.

After the meal and the night of death, the Children of Yisrael plundered the Egyptians and departed in a calm and organized fashion. They were loaded with gold and silver and along with a mixed multitude of people, they left Egypt and camped at Succot.

It is no coincidence that the first place that they camped was Succot, just as their father Yisrael had first camped at Succot when he

returned to the Land.[86] These were not the same physical locations, but they obviously are meant to tell us something. Succot, as it turns out, is more than just a place – it is a time. It is a very important Appointed Time where all who love and obey YHWH are to meet with Him and dwell in Succas, which are temporary dwellings.

All who follow YHWH are supposed to celebrate Succot every year as a rehearsal for a future event. It is an Appointed Time of YHWH, not a Jewish Holiday as some incorrectly believe. It is a time for everyone to obey, and some day the entire planet will be observing this Feast.[87] After leaving Succot the Yisraelites then proceeded to different camps led by "the Angel of YHWH" Who appeared as a pillar of fire by night and a cloud by day.

This imagery should immediately remind the reader of the smoking furnace and the lamp of fire that passed through the cuttings of the Covenant made with Abraham. This fire and cloud was YHWH fulfilling His promise to Abraham. Notice that just as the household of Abraham had originally contained numerous individuals who were not his physical descendants, so too this great assembly included the physical offspring of Yisrael as well as a mixed multitude of people.

The Scriptures record that the assembly was led to the edge of the Red Sea where they found themselves trapped between water and the army of Pharaoh. "*Then Mosheh stretched out* את *his hand over the sea; and YHWH caused* את *the sea to go back by a strong east wind all that night, and made* את *the sea into dry land, and the waters were divided.*" Shemot 14:21. In this passage there are three instances of the Aleph Taw (את) related directly to the waters of the sea.

The waters have always symbolized judgment and cleansing. The Yisraelites, led by Mosheh then passed through the parted waters of the Red Sea. They literally passed through judgment and were cleansed. The very same waters that were used to cleanse this people were later used to judge Egypt. This act of passing through the waters was symbolic immersion or "mikvah."[88]

Remember, they were on their way to the Land promised to Abraham. These people were like a bride preparing to be married to YHWH. Their journey was symbolic of the preparations for wedding. As the Bride of YHWH they first needed to be separated from the abominations of the Egyptians and then they needed to be cleansed. Once this occurred, they needed to prepare themselves for the wedding ceremony.

When a bride and groom would enter into their marriage relationship, they would traditionally stand underneath a Huppa which consists of the four cornerd garment of the husband, known as a tallit. This symbolized the protection or the covering of YHWH over the relationship. When YHWH prepared to marry Yisrael His Huppa of smoke descended over them. They then camped at the base of Mount Sinai and preparations were made for the wedding ceremony.

As YHWH began to speak the terms of the Covenant, which was the wedding contract, the people began to experience the awesome presence of YHWH and became afraid. *"¹⁸ Now all the people witnessed* את *the thunderings and* את *the lightning flashes and* את *the sound of the shofar, and* את *the mountain smoking; and when the people saw it, they trembled and stood afar off. ¹⁹ Then they said to Mosheh, You speak with us, and we will hear; but let not Elohim speak with us, lest we die."* Shemot 20:18-19.

After Elohim had spoken ten commandments the people could not take anymore. They asked Mosheh to listen to the commandments and then relay them to the people. This is very important because they are asking Mosheh to represent YHWH in their marital relationship. They are asking a man to act in place of YHWH.

YHWH agreed to this request, so Mosheh, as the mediator of the Covenant, went up the mountain to meet with YHWH and hear the rest of the words to transmit to the people.

While the instructions had been revealed to mankind from the beginning, something different was happening at Mount Sinai - just like something different happened with Abraham. It was another step in the process of restoring mankind with the Creator. This time the Torah was written and incorporated into a Covenant with these redeemed people called Yisrael. It was now written in stone.

YHWH had told Abraham that his seed would be afflicted for 400 years. When the time was up - the promise was fulfilled through the seed of Abraham that passed through Yitshaq to Yaakov - whose name was changed to Yisrael.

At Sinai YHWH was completing the marriage Covenant and included within that Covenant were those who dwelled with Yisrael. You see, anybody could sojourn with Yisrael as long as they agreed to obey the Holy One of Yisrael - just like anyone could live with Abraham and enter into the Covenant if they were circumcised and followed the ways of YHWH.

The Torah was still at the center of the Covenant - like a Ketubah or a written marriage contract between a husband and a wife. The Covenant was made between YHWH and Yisrael through

Mosheh the Mediator.[89]

The Torah was for all mankind, as it was from the beginning. Remember, Adam was not a Hebrew, a Yisraelite, a Jew or a Christian - he was a man created in the Image of YHWH. After the sin of Adam and Hawah, it was then necessary to restore individuals and mankind back into a right relationship and standing before the Creator.

YHWH was always concerned about the individual, and when He established Yisrael as a nation, it did not mean that He forgot about those who came prior to Yisrael, nor does it mean that He was not concerned about the other nations that inhabited the planet. In fact, He established Yisrael to reveal Himself to those very nations.[90]

Therefore, anyone who wanted to enter into this Covenant relationship with the Creator could do so provided that they observed the terms of the Covenant - which was the Torah. This is specifically stated in Vayiqra 19:33-34: "*[33] And if a stranger dwells with you in your Land, you shall not mistreat him. [34] The stranger who dwells among you <u>shall be to you as one born among you, and you shall love him as yourself</u>; for you were strangers in the land of Egypt: I am YHWH your Elohim.*"

There were plenty of non-native Yisraelites who had joined with Yisrael and were redeemed from Egypt. It was this mixed group of people, including the native Yisraelites, who grew impatient when Mosheh failed to return to them.

"*[1] Now when the people saw that Mosheh delayed coming down from the mountain, the people gathered together to Aaron, and said to him, Come, make us Elohim that shall go before us; for as for this Mosheh, the man who brought us up out of the land of Egypt, we do not know what has become of him. [2] And Aharon said to them, Break off the golden earrings which are in the ears of your wives, your sons, and your daughters, and bring them to me. [3] So all the people broke off the golden earrings which were in their ears, and brought them to Aharon. [4] And he received the gold from their hand, and he fashioned it with an engraving tool, and made a molded calf. Then they said, 'These are <u>your Elohika</u>, O Yisrael, that brought you out of the land of Egypt!' [5] So when Aharon saw it, he built an altar before it. And Aharon made a proclamation and said, 'Tomorrow is a Feast to YHWH.' [6] Then they rose early on the next day, offered burnt offerings, and brought peace offerings; and the people sat down to eat and drink, and rose up to play.*" Shemot 32:1-6.

The problem with growing up in a pagan society is that it is hard to stay set apart from all of the pagan elements that impact your day to day life. A casual observer might ask: Why on earth would they construct

a golden calf? It seems utterly absurd until you realize that they were doing what was familiar to them. They were worshipping "god" the way that the gods had been worshipped in Egypt.

Most English texts render Aharon's statement as: "These are your gods" – plural. There were likely multiple gods being worshipped at this event with the calf as the focal point. You see, pagan societies such as Egypt did not worship one god - they worshipped many gods. There were a multitude of gods and goddesses that symbolized different aspects of life on the earth and in the spirit realm. So, as it turns out, Yisrael was actually worshipping a pagan trinity, including a father, a mother and a son. While these were Egyptian gods it was the same system that originated in Babylon.[91]

They were actually involved in a form of messiah worship when they built the golden calf. You see while Horus was most often depicted as a falcon, as the child of Hathor, he was also depicted as a calf. In fact, there are numerous historical references to Horus as the "calf of gold" and of the "golden calf of Horus.[92]

So Aharon constructed an image of a god, a son of god, in direct contravention to the command not to make or worship any images.[93] He declared a feast day which was possibly in accordance with an Egyptian Apis Feast. The people made offerings to this image, they sat down to eat and drink and "rose up to play." That is a nice way of saying that they fornicated.

Now mind you, they declared this a Feast to YHWH, not to Apis, Hathor or Horus. They apparently thought that what they were doing was fine since it was in honor of YHWH. Sadly, they were mistaken because they started to worship YHWH just as the pagans worshipped their gods. While their bodies may have been cleansed their hearts still contained the filth of Egypt. Interestingly, it was from the very plunder of the Egyptians that they made the Egyptian idols.

You see, while slaves and servants may have had pierced ears as marks, slaves did not generally wear gold earings. These earings may very likely have been part of the plunder of Egypt. In the desert wilderness there is not much use for gold if there are no markets to buy or trade food or items. They adorned themselves with this gold from Egypt and then they used it in a corrupted ceremony. It is a good example of how the very things that we desire from the world (Egypt) may be the very things that can get us into trouble although, ultimately, the problem was in their hearts.

So with their mouths they were worshipping YHWH, but their actions revealed otherwise. They had been tainted by Egypt and they brought Egypt out into the desert with them. Not just the gold that they made into an idol, but also the false system of worship. In other words, they were attempting to worship YHWH the way that the Egyptians worshipped their gods. They were attempting to put a familiar face on the Creator of the Universe. That familiar face, or rather faces, were those of Apis, Hathor and Horus.

While Christian tradition holds that Mount Sinai is in the Sinai Peninsula in Egypt, the actual location of Mount Sinai was likely in the Land of Midian, which is modern day Saudi Arabia. Remember when Mosheh was shepherding the sheep of Jethro in Midian he saw the burning bush at Horeb "the mountain of Elohim." Shemot 3:1. Horeb is the same mountain as Sinai. הר וייאדד׳׳ו

Recently, an excellent candidate for Mount Sinai was discovered in Saudi Arabia. The top of the mountain is charred black and at the base of the mountain is a large altar with carvings of bulls and calves – the Egyptian gods that the Yisraelites were worshipping as YHWH.[94]

The one thing that was not present was a golden calf. The reason for this is found in the Scriptures. When Mosheh came down from the mountain he made them eat their messiah – Horus. "[19] So it was, as soon as he came near the camp, that he saw את the calf and the dancing. So Moshehs' anger became hot, and he cast את the tablets out of his hands and broke them at the foot of the mountain. [20] Then he took את the calf which they had made, burned it in the fire, and ground it to powder; and he scattered it on the water and made את the children of Yisrael drink it." Shemot 32:19-20.

When Mosheh saw what was going on he broke the tablets because the Yisraelites had broken the Covenant. In this passage we see the Aleph Taw (את) near the words, calf, tablet and Children of Yisrael.

Mosheh then literally proceeded to cook the calf, and he prepared a meal for the Yisraelites – a meal of gold and water. This was no coincidence since the Yisraelites had just participated in the Passover wherein they ate the Passover lamb – a symbol of the true Messiah. (Shemot 12). They were not satisfied with the Lamb that YHWH had provided, they wanted to worship their calf.

This appears to be a precurser of what is known as The Trial by Ordeal or The Law of Jealousy. In the Torah, there is a ritual that a husband would follow if he suspected that his wife was unfaithful.[95] YHWH describes Himself as a jealous El and He does not tolerate

infidelity. (Shemot 20:5). Those that were guilty may have become visibly affected by drinking the gold laced water and this may have been the first occurrence of this ritual.

Through this process Mosheh was demonstrating that if the golden calf of Horus was their messiah then they needed to eat his flesh of gold. Horus did not save anyone after Mosheh made them drink the gold and the water. In fact, the Levites proceeded to kill 3,000 men and YHWH then plagued the people. Worst of all He indicated: *"Whoever has sinned against Me, I will blot him out of My Book."* Shemot 32:33.

Therefore, those who chose to worship the calf were blotted out of the Book which is generally believed to be The Book of Life. This is the punishment for all who participate in idolatry.

Sadly, the Yisraelites only listened to ten of the commandments. YHWH made it very clear in the second commandment that they were not to make idols, that He was a jealous El and that idolatry would not go unpunished.

If they had continued to listen they would have heard the 11th Commandment which specifically prohibited gold or silver idols. These are the words spoken directly to Mosheh: *"22 Then YHWH said to Mosheh, Tell the Yisraelites this: You have seen for yourselves that I have spoken to you from heaven: 23 Do not make any gods to be alongside Me; do not make for yourselves gods of silver or gods of gold."* Shemot 20:22-23.

If they had only listened they probably would not have committed this sin and their names would not have been blotted out of the Book of Life. This is an important lesson for everyone. It is important to hear the commandments so that you can obey them.

What happened next is a powerful example of the work of the Messiah. After the Children of Yisrael broke the Covenant, YHWH was ready to destroy them and start over with the descendents of Mosheh - like He did with Abraham. In the custom of Abraham, Mosheh intervened which resulted in YHWH relenting. (Beresheet 18:22-33).

Mosheh was then instructed to bring two tablets up the mountain so YHWH could write the Commandments on those tablets. The first set of tablets, which were broken by Mosheh, were carved out of stone by YHWH on the mountain. This second set of tablets was carved by Mosheh and carried up the mountain. YHWH wrote the same words on this second set ,which was like the first set, and we see the Aleph Taw (את) present between the words "tablets" and "words" in the Hebrew passage describing the event. (Shemot 34:1).

This pattern is important in understanding how the Covenant

of YHWH is renewed. When it is broken, YHWH uses a man "like Mosheh" to mediate and renew the Covenant. Mosheh was not "The Messiah" but he was an important pattern for the anticipated Messiah. We know this because the Scriptures are quite clear on the matter.

"15 YHWH your Elohim will raise up for you a Prophet like me from your midst, from your brethren. Him you shall hear, 16 according to all you desired of YHWH your Elohim in Horeb in the day of the assembly, saying, Let me not hear again the voice of YHWH my Elohim, nor let me see this great fire anymore, lest I die. 17 And YHWH said to me: What they have spoken is good. 18 I will raise up for them a Prophet like you from among their brethren, and will put My words in His mouth, and He shall speak to them all that I command Him. 19 And it shall be that whoever will not hear My words, which He speaks in My Name, I will require it of him. 20 But the prophet who presumes to speak a word in My Name, which I have not commanded him to speak, or who speaks in the name of other gods, that prophet shall die' 21 And if you say in your heart, How shall we know the word which YHWH has not spoken? 22 When a prophet speaks in the Name of YHWH, if the thing does not happen or come to pass, that is the thing which YHWH has not spoken; the prophet has spoken it presumptuously; you shall not be afraid of him." Devarim 18:15-22.

Because of this passage, many look to Mosheh as the primary prototype for Messiah. In fact, there are some who have referred to Messiah ben Mosheh and look for a Messiah "like" Mosheh.

The essence of this passage is YHWH responding to the people's request to hear His commands from a mediator – not from YHWH directly. YHWH's response was "Fine – I will send you a Prophet like Mosheh Who will speak in My Name and you had better listen to Him." So this provides a clear litmus test for the Prophet that would be sent to Yisrael. He would be like Mosheh and He would speak in the Name of YHWH.

Interestingly, the name Mosheh in Hebrew, shares the root of the Hebrew word Moshiach. Mosheh is spelled משה in Hebrew while the word Moshiach is spelled משיח. Both the name and title start with the letter mem (מ). Remember that the numerical value for mem (מ) is forty (40).

Even the casual reader will recognize that there is something significant about the number forty (40) when dealing with Mosheh. He lived to be one hundred twenty (120) years old which has profound implications when viewing the length established for mankind.[96] His life is traditionally divided into three separate forty (40) year periods.[97] His journeys up and down the mountain are designated in forty (40) day

periods. Most of his life as a Servant of YHWH was lived and recorded in the Torah during the forty (40) year period in the Wilderness. As a result, we would expect to see the number forty (40) associated with Moshiach.

The mem (מ) represents water which can clearly be seen from the ancient Hebrew character - ᴟ. Since Mosheh was a pattern for Moshiach then we can safely assume that Moshiach would somehow be drawn out of water in an ark as with Mosheh. This becomes more significant when we understand that mem (מ) is also a picture of the womb. The womb is a place of safety and protection for an infant and it is filled with fluid. When a child is born it is drawn out of water so we know that Moshiach would come from a womb.

Mosheh was also considered to be like an El or Mighty One. "YHWH said to Mosheh: 'See, I have made you as Elohim to Pharaoh, and Aaron your brother shall be your prophet." Shemot 7:1. In that capacity, Mosheh was the representative of YHWH on Earth.

When the people became angry at YHWH they took it out on Mosheh. When people rebelled against YHWH, they rebelled against the authority of Mosheh. (Bemidbar 11-16). Even Aharon and Miriam rebelled against his authority. *"¹ Then Miriam and Aaron spoke against Mosheh because of the Ethiopian woman whom he had married; for he had married an Ethiopian woman. ² So they said, 'Has YHWH indeed spoken only through Mosheh? Has He not spoken through us also?' And YHWH heard it. ³ (Now the man Mosheh was very humble, more than all men who were on the face of the earth.) ⁴ Suddenly YHWH said to Mosheh, Aaron, and Miriam, 'Come out, you three, to the tabernacle of meeting!' So the three came out. ⁵ Then YHWH came down in the pillar of cloud and stood in the door of the tabernacle, and called Aaron and Miriam. And they both went forward. ⁶ Then He said, Hear now My words: If there is a prophet among you, I, YHWH, make Myself known to him in a vision; I speak to him in a dream. ⁷ Not so with My servant Mosheh; He is faithful in all My house. ⁸ I speak with him face to face, even plainly, and not in dark sayings; And he sees the form of YHWH. Why then were you not afraid to speak against My servant Mosheh?" Bemidbar 12:1-8.*

YHWH met with Mosheh personally and intimately. In that respect Mosheh was unique, he was not like any typical prophet, and he was described as being humble as well as the Servant of YHWH. He was a mediator between YHWH and the Children of Yisrael. He helped deliver them from slavery and he mediated the Covenant, He led them, ordered them into a nation and codified the Torah of YHWH for this new nation. He guided them and provided for them in the desert,

he led them into battle, judged their disputes and provided food and water. All of this was done with the power and authority of YHWH. He prayed for them when they sinned and he shepherded them as the flock of YHWH. He was a King, a judge, a priest, a prophet all in one role – the role was the pattern of the Messiah.

Mosheh was not necessarily what people would have expected from a deliverer. He was born a slave, adopted into royalty and fully immersed in Egyptian pagan culture at the beginning of his life. He was a murderer who was literally "on the lamb" and ended up becoming a sheep herder in a different pagan land and married the daughter of a pagan priest. He was then raised up to deliver an entire nation out of slavery.

The reason he was special was not because of any particular talent or skill. In fact, he needed a spokesperson to deliver his message. The reason why Mosheh was special was because he was chosen, he was obedient to the instructions of YHWH and he delivered the message of YHWH.

Those who YHWH chooses to use for His purpose do not always fit within our preconceived patterns or expectations. We need to be ready and willing to set aside our own ways and submit to His way. This is the chief prerequisite for living with Him and dwelling with His set apart people – Yisrael.

II

Yisrael

During the leadership of Mosheh we see the descendants of the man Yisrael become a great assembly of people collectively called Yisrael. Interestingly, Yisrael and his family originally numbered seventy (70) when they arrived in Egypt. The number seventy (70) commonly refers to "the nations" in Hebrew gematria. The irony is that these seventy (70) people grew into a nation while they were slaves in Egypt, and they left mixed with the nations.

It is important to always remember that this Assembly, known as qahal (קהל) in Hebrew, did not only include the physical descendants of their namesake, the Assembly also included a "mixed multitude" of people who likely came from many nations.

In the Hebrew this mixed multitude is referred to as the "ereb rab" (ערב רב). Thus, the significance of the emphasis on the nations cannot be overlooked. The Assembly of Yisrael was intended to be the conduit to bring the nations, also known as the Gentiles, to the Elohim of Yisrael. Historically, Yisrael has always been "interwoven" with the nations.

This great Assembly, which included a mixed multitude of people, eventually marched out of Egypt like an organized army (Shemot 13:18). There was no panic, they were not fleeing - they were the victors. Their Elohim had just conquered this powerful empire and they had plundered the land as a conquering army.

Their deliverance was a free gift. Their lives were saved - courtesy of the blood of the lamb placed on the doorpost. Yisrael constantly had to make a choice - whether to follow the One True Elohim or whether to chase after the false gods of the nations.

Yisrael consisted of anyone who wanted to follow the Elohim of Yisrael. It did not matter where you came from. If you were born outside of Yisrael you could join with Yisrael, but if you wanted to

dwell with the Redeemed people, you needed to live your life according to the instructions - the Torah. The Torah told Yisrael - the Bride - exactly what YHWH - the Husband - expected of her. It established boundaries for the marriage.

The Torah was, in essence, a wedding gift to Yisrael. It was never considered to be a burden by Yisrael; it was always understood to be a blessing and a privilege to be given the Torah. In fact, it showed them how to receive blessings and it warned them of how they could be cursed.

Who would not consider that to be a great gift? As a result, at Sinai, the Assembly of Yisrael willingly agreed to obey the Torah. It was not forced upon them. In fact, YHWH delivered them from slavery and freed them without any conditions other than to follow His instructions. This is so no one could ever state that they made a decision under duress.

Once the mixed multitude was delivered from slavery, they were <u>then</u> given the option to accept the Torah and their decision was unequivocal. After Mosheh told the people all of the words, they responded in Shemot 24:4: "*All the words that YHWH has commanded **we will do**.*" They freely chose to live in a manner which allowed them to dwell in the presence of a Holy Elohim - the manner prescribed by the Torah.

According to Bemidbar 15:29 "*You shall have **one Torah** for him who sins unintentionally, for him who is native-born among the children of Yisrael and for the stranger who dwells among them.*" Again, your skin color did not matter; neither did your genetic makeup. What mattered was what you believed and consequently what you obeyed. If you lived your life like many Christians do today, you would not be able to dwell with Yisrael and with YHWH because most Christians reject the Torah and do not obey the commandments.

Yisrael later rejected the promise of the Covenant by refusing to enter the Land. This demonstrated an utter lack of faith and trust in the promises of YHWH. While they passed the first test, leaving their homes, they failed to enter into the Land of Canaan, their promised inheritance.

How remarkable that their father Abraham did so with his relatively small entourage while this mighty band of people were too afraid to enter in. This is incredible because YHWH had just recently delivered them from arguably the most powerful nation on Earth. They were about to receive the Land which was promised to them but they were afraid, despite the miracles they had just witnessed.

Their fear demonstrated that they did not trust YHWH and ultimately they did not love Him. If they loved Him, they would have done what He said, even if it meant certain death. Sadly, YHWH was intent on blessing them and they still refused to obey. We should all meditate on this point because we too can miss the blessings if we fail to obey. There may come a time in the future when we must make a similar choice. Our response must be to obey no matter what we see with our eyes.

Despite all of the patterns, great signs, wonders and military victories given to Yisrael, they made a choice to succumb to fear rather than enter the Land. They were forced to wander in the wilderness for forty years until the next generation was raised up to enter into the Land. This was very merciful of YHWH. He could have destroyed them all because of their disobedience and moved ahead with His plan but instead, He let them live out the rest of their lives but they still did not comprehend the mercy of YHWH – they still grumbled along the way.

As a result, during their time in the wilderness they experienced many trials. One interesting event is described as follows: "⁵ *they spoke against Elohim and against Mosheh, and said, Why have you brought us up out of Egypt to die in the desert? There is no bread! There is no water! And we detest this miserable food!" ⁶ Then YHWH sent venomous snakes* את *among them; they bit* את *the people and many Yisraelites died. ⁷ The people came to Mosheh and said, We sinned when we spoke against YHWH and against you. Pray that YHWH will take the serpents* את *away from us. So Mosheh prayed for the people. ⁸ YHWH said to Mosheh, make a seraph and put it up on a pole; anyone who is bitten can look at it and live. ⁹ So Mosheh made a bronze serpent and put it up on a pole. Then when anyone was bitten by a snake and looked* את *at the bronze serpent, he lived.*" Bemidbar 21:5-9.

This incident has baffled many people who have tried to link it to pagan worship. Indeed, it appears that this serpent on the pole was kept by the Yisraelites and eventually placed in the Temple in Jerusalem where it became an article of worship. It was thus destroyed by King Hezekiah as described in 2 Kings 18:4. "*He removed the high places, and broke the images and cut down the groves, and broke in pieces the brazen serpent that Mosheh had made: for unto those days the children of Yisrael did burn incense to it: and he called it Nehushtan.*"

It is helpful to look at the original account in the Hebrew where it is possible to recognize that it is a pattern of great importance. When read in Hebrew, it is evident that this is a Messianic reference because the passage is filled with the untranslated Aleph Taw (את).

Notice that Mosheh is not instructed to make a serpent, he is instructed to make a seraph (שָׂרָף). The Hebrew word seraph (שָׂרָף) is the singular form of seraphim (שְׂרָפִים). The seraphim (שְׂרָפִים) are the ministers of YHWH who are above the throne and offer up praises to YHWH. They appear in the form of a man and they have six wings – six being the number of man. They are described in Isaiah 6:2-4 and are separate and distinct from the Cherubim that have four wings and four faces of a man, a lion, an ox and an eagle.

So Mosheh was commanded to make a seraph and place it on a pole. He thereafter made what is often described as a "bronze serpent." In Hebrew it reads n'chash n'chashet (נְחַשׁ נְחֹשֶׁת). Now bronze represents judgment and it is able to withstand great heat. It is the material used on the Altar. In the Hebrew, one cannot miss the word play in the text. The word for bronze (נְחֹשֶׁת) and the word for serpent (נָחָשׁ) share the same Hebrew root.

It was the serpent – n'chash (נָחָשׁ), that encouraged Adam and Hawah to transgress the commandments. Therefore, the serpent was involved in Adam and Hawah being cast out of the garden when they rebelled against YHWH. Yisrael was speaking against YHWH and Mosheh – the servant of YHWH. Specifically, they criticized the Manna – the Bread of Life also known as the Bread from Heaven.

Many sages have concluded that it was the act of looking or the obedience which saved the people – not the serpent itself. It was to show them that they needed faith to save them. And just as Mosheh had lifted up the rod in the past, now he was lifting up a pole with judgment upon it that is reminiscent of the Garden.

Could it be that this was prophetic, and the Yisraelites would eventually understand that they needed to look upon a man on a pole Who came from the very throne of YHWH to deliver them from the judgment of the Garden?

The serpent on the pole should immediately lead one to the events which occurred prior to the Exodus when Mosheh and Aharon confronted Pharaoh. "8 Then YHWH spoke to Mosheh and Aharon, saying, 9 When Pharaoh speaks to you, saying, Show a miracle for yourselves, then you shall say to Aharon, Take אֵת your rod and cast it before Pharaoh, and let it become a serpent. 10 So Mosheh and Aharon went in to Pharaoh, and they did so, just as YHWH commanded. And Aharon cast down אֵת his rod before Pharaoh and before his servants, and it became a serpent. 11 But Pharaoh also called the wise men and the sorcerers; so the magicians of Egypt, they also did in like manner with their enchantments. 12 For every man threw down his rod, and they became serpents. But Aaron's rod אֵת swallowed up their rods."

Shemot 7:8-13.

Three times when the text speaks of Aharon's rod we see the untranslated Aleph Taw (את) in the text. The word for rod is "matteh" (מטה) and it can mean "branch" or "extension."

As we continue to examine this rod or branch we see that it is, in fact, an extension of YHWH and it is typically paired with the Aleph Taw (את). There is a powerful tradition concerning this particular rod and according to the Book of Yasher this rod was first used by Elohim after creation and handed down from Adam through the aforementioned righteous line to Noah, through Shem, until it came to Abraham. It was then handed to Yitshaq, to Yaakov and to Joseph until it eventully came into the hand of Mosheh.[98]

Mosheh with Aharon struck the waters of the Nile and executed the plagues on Egypt through the rod and interestingly we continually see the Aleph Taw (את) associated with this rod in the Hebrew text.

When the Children of Yisrael had left Egypt and were pursued by Pharaoh's army Mosheh was instructed as follows: "lift up את your rod, and stretch out את your hand over the sea and divide it. And the Children of Yisrael shall go on dry ground through the midst of the sea." Shemot 14:16.

Mosheh struck the rock with the Rod at Massah and Mirebah and water poured forth from the rock. (Shemot 17:5). This rod was very important to Yisrael and no doubt symbolized the Messiah. It was the strength and power of YHWH and when it was raised up, YHWH would perform mighty deeds through this rod. In fact, it also became known as The Rod of Elohim.

In battle it was a sign of victory and the strength of YHWH. "8 Now Amalek came and fought with Yisrael in Rephidim. 9 And Mosheh said to Joshua, Choose us some men and go out, fight with Amalek. Tomorrow I will stand on the top of the hill with the rod of Elohim in my hand. 10 So Joshua did as Mosheh said to him, and fought with Amalek. And Mosheh, Aharon, and Hur went up to the top of the hill. 11 And so it was, when Mosheh held up his hand, that Israel prevailed; and when he let down his hand, Amalek prevailed. 12 But Mosheh's hands became heavy; so they took a stone and put it under him, and he sat on it. And Aharon and Hur supported his hands, one on one side, and the other on the other side; and his hands were steady until the going down of the sun. 13 So Joshua defeated Amalek and his people with the edge of the sword." Shemot 17:8-13.

Whenever the rod was lifted high above Yisrael they would be victorious. Whenever it was lowered they would not be victorious. It is also interesting to note that Joshua was leading the army. This will become more significant later in this discussion. YHWH certainly

made it clear that the rod or branch was the focus of this battle. I am certain that people must have pondered this Branch and seen the significance.

This Rod was also the one that sprouted, budded and produced almonds when left in the Tabernacle overnight. It actually became an almond tree and was kept in the Tabernacle from that time forward. (Bemidbar 17:2-10). Some traditions hold that this was an actual branch from the Tree of Life that had been passed on through Adam from the garden.[99] The placement of the almond-producing Rod in the Tabernacle certainly created a vivid picture of the Tree of Life, since the Tabernacle was a representation of the Garden – an enclosed space where YHWH would meet with mankind.[100]

This allusion to the Garden brings us back to the fiery serpents in the desert. The serpent, after all, was one of the primary players in the Garden incident and we now see the serpent in the desert, only not as we might imagine. In this instance YHWH forced the Yisraelites to look at the bronze serpent on the pole as if to refocus their attention.

It was a prophetic picture given to the Yisraelites that they could not fully appreciate or understand until their eyes were opened concerning the Messiah. In fact, it would only be the Messiah Who could explain this great mystery.

When their forty (40) year period in the wilderness was over the time had come to enter into the Land. Since the Land was an integral part of the Covenant made with Abraham and confirmed at Sinai, it was important for Yisrael to enter into the Land of promise. If you do not want to live in the Land then you should not expect to enter into the Covenant. The Land and the Covenant are inseparable. This, of course, is the pattern of restoration which YHWH has provided and the Messiah plays an integral part in that journey. The Promised Land represents the Garden – a place where the Torah is obeyed and where the inhabitants can once again reside with YHWH.

Some erroneously try to differentiate or divide elements of the Covenant by stating that the Land was a part of the Covenant made with Abraham, and they are part of a different Covenant that does not include the Land. This is simply not possible. All Covenants made between YHWH and Yisrael after Abraham were, in essence, the same Covenant renewed or refreshed.[101]

An important point to recognize is that only two adults from the generation that left Egypt in the Exodus actually crossed over into the Promised Land: Joshua and Caleb - two of the twelve who previously explored the Land. They were the two who gave a good report to

the people and encouraged them to enter into the Land - despite the presence of giants. They also took the trouble to carry out a large cluster of grapes as proof of the bounty that awaited them. The reason why these two were different is specifically detailed in the Scriptures: *"not one except Caleb son of Yephunneh the Kenizzite and Joshua son of Nun, for they followed YHWH wholeheartedly."* Bemidbar 32:12.

These two followed YHWH wholeheartedly and notice that Caleb was not a native Yisraelite. The Scriptures record that his father was a Kenizzite yet they became part of Yisrael. Despite the fact that his father was from a foreign land, the Scriptures list Caleb as being part of the Tribe of Judah. This means that at some point his family was "grafted in" to the tribe of Yahudah.

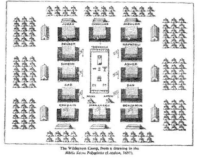

The Wilderness Camp, from a drawing in the *Biblia Sacra Polyglotta* (London, 1657).

This is how it worked when Yisrael camped after the Exodus. They divided into tribes and they camped around the Tabernacle. There was no "Tribe of the Mixed Multitude" - no "Tribe of the Nations." The mixed multitude was not separated from the other tribes - they became part of Yisrael as Caleb's family joined Yisrael through the Tribe of Yahudah.

Anyone that wanted to join with Yisrael was ultimately "grafted in" through a tribe. Thus Yisrael, the Bride of YHWH consisted of a multitude representing the nations. Just as the seventy (70), representing the nations, entered into Egypt, the multitude, representing the nations, departed from Egypt.

Before Yisrael could finally enter the Promised Land, the Covenant was renewed at Moab. We read in Devarim 29:1 *"These are the terms of the covenant YHWH commanded Mosheh to make with the Yisraelites in Moab, in addition to the covenant he had made with them at Horeb."* All of Yisrael was assembled, including sojourners in the midst of the Assembly, to hear the words of the Renewed Covenant.

"10 All of you are standing today in the presence of YHWH your Elohim - your leaders and chief men, your elders and officials, and all the other men of Yisrael, 11 together with your children and your wives, and the aliens living in your camps who chop your wood and carry your water. 12 You are standing here in order to enter into a Covenant with YHWH your Elohim, a Covenant YHWH is making with you this day and sealing with an oath, 13 to confirm you this day as His people, that He may be your Elohim as He promised

you and as He swore to your fathers, Abraham, Yitshaq and Yaakov. [14] *I am making this Covenant, with its oath, not only with you* [15] *who are standing here with us today in the presence of YHWH our Elohim but also with those who are not here today.*" Deuteronomy 29:10-15.

The Covenant was renewed with that new generation as well as with those who were not there. This points to a future people who would enter into the same Covenant - which would again be renewed. It also specifically includes those dwelling with Yisrael – aliens who were once living in the nations, but now part of Yisrael. These aliens were eligible to be grafted into Yisrael if they joined into the Covenant.

We are given a vivid example of this grafting process in the Book of Ruth. Ruth just happened to be a Moabite from the very land where this Covenant was renewed. The story of Ruth provides a beautiful picture of an alien being grafted into Yisrael and becoming an important part of the Messianic bloodline. Her famous words are the formula for becoming grafted into Yisrael: "*For wherever you go, I will go; and wherever you lodge, I will lodge; Your people shall be my people, and your Elohim, my Elohim.*" Ruth 1:16. Through this story we see a vivid example of redemption for those originally outside of Yisrael.[102]

Before entering in to the Promised Land, the Assembly of Yisrael was specifically commanded not to worship false gods. "*You shall not bow down to their gods or serve them or do after their works; but you shall utterly overthrow them and break down their pillars and images.*" Shemot 23:24. They were also instructed not to set up poles and pillars in order to worship false gods. "[21] *You shall not plant for yourself any tree, as a wooden image, near the altar which you build for yourself to YHWH your Elohim.* [22] *You shall not set up a sacred pillar, which YHWH your Elohim hates.*" Devarim 16:21-22.

The Yisraelites were supposed to live holy, set apart lives according to the Torah – their marriage contract. They were supposed to stay true to their Husband YHWH and not commit spiritual idolatry with other gods – which would constitute adultery. In other words, as the Bride of YHWH, if they wanted to live in His House - the Land – then they needed to remain faithful to Him and His ways.

After Mosheh led the people out of Egypt and through the desert for forty (40) years it came time for the Bride to enter the Promised Land, which was the marital residence. Mosheh was permitted to see the Land but would not be permitted to enter because of an incident at the waters of Meribah Kadesh in the Wilderness of Zin.[103]

As a result, it was now time for a new leader, one who would lead the Assembly of Yisrael into the Land. It was now time for Joshua to take command and lead the Bride into the Promised Land.

12

Joshua

While Mosheh was permitted to see the Promised Land He was not allowed to enter in. We read the account in the Book of Bemidbar. *"¹² Then YHWH El said, Mosheh, Go up this mountain in the Abarim range and see אֵת the Land I have given the Yisraelites. ¹³ After you have seen it, you too will be gathered to your people, as your brother Aharon was, ¹⁴ for when the community rebelled at the waters in the Desert of Zin, both of you disobeyed My command to honor Me as Set Apart before their eyes. (These were the waters of Meribah Kadesh, in the Desert of Zin.) ¹⁵ Mosheh said to YHWH, ¹⁶ May YHWH, the Elohim of the spirits of all mankind, appoint a man over this community ¹⁷ to go out and come in before them, one who will lead them out and bring them in, so YHWH's people will not be like sheep without a shepherd. ¹⁸ So YHWH said to Mosheh, take אֵת Joshua son of Nun, a <u>man in whom is the Spirit</u>, and lay אֵת your hand on him. ¹⁹ Have him stand before Eleazar the priest and the entire assembly and commission him אֵת in their presence. ²⁰ Give him some of your authority so the whole Yisraelite community will obey him. ²¹ He is to stand before Eleazar the priest, who will obtain decisions for him by inquiring of the Urim before YHWH. At his command they shall go out and at his command they shall come in, he and all of the children of Yisrael אֵת even all of the congregation."* Bemidbar 27:12-21.

So YHWH appointed Joshua to be a shepherd for the flock of Yisrael. He was a leader and Commander. The Scripture says that the Spirit "ruach" (רוּחַ) was in him. There are five occurrences of the Aleph Taw (אֵת) so it is clear that there is a Messianic hint that Messiah would be a Shepherd over Yisrael. Also, the Aleph Taw (אֵת) is present in another even more amazing fashion through the mention of the Urim (אוּרִים). The Urim (אוּרִים) and Thummim (תֻּמִּים) were both contained in the ephod of the High Priest.

The command concerning the placement of the Urim and Thummim in the ephod is found in Shemot 28:30-31 as follows: *"³⁰ And* you shall put in the breastplate of judgment את the Urim and the Thummim and they shall be upon Aharon's heart whenever he enters the presence of YHWH and Aharon shall bear את the judgment of the children of Yisrael upon his heart before YHWH continually. ³¹ And you shall make את the robe of the ephod all blue."

The three instances of the untranslated Aleph Taw (את) reveal that the Urim and Thummim have something to do with the Messiah. In fact, the very words Urim (אורים) and Thummim (תמים) are the Aleph Taw (את) as you can see that the Urim begins with Aleph (א) and the Thummim begins with Taw (ת).

The Urim and the Thummim mean "lights" and "perfections" and the light of the Urim is the same Light (אור) that was brought forth on the first day of creation. (Beresheet 1:3). Therefore, Joshua would stand before the High Priest and would be given answers from the Light by YHWH. This image of a man filled with the Spirit, communicating with YHWH through lights and leading the Bride is a powerful Messianic pattern.

Before we continue our examination of the role of Joshua son of Nun, it is important that we start by getting his name right. While tradition in the English language has his name beginning with a "J", his actual Hebrew name was Yahushua or Yahusha.[104] This was not always his name because, as with Abraham and Sarah, his name was also changed.

He was originally known as Hoshea (הושע) which means: "salvation." His name was later changed to Yahushua (יהושע) which means: "Yah is salvation." (Bemidbar 13:16). Yah is the short form of YHWH so the name is a declaration that it is YHWH Who saves. The change involved adding a yud (י) to the beginning of his name.

Yahushua was from the Tribe of Ephraim. The Tribe of Ephraim is extremely interesting because the name itself means: "doubly fruitful." Remember that Ephraim was the son of Joseph (Yoseph)[105] and he was born in Egypt along with his brother Manasheh - unlike the other children of Yisrael. His mother Asenath was an Egyptian - the daughter of a pagan priest - just as Mosheh's wife was the daughter of a pagan priest.[106] Yisrael has always been mixed with the other nations.

Ephraim was the youngest son of Yoseph yet he received the blessing and birthright of a firstborn son. He was adopted by his grandfather Yisrael and elevated as a son. So we have this powerful picture of a child born into a pagan culture and then being adopted by a veritable stranger – Yisrael. Through this adoption process Yisrael pronounced a blessing upon Ephraim as a firstborn son! (Beresheet 48:8-22).

Yahushua, Son of Nun, was called the assistant of Mosheh. The word used to describe his function was sharat (שרת), which can mean a minister or a servant. So in essence we see the pattern of Yahushua as a servant or a priest while Mosheh is alive and while Yisrael is in the wilderness.

When others were commanded not to go near Mount Sinai or touch the Mountain, we see Yahushua up on the Mountain receiving the Tablets with Mosheh. While Mosheh would come and go from the Tabernacle of Meeting, Yahushua would remain in the Tabernacle. (Shemot 33:11). While Mosheh was alive, he was like an El to the people and Yahushua was a high servant who remained in the presence of YHWH.

Immediately prior to the death of Mosheh we see Yahushua, along with Mosheh, renewing the Covenant with Yisrael at Moab. When Mosheh passed on, Yahushua then stepped into the role that Mosheh had vacated. He went from a servant to being the undisputed leader of Yisrael. From this point on we see an interesting transition as Yahushua moves from the servant of Mosheh to the servant of YHWH. Also, all throughout the text of the Book of Yahushua it refers to Mosheh in the past tense as "the servant of YHWH." So through both the lives of Mosheh and Yahushua we see servanthood as a predominant characteristic.

The Scriptures record the following: "⁹ Now Yahushua the son of Nun was full of the Spirit of wisdom, for Mosheh had laid his hands on him; so the children of Yisrael heeded him, and did as YHWH had commanded Mosheh." Devarim 39:9.

Yahushua was then given a commission directly from YHWH: "¹ After the death of Mosheh the servant of YHWH, it came to pass that YHWH spoke to Yahushua the son of Nun, Mosheh's assistant, saying: ² Mosheh My servant is dead. Now therefore, arise, go over this Jordan, you and all this people, to the Land which I am giving to them - the children of Yisrael. ³ Every place that the sole of your foot will tread upon I have given you, as I said to Mosheh. ⁴ From the wilderness and this Lebanon as far as the great river, the River Euphrates, all the land of the Hittites, and to the Great Sea toward the going down of the sun, shall be your territory. ⁵ No man shall be able to stand before you all the days of your life; as I was with Mosheh, so I will be with you. I will not leave you nor forsake you. ⁶ Be strong and of good courage, for to this people you shall divide as an inheritance the Land which I swore to their fathers to give them. ⁷ Only be strong and very courageous, that you may observe to do according to all the Torah which Mosheh My servant commanded you; do not turn from it to the right hand or to the left, that you

may prosper wherever you go. ⁸ *This Scroll of the Torah shall not depart from your mouth, but you shall meditate in it day and night, that you may observe to do according to all that is written in it. For then you will make your way prosperous, and then you will have good success.* ⁹ *Have I not commanded you? Be strong and of good courage; do not be afraid, nor be dismayed, for YHWH your Elohim is with you wherever you go."* Yahushua 1:1-9.

Therefore, Yahushua was elevated before the people to the same stature as Mosheh and the Torah was at the heart of his mission. Yahushua was to fulfill the Torah with Yisrael. While Mosheh delivered Yisrael from bondage, set them apart and established the marriage Covenant, the work was not finished. It was through Yahushua that the Torah would come alive to Yisrael. It was under the leadership of Yahushua that the Bride would "move in" with YHWH and consummate their marital relationship.

After Mosheh, Aharon and their generation of Yisraelites had passed away in the wilderness it was time for the next generation to cross the Jordan into the Promised Land. Their first obstacle would involve the fortified city of Jericho.

Prior to crossing the Jordan River and entering into the Promised Land, Yahushua sent out spies and this time the result was different. Yahushua sent only two spies out and it was done secretly. The spies entered into the city and went to the house of an adulterous woman, or rather a harlot named Rahab. We are told that they lodged there, literally the word for "lie down" is used in the Hebrew. This was probably a good cover for strangers entering the city, although not good enough. Soon the King found out that Yisraelites were in the city and an inquiry was made of Rahab.

Rahab had hidden the men under stalks of flax that she had laid out on her roof. She explained that the men had left at dusk and suggested pursuit to catch them. This provides some interesting information regarding the time of this incident. Since drying of flax was a customary procedure before the flax could be processed into linen, wicks or rope, this must have occurred around the flax harvest, otherwise it would have raised suspicion.

The climate in the Jordan River Valley is warmer than the other temperate areas of the Land and crops generally ripen sooner in that region. It is generally held that the flax and the barley ripen at the same time in the Jordan Valley.¹⁰⁷ We therefore know that this event took place shortly before Passover.

Rahab then aided the two spies in their escape and appeared to enter into covenant with the men. She gives testimony to the greatness

of YHWH and essentially goes through a conversion process. It is important to understand that each major Canaanite city was a miniature spiritual kingdom with the king being viewed as a descendent of El or rather a "son of El."

By her words, Rahab was disassociating from that system and was aligning with Yisrael. The spies then proceeded to swear by their lives that when YHWH gave them the Land they would deal with her "in kindness and truth."

Rahab asks for a sign and it is given – a scarlet thread from her window. They instructed her to bind to her window "this cord of thread of scarlet." If she followed those instructions both she and her family would be saved from death if they were located in her house. Anyone outside the house was outside the protection of the covenant. One cannot help but recall the scarlet thread tied around the wrist of Zerah and it turns out that Rahab becomes a significant part of the Messianic lineage.

Rahab then lowered the men out of the window with instructions for a safe return to their camp. The men were instructed to go to the

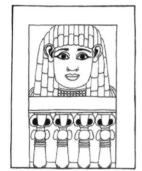

mountain and hide for three days. They did as instructed then crossed the Jordan River and returned to their camp. The symbology in this text is amazing. To begin, it is filled with the untranslated Aleph Taw (את). When you read this passge in the Hebrew it is abundantly clear that there is something important to do with the Messiah.

In ancient times the symbol of the prostitute was the woman in the window. Rahab lived on the outside wall with a window which was literally how she advertised. Not only were the Yisraelites delivered through this symbol of her trade, also the oath made between the Yisraelites and Rahab was intimately tied to that window.

The text records that the oath was made shavatanu (שבעתנו) which literally means to: "seven oneself" or "bind oneself by seven things." One cannot help but make the connection with the approaching Feast of Sevens called Shabuot.[108] This pattern of sevens will continue through the assault on the city.

The spies returned to Yahushua with the following report: "Truly YHWH has delivered all the Land into our hands, for indeed all the inhabitants of the country are fainthearted because of us." Yahushua 2:24. The spies could have come back with a bad report, but the selection of two spies instead of twelve likely helped. If I had to guess, those men were probably from the tribes of Yahudah and Ephraim. Interestingly, after bringing Egypt to its knees on the way out, YHWH would now require His Bride to fight her way into the Promised Land.

Jericho represented the first major obstacle to conquering the Land. Jericho means "moon city" and it was the seat of Canaanite moon worship. The name of the city, is actually pronounced Yeracho and derives from the Canaanite moon god Yerach, who can be directly traced to the Babylonian worship.

"Early in Canaanite religion, the male moon-god, Yerach, was the chief god of the pantheon. And the female sun-god, Shamash, was his cohort. Later, these were changed to Baal and Ashteroth. To judge from Canaanite place-names of the earliest period, such as Jericho and Beit-Yerach, as well as from Non-Semitic personal and place names of the 2nd millenium BCE, the cult of the sun-god and moon-god (or goddess) was at its height in very early times and steadily declined thereafter."[109]

In the land of Canaan " . . . there seem to have been two cities associated with moon worship, both "facing" east. One was Beit-Yerach ("Temple of the Moon") on the southwest shore of the Sea of Galilee. The other was Jericho with the broad Jordan valley extending eastward. The former ceased to be inhabited by ca. 2000 BCE. But Jericho was a leading city in Joshua's time (1400 BCE) and likely the seat of moon worship then. If the moon was the chief of the Canaanite pantheon, it would be a very strategic city indeed!"[110]

Canaanite worship was a depraved system driven by sex and violence and stood in stark contrast to the Torah of YHWH. The King of Jericho would have been considered a god king, and this City would have been a reproach in every way to the worship of YHWH.

Therefore, the taking of Jericho was an important event for the Yisraelites as they began to replace this Babylonian derived system with the Kingdom of YHWH. Each successive taking of a city was the defeat of a kingdom by the Kingdom of YHWH.

Prior to engaging Jericho, Yahushua met the prince or commander of the Army of YHWH. (Yahushua 5:13-15). Not much detail is provided concerning this encounter although we can discern that this was a fulfillment of the promise given to Mosheh. *"20 See, I am sending a messenger ahead of you to guard you along the way and to bring you to the place I have prepared. 21 Pay attention to Him and listen to what He says. Do not rebel against Him; He will not forgive your transgressions, since My Name is in Him."* Shemot 23:20-21.

Some translations indicate that this was an angel, but the Hebrew word is melek (מלאך) and can mean many things, primarily "messenger." We know that this was not simply a man or an angel because, as when YHWH met with Mosheh at the burning bush, Yahushua was instructed. *"Take your sandal off your foot, for the place where you stand is holy. And Yahushua did so."* Yahushua 5:15. In fact, this was the same "Melek YHWH" that appeared before Mosheh.

Interestingly, when asked whether the Commander was for Yisrael or their enemies the response given was "no." A series of directives are then given to Yahushua which would result in the miraculous victory over Jericho. It is an important point to remember that Yisrael would only be successful if and when they follow the directives of YHWH.

If Yisrael was with YHWH then they would be blessed. If not, then they would be cursed. YHWH created the Canaanites just as He had the Yisraelites. He did not hate the Canaanites, it was their abominable conduct that He hated and that was why He would lead Yisrael in to conquer them – so that the Land could be cleansed and He could be honored.

Yisrael crossed the river Jordan on the tenth day of the first month, often referred to as the month of the Abib. This is interesting because this was not just any random day. It was four days before the Passover which made it Lamb Selection Day. This was the day that all of the Yisraelites would select a lamb to be slaughtered. So just as the prior generation had observed this day in Egypt while still slaves preparing for deliverence, this new generation observed this day by crossing into the promised inheritance.

As with Mosheh the waters "piled up" and the Yisraelites crossed over on dry ground. This miraculous event, as with the Exodus from Egypt, was a corporate immersion or mikvah. The prior generation was cleansed while leaving Egypt on their way to the Promised Land. This new generation was cleansed while leaving the wilderness and entering the Land.

This entire process shows the redemptive process of YHWH. Yisrael was delivered from slavery by the blood of the lamb and the Rod (Branch) of YHWH in the hand of Mosheh. The enemies of Yisrael were decimated in the process. Yisrael was then washed in the waters of the Yom Suph (Sea of Reeds) and brought to the wedding at Sinai. They were then supposed to move in with their new Husband, however the incident involving the golden calf prevented this. The new generation crossed the Jorden River to cleanse then from their

transgressions, picking up where their ancestors left off forty (40) years earlier.

After crossing the Jordan, they then proceeded to Gilgal where Yahushua circumcised those who had crossed over. This is significant because we know that Yisrael was circumcised before they left Egypt. Shemot 12:43-51. All those who partake of the Passover must be circumcised. It seems that none of the Yisraelites born in the wilderness were circumcised on the eighth day as was commanded to Abraham, so none of them could have participated in the Passover.

Since circumcision was a sign of the Covenant, it was imperative that the Yisraelites be circumcised so that they could obey the Torah in the Land. What we can learn from this is that you must be in the Covenant in order to be delivered from death. We can also see that just because you bear the sign of the Covenant does not mean that you will automatically enter in to the Promised Land.

The path of restoration is plotted out through the Appointed Times. Yisrael was supposed to be delivered through the Passover, receive the Torah at Shabuot, and enter in to the Land at Succot during the first year of their deliverence.

Because of the bad report, Yisrael did not immediately enter the Land. This is a good example of why majority rule and the democratic system are not necessarily ideal and do not exist in the Kingdom of YHWH. The Children of Yisrael initially failed because of their sin, their fear and their unbelief. As a result, their entry into the Promised Land was delayed by forty (40) years. Remember the symbolism of the number four (4) and forty (40) as they relate to the Messsiah. This forty (40) year period emphasizes the need for the Messiah.

The process of preparation and redemption was repeated by Yahushua as Yisrael entered the Land. When they came out of the wilderness they were cleansed, circumcised and observed the Passover. They were now ready to take the Land, but first they had to get past Jericho.

The taking of Jericho was quite interesting because during this occurrence very specific instructions were given to Yahushua as follows: "*2 Then YHWH said to Yahushua, 'See, I have delivered Jericho* את *into your hands, along with its king and its fighting men. 3 You shall compass* את *the city, all the men of war go round about* את *the city once. Do this for six days. 4 Have seven priests carry the <u>seven yovelim shofarot</u> in front of the ark. On <u>the seventh day</u>, march around* את *the city <u>seven times</u>, with the priests blowing the shofarot. 5 And it shall come to pass when they make a long yovel b'qeren, when you hear* את *the sound of the shofarot, have all the people give a*

loud shout; then the wall of the city will collapse and the people will go up, every man straight in.'" Yahushua 6:2-5.

One cannot ignore the appearance of the sevens in these instructions which, at first glance would seem to indicate that this occurred at a specific Appointed Time known as Shabuot. We know from the Torah that beginning with the Firstfruits offering after Passover the Children of Yisrael were counting the Omer for a period of seven sevens or seven weeks. This counting leads up to the Feast of sevens or weeks which is called Shabuot. Tradition holds that this event actually occurred during Succot.

The English translation misses some very important meaning in this text. To begin, there are many instances of the Aleph Taw (את) which not only hints to the Messiah, but creates an even stronger link with the Commander of the Hosts of YHWH. Was this in fact the Messiah? Another problem with most English translations is that they simply mention "trumpets of ram's horns." The Hebrew text specifically mentions seven "yovelim shofarot" which provides a much deeper meaning.

You see a shofar (שופר) is a ram's horn so it is clear that the seven priests were to carry seven ram's horns. The key to this text is the word "yovelim" (יובל'ם). In fact, the text specifically refers to The Yovelim Shofarot or The Jubilee Ram's Horns.

The meaning could not be any clearer – these ram's horns, when blown on the seventh day, were to sound the yovel (יובל) – the Jubilee. This would have been Yom Kippur, the Day of Atonement, which marks the Jubilee Year every fifty years immediately preceding Succot.

Read what the Torah provides regarding this very special time. *"8 Count off seven sabbaths of years - seven times seven years - so that the seven sabbaths of years amount to a period of forty-nine years. 9 Then have the shofar blast everywhere on the tenth day of the seventh month; on the Day of Atonement sound the shofar throughout your Land. 10 Set apart* את *the fiftieth year and proclaim liberty throughout the Land to all its inhabitants. It shall be a yovel (יובל) for you; each one of you is to return to his family property and each to his own clan. 11 The fiftieth year shall be a jubilee for you; do not sow and do not reap* את *what grows of itself or harvest* את *the untended vines. 12 For it is a yovel and is to be set apart for you; you shall eat out of the field* את *the increase thereof."* Vayiqra 25:8-12.

The existence of the Aleph Taw (את) four (4) times clearly points to the Messianic significance surrounding the Yovel. Interestingly, we can discern from the Scriptures and tradition that Yisrael was actually forty (40) years into a Yovel cycle when they crossed the Jordan so it was not a Jubilee year for them. It is traditionally believed that Mosheh brought down the second set of tablets on Yom Kippur, which began a Year of Jubilee.

The fact that it was year forty (40) in the Yovel cycle confirms that there are clearly prophetic implications concerning the Jubilee and the Messiah which cannot be ignored. This event points to a future Yovel, likely the 120th Yovel, when Messiah will redeem Yisrael and lead the flock of Yisrael into the Land and restore all things.

After being given the unique instructions on how they would take the Land, The Scriptures then record the following "battle" scene: "[12] *And <u>Yahushua rose early in the morning</u>, and the priests took up the Ark of YHWH.* [13] *Then seven priests bearing seven yovelim shofarot before the Ark of YHWH went on continually and blew with the shofarot. And the armed men went before them. But the rear guard came after the Ark of YHWH, while the priests continued blowing the shofarot.* [14] *And the second day they marched around the city once and returned to the camp. So they did six days.* [15] *But it came to pass <u>on the seventh day that they rose early</u>, <u>about the dawning of the day</u>, and marched around the city seven times in the same manner. On that day only they marched around the city seven times.* [16] *And the seventh time it happened, when the priests blew the shofarot, that Yahushua said to the people: 'Shout, for YHWH has given you the city!'* [17] *Now the city shall be doomed by YHWH to destruction, it and all who are in it. Only Rahab the harlot shall live, she and all who are with her in the house, because she hid the messengers that we sent.* [18] *And you, by all means abstain from the accursed things, lest you become accursed when you take of the accursed things, and make the camp of Yisrael a curse, and trouble it.* [19] *But all the silver and gold, and vessels of bronze and iron, are consecrated to YHWH; they shall come into the treasury of YHWH.* [20] *So the people shouted when the priests blew the shofarot. And it happened when the people heard the sound of the shofarot, and the people shouted with a great shout, that the wall fell down flat. Then the people went up into the city, every man straight before him, and they took the city.* [21] *And they utterly destroyed all that was in the city, both man and woman, young and old, ox and sheep and donkey, with the edge of the sword.*" Yahushua 6:12-21.

Again, one cannot overlook the significance of the number (7) seven in this encounter and anyone familiar with the Book of Revelation should make an immediate connection.[III] Also notice when they began each day in the early morning, or "the dawning of the day."

The dawning of the day is that time in a day which perfectly parallels the morning twilight. Remember, the Hebrew day starts in the evening, when the sun has set. The dawning of the day is the opposite

time of day when the light of day begins to appear. It is the time when the Light of the first day was brought forth. It is an important time of day and it is closely linked with the Messiah. In fact, this entire event is a giant signal regarding when and how the Messiah will some day redeem Yisrael.[112]

After Jericho, Yisrael proceeded to conquer the Promised Land. Before they entered into the Land and before Mosheh died he instructed them as follows: "[11] *And Mosheh commanded the people on the same day, saying,* [12] *These shall stand on Mount Gerizim to bless the people, when you have crossed over the Jordan: Simeon, Levi, Judah, Issachar, Joseph, and Benjamin;* [13] *and these shall stand on Mount Ebal to curse: Reuben, Gad, Asher, Zebulun, Dan, and Naphtali.*" Devarim 27:12-13.

Shechem was the place where the Way would be physically presented to Yisrael. The blessings and the curses were found "between the shoulders." Yahushua obeyed the commandment given by YHWH through Mosheh after they entered the Land. "[30] *Now Yahushua built an altar to YHWH Elohim of Yisrael in Mount Ebal,* [31] *as Mosheh the servant of YHWH had commanded the children of Yisrael, as it is written in the Scroll of the Torah of Mosheh: 'an altar of whole stones over which no man has wielded an iron tool.' And they offered on it burnt offerings to YHWH, and sacrificed peace offerings.* [32] *And there, in the presence of the children of Yisrael, he wrote on the stones a copy of the Torah of Mosheh, which he had written.* [33] <u>*Then all Yisrael, with their elders and officers and judges, stood on either side of the Ark before the priests, the Levites, who bore the Ark of the Covenant of YHWH, the stranger as well as he who was born among them.*</u> *Half of them were in front of Mount Gerizim and half of them in front of Mount Ebal, as Mosheh the servant of YHWH had commanded before, that they should bless the people of Yisrael.* [34] *And afterward he read all the words of the Torah, the blessings and the cursings, according to all that is written in the Scroll of the Torah.* [35] *There was not a word of all that Mosheh had commanded which Yahushua did not read before all the assembly of Yisrael, <u>with the women, the little ones, and the strangers who were living among them.</u>*" Yahushua 8:30-35.

Notice that the altar was built on Mount Ebal – the mountain of the curses. It is disobedience which results in curses and death. Thus the need for an altar where blood is shed. On the stones of that altar the words of the Torah were written. All of Yisrael - the stranger and the native born – were involved in confirming the Covenant.

Yisrael was expected to obey those words. If they were obedient they would be blessed. If they disobeyed they would be cursed. It was really that simple and no different than any properly functioning

household. In my house, if my children obey there is peace and happiness for all. If they do not obey, there is discipline which involves varying degrees of punishment.

If Yisrael wanted to live peaceably in the Land they needed to obey the Head of the House - YHWH. Sadly we can see a literal illustration of the division that would come upon Yisrael in the future. At this place Shechem - "between the shoulders" where YHWH first appeared to Abram in the Land, where Abram had built the first Altar in the Land before he went to Beth El. This was the place where their forefathers had once slain the men of the area after deceiving them into being circumcised. It was after that incident that they rid themselves of their foreign gods and purified themselves before continuing to Beth El.

Yisrael, under the leadership of Yahushua needed to go to this very significant place and set the record straight. The ground rules needed to be firmly established before they could literally move into Beth El - The House of El.

Interestingly, under the leadership of Yahushua we see Yisrael united and fulfilling their destiny. After living in the wilderness in expectation, Yisrael was finally permitted to receive the promises of the wedding Covenant made at Sinai. Through the mediator Yahushua, the Bride was in a real way able to live the Torah.

The role of Yahushua was to help fulfill the Torah. The Torah is intended to be lived daily although Yisrael did not obey the Torah when they were in the wilderness. They did not circumcise their males on the eighth day as was expressly prescribed by the Torah. It was not until they were ready to move into the marital residence that they were cleansed and circumcised. They then celebrated the Appointed Times in the Land and entered into their inheritance.

Through Yahushua we see that Yisrael can be victorious and dwell in the Land when they remain in Covenant with YHWH and follow His commandments. Through the life of Yahushua we see a humble servant turned into a conquering leader who ruled over Yisrael and helped them fulfill the Torah by actually living out the Commandments in the Promised Land. As we shall soon see, his life was actually a pattern for the Messiah to come.

13

The Judges

If Yisrael had simply obeyed, they would have only received blessings, but sadly that is not what happened. Of course, none of this was a surprise to YHWH – He knew they would fall away. He actually predicted it through Mosheh.

"*When I have brought them to the Land flowing with milk and honey, of which I swore to their fathers, and they have eaten and filled themselves and grown fat, <u>then they will turn to other gods and serve them; and they will provoke Me and break My Covenant</u>.*" Devarim 31:20.

The Book of Judges describes a time after the death of Yahushua when the children of Yisrael had no cohesive leadership. This period is known as the time of the judges or rather "shoftim" in Hebrew. It provides various accounts of the problems that the tribes experienced and their struggle to settle and dwell in the Land.

The Book also provides a recurring theme as follows: "*In those days there was no king in Yisrael – everyone did what was right in his own eyes.*" The problem was, what was right in the eyes of one man was not necessarily right in the eyes of another, and particularly in the eyes of YHWH.

The text describes various men and women who were raised up by YHWH to rule over the children of Yisrael, often to "save" them from their enemies. This would typically lead to a recommitment to YHWH which was coupled with peace. Ultimately though they would fall back into idolatry which was the same as adultery in the eyes of YHWH.

Throughout the Book of Judges we see a repeating pattern of Yisrael "playing the harlot." This phrase was used to describe any number of forms of idolatry practiced by the Yisraelites, often with Baal. The word Baal means "lord" and was applied to the various Canaanite deities.

"In Babylonia it was the title specially applied to Merodach of Babylon, which in time came to be used in place of his actual name . . . The Babylonian Bel-Merodach was a Sun-god, and so too was the Canaanite Baal whose full title was Baal-Shemaim, "lord of heaven" . . . As the Sun-god, Baal was worshipped under two aspects, beneficent and destructive. On the one hand he gave light and warmth to his worshippers; on the other hand the fierce heats of summer destroyed the vegetation he had himself brought into being. Hence, human victims were sacrificed to him in order to appease his anger in time of plague or other trouble, the victim being usually the first-born of the sacrificer and being burnt alive. In the Old Testament this is euphemistically termed "passing" the victim "through the fire" (2 Kings 16:3; 21:6). The forms under which Baal was worshipped were necessarily as numerous as the communities which worshipped him. Each locality had its own Baal or divine "Lord" who frequently took his name from the city or place to which he belonged. Hence, there was a Baal-Zur, "Baal of Tyre"; Baal-hermon, "Baal of Hermon" (Judges 3:3); Baal-Lebanon, "Baal of Lebanon"; Baal-Tarz, "Baal of Tarsus." At other times the title was attached to the name of an individual god; thus we have Bel-Merodach, "the Lord Merodach" (or "Bel is Merodach") at Babylon, Baal-Melkarth at Tyre, Baal-gad (Joshua 11:17) in the north of Palestine. Occasionally the second element was noun as in Baal-Shemaim, "lord of heaven," Baalzebub (2 Kings 1:2), "Lord of flies," Baal-Hamman, usually interpreted "Lord of heat," but more probably "Lord of the sunpillar," the tutelary deity of Carthage. All these various forms of the Sun-god were collectively known as the Baalim or "Baals" who took their place by the side of the female Ashtaroth and Ashtrim."[113]

So we see that the Children of Yisrael continued to fall back into Babylonian sun worship. After the death of Gideon the text mentions specifically that some Yisraelites began to worship Baal-Berith who the Yisraelites made their god. Baal-Berith actually means "Lord of the Covenant" and this particular Baal was worshipped at Shechem – the very place where the Yisraelites recited the blessings and the curses when they renewed the Covenant with YHWH.

The text also records the Yisraelites worshipping all of the gods of the surrounding nations. After the death of Yair we read: *"Then the children of Yisrael again did evil in the sight of YHWH, and served the Baals and the Ashtoreths, the gods of Syria, the gods of Sidon, the gods of Moab, the gods of the people of Ammon, and the gods of the Philistines; and they forsook YHWH and did not serve Him."* Judges 10:6

It appears if left to their own devices the children of Yisrael

would be influenced by the gods of the neighboring nations as well as the gods of those inhabitants who were not removed from the Land. The Yisraelites required strong and righteous leaders to keep them on the straight path, otherwise they would fall away and whore after other gods. This cycle continued for over four centuries.

The Book of Judges ends after describing a tragic incident that begins with the words *"and it came to pass, when there was no king in Yisrael . . ."* (Judges 19:1). We are told of a certain Levite staying in the remote mountains of Ephraim who took a concubine from Bethlehem in Yahudah. She played the harlot and returned to Bethlehem for four months.

Her husband came to bring her home, and after some delay, retrieved her and began their journey back. On their way home "on the fifth day" the evening was drawing near. Instead of staying in Jerusalem for the night, a city then occupied by the Jebusites, the Levite chose to stay in Gibeah, a city of the Benjamites.

While in Gibeah an incident occured which reckons back to Lot and the events of Sodom and Gomorah. In this case, there was more than an attempted defilement. Here the concubine was actually abused by the men of Gibeah.[114] As a result, all of the tribes of Yisrael eventually came together to punish the tribe of Benjamin, except for those from Yabesh Gilead.

The united tribes decimated the tribe of Benjamin, which came close to being cut off completely. The account ends with another four month period where the six hundred remaining Benjamites were provided with four hundred wives. The wives were virgins from Yabesh Gilead which was also annihilated by twelve thousand Yisraelites for not participating in the massacre of the tribe of Benjamin. So we see this strange story bracketed by periods of four months which draws our attention to the content found within those brackets of time.

The Benjamites were then instructed to take their remaining wives from the daughters of Shiloh at a yearly feast to YHWH that occurred in Shiloh. At this time in history, the Tabernacle was in Shiloh and the Yisraelites were to appear in Shiloh before YHWH at His Appointed Times three times each year.[115]

It seems bizarre that fellow Yisraelites would encourage the Benjamites to "catch" their wives from their brethren, but the logic was apparently meant to preserve the seed of Benjamin, while allowing those from whom they were taken to remain guiltless from breaking their oath. They all had made an oath at Mizpah wherein they agreed that no one would give their daughter to Benjamin as a wife.

There is something very interesting that is occurring here. Read what follows: *"¹⁹ Then they said, 'In fact, there is a yearly feast of YHWH in Shiloh, which is north of Bethel, on the east side of the highway that goes up from Bethel to Shechem, and south of Lebonah. ²⁰ Therefore they instructed the children of Benjamin, saying, 'Go, lie in wait in the vineyards, ²¹ and watch; and just when the daughters of Shiloh come out to perform their dances, then come out from the vineyards, and every man catch a wife for himself from the daughters of Shiloh; then go to the land of Benjamin. ²² Then it shall be, when their fathers or their brothers come to us to complain, that we will say to them, Be kind to them for our sakes, because we did not take a wife for any of them in the war; for it is not as though you have given the women to them at this time, making yourselves guilty of your oath. ²³ And the children of Benjamin did so; they took enough wives for their number from those who danced, whom they caught. Then they went and returned to their inheritance, and they rebuilt the cities and dwelt in them. ²⁴ So the children of Yisrael departed from there at that time, every man to his tribe and family; they went out from there, every man to his inheritance. ²⁵ In those days there was no king in Yisrael; everyone did what was right in his own eyes."* Judges 21:19-25.

Interestingly, the text provides pinpoint directions to Shiloh *"north of Bethel, on the east side of the highway that goes up from Bethel to Shechem, and south of Lebonah."* Previously, under the leadership of Yahushua, Shiloh was established as the location of the Tabernacle and it was a focal point in Yisrael. (Yahushua 18:1).

Why the need to give such specific directions? They were all supposed to be meeting at Shiloh three times a year so everybody should have been well familiar with the way to Shiloh, but apparently this was not occurring.

The fact that the daughters of Shiloh were dancing in the vineyards leads many to believe that this was Tu B'Av or rather a celebration which was held on the 15ᵗʰ day of the 5ᵗʰ month. Tu B'Av was not an Appointed Time found within the commandments and since this event occurred shortly after the death of Yahushua it seems difficult to believe that such a traditional celebration was observed by Yisrael so soon after the giving of the Torah.

The text is clear that this was an "annual festival" to YHWH and that points specifically to those prescribed in the Torah – one of the Appointed Times referred to as moadim.[116] The problem is that one cannot help to view this as something pagan. Such a scene was typically associated with various fertility rites.

This text deserves additional examination as it contains an interesting statement. The statement "Behold a Feast to YHWH in

Shiloh yearly" is not necessarily an accurate translation. The text actually reads "yearly yearly" or "year to year" which is "miyamim yamiyamah" (מימים ימימה) in Hebrew. It is actually the same Hebrew word repeated twice.

This phrase is found only one time in the Torah and four other times in the Tanak, specifically in the texts of Shoftim and Shemuel. In the Torah the reference is in Shemot 13:10 when it refers to the Feast of Unleavened Bread. "*⁵ And it shall be, when YHWH brings you into the land of the Canaanites and the Hittites and the Amorites and the Hivites and the Jebusites, which He swore to your fathers to give you, a land flowing with milk and honey, that you shall keep את this service in this month. ⁶ seven days you shall eat unleavened bread, and on the seventh day there shall be a feast to YHWH. ⁷ Unleavened bread shall be eaten את seven days. And no leavened bread shall be seen among you, nor shall leaven be seen among you in all your quarters. ⁸ And you shall tell your son in that day, saying, This is done because of what YHWH did for me when I came up from Egypt. ⁹ It shall be as a sign to you on your hand and as a memorial between your eyes, that YHWH's Torah may be in your mouth; for with a strong hand YHWH has brought you out of Egypt. ¹⁰ You shall therefore keep this ordinance את at the Appointed Time from year to year.*" Shemot 13:5-10.

This passage contains three instances of the Aleph Taw (את). It was a time to remember the deliverance from Egypt and to be free from leaven, which often symbolized sin. This particular Feast occurred in the first month, often referred to as the month of the Abib, which fell in the season commonly referred to as spring. It often coincides with the vernal equinox which is the traditional time that the pagans would practice fertility rites.

The Yisraelites had conquered the Land of Canaan which was filled with the worship of Baal and Ashtoreth. It is well known that the Yisraelites absorbed the Canaanite ways and learned to identify their Elohim with Baal, whose rains allegedly brought fertility to the Land. Virgins dancing in vineyards was a custom common in pagan spring fertility rites and wine was intimately associated with these practices.

Therefore, the "Feast" occurring at Shiloh is questionable since there is a specific commandment concerning this Appointed Time, but no mention of virgins dancing in vineyards. Could it be that the Yisraelites were repeating the actions of their forefathers at Sinai? Were they celebrating "a Feast to YHWH" which was really pagan?

When examining this entire story it is important to remember that the underlying theme is the harlot. The priest's concubine played the harlot just as the children of Yisrael played the harlot. It appears

that the Children of Yisrael may have been profaning one of the Feasts of YHWH, just as they had done at Sinai.

This story was preceded by a description of the brutality and abominations committed by Dan and it concludes the book of Judges. The story ends as it began . . . *"In those days there was no king in Yisrael"* and it adds the phrase *"everyone did what was right in his own eyes."* Judges 21:25. These are the final words in the Book of Judges but they are preceded by a very interesting statement. *"At that time the Yisraelites left that place and went home to their tribes and clans, each to his own inheritance."* Judges 21:24. This is telling us that it was at or near a Jubilee Year as people were being restored to their inheritance according to Vayiqra 25:10. It is also emphasizing their need for a king as we see these two concepts – the Jubilee and the King brought together at the end of the text.

In their repetitive condition of disunity and idolatry they were living in sin and things were essentially chaotic. Even when they were united they were killing themselves, not just their enemies. Things were not going so well in the Promised Land. The message of Judges is clear – without a righteous leader the people continually stray into idolatry and "play the harlot."

The people of Yisrael required a righteous leader in order to follow YHWH, but the Judges did not adequately bring the tribes together, nor were they all righteous. The Children of Yisrael needed more than a judge. They needed a leader who was righteous by remaining obedient to the commandments of YHWH. They needed one who could unite all of the tribes and keep them united – they needed a king.

14

The Kings

There came a time when the people eventually cried out for a king. This was no surprise and was foretold by Mosheh. "¹⁴ *When you come to the Land which YHWH your Elohim is giving you, and possess it and dwell in it, and say, 'I will set a king over me like all the nations that are around me,' ¹⁵ you shall surely set a king over you whom YHWH your Elohim chooses; one from among your brethren you shall set as king over you; you may not set a foreigner over you, who is not your brother. ¹⁶ But he shall not multiply horses for himself, nor cause the people to return to Egypt to multiply horses, for YHWH has said to you, 'You shall not return that way again.' ¹⁷ Neither shall he multiply wives for himself, lest his heart turn away; nor shall he greatly multiply silver and gold for himself. ¹⁸ 'Also it shall be, when he sits on the throne of his kingdom, that he shall write for himself a copy of this Torah in a scroll, from the one before the priests, the Levites. ¹⁹ And it shall be with him, and he shall read it all the days of his life, that he may learn to fear YHWH his Elohim and be careful to observe all the words of this Torah and these statutes, ²⁰ that his heart may not be lifted above his brethren, that he may not turn aside from the commandment to the right hand or to the left, and that he may prolong his days in his kingdom, he and his children in the midst of Yisrael.*" Devarim 17:14-20.

During the transition between the period of the Judges and the Monarchy we read about Eli, who was a High Priest and Judge. The Tabernacle was located in Shiloh but as we already read, things were not necessarily going well in Shiloh. The sons of Eli were not conducting themselves well as priests and had perverted the priesthood. They were operating outside the will of YHWH and lost the Ark of the Covenant to the Philistines. During this time YHWH raised up a boy named Shemuel from the Tribe of Ephraim.

Shemuel was born to a barren woman and his life was devoted to the service of YHWH. He was a Nazarite from birth and he led a

set apart life. He functioned as a High Priest and a Judge which is quite intriguing since he was not born into the Tribe of Levi. He helped free Yisrael from the oppression of the Philistines after the deaths of Eli and his sons Hophni and Phineas.

With the loss of the Ark of the Covenant to the Philistines, the Tabernacle at Shiloh likely ceased to function. The Scriptures record that after seven months the Philistines returned the Ark and it remained in the house of Abinidab for twenty years.

"*¹ Then the men of Kirjath Jearim came and took the Ark of YHWH, and brought it into the house of Abinadab on the hill, and consecrated Eleazar his son to keep the Ark of YHWH. ² So it was that the Ark remained in Kirjath Jearim a long time; it was there twenty years. And all the House of Yisrael lamented after YHWH.*" 1 Shemuel 7:1-2.

Thereafter we read about Shemuel travelling throughout the Land and ruling over Yisrael with no central location for worship. The Scriptures detail him setting up altars and performing slaughterings throughout the Land. This appears to be in direct conflict with the prohibitions in the Torah until you recognize that he was operating in the capacity of the Melchizedek priesthood.[117]

He was also a prophet and in this capacity he was authorized to anoint Kings. The first King that YHWH chose was Shaul from the Tribe of Benjamin. Interestingly, Shaul came from the same tribe that came close to extinction. As a result, it was the smallest tribe in Yisrael and the only tribe that could lay claim to having its patriarchal namesake born in the Land.

Shaul was quite tall and a handsome man, just the characteristics that you would expect in a king. While Shaul was on a journey to find his father's missing donkeys, he ended up being anointed by Shemuel. (1 Shemuel 10:1). After being anointed by Shemuel, the Spirit of YHWH came upon him in power and he prophesied and was "*changed into a different person.*" 1 Shemuel 10:6.

Later, when it was time for him to become King, Shemuel called Yisrael together at Mizpah during the wheat harvest which would place it around the Feast of Shabuot. "*¹⁷ Then Shemuel called the people together to YHWH at Mizpah, ¹⁸ and said to the children of Yisrael, Thus says YHWH Elohim of Yisrael: I brought up Yisrael out of Egypt, and delivered you from the hand of the Egyptians and from the hand of all kingdoms and from those who oppressed you. ¹⁹ But you have today rejected your Elohim, who Himself saved you from all your adversities and your tribulations; and you have said to Him, 'No, set a king over us!' Now therefore, present yourselves before YHWH by your tribes and by your clans. ²⁰ And when Shemuel had caused*

all the tribes of Yisrael to come near, the tribe of Benjamin was chosen. [21] When he had caused the tribe of Benjamin to come near by their families, the family of Matri was chosen. And Shaul the son of Kish was chosen. But when they sought him, he could not be found. [22] Therefore they inquired of YHWH further, 'Has the man come here yet?' And YHWH answered, 'There he is, hidden among the equipment.' [23] So they ran and brought him from there; and when he stood among the people, he was taller than any of the people from his shoulders upward. [24] And Shemuel said to all the people, 'Do you see him whom YHWH has chosen, that there is no one like him among all the people?'" 1 Shemuel 10:17-24.

Shaul was hiding and YHWH had to tell the people where to find him. Yisrael now had their King. He looked good on the outside, but was lacking something on the inside – a heart for YHWH. Not long after his anointing he failed a serious test. He was specifically instructed to go to Gilgal and wait seven days until Shemuel arrived. Instead, he grew impatient and acted presumptuously.

"'[13] You acted foolishly,' Shemuel said. 'You have not kept the command YHWH your Elohim gave you; if you had, he would have established your kingdom over Yisrael for all time. [14] But now your kingdom will not endure; YHWH has sought out a man after his own heart and appointed him leader of his people, because you have not kept YHWH's command.'" 1 Shemuel 13:13-14.

This would mark the reign of Shaul. He acted foolishly on many occasions and he failed to obey the commands of YHWH. What seemed like a momentous turning point for the scattered Yisraelites, sadly did not live up to expectations. While Shaul may have been handsome, he was not a man who was completely obedient.

Because of Shaul's disobedience, YHWH chose another. It was not just anyone, rather it was David, who was someone who had already gained the attention of Shaul through the incident with Goliath. (1 Shemuel 17).

David stood up against the enemy of Yisrael when no other men would. He did this when he was not even a member of the standing army. He refused to wear the King's armour and relied solely on YHWH. It was at that moment in the Valley of Elah that we see the clear difference between Shaul and David.

David was the eighth and youngest son of a man named Jessie – Yeshai. Yeshai was a descendant of Obed, the son of Ruth and Boaz. While he was from the tribe of Yahudah, he was of mixed lineage, Ruth being a Moabite.

The selection of David is interesting because he was chosen by

YHWH while Shaul was still King over Yisrael. He was even anointed by Shemuel while Shaul was still King. So David was anointed, but he did not begin his reign for several years.

Shaul and his sons were later killed by the Philistines in Mount Gilboa (1 Shemuel 31:8). Their bodies had been hung from the walls of Beit Shean and the men of Yabesh Gilead came by night and took down their corpses from the walls. They burned the bodies, buried the bones under a tree and observed a fast for seven days. They did this out of honor and appreciation to Shaul.

Several years prior to his death, Shaul saved them from undergoing a terrible surrender agreement with Nahash, king of the Ammonites, which would involve gouging out their right eyes. These people who were nearly annihilated by the Yisraelites during the period of the Judges, and nearly maimed by the Ammonites acted nobly. As a result, the new King of Yisrael showed his appreciation.

It was not until the death of Shaul that David began to reign, and even then he only ruled over Yahudah. It is important to recognize that the tribes of Yisrael were essentially divided into two groups: The House of Yahudah and The House of Yisrael – the South and the North.

David inquired of YHWH and only acted when told to do so. *"1 It happened after this that David inquired of YHWH, saying, 'Shall I go up to any of the cities of Yahudah?' And YHWH said to him, 'Go up.' David said, 'Where shall I go up?' And He said, 'To Hebron.' 2 So David went up there, and his two wives also, Ahinoam the Jezreelitess, and Abigail the widow of Nabal the Carmelite. 3 And David brought up the men who were with him, every man with his household. So they dwelt in the cities of Hebron. 4 Then the men of Yahudah came, and there they anointed David king over the house of Yahudah. And they told David, saying, The men of Yabesh Gilead were the ones who buried Shaul. 5 So David sent messengers to the men of Yabesh Gilead, and said to them, You are blessed of YHWH, for you have shown this kindness to your lord, to Shaul, and have buried him. 6 And now may YHWH show kindness and truth to you. I also will repay you this kindness, because you have done this thing. 7 Now therefore, let your hands be strengthened, and be valiant; for your master Shaul is dead, and also the house of Yahudah has anointed me king over them."* 2 Shemuel 2:1-7.

David began his reign in Hebron and ruled over Yahudah for seven years and six months from that important city. It was not until the expiration of that time that he began to rule over all Yisrael.

"3 Therefore all the elders of Yisrael came to the king at Hebron, and King David made a covenant with them at Hebron before YHWH. And they

anointed David king over Yisrael. ⁴ *David was thirty years old when he began to reign, and he reigned forty years.* ⁵ In Hebron he reigned over Yahudah *seven years and six months, and in Jerusalem he reigned thirty-three years over all Yisrael and Yahudah."* 2 Shemuel 5:3-5.

So the greatest King of Yisrael became King over Yahudah when he was thirty (30) years old. He began his reign in a divided Kingdom – the House of Yisrael and the House of Yahudah. Under his reign the Kingdom was united and at the age of thirty seven (37) he became King over all of Yisrael. It was only when the Kingdom was restored that he reigned from the area known as the City of David in Jerusalem. These numbers should make us think about Joseph, a Messianic figure who began to rule at the age of thirty (30) and stored grain for a period of seven (7) years before being reunited with his brothers – The Tribes of Yisrael. David's reign spanned forty (40) years, a number that has great Messianic significance.

It is a remarkable fact that David was anointed three times. He was first privately anointed at Bethlehem (1 Shemuel 16:13). He was then anointed a second time by the men of Yahudah (2 Shemuel 2:4). Last and thirdly he was anointed by the elders of Yisrael (2 Shemuel 5:3). Remember that the word moshiach in Hebrew means "anointed" and therefore David was a moshiach – as King he was anointed by YHWH.

We read the following Mizmor concerning the anointing of David: "²⁰ *I have found My servant David; with My holy oil I have anointed him,* ²¹ *With whom My Hand shall be established; also My Arm shall strengthen him.* ²² The enemy shall not outwit him, nor the son of wickedness afflict him. ²³ I will beat down his foes before his face, and plague those who hate him. ²⁴ But My faithfulness and My mercy shall be with him, *and in My Name his horn shall be exalted.* ²⁵ *Also I will set his hand over the sea, and his right hand over the rivers.* ²⁶ *He shall cry to Me, You are my Father, My Elohim, and the rock of my salvation.* ²⁷ *Also I will make him My firstborn, the highest of the kings of the earth.* ²⁸ *My mercy I will keep for him forever, and My covenant shall stand firm with him.* ²⁹ His seed also I will make to endure forever, and his throne as the days of heaven. ³⁰ If his sons forsake My Torah and do not walk in My judgments, ³¹ If they break My statutes and do not keep My commandments, ³² *Then I will punish their transgression with the rod, and their iniquity with stripes.* ³³ Nevertheless My lovingkindness I will not utterly take from him, nor allow My faithfulness to fail. ³⁴ My Covenant I will not break, nor alter the word that has gone out of My lips. ³⁵ Once I have sworn by My holiness; I will not lie to David: ³⁶ His seed shall endure forever, and his throne as the sun before Me; ³⁷ It shall be established forever like the moon, even like the faithful *witness in the sky.*" Tehillim 89:20-37.

These are powerful words concerning David who had an intimate relationship with YHWH. Clearly David was special. He was anointed and his throne would be established "forever." He is considered to be a great example of Messiah the King and some actually refer to the Messiah ben David or Messiah Son of David.

After David had established his reign in Jerusalem and moved into his palace, he desired to build a House for YHWH. It was then that YHWH told David that He would make a house for him. In other words, YHWH would extend the reign of David through his progeny.

These words were spoken through the prophet Nathan: *"¹¹ Also YHWH tells you that He will make you a house. ¹² When your days are fulfilled and you rest with your fathers, I will set up אֵת your seed after you, who will come from your body, and I will establish אֵת his kingdom. ¹³ He shall build a house for My name, and I will establish אֵת the throne of his kingdom forever. ¹⁴ I will be his Father, and he shall be My son. If he commits iniquity, I will chasten him with the rod of men and with the blows of the sons of men. ¹⁵ But My mercy shall not depart from him, as I took it from Shaul, whom I removed from before you. ¹⁶ And your house and your kingdom shall be established forever before you. Your throne shall be established forever.*" 2 Shemuel 7:11-16.

The seed of David would call YHWH Father. This is the language of adoption. David was actually adopted by YHWH. As such, he was a son of Elohim. What started out as David being a servant ended up being an adopted son. Notice also the language used for the duration of his house, his kingdom and his throne – forever. In the Hebrew the text reads "ad olam" (עד עולם) which can be rendered "through all the ages" or "through all the ages to eternity." This is a long time, arguably eternity, so it stands to reason that this throne goes beyond simply mortal descendants of this great King.

This is a profound step in man's relationship with YHWH. We see this righteous king chosen and adopted by YHWH. His seed will be a son of YHWH. As it turns out this prophecy has both a physical fulfillment and a spiritual fulfillment. There would indeed be a "seed" who would build a physical House but there would also be a Seed Who would build a Spiritual House, an Eternal House for the Name of YHWH. This is clearly understood by the presence of the three instances of the untranslated Aleph Taw (את). Therefore, the Messiah would be a Seed or rather a Son of David who would also be a Son of YHWH.

This becomes even more evident when we see the failure of the

physical seed of David during the life of David – surely his physical seed was unable to continue to rule the Kingdom as He had done.

He was considerd to be a righteous King, but he also played an active role in the worship of YHWH. He made plans and preparations for the building of the House of YHWH, he wrote songs and helped develop the worship service. He also helped establish the priestly courses wherein the duties of the priests were divided into 24 shifts, called "courses." (see 1 Chronicles 24).[118]

Thus David played a major role in the worship of YHWH and he also united the Kingdom of Yisrael. He was a sort of Priestly King in the Order of Melchizedek. While his reign is looked upon as the Golden Years of Yisrael, things declined during and after the reign of his successor son Solomon (Shlomo).[119]

In fact, after the death of King David things deteriorated very rapidly. His son, Shlomo did, in fact, build and dedicate the House of YHWH. He also built other great structures and he accrued incredible wealth. He was known for his great wisdom, but sadly he fell into serious idolatry at the end of his life.

Read how his heart turned away from YHWH: *"¹ But King Shlomo loved many foreign women, as well as the daughter of Pharaoh: women of the Moabites, Ammonites, Edomites, Sidonians, and Hittites - ² from the nations of whom YHWH had said to the children of Yisrael, 'You shall not intermarry with them, nor they with you. Surely they will turn away your hearts after their gods.' Shlomo clung to these in love. ³ And he had seven hundred wives, princesses, and three hundred concubines; and his wives turned away his heart. ⁴ For it was so, when Shlomo was old, that his wives turned his heart after other gods; and his heart was not loyal to YHWH his Elohim, as was the heart of his father David. ⁵ For Shlomo went after Ashtoreth the goddess of the Sidonians, and after Milcom the abomination of the Ammonites. ⁶ Shlomo did evil in the sight of YHWH, and did not fully follow YHWH, as did his father David. ⁷ Then Shlomo built a high place for Chemosh the abomination of Moab, on the hill that is east of Jerusalem, and for Molech the abomination of the people of Ammon. ⁸ And he did likewise for all his foreign wives, who burned incense and sacrificed to their gods. ⁹ So YHWH became angry with Shlomo, because his heart had turned from YHWH Elohim of Yisrael, who had appeared to him twice, ¹⁰ and had commanded him concerning this thing, that he should not go after other gods; but he did not keep what YHWH had commanded. ¹¹ Therefore YHWH said to Shlomo, because you have done this, and have not kept My Covenant and My statutes, which I have commanded you, I will surely tear the kingdom away from you and give it to your servant. ¹² Nevertheless I will not do it in your days, for the sake of your*

father David; I will tear it out of the hand of your son. ¹³ *However <u>I will not</u>* <u>*tear away the whole kingdom; I will give one tribe to your son for the sake*</u> <u>*of My servant David, and for the sake of Jerusalem which I have chosen.*</u>" 1 Kings 11:1-13.

So a man who began his reign renowned for his wisdom ended up an idolater. He failed to keep (shamar) the commandments which separated him from the One Who had blessed him so greatly. The Scriptures are very clear that it was his disobedience which led to his demise. The Torah specifically forbids kings from obtaining great wealth or taking many wives. (Devarim 17:16-17) All kings of Yisrael were supposed to prepare their own Torah Scroll to remind them to live and rule according to the instructions of YHWH. (Devarim 17:18).

Shlomo was provided with everything he needed to be a great king, but he failed miserably and ended up being involved in abominable conduct. In fact, he was involved in some of the worst pagan rituals that existed.

Some legends provide that he used to summon demons using The Seal of Solomon – a two sided pendant with a pentagram on one side and a hexagram on the other side. It is clear that Shlomo blatantly disobeyed the commandments and the Kingdom would suffer as a result. Before his death, it was prophesied by Ahiyah of Shiloh that the Kingdom would be torn apart.

The prophet confronted the servant of Shlomo, Jeroboam, as he was leaving Jerusalem. Ahiyah took a new cloak and tore it into 12 pieces. He told Jeroboam to take 10 pieces and spoke the following to him:

"³¹ *See, I am going to tear the kingdom out of Shlomo's hand and* *give you ten tribes.* ³² *But for the sake of My servant David and the* *city of Jerusalem, which I have chosen out of all the tribes of Yisrael,* *he will have one tribe.* ³³ *I will do this because they have forsaken* *Me and worshiped Ashtoreth the goddess of the Sidonians, Chemosh* *the god of the Moabites, and Molech the god of the Ammonites, and* *have not walked in My ways, nor done what is right in My eyes, nor* *kept My statutes and laws as David, Shlomo's father, did.* ³⁴ *But I* *will not take the whole kingdom out of Shlomo's hand; I have made* *him ruler all the days of his life for the sake of David My servant,* *whom I chose and who observed My commands and statutes.* ³⁵ <u>*I will*</u> <u>*take the kingdom from his son's hands and give you ten tribes.*</u> ³⁶ <u>*I*</u> <u>*will give one tribe to his son so that David My servant may always*</u> <u>*have a lamp before Me in Jerusalem, the city where I chose to put*</u> <u>*My Name.*</u> ³⁷ *However, <u>as for you, I will take you, and you will rule</u>*

over all that your heart desires; you will be king over Yisrael. 38 If you do whatever I command you and walk in My ways and do what is right in My eyes by keeping My statutes and commands, as David My servant did, I will be with you. I will build you a dynasty as enduring as the one I built for David and will give Yisrael to you. 39 I will humble David's descendants because of this, but not forever." 1 Kings (Melakim) 11:31-39.

This was quite a prophecy given to Jeroboam – an Ephraimite. The Scriptures record that Jeroboam was a mighty man of valour - he was a powerful man. Shlomo recognized this and placed him in charge of the whole labor force of the House of Yoseph, but Jeroboam rebelled against Shlomo. His people were being oppressed and YHWH chose Jeroboam to punish Shlomo. He also gave Jeroboam great promises if he would only do what Shlomo failed to do – be like David. All he needed to do was obey and guard (shamar) the commands, walk in His ways and do what was right.[120]

After the death of King Shlomo, the prophecy given by Ahiyah came to pass. The House of Yisrael, also known as the Northern Kingdom, petitioned Solomon's son, King Rehoboam, essentially asking for tax relief. In the past, King Shlomo, had put a heavy burden on the people amassing great wealth and funding his many building projects, which included pagan structures.

Instead of taking the advice of the elders, Rehoboam took the advice of his young friends and responded to the apparent reasonable request by stating: *"My father laid on you a heavy yoke; I will make it even heavier. My father scourged you with whips; I will scourge you with scorpions."* 1 Kings (Melakim) 12:11.

His "unwise" response resulted in a split in the Kingdom of Yisrael. The House of Yisrael, which consisted of the Ten Northern Tribes, aligned with Jeroboam son of Nebat. The House of Yahudah, which consisted of the Southern Tribes, aligned with Rehoboam. While the House of Yahudah maintained the worship of YHWH in Jerusalem the Northern Tribes set up their own false worship system. This is where things started to go bad for the House of Yisrael.

Apparently, Jeroboam feared that if the House of Yisrael continued to go to Jerusalem for the Appointed Times they would eventually join up with the House of Yahudah and reunite the Kingdom of Yisrael. This notion was unfounded, self serving and contrary to the promise given to him by YHWH. Therefore, after seeking some bad advice he set up pagan worship in the north.

"26 Jeroboam thought to himself, the Kingdom will now likely

revert to the house of David. ²⁷ *If these people go up to offer sacrifices at the temple of YHWH in Jerusalem, they will again give their allegiance to their master, Rehoboam king of Yahudah. They will kill me and return to King Rehoboam.* ²⁸ *After seeking advice, the king made two golden calves. He said to the people, 'It is too much for you to go up to Jerusalem. Here are your gods, O Yisrael, who brought you up out of Egypt.* ²⁹ *One he set up in Bethel, and the other in Dan.'* ³⁰ *And this thing became a sin; the people went even as far as Dan to worship the one there.* ³¹ *Jeroboam built shrines on high places and appointed priests from all sorts of people, even though they were not Levites.* ³² *He instituted a festival on the fifteenth day of the eighth month, like the festival held in Yahudah, and offered sacrifices on the altar. This he did in Bethel, sacrificing to the calves he had made. And at Bethel he also installed priests at the high places he had made.* ³³ *On the fifteenth day of the eighth month, a month of his own choosing, he offered sacrifices on the altar he had built at Bethel. So he instituted the festival for the Yisraelites and went up to the altar to make offerings.*"
1 Kings (Melakim) 12:26-33.

This is really quite incredible because Jeroboam was already promised a perpetual throne, like David's, if he would simply obey. Instead of trusting the word of YHWH, he tried to hold onto power using his own intellect and setting up his own system of worship – in direct contravention to the ways of YHWH! He told the people "Here are your gods" which is the same statement Aharon made to the people when they "played the harlot" at Sinai. Jeroboam even used the same gods that were worshipped at Sinai.

Jeroboam not only established new places of worship, he also established different appointed times and set up a false priesthood.[121] The sin of Jeroboam was even worse than the sin of his predecessors at Sinai. Despite warnings, Jeroboam refused to repent and therefore, as a result of this great sin, Yisrael was scheduled for punishment. It was not a mystery that they would be punished. Mosheh had told them long ago, but they apparently did not remember or they just did not care.

As you can probably imagine, not everyone in this new breakaway kingdom was pleased with the idolatry which was introduced by Jeroboam. While everyone must have surely appreciated the tax relief, they needed to choose whether the trade was worth it or not – they all had a choice to make.

The Scriptures record the following: "¹³ *And from all their territories the priests and the Levites who were in all Yisrael took their stand with him.* ¹⁴ *For the Levites left their common-lands and their possessions and*

came to Yahudah and Jerusalem, for Jeroboam and his sons had rejected them from serving as priests to YHWH. ¹⁵ Then he appointed for himself priests for the high places, for the goat and the calf idols which he had made. ¹⁶ And after them, those from all the tribes of Yisrael, such as set their heart to seek YHWH Elohim of Yisrael, came to Jerusalem to sacrifice to YHWH Elohim of their fathers. ¹⁷ So they strengthened the kingdom of Yahudah, and made Rehoboam the son of Shlomo strong for three years, because they walked in the way of David and Shlomo for three years." 2 Chronicles 11:13-17

So we see that at least the Levites from the Northern Kingdom left and went to dwell with Yahudah. While others from the Northern Kingdom "*came to Jerusalem to sacrifice,*" we do not know for sure if they moved there. We can safely assume from the language that the statement: "*they strengthened the kingdom of Yahudah*" means that they were added to the kingdom by moving to Judea. This will be important to remember later in the discussion because it is highly likely that the resulting Southern Kingdom was a mixture of all of the tribes, although primarily Yahudah, Benyamin and Levi.

Sadly, the entire ordeal stemmed from a continuing sibling rivalry between Ephraim (Joseph) and Yahudah. Jeroboam, after all, was from the tribe of Ephraim (1 Melakim 7:46) and Rehoboam was from the tribe of Yahudah. We will see this as a common theme throughout the Scriptures and it is a very important concept to understand – the battle between the first born status and the rulership.

The matter was aptly summarized in 1 Melakim 12:19: "*So Yisrael has been in rebellion against the house of David to this day.*" The split in the kingdom was no accident as proclaimed by Shemayah, the man of Elohim, as Rehoboam was about to suppress the rebellion of the House of Yisrael. "*This is what YHWH says: 'Do not go up to fight against your brothers, the Yisraelites. Go home, every one of you, **for this is My doing**. So they obeyed the word of YHWH and went home again, as YHWH had ordered.*'" 1 Melakim 12:24. YHWH had a plan for this division which was much greater than people could imagine.

They would need one like David - a Messiah Son of David who could reunite these divided Kingdoms. Sadly, things would get worse before they would get better as both of these Kingdoms would experience punishment through exile.

15

Exile

There were serious problems in Yisrael before the division and things continued to worsen afterward. Despite the fact that Shlomo had brought idolatry into Jerusalem, that city remained the spiritual capital of Yahudah and the Levitic priesthood continued to function in the House of YHWH. In fact, most of the Levites in the north moved to the south when Jeroboam set up his false system of worship.

While individuals from some of the northern tribes moved with them, in general the Kingdom of Yisrael was divided into two kingdoms. The Northern Kingdom was called the House of Yisrael and consisted of ten tribes while the Southern Kingdom was called the House of Yahudah and consisted of the three tribes of Yahudah, Benjamin and Levi.

The line of David continued to reign in the Southern Kingdom in accordance with the Covenant made by YHWH. While the House of Yahudah essentially continued the Torah based worship of YHWH, they clearly continued the idolatry precipitated by Shlomo and his wives. There were brief periods of restoration and purification when a righteous king would arise and actually lead the people, but generally Yahudah was in a perpetual period of backsliding and decline.

The Northern Kingdom, on the other hand, did not delay in their departure from the ways of YHWH. In an attempt to be different from their brethren in Yahudah, they changed the place of worship, the Appointed Times and the priesthood.

Interestingly, Jeroboam who essentially delivered the Northern Kingdom from bondage by the Hand of YHWH did not follow the example of Mosheh. Instead, he followed in the error of his ancestors by building not just one, but two golden calves.

Jeroboam was promised a great kingdom but he set up abominations instead. He was not fit to be king nor were the errant

Yisraelites fit to live in the Land any longer. The stage was set for them to be the first to experience the punishment set forth in the Torah – the punishment of exile.

Before the tribes of Yisrael entered the Land, they were given detailed and repeated guidance concerning the blessings of obedience and the curses of disobedience. Just as with Adam and Hawah, they were given instructions and they were warned of the punishment that awaited them if they disobeyed. Likewise, as with Adam and Hawah, if they wanted to dwell in the Household of YHWH they needed to obey the rules of the House. Yisrael could live in the Land as long as they obeyed the Torah.

There are many who proclaim that the Torah, which they call "the Law," was too difficult for Yisrael to obey. This is simply untrue. After detailing the blessings and the curses to Yisrael, Mosheh specifically stated: "*¹¹ Now what I am commanding you today is not too difficult for you or beyond your reach. ¹² It is not up in heaven, so that you have to ask, 'Who will ascend into heaven to get it and proclaim it to us so we may obey it?' ¹³ Nor is it beyond the sea, so that you have to ask, 'Who will cross the sea to get it and proclaim it to us so we may obey it?' ¹⁴ No, the Word is very near you; it is in your mouth and in your heart so you may obey it.*" Devarim 30:11-14.

One of the penalties of disobedience was exile. It was specifically provided that if Yisrael did not obey the Torah: "*³⁶ YHWH will drive you and the king you set over you to a nation unknown to you or your fathers. There you will worship other gods, gods of wood and stone. ³⁷ You will become a thing of horror and an object of scorn and ridicule to all the nations where YHWH will drive you.*" Devarim 28:36-37.

Again they were told: "*⁶⁴ Then YHWH will scatter you among all nations, from one end of the earth to the other. There you will worship other gods - gods of wood and stone, which neither you nor your fathers have known. ⁶⁵ Among those nations you will find no repose, no resting place for the sole of your foot. There YHWH will give you an anxious mind, eyes weary with longing, and a despairing heart. ⁶⁶ You will live in constant suspense, filled with dread both night and day, never sure of your life. ⁶⁷ In the morning you will say, 'If only it were evening!' and in the evening, 'If only it were morning!' - because of the terror that will fill your hearts and the sights that your eyes will see. ⁶⁸ YHWH will send you back in ships to Egypt on a journey I said you should never make again. There you will offer yourselves for sale to your enemies as male and female slaves, but no one will buy you.*" Devarim 28:64-68.

There was also provision for multiplying their punishment. In Vayiqra 26 the Yisraelites were told on three separate occasions that

their punishment would be multiplied **seven times** if they continued to disobey. This is extremely important to understand when examining the duration of the exiles for the different kingdoms.

Mosheh told the children of Yisrael that they would, in fact, be exiled. He also provided them with the hope of an eventual restoration described as follows:

"¹ *When all these blessings and curses I have set before you come upon you and you take them to heart wherever YHWH your Elohim disperses you among the nations,* ² *and when you and your children return to YHWH your Elohim and obey him with all your heart and with all your soul according to everything I command you today,* ³ *then* <u>YHWH your Elohim will restore your fortunes and have compassion on you and gather you again from all the nations where he scattered you.</u> ⁴ ***Even if you have been banished to the most distant land under the heavens, from there YHWH your Elohim will gather you and bring you back.*** ⁵ *He will bring you to the Land that belonged to your fathers, and you will take possession of it. He will make you more prosperous and numerous than your fathers.* ⁶ <u>YHWH your Elohim will circumcise your hearts and the hearts of your descendants, so that you may love him with all your heart and with all your soul, and live.</u> ⁷ *YHWH your Elohim will put all these curses on your enemies who hate and persecute you.* ⁸ *You will again obey YHWH and follow all his commands I am giving you today.* ⁹ <u>Then YHWH your Elohim will make you most prosperous in all the work of your hands and in the fruit of your womb, the young of your livestock and the crops of your Land. YHWH will again delight in you and make you prosperous, just as He delighted in your fathers,</u> ¹⁰ <u>if you obey YHWH your Elohim and keep His commands and decrees that are written in this Scroll of the Torah and turn to YHWH your Elohim with all your heart and with all your soul.</u>" Devarim 30:1-10.

So we see a pattern being repeated. In the Garden, Adam was divided and then he and Hawah were cut off and expelled from the "household" because of their disobedience. So we also see Yisrael divided and then expelled from the Land. Just as Adam and Hawah experienced individual and unique curses so would the two kingdoms. They were not exiled together nor did they receive the same punishments, rather the Kingdom was divided in two and the House of Yisrael was exiled separate from the House of Yahudah. Their sins were different so their punishments were different.[122]

Let us first read what happened to the House of Yisrael:

"¹ *In the twelfth year of Ahaz king of Yahudah, Hoshea son of Elah*

became king of Yisrael in Samaria, and he reigned nine years. ² He did evil in the eyes of YHWH, but not like the kings of Yisrael who preceded him. ³ Shalmaneser king of Assyria came up to attack Hoshea, who had been Shalmaneser's vassal and had paid him tribute. ⁴ But the king of Assyria discovered that Hoshea was a traitor, for he had sent envoys to So king of Egypt, and he no longer paid tribute to the king of Assyria, as he had done year by year. Therefore Shalmaneser seized him and put him in prison. ⁵ The king of Assyria invaded the entire land, marched against Samaria and laid siege to it for three years. ⁶ In the ninth year of Hoshea, the king of Assyria captured Samaria and deported the Yisraelites to Assyria. He settled them in Halah, in Gozan on the Habor River and in the towns of the Medes. ⁷ All this took place because the Yisraelites had sinned against YHWH their Elohim, who had brought them up out of Egypt from under the power of Pharaoh king of Egypt. They worshiped other gods ⁸ and followed the practices of the nations YHWH had driven out before them, as well as the practices that the kings of Yisrael had introduced. ⁹ The Yisraelites secretly did things against YHWH their Elohim that were not right. From watchtower to fortified city they built themselves high places in all their towns. ¹⁰ They set up sacred stones and Asherah poles on every high hill and under every spreading tree. ¹¹ At every high place they burned incense, as the nations whom YHWH had driven out before them had done. They did wicked things that provoked YHWH to anger. ¹² They worshiped idols, though YHWH had said, 'You shall not do this. ¹³ YHWH warned Yisrael and Yahudah through all his prophets and seers: Turn from your evil ways. Observe My commands and decrees, in accordance with the entire Torah that I commanded your fathers to obey and that I delivered to you through My servants the prophets.' ¹⁴ But they would not listen and were as stiff-necked as their fathers, who did not trust in YHWH their Elohim. They rejected His decrees and the Covenant He had made with their fathers and the warnings He had given them. They followed worthless idols and themselves became worthless. They imitated the nations around them although YHWH had ordered them, 'Do not do as they do,' and they did the things YHWH had forbidden them to do. ¹⁶ They forsook **all** the commands of YHWH their Elohim and made for themselves two idols cast in the shape of calves, and an Asherah pole. They bowed down to all the starry hosts, and they worshiped Baal. ¹⁷ They sacrificed their sons and daughters in the fire. They practiced divination and sorcery and sold themselves to do evil in the eyes of YHWH,

provoking him to anger. *¹⁸ So YHWH was very angry with Yisrael and removed them from His presence. **Only the branch (clan) of Yahudah was left,** ¹⁹ and even Yahudah did not keep the commands of YHWH their Elohim. They followed the practices Yisrael had introduced. ²⁰ Therefore* **YHWH rejected all the people of Yisrael;** *He afflicted them and gave them into the hands of plunderers, until He thrust them from His presence.* ²¹ When He tore Yisrael away from the house of David, they made Jeroboam son of Nebat their king. Jeroboam enticed Yisrael away from following YHWH and caused them to commit a great sin. ²² The Yisraelites persisted in all the sins of Jeroboam and did not turn away from them ²³ until YHWH removed them from His presence, as He had warned through all His servants the prophets. *So the people of Yisrael were taken from their homeland into exile in Assyria, and they are still there.*" 2 Melakim 17:1-24.

The Assyrians actually removed all of the House of Yisrael from the Land. This is a fact debated by some but the Scriptures clearly state that "*YHWH rejected ALL the people of Yisrael*"

and "*ONLY the branch (clan) of Yahudah was left.*" Remember that a remnant of the Northern Tribes, along with the Levites, likely "moved in" with the House of Yahudah and became part of that clan after Jeroboam set up his idolatrous system of worship. While Assyria removed the Northern Tribes from their Land, there was probably a remnant of these Tribes who lived in Judea and joined the House of Yahudah. The Olive Tree of Yisrael had been cut down and only the branch of Yahudah remained in the Land.

As was their custom, Assyrian Kings did not just defeat their enemies – they transplanted them in order to better gain control of the territories that they conquered. In the case of the House of Yisrael, this appears to have been a process which took place through the reigns of three Assyrian Kings, Tiglath-pileser III, Shalmaneser V and Sargon II – possibly others.

One can read in the Khorsebad Annals how Sargon II took Samaria and carried away 27,290 of the population of Yisrael. This is often used by those who desire to contradict the Scriptures by claiming that not all of the House of Yisrael was sent into exile. That is a weak argument because this particular incident recorded by Sargon II was only one event of many which occurred in the eighth century BCE.

"In the late 1800's some clay Assyrian cuneiform tablets were discovered and they were finally translated in the 1930's. These

tablets were Assyrian records of this . . . [Y]israelite deportation [in the eighth century BCE]. There were records of four deportations, which proved the ten tribes of the northern Nation of [Y]israel were assembled into Assyrian culture and became identifiable as the C[i]merians, the Sythians, and the Goths. Our records of ancient history show that over several hundred years, and through different paths, the Sycthians, C[i]merians and the Goths migrated essentially to northwest Europe and became known as the Anglo-Saxon Celtic people. Linguistic analysis of the word 'Anglo-Saxon' shows the word 'Saxon' means 'sons of Isaac.'"[123]

The exile of the northern tribes was a result of their grievous sins – YHWH had to remove them from His presence. They were participating in the worst forms of idolatry, even offering their children as sacrifices – likely to the god Chemosh. Not only were the Yisraelites removed from their Land, they were replaced by foreigners.

"[24] *The king of Assyria brought people from Babylon, Cuthah, Avva, Hamath and Sepharvaim and settled them in the towns of Samaria to replace the Yisraelites. They took over Samaria and lived in its towns. [25] When they first lived there, they did not worship YHWH; so He sent lions among them and they killed some of the people. [26] It was reported to the king of Assyria: The people you deported and resettled in the towns of Samaria do not know what the god of that country requires. He has sent lions among them, which are killing them off, because the people do not know what he requires. [27] Then the king of Assyria gave this order: 'Have one of the priests you took captive from Samaria go back to live there and teach the people what the god of the Land requires.' [28] So one of the priests who had been exiled from Samaria came to live in Bethel and taught them how to worship YHWH. [29] Nevertheless, each national group made its own gods in the several towns where they settled, and set them up in the shrines the people of Samaria had made at the high places. [30] The men from Babylon made Succoth Benoth, the men from Cuthah made Nergal, and the men from Hamath made Ashima; [31] the Avvites made Nibhaz and Tartak, and the Sepharvites burned their children in the fire as sacrifices to Adrammelech and Anammelech, the gods of*

Sepharvaim. [32] They worshiped YHWH, but they also appointed all sorts of their own people to officiate for them as priests in the shrines at the high places. [33] They worshiped YHWH, but they also served their own gods in accordance with the customs of the nations from which they had been brought. [34] To this day they persist in their former practices. They neither worship YHWH nor adhere to the decrees and ordinances, the laws and commands that YHWH gave the descendants of Yaakov, whom He named Yisrael. [35] When YHWH made a Covenant with the Yisraelites, He commanded them: 'Do not worship any other gods or bow down to them, serve them or sacrifice to them. [36] But YHWH, who brought you up out of Egypt with mighty power and outstretched arm, is the one you must worship. To Him you shall bow down and to Him offer sacrifices. [37] You must always be careful to keep the decrees and ordinances, the laws and commands He wrote for you. Do not worship other gods. [38] Do not forget the Covenant I have made with you, and do not worship other gods. [39] Rather, worship YHWH your Elohim; it is He who will deliver you from the hand of all your enemies.' [40] They would not listen, however, but persisted in their former practices. [41] Even while these people were worshiping YHWH, they were serving their idols. To this day their children and grandchildren continue to do as their fathers did." 2 Melakim 17:24-41.

So the House of Yisrael was removed from the Land and replaced by foreigners. The King of Assyria sent back a priest to instruct the foreigners how to serve YHWH, which they did <u>along</u> with their pagan worship. To this very day, descendants of those people, known as Samaritans, continue their religious system on Mount Gerizim in Samaria.

How interesting that the Kingdom of Yisrael was chosen to be a kingdom of priests who, through their obedience were to shine as a light to the nations. They were delivered from Egypt and brought to their own Land so that they could be set apart and obey YHWH.

Through their obedience they would be blessed and all the world would see it. Instead, they disobeyed, but even through their disobedience they would give testimony to the nations, only now they would be scattered throughout the nations and the nations were brought into the Land.

The Scriptures indicate that the House of Yahudah also followed the ways of the House of Yisrael. Their punishment was withheld due to their repentance and restoration which occurred under the reigns of various kings. While the tribes of the House of Yisrael were removed

from their Land and scattered between 723 – 714 BCE, the House of Yahudah was exiled between 618 – 595 BCE. The year 586 BCE has long been the accepted date for the destruction of the First Temple at Jerusalem, but new astronomical data tends to point to 599 BCE.[124]

Ezekiel (Yehezqel)[125] was one of the major prophets who prophesied to the House of Yahudah concerning their sin during their exile. He began his prophetic ministry in the *"fifth year of King Jehoiachin's captivity."* Yehezqel 1:2. Yehezqel described the idolatrous conduct of the House of Yahudah as well as the abominations that were occurring in the House of Yahudah and in the Temple.

"[14] Then he brought me to the entrance to the north gate of the House of YHWH, and I saw women sitting there, mourning for Tammuz. [15] He said to me, Do you see this, son of man? You will see things that are even more detestable than this. [16] He then brought me into the inner court of the House of YHWH, and there at the entrance to the House, between the portico and the altar, were about twenty-five men. With their backs toward the House of YHWH and their faces toward the east, they were bowing down to the sun in the east. [17] He said to me, Have you seen this, son of man? Is it a trivial matter for the House of Yahudah to do the detestable things they are doing here? Must they also fill the Land with violence and continually provoke me to anger? Look at them putting the branch to their nose! [18] Therefore I will deal with them in anger; I will not look on them with pity or spare them. Although they shout in my ears, I will not listen to them." Yehezqel 8:14-18.

The prophet Jeremiah (Yirmeyahu)[126] who prophesied before and during the exile also described the sins of the House of Yahudah. *"[17] Do you not see what they are doing in the towns of Yahudah and in the streets of Jerusalem? [18] The children gather wood, the fathers light the fire, and the women knead the dough and make cakes of bread for the Queen of Heaven. They pour out drink offerings to other gods to provoke me to anger. [19] But am I the one they are provoking? declares YHWH. Are they not rather harming themselves, to their own shame? [20] Therefore this is what the Sovereign YHWH says: My anger and my wrath will be poured out on this place, on man and beast, on the trees of the field and on the fruit of the ground, and it will burn and not be quenched. [21] This is what YHWH Almighty, the Elohim of Yisrael, says: Go ahead, add your burnt offerings to your other sacrifices and eat the meat yourselves! [22] For when I brought your forefathers out of Egypt and spoke to them, I did not just give them commands about burnt offerings and sacrifices, [23] but I gave them this command: <u>Obey Me, and I will be your Elohim and you will be My people. Walk in all the ways I command you, that it may go well with you</u>. [24] But they did not listen or pay attention; instead, they followed the stubborn inclinations of their evil hearts. They went backward* and not forward. [25] From the time your forefathers left Egypt until now, day after day, again and again I sent you My servants the prophets. [26] But they did not listen to me or pay attention. They were stiff-necked and did more evil than their forefathers. [27] When you tell them all this, they will not listen to you; when you call to them, they will not answer. [28] Therefore say to them, This is the nation that has not obeyed YHWH its Elohim or responded to correction. Truth has perished; it has vanished from their lips. [29] Cut off your hair and throw it away; take up a lament on the barren heights, for YHWH has rejected and abandoned this generation that is under His wrath. [30] *The people of Yahudah have done evil in My eyes, declares YHWH. They have set up their detestable idols in the House that bears My Name and have defiled it.* [31] *They have built the high places of Topheth in the Valley of Ben Hinnom to burn their sons and daughters in the fire - something I did not command, nor did it enter My mind.* [32] So beware, the days are coming, declares YHWH, when people will no longer call it Topheth or the Valley of Ben Hinnom, but the Valley of Slaughter, for they will bury the dead in Topheth until there is no more room. [33] Then the carcasses of this people will become food for the birds of the air and the beasts of the earth, and there will be no one to frighten them away. [34] I will bring an end to the sounds of joy and gladness and to the voices of bride and bridegroom in the towns of Yahudah and the streets of Jerusalem, for the Land will become desolate." Yirmeyahu 7:17-34.

Both Yehezeqel and Yirmeyahu are describing Babylonian sun worship. They faced the east and bowed to the sun – Nimrod. They participated in the ceremony of weeping for Tammuz, the son of the sun god. This was a forty (40) day period when they mourned the death of Tammuz, who was later allegedly resurrected. They baked cakes to the Queen of Heaven, known as Ishtar or Easter. These cakes are still baked to this day, known as hot cross buns, they are marked with the cross or "+" of Tammuz.

They were continuing the sins perpetrated by Shlomo by burning their children in the fires of Moloch. The word moloch, shares the root of the Hebrew word "king" which is melech (מלך) in Hebrew. The worship of Moloch is a profane affront to the worship of YHWH.

"Moloch answered to Baal the Phoenician sun god, to whom also human burnt offerings were sacrificed; also to Chemosh, to whom Mesha sacrificed his son (2 Kings 3:27; Micah 6:7; Ezekiel 16:20; 23:39). Kimchi (on 2 Kings 23:10) represents Moloch as a hollow brass humanlike body, with ox's head, and hands stretched forth to receive. When it was thoroughly heated the priests put the babe into its hands, while drums (Tophiym from whence came Tophet) were beat to drown the infant cries, lest the parent should relent. The image was set within seven

chapels: the first was opened to any one offering fine flour; the second to one offering turtle doves or young pigeons; the third to one offering a lamb; the fourth to one offering a ram; the fifth to one offering a calf; the sixth to one offering an ox; the seventh to one offering his son."[127]

Notice the similarity in the sacrifices to YHWH - only they also offered their sons to Moloch. This stands in stark contrast to the worship of YHWH. YHWH specifically told Abraham not to sacrifice his son because YHWH would provide the Lamb. This was an honor reserved for YHWH alone. Yahudah was supposed to redeem their firstborn sons, not offer them to a pagan god - this was an abomination.

Accordingly, the House of Yahudah was subsequently taken over and then placed into exile by the Babylonians. This process occurred during the reigns of Jehoiakim and his son Jehoiachin, who only reigned for three months and ten days. Jerusalem was besieged and King Jehoiachin was taken captive around 610 BCE. The Temple was looted and destroyed and all of the the treasures, nobility and talent of Yahudah were taken to Babylon.

Zedekiah was thereafter made the King of Yahudah after the capitulation of Jerusalem and this small group remaining was likened by YHWH as a basket of "rotten figs." Yirmeyahu was shown by YHWH that those who remained with Zedekiah were the "residue" and things would not go well for them. *"9 I will deliver them to trouble into all the kingdoms of the earth, for their harm, to be a reproach and a byword, a taunt and a curse, in all places where I shall drive them. 10 And I will send the sword, the famine, and the pestilence among them, till they are consumed from the Land that I gave to them and their fathers."* Yirmeyahu 24:9-10.

On the other hand, those who were taken captive were likened as a basket of "good figs." A good word was prophesied concerning these individuals. *"5 Like these good figs, so will I acknowledge those who are carried away captive from Yahudah, whom I have sent out of this place for their own good, into the land of the Chaldeans. 6 For I will set My eyes on them for good, and I will bring them back to this Land; I will build them and not pull them down, and I will plant them and not pluck them up. 7 Then I will give them a heart to know Me, that I am YHWH; and <u>they shall be My people, and I will be their Elohim,</u> for they shall return to Me with their whole heart."* Yirmeyahu 24:5-7.

While Babylon was used to carry out the punishment upon Yahudah, they too would be punished for their deeds after seventy years had elapsed. *"12 Then it will come to pass, when seventy years are*

completed, that I will punish the king of Babylon and that nation, the land of the Chaldeans, for their iniquity, says YHWH; and I will make it a perpetual desolation. ¹³ So I will bring on that land all My words which I have pronounced against it, all that is written in this scroll, which Yirmeyahu has prophesied concerning all the nations. ¹⁴ (For many nations and great kings shall be served by them also; and I will repay them according to their deeds and according to the works of their own hands.)" Yirmeyahu 25:12-14.

Thus we have the House of Yisrael, often referred to as Ephraim or Joseph, separated from the House of Yahudah and completely removed from the Land by the Assyrians. We later see the House of Yahudah removed by the Babylonians. Both Kingdoms strayed from YHWH. We previously saw Ephraim, represented by Yahushua, and Yahudah, represented by Caleb, enter in to the Land because they followed YHWH wholeheartedly (Devarim 1:36). Now both Houses were expelled because of their disobedience.

Over the decades that followed, many prophets were sent to try to restore them to a right relationship with YHWH by pointing the way back to the Torah. This, after all, is the primary function of a prophet - restoration.

There were different prophets sent to the different Kingdoms to warn them and they would often stand in the gap and encourage the House of Yisrael (Ephraim) and the House of Yahudah to get cleaned up and get right with their Creator. These prophets acted like marriage counselors, but both Kingdoms failed to heed their warnings. They refused to give up their whoring and thus they remained separated from their Husband - YHWH.

Read what YHWH spoke through the Prophet Hoshea: "⁴ What can I do with you, Ephraim? What can I do with you, Yahudah? Your love is like the morning mist, like the early dew that disappears. ⁵ Therefore I cut you in pieces with my prophets, I killed you with the words of my mouth; my judgments flashed like lightning upon you. ⁶ For I desire mercy, not sacrifice, and acknowledgment of Elohim rather than burnt offerings. ⁷ Like Adam, they have broken the Covenant - they were unfaithful to me there." Hoshea 6:4-7.

Notice how YHWH speaks to Ephraim and Yahudah separately, and notice the connection with Adam. Adam was supposed to commune with YHWH. Adam was literally and metaphorically divided in two when Hawah was taken from his side - and both Adam and Hawah broke the Covenant. This was similar to what happened with Yisrael. The Kingdom was divided into Ephraim and Yahudah and both of them broke the Covenant.

Sadly, it turned out that kings were not the solution to Yisrael's

problems. Even with kings the people failed to follow YHWH, and because of their disobedience they were subjected to the penalties provided through Mosheh.

Mosheh told the children of Yisrael that they would, in fact, be exiled. He also provided them with the hope of an eventual restoration. So it was inevitable that they would indeed be cursed and dispersed, but they would one day be regathered, just as they had been from Egypt. For this to occur they would need a king like Mosheh, one who could deliver the people from their exile and reunite them with their Elohim around the Torah. "⁴ *Mosheh commanded a Torah for us, a heritage of the congregation of Jacob.* ⁵ *And He was King in Yahshurun, when the leaders of the people were gathered, all the tribes of Yisrael together.*" Devarim 33:4-5.

They would also need a Prophet like Mosheh to direct and lead the people. "*YHWH your Elohim will raise up for you a Prophet like me from your midst, from your brethren. Him you shall hear,* ¹⁶ *according to all you desired of YHWH your Elohim in Horeb in the day of the assembly, saying, 'Let me not hear again the voice of YHWH my Elohim, nor let me see this great fire anymore, lest I die.'* ¹⁷ *And YHWH said to me: 'What they have spoken is good.* ¹⁸ <u>*I will raise up for them a Prophet like you from among their brethren, and will put My words in His mouth, and He shall speak to them all that I command Him.* ¹⁹ *And it shall be that whoever will not hear My words, which He speaks in My Name, I will require it of him.*</u>'" Devarim 18:15-19.

It is through the Writings and the Prophets that we begin to see the function and identity of this One "like Mosheh" who would become known as the Messiah. While the Torah provides us with Messianic hints, patterns and Appointed Times, nowhere in that text does it ever provide an itemized checklist of the identity and character of that Messiah.

Rather, what you discover is that there are clues and allusions scattered all throughout which must be put together like pieces to a puzzle. This endeavor is much more difficult for people using translations because there is information in the Hebrew text, such as the Aleph Taw (את), which is completely missing from translations in to other languages.

Up to this point we have read the history of Yisrael and we have seen the problems that Yisrael experienced, similar to what Adam and Hawah experienced in the Garden. Just as a promise was given to them when they were expelled from the Garden, so too Yisrael received promises of hope through the Messiah. We will now explore some of those Messianic promises found in the portion of the Tanak known as the Writings.

16

The Writings

Besides the Torah, the Tanak also contains a collection of texts referred to collectively as the "ketubim." The ketubim represent the k̲ in the acronym TaNaK̲ and ketubim means "writings" in Hebrew. A significant portion of the writings are historical in nature, books such as: Joshua, Judges, I and II Shemuel, Kings, Chronicles, Ezra, Nehemiah, Ruth and Esther.

All of these texts give historical accounts of Yisrael and we have already examined the progression of Yisrael from the period of Joshua through the exiles of both the House of Yisrael and the House of Yahudah. The Writings also provide an account of the return of the House of Yahudah after their 70 year exile in Babylonia.

What is clearly missing from the Tanak is a description of the return of the House of Yisrael from their Assyrian exile and the restoration of the Kingdom of Yisrael. Also, the Writings fail to provide the fulfillment of the many patterns and prophecies concerning the Messiah. While these events are prophesied, their realization is not included in the text. Therefore, you could say that the Tanak is an unfinished work, at least in the sense of providing needed historical data.

The writings are much more than historical though, they include poetry, proverbs and psalms, all of which contain a prophetic element. For instance, the Song of Songs is about two lovers, which could simply be speaking of two individuals, but the entire text could also be viewed to encompass YHWH and His Bride.

A major portion of the writings are found in the Tehillim, often referred to as the Psalms. The Hebrew word mizmor (מזמור) is also used to describe a Psalm, which is by implication a poem or a song set to music. The Tehillim are filled with Messianic hints and prophetic imagery.

The Writings help to confirm that the Torah is about the Messiah. For instance, in Tehillim 40:7 we read: *"Behold, I come in the volume (megillah) of the scroll - it is written of Me. I delight My El to do Your will. Your Torah is within My heart."* This is a Messianic reference and it could be argued that the Scrolls of the Torah were all written about the Messiah and the Messiah is all about the Torah. In fact, to make this very clear the Psalms start off by laying the foundation of the Torah and the Messiah.

Read how these writings begin: *"¹ Blessed is the man who walks not in the counsel of the ungodly, nor stands in the path of sinners, nor sits in the seat of the scornful; ² But his delight is in the Torah of YHWH, and in His Torah he meditates day and night. ³ He shall be like a tree planted by the rivers of water, that brings forth its fruit in its season, whose leaf also shall not wither; and whatever he does shall prosper. ⁴ The ungodly are not so, but are like the chaff which the wind drives away. ⁵ Therefore the ungodly shall not stand in the judgment, nor sinners in the congregation of the righteous. ⁶ For YHWH knows the way of the righteous, but the way of the ungodly shall perish."* Tehillim 1:1-6.

The first words of the Tehillim are reminiscent of the Garden and the Tree of Life and the emphasis is on the Torah. Obeying the instructions of YHWH is the way to blessing. The righteous will be able to stand after the judgment of YHWH, the ungodly will perish.

Now read what King David, a Messianic figure himself, wrote concerning the Son: *"¹ Why do the nations conspire and the peoples plot in vain? ² The kings of the earth take their stand and the rulers gather together against YHWH and against his Anointed One (Moshiach). ³ 'Let us break their chains,' they say, 'and throw off their fetters.' ⁴ The one enthroned in heaven laughs; YHWH scoffs at them. ⁵ Then He rebukes them in His anger and terrifies them in His wrath, saying, ⁶ 'I have installed my King on Zion, My holy hill.' ⁷ I will proclaim the decree of YHWH: He said to me, 'You are my Son; today I have become your Father. ⁸ Ask of me, and I will make the nations your inheritance, the ends of the earth your possession. ⁹ You will rule them with an iron scepter; you will dash them to pieces like pottery.' ¹⁰ Therefore, you kings, be wise be warned, you rulers of the earth. ¹¹ Serve YHWH with fear and rejoice with trembling. ¹² Kiss the Son, lest he be angry and you be destroyed in your way, for his wrath can flare up in a moment. Blessed are all who take refuge in Him."* Tehillim 2:1-12.

Mizmor 1 speaks of the way of the righteous, which is the Torah while Mizmor 2 also makes an interesting connection between the Messiah and the Son of YHWH. Some question this transalation as the word for "son" in the text is "bar," which is Aramaic versus the

Hebrew word "ben." The consensus appears to support the rendering "kiss the Son" or "Do homage to the Son." This would imply submission to the authority of the Messiah, the Son of Elohim. Therefore those who obey the Torah would do well to do homage to this Son and take refuge in Him while the rest of the Earth rebels against YHWH. A literal translation could read that we should yearn for purity and be clean. This is also consistent with how we should serve YHWH.[128]

There are other Tehillim which also speak of a Son of YHWH. "¹ Hear us, O Shepherd of Yisrael, you who lead Joseph like a flock; you who sit enthroned between the cherubim, shine forth ² before Ephraim, Benjamin and Manasseh. Awaken Your might; come and save us. ³ Restore us, O Elohim; make Your face shine upon us, that we may be saved. ⁴ YHWH Elohim of Hosts, how long will your anger smolder against the prayers of your people? ⁵ You have fed them with the bread of tears; you have made them drink tears by the bowlful. ⁶ You have made us a source of contention to our neighbors, and our enemies mock us. ⁷ Restore us, O Elohim of Hosts; make Your face shine upon us, that we may be saved. ⁸ You brought a vine out of Egypt; you drove out the nations and planted it. ⁹ You cleared the ground for it, and it took root and filled the Land. ¹⁰ The mountains were covered with its shade, the mighty cedars with its branches. ¹¹ It sent out its boughs to the Sea, its shoots as far as the River. ¹² Why have you broken down its walls so that all who pass by pick its grapes? ¹³ Boars from the forest ravage it and the creatures of the field feed on it. ¹⁴ Return to us, O Elohim Almighty! Look down from heaven and see! Watch over this vine, ¹⁵ the root Your Right Hand has planted, the Son you have raised up for yourself. ¹⁶ Your vine is cut down, it is burned with fire; at Your rebuke Your people perish. ¹⁷ Let Your Hand rest on the man at Your Right Hand, the Son of Adam you have raised up for yourself. ¹⁸ Then we will not turn away from you; revive us, and we will call on your Name. ¹⁹ Restore us, YHWH Elohim of Hosts; make your face shine upon us, that we may be saved." Tehillim 80:1-19.

This particular passage is very interesting as it speaks of a vine and a son. The word for vine is gephen (גֶּפֶן) and typically refers to Yisrael, but in the context of this passage it is more directed at Joseph – the House of Yisrael. The text was written before the Assyrian captivity, but it seems to be prophetic concerning that event. It then speaks to their restoration, and in that process we see a Son at the Right Hand of YHWH – a Son of Adam raised up by YHWH for Himself. The word for son is ben (בֵּן).

The Mizmor appears to be a direct reference to the blessing given over Joseph by Yaakov. (Yisrael was called Yaakov because he was in Egypt and not in the Land). Let us take a moment and read that blessing so that you can see the connection.

"²² *Joseph is <u>a fruitful vine</u>, <u>a fruitful vine</u> near a spring, whose branches climb over a wall. ²³ With bitterness archers attacked him; they shot at him with hostility. ²⁴ But his bow remained steady, his strong arms stayed limber, because of the Hand of the Mighty One of Jacob, because of the Shepherd, the Rock of Yisrael, ²⁵ because of your father's Elohim, who helps you, אֵת because of the Almighty, who blesses you with blessings of the heavens above, blessings of the deep that lies below, blessings of the breast and womb. ²⁶ Your father's blessings are greater than the blessings of the ancient mountains, than the bounty of the age-old hills. Let all these rest on the head of Joseph, on the brow of the prince among his brothers.*" Beresheet 49:22-26.

An interesting thing about this blessing is the hidden element of the son. The word translated as "vine" twice at the beginning of the blessing is ben (בֵן) which means: "son." Therefore, Joseph is a fruitful "son" who is endowed with incredible blessings. In fact, the word barak (ברך) is used six times to describe the blessings upon Joseph who is a prince among his brothers.

It appears that the House of Yisrael will be helped by the Aleph Taw (את) - The Messiah. Notice the relationship between Joseph and the Shepherd - the Rock of Yisrael - which are both references to the Messiah. This Rock or Stone is represented by the word "aben" (אבן) in Hebrew. Some believe that this was a literal reference to the stone from Beth El which Yaakov rested his head upon, raised up as a pillar and later anointed. Since Beth El was in the Land allotted to Joseph it is believed that the Tribe of Joseph actually carried this Rock as a sign of their birthright.

There are three instances of the Aleph Taw (את) in the passage describing the "aben" (אבן) at Beth El. (see Beresheet 28:18-19). If we look at this Rock in the same sense as we did the Rod, we can see numerous patterns concerning the Messiah.

A literal translation of the blessing over Joseph reads: "The arms of his hands were made strong by the Hand of the Mighty of Yaakov - the Shepherd, the Stone (Rock) "aben" (אבן) of Yisrael." It is interesting that the word for Rock "aben" (אבן) has at its root the word for son, which is "ben" (בֵן).

There is clearly a special relationship between this "first born" son of Yisrael and the Hand or Arm of YHWH, The Shepherd, the Rock of Yisrael. Both the Mizmor and the Blessing of Joseph speak of sonship and the "Hand" or "Arm" of YHWH.

In fact, the Tehillim refer repeatedly to the Right Hand and the Arm of YHWH. It was by the Right Hand, the Arm of YHWH, that Yisrael was saved and gained possession of the Land. *"For they did not gain possession of the Land by their own sword, nor did their own arm save them; but it was Your Right Hand, Your Arm, and the light of Your countenance, because You favored them."* Tehillim 44:3.

The Scriptures record on numerous occasions that salvation comes from the Right Hand of YHWH. *"That Your beloved may be delivered, save with Your Right Hand, and hear me."* Tehillim 60:5. The word for "beloved" in the Hebrew is "yideyideka" (ידידיך). It is the same language used to refer to a bride or a lover. Clearly, the love of YHWH is expressed through His Right Hand. *"Show the wonder of your great love, you who save by your Right Hand those who take refuge in you from their foes."* Tehillim 17:7.

The Right Hand and the Moshiach are even combined in places. *"Now I know that YHWH saves His anointed (moshiach) He answers Him from His holy heaven with the saving power of His Right Hand."* Tehillim 20:6. Most translations place a semi-colon after "anointed" but the punctuation is not in the original text. I have removed the semi-colon to demonstrate the depth of this text.

Read how the Arm of YHWH is detailed in Tehillim 89 which has numerous Messianic undertones, linking the line of David with the Rule of the Messiah.

"¹ I will sing of YHWH's great love forever; with my mouth I will make your faithfulness known through all generations. ² I will declare that your love stands firm forever, that you established your faithfulness in heaven itself. ³ You said, I have made a Covenant with My chosen one, I have sworn to David My servant, ⁴ <u>I will establish your seed forever and make your throne firm through all generations.</u> Selah ⁵ The heavens praise your wonders, O YHWH, your faithfulness too, in the assembly of the holy ones. ⁶ For who in the skies above can compare with YHWH? Who is like YHWH among the heavenly beings? ⁷ In the council of the holy ones Elohim is greatly feared; He is more awesome than all who surround him. ⁸ O YHWH Elohim Almighty, who is like you? You are mighty, O YHWH, and your faithfulness surrounds you. ⁹ You rule over the surging sea; when its waves mount up, you still them. ¹⁰ You crushed Rahab like one of the slain; with your strong arm you scattered your enemies. ¹¹ The heavens are yours, and yours also the earth; you founded the world and all that is in it. ¹² You created the north and the south; Tabor and Hermon sing for joy at Your Name. ¹³ <u>Your Arm is endued with power; Your Hand is strong, Your Right Hand exalted.</u> ¹⁴ Righteousness and justice are the foundation of Your throne; love and faithfulness go before You. ¹⁵

Blessed are those who have learned to acclaim You, who walk in the light of Your presence, O YHWH. ¹⁶ *They rejoice in Your Name all day long; they exalt in Your righteousness.* ¹⁷ *For You are their glory and strength, and by Your favor You exalt our horn.* ¹⁸ *Indeed, our shield belongs to YHWH, our king to the Holy One of Yisrael.* ¹⁹ *Once you spoke in a vision, to Your faithful people You said: I have bestowed strength on a warrior; I have exalted a young man from among the people.* ²⁰ *I have found David My servant; with My sacred oil I have anointed him.* ²¹ *My Hand will sustain him; surely My Arm will strengthen him.* ²² *No enemy will subject him to tribute; no wicked man will oppress him.* ²³ *I will crush his foes before him and strike down his adversaries.* ²⁴ *My faithful love will be with him, and through My Name his horn will be exalted.* ²⁵ *I will set his hand over the sea, his right hand over the rivers.* ²⁶ *He will call out to me, You are my Father, my Elohim, the Rock my Savior.* ²⁷ *I will also appoint him My firstborn, the most exalted of the kings of the earth.* ²⁸ *I will maintain My love to him forever, and My Covenant with him will never fail.* ²⁹ *I will establish his line forever, his throne as long as the heavens endure.* ³⁰ *If his sons forsake My Torah and do not follow My statutes,* ³¹ *if they violate My decrees and fail to keep My commands,* ³² *I will punish their sin with the rod, their iniquity with flogging;* ³³ *but I will not take My love from him, nor will I ever betray My faithfulness.* ³⁴ *I will not violate My Covenant or alter what My lips have uttered.* ³⁵ *Once for all, I have sworn by My holiness - and I will not lie to David -* ³⁶ *that his line will continue forever and his throne endure before Me like the sun;* ³⁷ *it will be established forever like the moon, the faithful witness in the sky.* ³⁸ *But you have rejected, you have spurned, you have been very angry with your anointed one.* ³⁹ *You have renounced the Covenant with Your servant and have defiled his crown in the dust.* ⁴⁰ *You have broken through all his walls and reduced his strongholds to ruins.* ⁴¹ *All who pass by have plundered him; he has become the scorn of his neighbors.* ⁴² *You have exalted the right hand of his foes; you have made all his enemies rejoice.* ⁴³ *You have turned back the edge of his sword and have not supported him in battle.* ⁴⁴ *You have put an end to his splendor and cast his throne to the ground.* ⁴⁵ *You have cut short the days of his youth; You have covered him with a mantle of shame.* ⁴⁶ *How long, O YHWH? Will You hide yourself forever? How long will Your wrath burn like fire?* ⁴⁷ *Remember how fleeting is my life. For what futility You have created all men!* ⁴⁸ *What man can live and not see death, or save himself from the power of the grave?* Selah ⁴⁹ *O YHWH, where is Your former great love, which in*

Your faithfulness You swore to David? [50] *Remember, YHWH, how Your servant has been mocked, how I bear in my heart the taunts of all the nations,* [51] *the taunts with which Your enemies have mocked, O YHWH, with which they have mocked every step of Your anointed one.* [52] *Praise be to YHWH forever! So be it."* Tehillim 89:1-52.

The Arm of YHWH is accounted for crushing Rahab, which is another name for Egypt. This Mizmor also seems to support a Messiah from the line of David – thus a tradition established concerning the Messiah Son of David. This is confirmed in the following Mizmor: *"*[11] *YHWH swore an oath to David, a sure oath that He will not revoke: One of your own descendants I will place on your throne* [12] *if your sons keep My Covenant and the statutes I teach them, then their sons will sit on your throne for ever and ever.* [13] *For YHWH has chosen Zion, He has desired it for His dwelling:* [14] *This is my resting place for ever and ever; here I will sit enthroned, for I have desired it.* [15] *I will bless her with abundant provisions; her poor will I satisfy with food.* [16] *I will clothe her priests with salvation, and her saints will ever sing for joy.* [17] *Here I will make a horn grow for David and set up a lamp for My Anointed One.* [18] *I will clothe His enemies with shame, but the crown on His head will flourish."* Tehillim 132:11-18.

Besides being a metaphorical reference, the Right Hand is also a place of honor where the Messiah sits. This Mizmor speaks directly about the Messiah *"*[1] *YHWH said to my Adonai, 'Sit at My Right Hand, till I make Your enemies Your footstool.* [2] *YHWH shall send the rod of Your strength out of Zion. Rule in the midst of Your enemies!* [3] *Your people shall be volunteers in the day of Your power; In the beauties of holiness, <u>from the womb of the morning</u>, You have the dew of Your youth.* [4] *YHWH has sworn and will not relent, You are a priest forever according to the order of Melchizedek.* [5] *YHWH is at Your Right Hand; He shall execute kings in the day of His wrath.* [6] *He shall judge among the nations, He shall fill the places with dead bodies, He shall execute the heads of many countries.* [7] *He shall drink of the brook by the wayside; therefore He shall lift up the head."* Tehillim 110:1-7.

He is *"from the womb of the morning"* which is likened to the dawning of the day and a reference to the Light of Beresheet 1:3,4. This text speaks of the Messiah as a Priest according to the Order of Melchizedek. This is a very important concept to understand. It is an eternal priesthood established at the beginning of creation separate and distinct from the Levitic priesthood. Abraham, the great grandfather of Levi actually tithed to the Melchizedek priest. (Beresheet 14:18-20).

The following Mizmor envisions the Messiah as a mighty and strong King from the line of David with an everlasting throne. *"*[1] *My heart is overflowing with a good theme. I recite my composition concerning the*

King. My tongue is the pen of a ready writer. ² You are fairer than the sons of men. Grace is poured upon Your lips, therefore Elohim has blessed You forever. ³ Gird Your sword upon Your thigh, O Mighty One, with Your glory and Your majesty. ⁴ And in Your majesty ride prosperously because of truth, humility, and righteousness; and Your Right Hand shall teach You awesome things. ⁵ Your arrows are sharp in the heart of the King's enemies; The peoples fall under You. ⁶ <u>Your throne, O Elohim, is forever and ever; a scepter of righteousness is the scepter of Your kingdom.</u> ⁷ <u>You love righteousness and hate wickedness; therefore Elohim, Your Elohim, has anointed You With the oil of gladness more than Your companions.</u>" Tehillim 45:1-7.

This vision of the Messiah as an anointed King, even a righteous King and Priest (Melchizedek), is easy to understand. All people want to live under righteous leaders who deal fairly with justice and truth. The notion of a Messiah that would rule in the ways of David is pleasing and desirous. Interestingly, this is not the only Messianic vision provided by the Tehillim.

There is another description of the Messiah which is quite different and harder to comprehend.

"¹ Eli, Eli, why have you spared Me? Why are you so far from saving Me, so far from the words of My groaning? ² O My Elohim, I cry out by day, but You do not answer, by night, and am not silent. ³ Yet you are enthroned as the Holy One; you are the praise of Yisrael. ⁴ In You our fathers put their trust; they trusted and You delivered them. ⁵ They cried to You and were saved; in You they trusted and were not disappointed. ⁶ But I am a worm and not a man, scorned by men and despised by the people. ⁷ All who see Me mock Me; they hurl insults, shaking their heads: ⁸ He trusts in YHWH; let YHWH rescue Him. Let Him deliver Him, since He delights in Him. ⁹ <u>Yet You brought Me out of the womb. You made Me trust in You even at My mother's breast.</u> ¹⁰ <u>From birth I was cast upon You. From My mother's womb you have been My Elohim.</u> ¹¹ Do not be far from Me, for trouble is near and there is no one to help. ¹² Many bulls surround Me; strong bulls of Bashan encircle Me. ¹³ Roaring lions tearing their prey open their mouths wide against Me. ¹⁴ <u>I am poured out like water, and all My bones are out of joint. My heart has turned to wax; it has melted away within Me.</u> ¹⁵ <u>My strength is dried up like a potsherd, and My tongue sticks to the roof of My mouth; you lay Me in the dust of death.</u> ¹⁶ <u>Dogs have surrounded Me; a band of evil men has encircled Me, they have pierced My hands and My feet.</u> ¹⁷ <u>I can count all My bones; people stare and gloat over Me.</u> ¹⁸ <u>They divide My garments among them and cast lots for My clothing.</u> ¹⁹ But You, O YHWH, be not far off; O My Strength, come quickly to help Me. [20] Deliver My life from the sword, My precious life from the power of the dogs. [21] Rescue Me from the mouth of the lions; save Me from the horns of the wild oxen. [22] _I will declare Your Name to my brothers; in the congregation I will praise You._ [23] You who fear YHWH, praise Him! All you descendants of Yaakov, honor Him! Revere Him, all you descendants of Yisrael! [24] For He has not despised or disdained the suffering of the afflicted one; He has not hidden His face from Him but has listened to His cry for help. [25] From you comes the theme of My praise in the great assembly; before those who fear You will I fulfill My vows. [26] The poor will eat and be satisfied; they who seek YHWH will praise Him - may your hearts live forever! [27] All the ends of the earth will remember and turn to YHWH, and all the families of the nations will bow down before Him, [28] for dominion belongs to YHWH and He rules over the nations. [29] All the rich of the earth will feast and worship; all who go down to the dust will kneel before Him - those who cannot keep themselves alive. [30] Posterity will serve Him; future generations will be told about YHWH. [31] _They will proclaim His righteousness to a people yet unborn - for He has done it._" Tehillim 22:1-31.

This stands in stark contrast to the Messiah Son of David. This passage describes one who was born from a womb and was with YHWH from birth, although at some point he becomes separated from YHWH. He is despised and undergoes horrific physical pain and suffering. He finds himself in a position where people can look at him, shake their heads at him, mock him and hurl insults at him. They will actually look at him and say: "_He trusts in YHWH; let YHWH rescue him. Let Him deliver Him, since He delights in Him._" Tehillim 22:8.

He will be encircled by evil men - his hands and his feet will be pierced. People will stare and gloat over him. They will take away His garments and cast lots for His clothes. Most recognize this as a description of a person who is being crucified, only at the time that this Mizmor was written, crucifixion had not even been invented as a form of punishment.

So this Messiah will be tortured by a method not yet invented and will be placed in a position where he actually looks like He needs saving Himself. Because of this description, along with similar accounts such as Mizmor 69, many have attributed this to a different Messiah called Messiah ben Joseph – Messiah Son of Joseph.

There are numerous other writings which speak of the Messiah and we can only view a small portion, but from the patterns of the

Torah along with the descriptions and titles provided through the Writings we have a good picture, although sometimes contradictory, of what the Messiah would do.

The writings seem to indicate that the Messiah has been involved with Yisrael and creation from the very beginning. They also show that as the Right Hand or Arm of YHWH, He will restore Yisrael and rule over Yisrael. He would function in two capacities: The Suffering Servant – the Son of Joseph and The Conquering King – the Son of David.

Also, one cannot deny the strong implication that the Messiah will be the Son of Elohim and will come in the Name of YHWH. *"[15] Shouts of joy and victory resound in the tents of the righteous: YHWH's Right Hand has done mighty things! [16] YHWH's Right Hand is lifted high; YHWH's Right Hand has done mighty things! [17] I will not die but live, and will proclaim what YHWH has done. [18] YHWH has chastened me severely, but he has not given me over to death. [19] Open for me the gates of righteousness; I will enter and give thanks to YHWH. [20] This is the gate of YHWH through which the righteous may enter. [21] I will give you thanks, for you answered me; you have become my salvation. [22] The Stone the builders rejected has become the capstone* את *[23] YHWH has done this, and it is marvelous in our eyes. [24] This is the day YHWH has made; let us rejoice and be glad in it. [25] I pray YHWH, save us now I pray YHWH, grant us success. [26] Blessed is He who comes in the Name of YHWH. From the House of YHWH we bless you. [27] YHWH is Elohim, and He has made His Light shine upon us. Bind the festal offering with cords to the horn of the altar. [28] You are my Elohim, and I will give You thanks; You are my Elohim, and I will exalt You. [29] Give thanks to YHWH, for He is good; His love endures forever."* Tehillim 118:15-29.

This passage is very telling as it speaks of the Right Hand and the Stone, aben (אבן), of YHWH. We have seen that these are Messianic references. In fact, the capstone in the text is directly linked with the Aleph Taw (את). The Mizmor is indicating that the Messiah will "become" - which is hayah (היה) in Hebrew - "salvation." Hayah is part of the Name of YHWH and it is how YHWH described Himself to Mosheh.

In Shemot 3:13-14 we read the following: *"[13] Mosheh said to Elohim, Suppose I go to the Yisraelites and say to them, the Elohim of your fathers has sent me to you, and they ask me, What is His Name? Then what shall I tell them? [14] Elohim said to Mosheh, I AM THAT I AM. This is what you are to say to the Yisraelites: I AM has sent me to you."* In the Hebrew we read Eyah Asher Eyah (אהיה אשר אהיה). So the Messiah "becoming" salvation links Him directly and intimately with YHWH.

In verse 25 of Tehillim 118 we read: "*Aana YHWH hoshiya na aana YHWH*" – "*I pray YHWH save now I pray YHWH.*" This is a very popular and powerful prayer linked to the Messiah often translated as "Hosanna." We read in verse 26 that He will come at a time when the House of YHWH is standing because the people will bless Him from the House of YHWH.

From that passage we also see that the Messiah will come in the Name of YHWH. This is an important hint because so far, through the Torah and the Writings, we have seen patterns, shadows and word pictures concerning what the Messiah will do, but there has been an absence of specificity concerning the identity of Messiah. The Hebrew word for name is shem (שֵׁם) and means more than just a label – it means "authority." So the Messiah will come in the authority of YHWH and would also likely carry the Name of YHWH in His Name.

This was actually quite common and many individuals in the Scriptures share or include the Name of YHWH. For example, Elijah is Eliyahu which means: "YHWH is El." Isaiah is Yeshayahu which means: "YHWH will save His people." Interestingly, Joshua, which is Yahushua in Hebrew, means the same thing: "YHWH will save His people." It is a combination of Yah (YHWH) and Hoshea (salvation).

The Writings go further than tell us that the Messiah will come in the Name of YHWH, they even indicate that we can know His name. In the writings known as the Proverbs, we are posed a riddle concerning the Name of the Messiah – the Son of Elohim. "*Who has gone up to heaven and come down? Who has gathered up the wind in the hollow of His hands? Who has wrapped up the waters in His cloak? Who has established all the ends of the earth? What is His Name, and the Name of His Son? Tell me if you know!*" Proverbs (Mishle) 30:4.

This passage poses a riddle for those who have wisdom. It clearly implies that the Creator has a Son and they both have a Name. That Name is actually found in the Tanak, along with an enormous amount of information concerning the Messiah, in the scrolls of the Prophets.

17

The Prophets

Thus far we have examined the Torah and the Ketubim which represent the T and the K in acronym - TaNaK. The final portion to review is the Nebi'im which represents the N in TaNaK. Nebi'im means "prophets" and the Tanak contains a variety of prophecies given to Yisrael. Interestingly, it does not contain all of the prophecies of YHWH, nor does it exclusively contain prophecies since we have already seen that both the Torah and the Ketubim are full of prophetic content.

There were always prophets in Yisrael who would guide her on the path of righteousness given through the instructions and commandments in the Torah. They would point out error and direct people back to YHWH. This after all is the primary role of the prophet. They are not to be confused with fortune tellers.

While they would, at times, predict the future it was typically in the context of providing the details of the punishment that would occur upon disobeying the commandments. They also provided information concerning the redemption of YHWH and His Messiah.

The collection of texts known as the Nebi'im generally focus upon the warnings and subsequent punishments given to the two kingdoms - the House of Yisrael and the House of Yahudah. It is important when reading the prophets to understand the context as well as the recipient of a particular prophecy.

Sometimes prophecies were given in the Land prior to the punishment, while at times they were given in exile while the punishment was in effect. YHWH sent prophets to the House of Yisrael and to the House of Yahudah. These prophets warned of impending punishment – they even revealed how long the punishments would last. Ezekiel and Jeremiah each gave specific time periods for the exiles of Yisrael and Yahudah. We are actually at the end of the period of punishment for

the House of Yisrael.

When each House was finally punished the prophets not only explained the punishments to the people, but also gave them hope. Since the Kingdom had been divided and exiled, the ultimate hope was that there would be an eventual return from exile for each House and a reunification of the Kingdom.

This was not only the hope, it was also the promise given by YHWH through His prophets. YHWH told them that He would once again gather His people as He had done from Egypt, only this time he would do it from the entire planet.

Sometimes these prophets spoke words, sometimes they acted out the prophecy, and at times they even lived it. Take for example the life and the words of the prophet named Hosea, also known as Hoshea. The name Hoshea, as we have already seen means "salvation." It was the original name of Yahushua (Joshua) before his name was changed by Mosheh. This is of particular interest because Yahushua was from the Tribe of Ephraim (Joseph) and the Prophet Hoshea was primarily called to speak to the House of Yisrael. Through his life, YHWH provided a vivid depiction of what would happen to the House of Yisrael.

"*¹ The word of YHWH that came to Hoshea son of Beeri <u>during the reigns of Uzziah, Jotham, Ahaz and Hezekiah, kings of Yahudah, and during the reign of Jeroboam son of Jehoash king of Yisrael</u>: ² When YHWH began to speak through Hoshea, YHWH said to him, <u>Go, take to yourself an adulterous wife and children of unfaithfulness, because the Land is guilty of the vilest adultery in departing from YHWH</u>. ³ So he married Gomer daughter of Diblaim, and she conceived and bore him a son. ⁴ Then YHWH said to Hoshea, <u>Call him Jezreel, because I will soon punish the house of Jehu for the massacre at Jezreel, and I will put an end to the kingdom of Yisrael</u>. ⁵ In that day I will break Yisrael's bow in the Valley of Jezreel. ⁶ Gomer conceived again and gave birth to a daughter. Then YHWH said to Hoshea, <u>Call her Lo-Ruhamah, for I will no longer show love to the House of Yisrael, that I should at all forgive them</u>. ⁷ <u>Yet I will show love to the House of Yahudah; and I will save them</u> - not by bow, sword or battle, or by horses and horsemen, but by YHWH their Elohim. ⁸ After she had weaned Lo-Ruhamah, Gomer had another son. ⁹ Then YHWH said, <u>Call him Lo-Ammi, for you are not my people, and I am not yours</u>. ¹⁰ <u>Yet the Yisraelites will be like the sand on the seashore, which cannot be measured or counted. In the place where it was said to them, You are not My people, they will be called sons of the living El</u>. ¹¹ <u>The people of Yahudah and the people of Yisrael will be reunited, and they will appoint one leader and will come up out of the land, for great will be the day of</u>*

Jezreel." Hoshea 1:1-11.

Now we know from the first verse that Hoshea prophesied while both the Kingdoms were still in the Land. They were given fair warning of what would happen, particularly to the Northern Kingdom - the House of Yisrael. In fact, the words of Hoshea occurred exactly as spoken. The Kingdom of Yisrael was taken captive by the Assyrians and utterly removed from the Land. YHWH put an end to the Kingdom of Yisrael. Thus the child named Jezreel.

We later see that YHWH, in essence, fell out of love with Yisrael due to her repeated acts of adultery - Thus the child Lo-Ruhamah. Because of this breakdown in their relationship there was finally a severence. Many English translations insert the word God in this text by providing _"you are not My people and I am not your God."_ This is not accurate because the word God, or rather Elohim, is not in the text. It simply states: _"You are not My people and I will not be yours"_ - Thus the child Lo-Ami.

This stands in stark contrast to the language of lovers provided in the Song of Shlomo 2:16: _"My beloved is mine and I am his."_ The language spoken through Hoshea sounds like divorce language. YHWH did not say that He would not be their Elohim, he was saying that He would not be their Husband. This is an extremely important distinction which must be understood. YHWH still had a plan for the House of Yisrael - He was still their Elohim.

That leads us to the final portion of Hoshea's prophecy. There is much talk about the lost ten tribes of Yisrael because people understand that the prophecy concerning their exile was literally fulfilled. Those ten tribes that made up the House of Yisrael were taken and scattered throughout the world - their identity as Yisraelites was "lost." Their descendants are now mixed with the nations of the planet, and unlike their brethren in the House of Yahudah, currently identified as Jews, they lost their identity and forgot their relationship with YHWH.

I have seen documentaries where scholars have searched for pockets of people located in remote areas throughout the world who appear to be Jewish, or are maintaining Jewish traditions. This is really missing the point. These small clusters are no different than the Jews scattered throughout the world who are maintaining their heritage in the diaspora.

Yisrael is lost because they do not know who they are, and they therefore do not hold to the traditions of the Jews. They are not some small band of scattered people living in remote and hidden areas of the planet. They are a vast number of people who have multiplied

enormously while scattered.

Remember that the original clan of Yisrael, counting the direct descendants of Yaakov, numbered seventy (70) when they entered into Egypt. (Beresheet 46:7). The number seventy (70) represents "the nations" and it was when Yisrael was in Egypt that they became a great multitude of people. Likewise, the House of Yisrael has become a vast people while in their dispersion – a dispersion which is about to come to an end.

This should not be a surprise because, it fulfills the prophecy provided to the Tribes of Joseph (Ephraim and Manasheh) by Yisrael himself when he adopted the two sons of Joseph. *"16 May they be called by my name and the names of my fathers Abraham and Yitshaq, and may they increase greatly upon the earth. 17 When Joseph saw his father placing his right hand on Ephraim's head he was displeased; so he took hold of his father's hand to move it from Ephraim's head to Manasheh's head. 18 Joseph said to him, No, my father, this one is the firstborn; put your right hand on his head. 19 But his father refused and said, I know, my son, I know. He too will become a people, and he too will become great. Nevertheless, his younger brother will be greater than he, and his descendants will become a group of nations. 20 He blessed them that day and said, In your name will Yisrael pronounce this blessing: May Elohim make you like Ephraim and Manasseh. So he put Ephraim ahead of Manasheh."* Beresheet 48:16-20.

Ephraim would be the largest among all the Tribes of Yisrael. This was later confirmed by Mosheh. *"13 About Joseph he said: May YHWH bless his land with the precious dew from heaven above and with the deep waters that lie below; 14 with the best the sun brings forth and the finest the moon can yield; 15 with the choicest gifts of the ancient mountains and the fruitfulness of the everlasting hills; 16 with the best gifts of the earth and its fullness and the favor of Him who dwelt in the burning bush. Let all these rest on the head of Joseph, on the brow of the prince among his brothers. 17 In majesty he is like a firstborn bull; his horns are the horns of a wild ox. With them he will gore the nations, even those at the ends of the earth. Such are the ten thousands of Ephraim; such are the thousands of Manasheh."* Beresheet 33:13-17.

Because of it's prophesied greatness, Ephraim often represented the Northern Tribes after the split in the Kingdom. This begs the question: How could the prophecy of Hoshea come to fruition with all of these incredible prophecies concerning Joseph? Thankfully there was hope provided by Hoshea. While the House of Yisrael would be punished severely for their sins, he stated that the Yisraelites would be so numerous that they could not be counted and they would be called

"sons of the living El." He further stated that Yahudah and Yisrael would be reunited under one leader and that one leader is believed to be the Messiah. (Hoshea 1:10-11).

The statement that Yisrael would be called "sons of the living El" is of particular interest. As we have already seen, in the Hebrew language, letters also have a numeric value so it is possible to place numeric values on certain words or phrases.[129] In the Hebrew Scriptures the phrase "Sons of Elohim" calculates to 153. Sons of Elohim in Hebrew is Beni Ha-Elohim (בני האלהים). The gematria calculation for Beni Ha-Elohim is as follows: (ב = 2), (נ = 50), (י = 10), (ה = 5), (א = 1), (ל = 30), (ה = 5), (י = 10), (ם = 40). Therefore 2+50+10+5+1+30+5+10+40 = 153. Keep this in mind as we look further at the Messiah of Yisrael.

The House of Yisrael had a serious problem that needed to be resolved. We saw that at Sinai YHWH married Yisrael – she was His Bride. She was not a faithful Bride and continually strayed. As a result, YHWH put her away. In other words, she was evicted from the marital home for her infidelity, just as Adam and Hawah were thrown out of the garden for their conduct.

The House of Yisrael was in exile and was given a certificate of divorce from YHWH. Read the words of YHWH as given through Yirmeyahu in the days of Josiah, King of Yahudah after the House of Yisrael had been taken into captivity.

"⁶ *Have you seen what backsliding Yisrael has done? She has gone up on every high mountain and under every green tree, and there played the harlot.* ⁷ *And I said, after she had done all these things, return to Me. But she did not return. And her treacherous sister Yahudah saw it.* ⁸ *Then I saw that for all the causes for which backsliding Yisrael had committed adultery, I had put her away and given her a certificate of divorce; yet her treacherous sister Yahudah did not fear, but went and played the harlot also.* ⁹ *So it came to pass, through her casual harlotry, that she defiled the Land and committed adultery with stones and trees.* ¹⁰ *And yet for all this her treacherous sister Yahudah has not turned to Me with her whole heart, but in pretense, says YHWH.* ¹¹ *Then YHWH said to me, backsliding Yisrael has shown herself more righteous than treacherous Yahudah.* ¹² *Go and proclaim these words toward the north, and say: Return, backsliding Yisrael, says YHWH; I will not cause My anger to fall on you. For I am merciful says YHWH; I will not remain angry forever.* ¹³ *Only acknowledge your iniquity, that you have transgressed against YHWH your Elohim, and have scattered your charms to alien deities under every green tree, and you have not obeyed My voice, says*

YHWH. ¹⁴ *Return, O backsliding children says YHWH for I am married to you. I will take you, one from a city and two from a family, and I will bring you to Zion.* ¹⁵ *And I will give you shepherds according to My heart, who will feed you with knowledge and understanding.* ¹⁶ *Then it shall come to pass, when you are multiplied and increased in the land in those days, says YHWH, that they will say no more, The Ark of the Covenant of YHWH. It shall not come to mind, nor shall they remember it, nor shall they visit it, nor shall it be made anymore.* ¹⁷ *At that time Jerusalem shall be called The Throne of YHWH, and all the nations shall be gathered to it, to the Name of YHWH, to Jerusalem. No more shall they follow the dictates of their evil hearts.* ¹⁸ *In those days the House of Yahudah shall walk with the House of Yisrael, and they shall come together out of the land of the north to the Land that I have given as an inheritance to your fathers.* ¹⁹ *But I said: How can I put you among the children and give you a pleasant Land, a beautiful heritage of the hosts of nations? And I said: You shall call Me, My Father, and not turn away from Me.* ²⁰ *Surely, as a wife treacherously departs from her husband, so have you dealt treacherously with Me, O House of Yisrael, says YHWH.* ²¹ *A voice was heard on the desolate heights, weeping and supplications of the children of Yisrael. For they have perverted their way; they have forgotten YHWH their Elohim.* ²² *Return, you backsliding children, and I will heal your backslidings. Indeed we do come to You, for You are YHWH our Elohim.*" Yirmeyahu 3:6 – 22.

This prophecy was given while the House of Yahudah was still in the Land. We know this because Josiah was the King of Yahudah at that time. Even though the House of Yahudah could clearly see the punishment that the House of Yisrael had experienced, she continued in her treacherous ways. She was called treacherous by YHWH, and the House of Yisrael, which had already been exiled, was actually considered to be more righteous than the House of Yahudah.

Since Yahudah was thereafter put away, as was done with Yisrael, the argument could be made that Yahudah was also given her "walking papers" or a "certificate of divorce" as was done with Yisrael. This is never implicitly stated in the Scriptures but could definitely be inferred by the language used by Yirmeyahu. On the other hand, it is probable that YHWH actually relented from completely divorcing Yahudah for the sake of His Covenant with David.[130]

According to the Torah a husband and wife could not remarry once they had been divorced and had relations with another. Read what the Torah has to say about this situation: "¹ *When a man takes a wife and*

marries her, and it happens that she finds no favor in his eyes because he has found some uncleanness in her, and he writes her a certificate of divorce, puts it in her hand, and sends her out of his house, ² when she has departed from his house, and goes and becomes another man's wife, ³ if the latter husband detests her and writes her a certificate of divorce, puts it in her hand, and sends her out of his house, or if the latter husband dies who took her as his wife, ⁴ then her former husband who divorced her must not take her back to be his wife after she has been defiled; for that is an abomination before YHWH, and you shall not bring sin on the Land which YHWH your Elohim is giving you as an inheritance." Devarim 24:1-4.

It would appear that there was no hope for Yisrael, but thankfully YHWH was not through with His Bride. We see through the example of Hoshea that the whoring wife could be redeemed for a price. "¹ YHWH said to me, Go, show your love to your wife again, though she is loved by another and is an adulteress. Love her as YHWH loves the Yisraelites, though they turn to other gods and love the sacred raisin cakes. ² So I bought her for fifteen shekels of silver and about an omer and a lethek of barley. ³ Then I told her, you are to live with me many days; you must not be a prostitute or be intimate with any man, and I will live with you. ⁴ For the Yisraelites will live many days without king or prince, without sacrifice or sacred stones, without ephod or idol. ⁵ <u>Afterward the Yisraelites will return and seek YHWH their Elohim and David their king. They will come trembling to YHWH and to His blessings in the last days.</u>" Hoshea 3:1-5.

So we see from Hoshea that the House of Yisrael would go a long time without a leader. In "the last days," which many would argue is now, they would seek out YHWH and His blessings which come from obeying the Torah. The question remains as to how this could be accomplished with the specific prohibition against remarriage found within the Torah.

We read the following prophecy given by Yeshayahu: "¹ Thus says YHWH: '<u>Where is your mother's certificate of divorce, with which I sent her away?</u> Or to which of My creditors did I sell you? Because of your sins you were sold, because of your transgressions your mother was sent away. ² When I came why was there no one? When I called, why was there no one to answer? Was My Arm too short to ransom you?" Yeshayahu 50:1-2.

The question is rhetorical. Obviously YHWH can ransom, or rather - redeem His Bride. He had done it before out of the land of Egypt through His servant Mosheh and now He would do it again from the entire planet where the tribes had been scattered to the four winds.

The answer to the question posed through Yeshayahu was answererd as follows:

"¹ _Surely the Arm of YHWH is not too short to save_, nor His ear too dull to hear. ² But your iniquities have separated you from your Elohim; your sins have hidden His face from you, so that He will not hear. ³ For your hands are stained with blood, your fingers with guilt. Your lips have spoken lies, and your tongue mutters wicked things. ⁴ No one calls for justice; no one pleads his case with integrity. They rely on empty arguments and speak lies; they conceive trouble and give birth to evil. ⁵ They hatch the eggs of vipers and spin a spider's web. Whoever eats their eggs will die, and when one is broken, an adder is hatched. ⁶ Their cobwebs are useless for clothing; they cannot cover themselves with what they make. Their deeds are evil deeds, and acts of violence are in their hands. ⁷ Their feet rush into sin; they are swift to shed innocent blood. Their thoughts are evil thoughts; ruin and destruction mark their ways. ⁸ The way of peace they do not know; there is no justice in their paths. They have turned them into crooked roads; no one who walks in them will know peace. ⁹ So justice is far from us, and righteousness does not reach us. We look for light, but all is darkness; for brightness, but we walk in deep shadows. ¹⁰ Like the blind we grope along the wall, feeling our way like men without eyes. At midday we stumble as if it were twilight; among the strong, we are like the dead. ¹¹ We all growl like bears; we moan mournfully like doves. We look for justice, but find none; for deliverance, but it is far away. ¹² For our offenses are many in Your sight, and our sins testify against us. Our offenses are ever with us, and we acknowledge our iniquities: ¹³ rebellion and treachery against YHWH, turning our backs on our Elohim, fomenting oppression and revolt, uttering lies our hearts have conceived. ¹⁴ So justice is driven back, and righteousness stands at a distance; truth has stumbled in the streets, honesty cannot enter. ¹⁵ Truth is nowhere to be found, and whoever shuns evil becomes a prey. YHWH looked and was displeased that there was no justice. ¹⁶ _He saw that there was no one, He was appalled that there was no one to intervene; so His own Arm worked salvation for Him, and His own righteousness sustained Him._ ¹⁷ _He put on righteousness as His breastplate, and the helmet of salvation on His head; He put on the garments of vengeance and wrapped Himself in zeal as in a cloak._ ¹⁸ According to what they have done, so will He repay wrath to His enemies and retribution to His foes. He will repay the islands their due. ¹⁹ From the west, men will fear the Name of YHWH, and from the rising of the sun, they will revere his glory. For He will come like a pent-up flood that the breath of YHWH drives along. ²⁰ _The Redeemer will come to Zion, to those in Yaakov who repent of their_

sins, declares YHWH. *²¹ As for Me, this is My Covenant with them, says YHWH. My Spirit, who is on you, and My words that I have put in your mouth will not depart from your mouth, or from the mouths of your children, or from the mouths of their descendants from this time on and forever, says YHWH.*" Yeshayahu 59:1-21.

So we see that it would be by the Arm of YHWH that those in the family of Yaakov, who repented, would be saved by the Redeemer. Yaakov was the name of Yisrael before he entered into the Covenant Land to live. Those who are scattered around the planet "in Yaakov" need to repent to receive their redemption – their salvation.

Salvation is a very important concept to this prophet whose Hebrew name Yeshayahu (ישעיהו) means: "YHWH has saved." The prophet uses three different Hebrew words for save. The first is "hoshea" (הושיע), also pronounced hoshiya. The second is "yeshua" (ישועה) and the third is "yasha" (ישע). They all refer to deliverance, freedom, liberation, safety and the like.

The Prophet Yeshayahu personifies the Arm of YHWH as if it were a person who would come in the future as "The Redeemer." This Redeemer will not only come in the future, but He also intervened in the past. "*⁹ Awake, awake, put on strength, O Arm of YHWH! Awake as in the ancient days, in the generations of old. Are You not the Arm that cut Rahab apart, and wounded the serpent? ¹⁰ Are You not the One who dried up the sea, the waters of the great deep; that made the depths of the sea a road for the redeemed to cross over? ¹¹ So the ransomed of YHWH shall return, and come to Zion with singing, with everlasting joy on their heads. They shall obtain joy and gladness; sorrow and sighing shall flee away. ¹² I, even I, am He who comforts you. Who are you that you should be afraid of a man who will die, and of the son of a man who will be made like grass? ¹³ And you forget YHWH your Maker, Who stretched out the heavens and laid the foundations of the earth; you have feared continually every day because of the fury of the oppressor, when he has prepared to destroy. And where is the fury of the oppressor? ¹⁴ The captive exile hastens, that he may be loosed, that he should not die in the pit, and that his bread should not fail. ¹⁵ But I am YHWH your Elohim, Who divided the sea whose waves roared - YHWH of hosts is His Name. ¹⁶ And I have put My words in your mouth. I have covered you with the shadow of My Hand, that I may plant the heavens, lay the foundations of the earth, and say to Zion, 'You are My people.'*" Yeshayahu 51:9-16.

Now Yeshayahu prophesied during the reign of King Hezekiah, King of Yahudah. During this period the House of Yisrael had already been removed from the Land by the Assyrians who were also pressing in on the House of Yahudah. Yeshayahu and Hezekiah called out to

YHWH and YHWH sent a messenger to cut down all of the mighty men of the Assyrian King who was soundly humiliated and defeated.

Notice the same language used by Hoshea except Hoshea said, "You are not my people." Yeshayahu is saying "You are my people" which, according to Hoshea, would make them Sons of the Living Elohim.

Interestingly, Yeshayahu speaks about the Arm of YHWH that cut Rahab apart and wounded the serpent. This was a similar reference that we read in the Ketubim. (Tehillim 89:10). This particular phrase should make us think of another writing in the Book of Job which stated: "*12 By His power He churned up the sea; by His wisdom He cut Rahab to pieces. 13 By His breath the skies became fair; His Hand pierced the fleeing serpent.*" Job 26:12-13. This is a common theme woven throughout the Scriptures.

Rahab is a reference to Egypt and His Hand and Arm were His method for deliverence in the past. In this same fashion, Yisrael will be saved in the future by the Arm of YHWH. Just as Yisrael was brought out of Egypt by Mosheh carrying the Rod or Branch - in like fashion - Yisrael will be saved and regathered by Messiah.

Read how Yeshayahu actually describes the Messiah as the salvation of YHWH personified as He comes to Zion to rule.

"*61:10 I delight greatly in YHWH; my soul rejoices in my Elohim. For He has clothed me with garments of salvation and arrayed me in a robe of righteousness, as a bridegroom adorns his head like a priest, and as a bride adorns herself with her jewels. 11 For as the soil makes the sprout come up and a garden causes seeds to grow, so the Sovereign YHWH will make righteousness and praise spring up before all nations. 62:1 For Zion's sake I will not keep silent, for Jerusalem's sake I will not remain quiet, till her righteousness shines out like the dawn, her salvation like a blazing torch. 2 The nations will see your righteousness, and all kings your glory; you will be called by a new name that the mouth of YHWH will bestow. 3 You will be a crown of splendor in YHWH's Hand, a royal diadem in the Hand of your Elohim. 4 No longer will they call you Deserted, or name your Land Desolate. But you will be called Hephzibah, and your Land Beulah; for YHWH will take delight in you, and your Land will be married. 5 As a young man marries a maiden, so will your sons marry you; as a bridegroom rejoices over his bride, so will your Elohim rejoice over you. 6 I have posted watchmen on your walls, O Jerusalem, they will never be silent day or night. You who call on YHWH, give yourselves no rest, 7 and give Him no rest till He establishes Jerusalem and makes*

her the praise of the earth. *8 YHWH has sworn by His Right Hand and by His Mighty Arm: Never again will I give your grain as food for your enemies, and never again will foreigners drink the new wine for which you have toiled; 9 but those who harvest it will eat it and praise YHWH, and those who gather the grapes will drink it in the courts of my sanctuary. 10 Pass through, pass through the gates! Prepare the way for the people. Build up, build up the highway! Remove the stones. Raise a banner for the nations. 11 YHWH has made proclamation to the ends of the earth: Say to the Daughter of Zion, See, your Savior comes! See, His reward is with Him, and His recompense accompanies Him. 12 They will be called the Holy People, the Redeemed of YHWH; and you will be called Sought After, the City No Longer Deserted.*" Yeshayahu 61:10 – 62:12.

Notice the marriage language following this great regathering. Just as Yisrael left Egypt to be married, the purpose of the final regathering will be for a marriage and a wedding feast. Yisrael will be marrying the One Who saves her.

We know that YHWH will somehow bring Yisrael back to Him as He previously delivered Yisrael from Egypt, but how could the problem be rectified? How can He remarry Yisrael with the prohibition found in Devarim 24.

We see the answer through the prophecy in Hoshea involving the 153. There is another Hebrew term that equals 153 – the Passover Sacrifice known as Ha-Pesach. In Hebrew it is spelled (הפסח). The gematria calculation for Ha-Pesach goes as follows: (ה= 5), (פ = 80), (ס = 60), (ח = 8). 5+80+60+8 = 153.

Therefore, we see a Messianic pattern in the Passover Lamb. Just as the Passover Lambs were slaughtered and the blood of the Lamb saved the Children of Yisrael from death, it was through the pattern provided by the Passover sacrifice that the House of Yisrael would be called the "sons of Elohim."

This Passover sacrifice was shown through Abraham as the Father sacrificing his son. So it appears that this pattern is showing that YHWH would sacrifice His Son, the Messiah, Who would become the Passover Lamb that would provide for this regathering. The blood of the Lamb of Elohim would save the Children of Yisrael and allow them to be delivered in the great regathering in the end.

This concept of the Messiah as the Son has long and ancient traditions, although as discussed previously, the Sages have been mystified because they saw the Messiah function through the Scriptures in two roles: 1) the son of Joseph and 2) the son of David.

The reason for these two Messianic roles should be evident as we just examined the division of Yisrael into two houses. It is important to recognize that Joseph represented the leadership of the Northern Kingdom through the Tribe of Ephraim and David represented the leadership of the Southern Kingdom through the Tribe of Yahudah.

These two kingdoms were punished differently and they needed One Who could resolve both of their unique circumstances. They both had sinned and needed to be restored into right relationship with YHWH. This was not a new problem – it goes back to the Garden.

Therefore, Yisrael and all of mankind needed One who could restore all of Creation to the Creator and atone for the sin that separated mankind from YHWH – the Son of Joseph. They also needed a King Who could unite the Tribes and restore the Kingdom of Yisrael – the Son of David.

No passage of Scripture better exemplifies this seeming contradiction between the roles of the Messiah than Yeshayahu 52 and 53 which provide the following description of the Arm of YHWH, also identified as the Servant.

"⁵²:¹⁰ _YHWH will lay bare His Holy Arm in the sight of all the nations, and all the ends of the earth will see the salvation of our Elohim._ ¹¹ _Depart, depart, go out from there! Touch no unclean thing! Come out from it and be pure, you who carry the vessels of YHWH._ ¹² _But you will not leave in haste or go in flight; for YHWH will go before you, the Elohim of Yisrael will be your rear guard._ ¹³ _See, My Servant will act wisely; He will be raised and lifted up and highly exalted._ ¹⁴ _Just as there were many who were appalled at Him - His appearance was so disfigured beyond that of any man and His form more than the sons of men-_ ¹⁵ _so will He sprinkle many nations, and kings will shut their mouths because of Him. For what they were not told, they will see, and what they have not heard, they will understand._ ⁵³:¹ _Who has believed our message and to whom has the Arm of YHWH been revealed?_ ² _He grew up before Him like a tender shoot (twig), and like a root out of dry ground. He had no beauty or majesty to attract us to Him, nothing in His appearance that we should desire Him._ ³ _He was despised and rejected by men, a Man of sorrows, and familiar with suffering. Like One from whom men hide their faces He was despised, and we esteemed Him not._ ⁴ _Surely He took up our infirmities and carried our sorrows, yet we considered Him stricken by Elohim, smitten by Him, and afflicted._ ⁵ _But He was pierced for our transgressions, He was crushed for our iniquities; the punishment that brought us peace was upon Him, and by His wounds we are healed._

⁶ We all, like sheep, have gone astray, each of us has turned to his own way, and YHWH has laid on Him the iniquity of us all. ⁷ He was oppressed and afflicted, yet He did not open His mouth. He was led like a lamb to the slaughter, and as a sheep before her shearers is silent, so He did not open His mouth. ⁸ By oppression and judgment He was taken away. And who can speak of His descendants? For He was cut off from the land of the living; for the transgression of my people he was stricken. ⁹ He was assigned a grave with the wicked, and with the rich in His death, though He had done no violence, nor was any deceit in His mouth. ¹⁰ Yet it was YHWH's will to crush Him and cause Him to suffer, and though YHWH makes His life a guilt offering. He will see His offspring and prolong His days, and the will of YHWH will prosper in His Hand. ¹¹ After the suffering of His soul, He will see the labor of His soul and be satisfied; by His knowledge My righteous Servant will justify many, and he will bear their iniquities. ¹² Therefore I will give Him a portion among the great, and He will divide the spoils with the strong, because He poured out His life unto death, and was numbered with the transgressors. For He bore the sin of many, and made intercession for the transgressors." Yeshayahu 52:10-53:12.

The appearance of the Aleph Taw (את) is found throughout this text and it is clearly a Messianic prophecy. This prophecy describes the Servant, the Son of Joseph, as one who was not handsome and one who was afflicted. Yeshayahu describes this Servant as one who would be despised and rejected by men although He would carry the punishment of Yisrael.

He would be led to the slaughter like a lamb – the Lamb of YHWH. He would be killed and actually bear the sins of many. His life would be a guilt offering yet He would later be satisfied by the labor of His soul. He would be "cut off" from the Land of the living and have no physical descendants, yet He will see His offspring and prolong His days.

The mouth of kings will be shut because of this Servant, who will divide the spoils with the strong and be given a portion with the great. The life of this Servant will actually atone for the sins of many and by His wounds Yisrael would be healed.

This is an incredible prophecy and very difficult for some to understand. It was hard to comprehend how this Servant could die, yet live. This was the solution that Yisrael needed, One who could atone for their sins and restore their relationship with their Husband, YHWH.

It is important to understand that the blood of animals could never accomplish such a feat. Blood was shed after the sin of Adam and Hawah, but they were still not permitted back into the Garden.

The sacrificial system was instituted by YHWH as a practical way of instructing mankind in matters of sin and atonement. YHWH wanted man to understand that if sin was committed, it would take the blood of an innocent to cover the sin.

Interestingly, the Servant will perform a work which will affect the Nations and the entire earth – not just Yisrael. "¹ *Behold! My Servant whom I uphold, My Elect one in whom My soul delights! I have put My Spirit upon Him; He will bring forth justice to the Gentiles (Nations).* ² *He will not cry out, nor raise His voice, nor cause His voice to be heard in the street.* ³ *A bruised reed He will not break, and smoking flax He will not quench; He will bring forth justice for truth.* ⁴ <u>*He will not fail nor be discouraged, till He has established justice in the earth; and the coastlands shall wait for His Torah.*</u> ⁵ *Thus says Elohim YHWH, Who created the heavens and stretched them out, Who spread forth the earth and that which comes from it, Who gives breath to the people on it.*" Yeshayahu 42:1-5.

In order for the nations to be justified, a sacrifice would have to be made that would clear the conscience from the effects of sin. This sacrifice would be accomplished by the Servant in Whom Elohim delighted. This Servant would bring justice, or rather judgment, to the Nations.

"¹ *Listen, O coastlands, to Me, and take heed, you peoples from afar!* <u>*YHWH has called Me from the womb; from the matrix of My mother He has made mention of My Name.*</u> ² *And He has made My mouth like a sharp sword; in the shadow of His Hand He has hidden Me, and made Me a polished shaft; in His quiver He has hidden Me.* ³ *And He said to Me, You are My servant, O Yisrael, in whom I will be glorified.* ⁴ *Then I said, I have labored in vain, I have spent my strength for nothing and in vain; yet surely my just reward is with YHWH, and my work with my Elohim.* ⁵ <u>*And now YHWH says, Who formed Me from the womb to be His Servant, to bring Yaakov back to Him, so that Yisrael is gathered to Him (For I shall be glorious in the eyes of YHWH, and My Elohim shall be My strength),*</u> ⁶ <u>*Indeed He says, It is too small a thing that You should be My Servant to raise up the tribes of Yaakov, and to restore the preserved ones of Yisrael; I will also give You as a light to the Gentiles (Nations), that You should be My salvation to the ends of the earth.*</u> ⁷ *Thus says YHWH, The Redeemer of Yisrael, their Holy one, to Him whom man despises, to Him whom the nation abhors, to the Servant of rulers: Kings shall see and arise, Princes also shall worship, because of YHWH who is faithful, The Holy One of Yisrael; and He has chosen You.* ⁸ *Thus says YHWH:* <u>*In*</u>

an acceptable time I have heard You, and in the day of salvation I have helped You; I will preserve You and give You as a Covenant to the people, to restore the earth, to cause them to inherit the desolate heritages; ⁹ That You may say to the prisoners, Go forth, to those who are in darkness, show yourselves. They shall feed along the roads, and their pastures shall be on all desolate heights. ¹⁰ They shall neither hunger nor thirst, neither heat nor sun shall strike them; for He who has mercy on them will lead them, even by the springs of water He will guide them. ¹¹ I will make each of My mountains a road, and My highways shall be elevated. ¹² Surely these shall come from afar; Look! Those from the north and the west, and these from the land of Sinim. ¹³ Sing, O heavens! Be joyful, O earth! And break out in singing, O mountains! For YHWH has comforted His people, and will have mercy on His afflicted." Yeshayahu 49:1-13.

There are some who argue the Servant is actually Yisrael, but when read in context that is clearly not the case. Yisrael was intended to be a light to the nations but she failed. It is the Messiah Who will now be that Light and it will be Messiah Who will *"raise up the tribes of Yaakov, and . . . restore the preserved ones of Yisrael."*

The prophecy clearly speaks of an individual Who will do the necessary work of YHWH. The Servant was hidden in the Hand of YHWH and would be formed in the womb, have a mother and obviously be born and live as a son of Adam. He would raise up and restore the Tribes of Yisrael. His life would be marked with suffering and He would actually become the Covenant with Yisrael which was broken. He would be the Renewed Covenant.

We have already discussed the Jubilee and anyone familiar with the concept of the yovel will quickly recognize that Yeshayuhu is referencing the Jubilee and all of the blessings attributed with it. (see Vayiqra 25). This is not just any Jubilee, this is describing the restoration of all things – the great Jubilee as foretold at the time of the flood.

Prior to that time there was no apparent limit set on creation. In fact, one could argue that man was set in Eden to live forever with YHWH. After the fall of man, sin and death entered into creation, which continued to be corrupted throughout the centuries. Finally, things deteriorated to such an extent that YHWH apparently became fed up. *"Then YHWH said, My Spirit will not contend with man forever, for he is mortal; his days will be a hundred and twenty years."* Beresheet 6:3.

As was previously mentioned in Chapter 3, people often believe that this passage is referring to the fact that men's individual lifespans would be shortened to a maximum of 120 years, but the Scriptures clearly record men living well beyond 120 years after this point. This passage is referring to all of mankind, not individual lifespans of men.

The passage provides that "the days" – yamayaw (ימיו) shall be 120 years - shanah (שנה).

The Hebrew word yamayaw (ימיו) or yom (ימ) is often used to describe a 24 hour period from evening to evening, but it can also refer to a general time period. The word shanah (שנה) is used most often to describe a year, but the word can be used more generally to describe a cycle, a revolution or a measure.

Thus, what is being revealed is that mankind was destined to live in mortal bodies in a fallen world for a period of no longer than 120 Jubilee Years. As there are fifty (50) years in a Jubilee cycle, 120 Jubilee cycles comprise 6,000 years

Therefore, mankind would be given 6,000 years until YHWH would come and restore His creation in the 120th Jubilee year which initiates a Sabbath millennia. This was the pattern established during the first week of creation. So we can expect the Messiah as the Servant, the Hand of YHWH, to have rulership over the world at the end of 120 Jubilee cycles after the full measure of the nations have been restored to the Covenant. This will fulfill the prophecy Yisrael made over his adopted son Ephraim in Beresheet 48:19.

We are given an outside date for the reign of man and we know that a lot went wrong that needed to be fixed. Yeshayahu shows that YHWH would save by His own Arm. This Arm is referred to as the Servant and the Servant is part of YHWH. We can deduce that the Servant is the Son - the Passover Lamb as shown from the pattern provided by Abraham and "his son, his only son" Yitshaq.

This is an important concept to grasp. The Messiah Son of Joseph was not going to suffer needlessly. His suffering was for a very important and specific purpose. Let us look at the words of Yeshayahu 53 again: "⁶ *We all, like sheep, have gone astray, each of us has turned to his own way; and YHWH has laid on Him* את *the iniquity of us all. ⁷ He was oppressed and afflicted, yet He did not open His mouth; He was led like a lamb to the slaughter, and as a sheep before her shearers is silent, so He did not open His mouth. ⁸* By oppression and judgment He was taken away. And who can speak of His descendants? For He was cut off from the land of the living; *for the transgression of My people He was stricken.* ⁹ He was assigned a grave with the wicked, and with the rich in His death, though He had done no violence, nor was any deceit in His mouth. ¹⁰ Yet it was YHWH's will to crush Him and cause Him to suffer, and though *YHWH makes His life a guilt offering,* He will see His offspring and prolong His days, and the will of YHWH will prosper in His hand. ¹¹ After the suffering of His soul, He will see the light [of life] and be satisfied; *by His knowledge my Righteous Servant*

will justify many, and He will bear their iniquities." Yeshayahu 53:6-11.

This Servant was specifically identified with the Aleph Taw (את). He would be slaughtered like a lamb – the Lamb of Elohim. He would bear the sins of the lost sheep – Yisrael. He will have offspring, but only after He has died. The text records that by His knowledge He would justify many. The root of the word "knowledge" is yada (ידע) which can refer to the intimacy of a marital relationship. Thus by "knowing" this Servant, by being intimate with Him, many would be saved.

This Servant, the Lamb of YHWH would be a guilt offering for Yisrael. It was through the death of the Servant that Yisrael, the Bride, could be remarried to YHWH. The Servant would then see life, after His suffering – this is resurrection from the dead.

Modern Judaism often proclaims that the Scriptures do not condone human sacrifice and that the Messiah is only a man – not God. These modern proclamations appear to be in direct response to Christianity and the death and resurrection of Jesus as portrayed in the New Testament. The position of Modern Judaism most certainly does not represent the beliefs of their predecessors – the House of Yahudah.

Judaism finds itself in a precarious position. Having rejected the Christian Jesus, they have no other Messianic candidate in history who could possibly have been the Messiah as described by Yeshayahu. As a result, they have chosen to rethink and refine their definition and expectations of the Messiah instead of reexamining history and the distortions perpetrated by both Judaism and Christianity. This is a subject which will be discussed in more depth later in this text.

One of the reasons why most in Judaism have a problem with the concepts found in Yeshayahu is because this particular portion of the prophecy is rarely, if ever, read in the Synagogue. As a result, many are not familiar with the fact that the Messiah was to suffer and be offered up to death as a guilt offering.

This, by the way, is perfectly consistent with the pattern provided by Abraham as well as the prophets and the writings. In fact, the prophet Zechariah, also known as Zekaryah, confirms that the method of death for the Messiah will be by crucifixion and that Yahudah will fail to recognize Him until their eyes are finally opened.

Read what the Prophet says in this regard: "¹⁰ *And I will pour out on the house of David and the inhabitants of Jerusalem a spirit of grace and supplication. They will look upon* את *Whom they have pierced, and they will mourn for Him as one mourns for an only child, and grieve bitterly for Him as one grieves for a firstborn son. ¹¹ On that day the weeping in Jerusalem will be* great, like the weeping of Hadad Rimmon in the plain of Megiddo. [12] The Land will mourn, each clan by itself, with their wives by themselves: the clan of the House of David and their wives, the clan of the House of Nathan and their wives, [13] the clan of the House of Levi and their wives, the clan of Shimei and their wives, [14] and all the rest of the clans and their wives." Zekaryah 12:10-14.

This prophecy confirms Tehillim 118 which speaks of piercing the Messiah. It specifically and unequivocally refers to the Aleph Taw (את) as being the One Who is pierced. It even compares Him to a firstborn son, which He is – the firstborn of Elohim.

Yehezqel prophesied that YHWH would provide atonement for Yisrael by renewal of the Covenant which had been broken. "[59] This is what the Sovereign YHWH says: I will deal with you as you deserve, because you have despised my oath by breaking the Covenant. [60] Yet I will remember the Covenant I made with you in the days of your youth, and I will establish an everlasting Covenant with you. [61] Then you will remember your ways and be ashamed when you receive your sisters, both those who are older than you and those who are younger. I will give them to you as daughters, but not on the basis of My Covenant with you. [62] So I will establish My Covenant with you, and you will know that I am YHWH. [63] Then, when I make atonement for you for all you have done, you will remember and be ashamed and never again open your mouth because of your humiliation, declares the Sovereign YHWH." Yehezqel 16:59-63

The concept of YHWH providing a Son who would atone for the sins of Yisrael is a difficulty that exists for some in the present day, but in the past the problem was different. Yisraelites fully understood and accepted the fact that there would be a Suffering Servant, although they could not synchronize this Suffering Servant with the Messiah Who would restore the Kingdom of Yisrael and rule over the entire Earth.

As a result, many previously believed that there would be two Messiahs - the Son of Joseph, who would suffer for the iniquities of Yisrael, and the Son of David, who would be exalted and rule over a united kingdom.

As stated, the notion of the Son of David was easy to understand. A righteous King who would unite the Tribes and reign over a united kingdom was something every one desired, and from all accounts, the prophecies seemed to indicate that one day this would occur. The suffering servant was not so easy to comprehend, although it clearly appears in the Scriptures.

Despite the seeming contradictions between these Messianic roles, it is quite clear that Yisraelites around the turn of the millennium fully anticipated Messiah Son of Joseph. In a discovery similar to the Dead Sea Scrolls, albeit on a much smaller scale, a text from that period, referred to as Gabriel's Revelation, was actually written on stone.

The contents of the revelation appear to be a message given by none other than Gabriel concerning the Messiah and refers to both the servant David as well as Ephraim – Messiah Son of Joseph.[131] The Revelation is dated around the turn of the millennium - the same period when the Dead Sea Scrolls were written.

The Messiah Son of Joseph was not a new idea introduced through Gabriel's revelation. In fact it was first specifically mentioned in the Babylonian Talmud at Sukkah 52a: " . . . But as the Messiah ben David will have seen that the Messiah ben Joseph who preceded Him was killed, He will say before the Lord: 'Lord of the Universe, I will ask nothing of Thee but life.' And the Lord will answer: 'This was prophesied already for thee by thy father David: Life hath he asked of thee, thou gavest it to him.'"

Other later writings such as "Joseph and Aseneth," written between 100 BCE and 115 CE describe Joseph as "son of Elohim" (6:3,5, 13:13) and Elohim's "firstborn son" (18:11, 21:4, 23:10).[132] These notions were not fabricated from thin air. They were actually founded upon an understanding of the Messianic pattern provided by Joseph, as well as prophecies which describe the Messiah as a suffering servant.

They may not have understood how it would all happen, but they fully expected to see the Messiah Son of Joseph, the Suffering Servant. Therefore, it would be through the death of the Servant that Yisrael would be restored to YHWH, and the Servant would then be raised to life. He would be the Renewed Covenant which would bring Yisrael back into right relationship with her Husband – YHWH.

So as we saw in the Writings, we also see in the Prophets, that the Messiah was to act in two unique roles, the conquering King – which is the Son of David and the Suffering Servant – which is the Son of Joseph. Both of the roles are functions of the anointed – the King and the Priest.

Through the various prophets, some other very specific and detailed information was given concerning the Messiah. Interestingly, the prophecies told where the Messiah would be born and where He would live. According to Micah: *"2 But you, Bethlehem Ephrathah, though you are little among the thousands of Yahudah, yet out of you shall come forth to Me, the One to be Ruler in Yisrael, whose goings forth are from of old, from everlasting. 3 Therefore He shall give them up, until the time that she who is in labor has given birth; then the remnant of His brethren shall return to the* children of Yisrael. *⁴ And He shall stand and feed His flock in the strength of YHWH, in the majesty of the Name of YHWH His Elohim; and they shall abide, for now He shall be great to the ends of the earth; ⁵ and this One shall be peace.*" Micah 5:2-5.

From Micah we learn that the Messiah will be born, like David, in Bethlehem. This Ruler of Yisrael is referred to as "eternal." He will come in the strength and majesty of the Name of YHWH. He will restore Yisrael and rule over the entire Earth in peace.

We also were told that the Messiah would shine as a light from the Galilee (Yeshayahu 9), and a further description was provided concerning the Messiah as follows: "*⁶ For to us a Child is born, to us a Son is given, and the government will be on his shoulders. And He will be called Wonderful Counselor, Mighty Elohim, Everlasting Father, Prince of Peace. ⁷ Of the increase of His government and peace there will be no end. He will reign on David's throne and over His kingdom, establishing and upholding it with justice and righteousness from that time on and forever. The zeal of YHWH Almighty will accomplish this.*" Yeshayahu 9:6-7.

From this passage we see that there will be a Son that will come from the lineage of David who will be called "*Wonderful Counselor, Mighty Elohim, Everlasting Father, Prince of Peace*" and will rule forever. This will occur through the zeal of YHWH. The word zeal is qinah (קנאה) in Hebrew which denotes "the jealous disposition of a husband" and "sexual passion." So then we can conclude that this Son will derive from YHWH as a Husband.

How can this be? We are given the answer in the same prophecy of Yeshayahu which states: "*¹³ Hear now, you house of David! Is it not enough to try the patience of men? Will you try the patience of my Elohim also? ¹⁴ Therefore YHWH Himself will give you a sign: The virgin will be with Child and will give birth to a Son, and will call Him Immanuel.*" Yeshayahu 7:13-14.

This promised Son will be called Immanuel which is a Hebrew word that means: "El is with us." So then this Son will be El and He will be born of a virgin. Many argue that this Son will not necessarily come from a virgin because the Hebrew word translated virgin - "alma'ah" could just as easily be translated as "maiden" or "damsel." That would raise the question of how or why this would be a sign from YHWH. There is obviously nothing unique about a young maiden conceiving.

We will see further in this discussion that Yeshayahu was clearly referring to a virgin. Therefore, this Messiah – Son of David would somehow be born from a virgin with YHWH as His Father. He would be an offspring of David who would be called Elohim.

Again, the Messiah as Son of David was easy for people to envisage. After all, most of these prophets lived and prophesied during and after the division of the Kingdom of Yisrael. The House of Yisrael – the Northern Tribes – had been removed from the Land and were "lost." The House of Yahudah had been exiled by the Babylonians. There was clearly the need for a King that could restore the shattered Kingdom.

This restoration was specifically promised and demonstrated by the Prophet Yehezqel using a stick – also known as a "branch" or a "rod."

"*¹⁶ As for you, son of man, take a stick for yourself and write on it: 'For Yahudah and for the children of Yisrael, his companions. Then take another stick and write on it, For Joseph, the stick of Ephraim, and for all the house of Yisrael, his companions. ¹⁷ Then join them one to another for yourself into one stick, and they will become one in your hand. ¹⁸ And when the children of your people speak to you, saying, Will you not show us what you mean by these? ¹⁹ say to them, Thus says YHWH Elohim: <u>Surely I will take the stick of Joseph, which is in the hand of Ephraim, and the tribes of Yisrael, his companions; and I will join them with it, with the stick of Yahudah, and make them one stick, and they will be one in My Hand</u>. ²⁰ And the sticks on which you write will be in your hand before their eyes. ²¹ Then say to them, Thus says YHWH Elohim: <u>Surely I will take the children of Yisrael from among the nations, wherever they have gone, and will gather them from every side and bring them into their own Land</u>; ²² <u>and I will make them one nation in the Land, on the mountains of Yisrael; and one king shall be king over them all; they shall no longer be two nations, nor shall they ever be divided into two kingdoms again</u>. ²³ They shall not defile themselves anymore with their idols, nor with their detestable things, nor with any of their transgressions; but I will deliver them from all their dwelling places in which they have sinned, and will cleanse them. <u>Then they shall be My people, and I will be their Elohim</u>. ²⁴ <u>David My Servant shall be king over them, and they shall all have One Shepherd; they shall also walk in My judgments and observe My statutes, and do them</u>.²⁵ Then they shall dwell in the Land that I have given to Jacob My servant, where your fathers dwelt; and they shall dwell there, they, their children, and their children's children, forever; and <u>My Servant David shall be their Prince forever</u>. ²⁶ <u>Moreover I will make a Covenant of Peace with them, and it shall be an everlasting covenant with them</u>; I will establish them and multiply them, and I will set My Sanctuary in their midst forevermore.²⁷ My*

Tabernacle also shall be with them; indeed *I will be their Elohim, and they shall be My people.*²⁸ *The nations also will know that I, YHWH, sanctify Yisrael, when My sanctuary is in their midst forevermore."* Yehezqel 37:16-28.

Notice the emphasis on servants, just as with Mosheh and Yahushua. This prophecy makes clear how the restoration of the divided Kingdom of Yisrael would be accomplished. The two Houses would be brought together as two sticks, and they would become one (Echad) in the Hand of YHWH. David will rule over this United Kingdom.

Yehezqel speaks further of this Covenant of Peace through the Servant David and uses clear language of this David acting as a Shepherd to the flock of Yisrael. *"²⁰ Therefore this is what the Sovereign YHWH says to them: See, I Myself will judge between the fat sheep and the lean sheep. ²¹ Because you shove with flank and shoulder, butting all the weak sheep with your horns until you have driven them away, ²² I will save My flock, and they will no longer be plundered. I will judge between one sheep and another. ²³ I will place over them One Shepherd, My Servant David, and He will tend them; He will tend them and be their Shepherd. ²⁴ I YHWH will be their Elohim, and My Servant David will be Prince among them. I YHWH have spoken. ²⁵ I will make a Covenant of peace with them and rid the Land of wild beasts so that they may live in the desert and sleep in the forests in safety. ²⁶ I will bless them and the places surrounding My hill. I will send down showers in season; there will be showers of blessing. ²⁷ The trees of the field will yield their fruit and the ground will yield its crops; the people will be secure in their land. They will know that I am YHWH, when I break the bars of their yoke and rescue them from the hands of those who enslaved them. ²⁸ They will no longer be plundered by the nations, nor will wild animals devour them. They will live in safety, and no one will make them afraid. ²⁹ I will provide for them a Land renowned for its crops, and they will no longer be victims of famine in the Land or bear the scorn of the nations. ³⁰ Then they will know that I, YHWH their Elohim, am with them and that they, the House of Yisrael, are My people, declares the Sovereign YHWH. ³¹ You My sheep, the sheep of My pasture, are people, and I am your Elohim, declares the Sovereign YHWH."* Yehezqel 34:20-31

Notice again the language from Hoshea concerning the House of Yisrael – YHWH will be their Elohim and the House of Yisrael will be His people. As with Hoshea, Yehezqel prophesies that there will be one ruler over them – the Messiah Son of David.

The Messiah is the Shepherd and the Hand of YHWH. The Messiah was and is the One Who operates on the planet as a representative of the Father, just like Mosheh represented YHWH. He

would come to gather the Sheep of YHWH, like a Shepherd, and direct the flock in the ways of the Torah as was the function of a prophet. He is, after all, The Prophet like Mosheh.

Yisrael needed One like Mosheh because they needed to renew the Covenant that they had broken. The Prophet Yirmeyahu gave hope that the Covenant would indeed be renewed. "*31 The time is coming, declares YHWH, when I will make a renewed Covenant with the House of Yisrael and with the House of Yahudah. 32 It will not be like the Covenant I made with their forefathers when I took them by the hand to lead them out of Egypt, because they broke My Covenant, though I was a Husband to them, declares YHWH. 33 This is the Covenant I will make with the House of Yisrael after that time, declares YHWH. I will put My Torah in their minds and write it on their hearts. I will be their Elohim, and they will be My people."* Yirmeyahu 31:31-33.

Again, notice the consistent language used specifically concerning the House of Yisrael – "*I will be their Elohim and they will be My people.*" This would occur when He circumcised their hearts. He would write His Torah on their hearts and in their minds. He would put His Spirit within them and by doing so they would become the "Sons of Elohim." This would occur by the work of the Messiah, the Son of Elohim.

Since the Yisraelites were punished for disobeying the Torah, they needed One who could reconcile them to YHWH and get them back to the Torah. This is the goal of the restoration – the Torah of YHWH as the rule of the Kingdom. This rule is to be established during the fifth and sixth millennia of mankind's history. The fifth and sixth millennial "days" are called the "latter days" in prophecy.

"*2 Now it shall come to pass in the latter days that the mountain of YHWH's House shall be established on the top of the mountains, and shall be exalted above the hills; and all nations shall flow to it. 3 Many people shall come and say, Come, and let us go up to the mountain of YHWH, to the House of the Elohim of Yaakov; He will teach us His ways, and we shall walk in His paths. For out of Zion shall go forth the Torah, and the word of YHWH from Jerusalem.*" Yeshayahu 2:2-3.

It was disobedience to the Torah which created all of the problems on the planet, and the restoration would clearly involve a return to the Torah. This is emphasized by the Prophet Malachi. "*1 Surely the day is coming; it will burn like a furnace. All the arrogant and every evildoer will be stubble, and that day that is coming will set them on fire, says YHWH Almighty. Not a root or a branch will be left to them. 2 But for you who revere my Name, the Sun of righteousness will rise with healing in its* wings. *And you will go out and leap like calves released from the stall.* ³ *Then you will trample down the wicked; they will be ashes under the soles of your feet on the day when I do these things, says YHWH Almighty.* ⁴ <u>*Remember the Torah of My servant Mosheh, the decrees and laws I gave him at Horeb for all Yisrael.*</u> ⁵ *See, I will send you the prophet Elijah before that great and dreadful day of YHWH comes.* ⁶ *He will turn the hearts of the fathers to their children, and the hearts of the children to their fathers; or else I will come and strike the Land with a curse."* Malachi 4:1-6.

So far we have not mentioned the prophet Elijah, whose correct name is Eliyahu. Eliyahu the Tishbite was a prophet who lived and ministered around 865 - 823 BCE*. He was unique from most of the other prophets, save Mosheh, because he operated in great signs and wonders. He raised the dead, called down fire from heaven, and controlled the weather, among other things. He is also closely linked with his counter part Elisha, who operated in the same spirit and power. Together, both Eliyahu and Elisha provide a hint to the Name of the Messiah, which will be discussed in the next chapter.

Eliyahu the Tishbite confronted corrupt political and religious leaders. In particular, he confronted the pagan gods that Yisrael was serving at the time. His actions of controlling the weather, so that there was no rain in the Land, was a direct affront to Baal. Baal was worshipped by Jezebel, and her husband King Ahab actually built a temple to Baal.

In response, Eliyahu rebuilt the Altar of YHWH and slaughtered outside of Jerusalem, acts typically forbidden by the Torah. This demonstrates that he operated in the Melchizedek priesthood. He ordered the massacre of the priests of Baal, and was eventually taken up in a whirlwind.

Eliyahu stands with Mosheh in that he has no tomb on this earth. He is closely linked with the Messiah, in fact, many believe that aside from the Messiah like Mosheh, the Messiah like Joseph and the Messiah like David, there is a fourth Messiah - the Messiah like Eliyahu.

The prophecy given by Malachi is particularly interesting because it refers to the "Sun of Righteousness," which is a clear Messianic reference, and should bring us back to the Light of the First Day. Instead of the physical sun that was created on the fourth day, we have the Sun of Righteousness Who existed before the world began and Whose Light was brought forth on the first day at the dawning of the day.

This Sun of Righteousness will come with healing in His

wings. These "wings" are kanaph (כנף) in Hebrew and refer to the edge of a garment, or tassels, otherwise known as tzitzit. The tzitzit were specifically commanded to be worn by the Yisraelites to remind them of the commandments – the Torah. Since the Messiah would come with healing in His tzitzit, it is obvious that He would be wearing tzitzit in obedience to the Torah.

Interestingly, Malachi proclaims that "not a root or branch" will be left for the evildoers when the judgment of YHWH comes. This could be taken two ways. First, it could mean that nothing will be left of evildoers. It could also mean that there will be no healing for the evildoers because both the root and the branch are terms used for the Messiah.

Read the words spoken by Yeshayahu: "¹ _A shoot will come up from the stump of Jesse; from his roots a Branch will bear fruit. ² The Spirit of YHWH will rest on him the Spirit of wisdom and of understanding, the Spirit of counsel and of power, the Spirit of knowledge and of the fear of YHWH ³ and He will delight in the fear of YHWH. He will not judge by what He sees with His eyes, or decide by what He hears with His ears; ⁴ but with righteousness He will judge the needy, with justice He will give decisions for the poor of the earth. He will strike the earth with the rod of His mouth; with the breath of His lips He will slay the wicked. ⁵ Righteousness will be His belt and faithfulness the sash around His waist. ⁶ The wolf will live with the lamb, the leopard will lie down with the goat, the calf and the lion and the yearling together; and a little child will lead them. ⁷ The cow will feed with the bear, their young will lie down together, and the lion will eat straw like the ox. ⁸ The infant will play near the hole of the cobra, and the young child put his hand into the viper's nest. ⁹ They will neither harm nor destroy on all my holy mountain, for the earth will be full of the knowledge of YHWH as the waters cover the sea. ¹⁰ In that day the Root of Jesse will stand as a banner for the peoples; the nations will rally to Him, and His place of rest will be glorious. ¹¹ In that day_ YHWH will reach out His Hand a second time to reclaim the remnant that is left of his people from Assyria, from Lower Egypt, from Upper Egypt, from Cush, from Elam, from Babylonia, from Hamath and from the islands of the sea. ¹² _He will raise a banner for the nations and gather the exiles of Yisrael; He will assemble the scattered people of Yahudah from the four quarters of the earth._ ¹³ Ephraim's jealousy will vanish, and Yahudah's enemies will be cut off; Ephraim will not be jealous of Yahudah, nor Yahudah hostile toward Ephraim. ¹⁴ They will swoop down on the slopes of Philistia to the west; together they will plunder the people to the east. They will lay hands on Edom and Moab, and the Ammonites will be subject to them. ¹⁵ YHWH will dry up the gulf of the Egyptian sea; with a scorching wind He will sweep His Hand over the

Euphrates River. He will break it up into seven streams so that men can cross over in sandals. <u>*¹⁶ There will be a highway for the remnant of His people that is left from Assyria, as there was for Yisrael when they came up from Egypt.*</u>" Yeshayahu 11:1-16.

We read again about the recurring theme of the restoration of the divided kingdom of Yisrael. This is a great promise and a fundamental purpose of the Messiah – to restore the Kingdom. He will regather the remnant of Yahudah and Yisrael as a shepherd gathers his sheep. They will be brought from the four corners of the earth where they are scattered. The Messiah will then deliver them in miraculous fashion – more spectacular than when Mosheh brought Yisrael out of Egypt.

The prophecy clearly shows that the Messiah will come from the stump or root of Jesse, the father of King David. He is actually called a "Branch." There are several other Scripture passages that show the "Branch" to be the future Messiah. *"In those days, and at that time, will I cause the Branch of righteousness to grow up to David; and He shall execute judgment and righteousness in the Land"* Yirmeyahu 33:15.

This appears to be hinting to the time of the birth of the Messiah. The Hebrew word for Branch is tsemach (צמח), and further on in this book we will discover how through the signs in the heavens we can discover the moment of the birth of the Messiah – to the minute.

The Messiah would no doubt come from the lineage of David. *"⁵ Behold, the days come, says YHWH, that I will raise to David a righteous Branch, and a King shall reign and prosper, and shall execute judgment and justice upon the earth."* Yirmeyahu 23:5.

The Branch is the same as the Servant. *"Hear now, O Yahushua the high priest, you and your companions that sit before thee: though they be men wondered at: for, behold, I will bring forth My אֵת Servant the Branch."* Zekaryah 3:8.

Interestingly, Zekaryah seems to tie things together by placing the Aleph Taw (את) at the point of "the Servant the Branch" so we know that the Servant is the Branch, and they are both the Messiah. While these passages referring to the Branch had immediate application in the time when they were spoken, they also had a deeper significance directing us to the Name of the Messiah.

18

The Name

We have discussed the Name of the Father, which is YHWH (יהוה), although there is dispute concerning the actual pronunciation of that Name. Many unknowingly use the Name when they say the word "halleluyah" which means: "Praise Yah." As a result, I believe that it is reasonable that we pronounce the beginning of YHWH as Yah, and Yah is agreed upon by most to constitute the short form poetic Name of YHWH.

We see an example of this in the New King James Version of Tehillim 68:4 which reads: "*Sing to God, sing praises to His Name; extol Him who rides on the clouds, by His Name YAH, and rejoice before Him.*"

The reason we are addressing this is because the Name of the Messiah is directly linked with the Name of the Father. We have already seen through the various Scriptures that there is a Son, and the Son has a Name which is discoverable if we have wisdom.

Remember the riddle in the Proverbs: "*Who has gone up to heaven and come down? Who has gathered up the wind in the hollow of His hands? Who has wrapped up the waters in His cloak? Who has established all the ends of the earth? What is His Name, and the Name of His Son? Tell me if you know!*" Proverbs 30:4.

The Tehillim refer to the Son as the Right Hand, and there are a number of Prophets who have referred to the Branch. In the Tehillim the word "branch" and "son" are even mixed in some translations because the meaning is so clear.

The Amplified Bible provides: "*[Protect and maintain] the stock which Your right hand planted, and the Branch (the Son) that You have reared and made strong for Yourself.*" Tehillim 80:15 AMP. The word is actually ben (בן) and in this context could refer to Yisrael or the Messiah coming from the line of David.

The prophecies of Yirmeyahu give us a clue as to the Name of

Messiah the Branch. *"⁵ Behold, the days are coming, says YHWH, That I will raise to David a Branch of righteousness; a King shall reign and prosper, and execute judgment and righteousness in the earth. ⁶ In His days Yahudah will be saved and Yisrael will dwell safely; Now this is His Name by which He will be called: YHWH OUR RIGHTEOUSNESS."* Yirmeyahu 23:5-6 (see also 33:16).

This prophecy clearly speaks of Messiah the King and the word for "branch" is tsemach (צמח). This will be important to remember later in our discussion. The prophecy does not mean that the full Name of the Messiah will literally be "YHWH OUR RIGHTEOUSNESS," or rather "YHWH Tsideqeenu," which is the transliteration of the Hebrew יהוה צדקנו. Rather, it provides a hint of His character as we understand that He will carry the Name of YHWH within His Name. The Hebrew name that means "YHWH our righteousness" is Yahuzadak (יהוצדק). We shall soon see that this name is an important link to the Name of the Messiah.

Armed with this information we now examine another clue provided through the Prophet Zekaryah. *"¹¹ Take the silver and gold and make a crown, and set it on the head of the high priest, Yahushua son of Yahuzadak (יהוצדק). ¹² Tell him this is what YHWH of Hosts says:* **Here is the man whose Name is the Branch,** *and He will branch out from His place and build the temple (hekal) of YHWH. ¹³ It is He who will build the temple (hekal) of YHWH, and He will be clothed with majesty and will sit and rule on His throne. And He will be a priest on His throne. And there will be harmony between the two."* Zekaryah 6:11-14.

This is profound because the prophecy describes what the Messiah will do. He will sit as King and High Priest – this is the Melchizedek that we read of in the Torah and the Writings. The text also tells us that His Name will be Yahushua son of Yahuzadak (יהוצדק), or rather Yahushua son of YHWH our righteousness.

So here we see that the Branch is the Son and the Son is the Messiah. The Name of the Branch – the Messiah is the same name as Yahushua, the commander of Yisrael. The same one who was the Servant, like Mosheh. The one who brought the children of Yisrael across the Jordan River into the Promised Land. The one who directed their circumcision and who led them into battle as they conquered their enemies.

It should now be apparent that the patterns provided in the Scripture are for the future, and that the redemptive plan for mankind is through the Son. How appropriate that the Messiah of Yisrael would bear the same Name as this great patriarch, Yahushua.

The answer to the riddle posed in the Proverbs concerning the Name of Messiah was provided through the Prophets while Yahudah was in the process of returning from their seventy (70) year exile.

Interestingly, there was more information forthcoming during this time through a Prophet named Daniel who was contemplating that 70 year punishment. Daniel was told when the Messiah would appear within another riddle surrounding a period of time involving the number seventy (70), in this case seventy (70) weeks.

19

Daniel

The book of Daniel is unique from all of the other texts in the Tanak. While it is filled with prophecies, in the Hebrew Scriptures it is generally included with The Writings. In most modern Bibles, it is located in The Prophets.[133] Therefore, this is a unique text which straddles both The Writings and The Prophets. As a result, this text will be treated separate from the others.

Read the following account at the beginning of Daniel: "*¹ In the third year of the reign of Jehoiakim king of Yahudah, Nebuchadnezzar king of Babylon came to Jerusalem and besieged it. ² And YHWH gave Jehoiakim king of Yahudah into his hand, with some of the articles of the House of Elohim, which he carried into the land of Shinar to the house of his god; and he brought the articles into the treasure house of his god. ³ Then the king instructed Ashpenaz, the master of his eunuchs, to bring some of the children of Yisrael and some of the king's descendants and some of the nobles, ⁴ young men in whom there was no blemish, but good-looking, gifted in all wisdom, possessing knowledge and quick to understand, who had ability to serve in the king's palace, and whom they might teach the language and literature of the Chaldeans. ⁶ Among these were some from Yahudah: Daniel, Hananiah, Mishael and Azariah. ⁷ The chief official gave them new names: to Daniel, the name Belteshazzar; to Hananiah, Shadrach; to Mishael, Meshach; and to Azariah, Abednego.*" Daniel 1:1-7.

Daniel was from the tribe of Yahudah and descended from nobility. It is important to understand that Daniel was taken into captivity by the Babylonians after the northern Kingdom of Yisrael had been taken in the Assyrian captivity.

Not unlike the House of Yisrael, the House of Yahudah was also found to be unfaithful, and the prophet Yirmeyahu prophesied the following: "*¹¹ this whole Land shall be a desolation and an astonishment, and these nations shall serve the king of Babylon seventy (70) years. ¹² Then it will*

come to pass, when seventy (70) years are completed, that I will punish the king of Babylon and that nation, the land of the Chaldeans, for their iniquity, says YHWH; and I will make it a perpetual desolation." Yirmeyahu 25:11-12.

We have already mentioned this prophecy which concerned the punishment of Babylon after the passage of seventy (70) years. There was another seventy (70) year prophecy concerning the return of Yahudah. "For thus says YHWH: After seventy (70) years are completed at Babylon, I will visit you and perform My good word toward you, and cause you to return to this place." Yirmeyahu 29:10.

These two prophecies are often considered to be the same, but they are not. They are two separate and distinct seventy (70) year prophecies. One deals with the punishment of Babylon and the other deals with the return of the House of Yahudah from exile.

True to the prophecies, the Kingdom of Yahudah was indeed conquered by the Babylonian King Nebuchadnezzar after a series of sieges and exiles that culminated in the destruction of Jerusalem. Along with the captivity of King Jehoiachin, King of the House of Yahudah, many of the royal family and nobility were forced into Nebuchadnezzar's service. Nebuchadnezzar conquered Yahudah over a period of twenty four (24) years, in which the people of Yahudah were taken captive at seven different times. In the very first captivity, four young men from Yahudah were taken named Daniel, Hananiah, Mishael and Azariah.

The Babylonian kingdom ruled by Nebuchadnezzar was not the same Babylon that was ruled by Nimrod. Some scholars refer to this empire as the 10th Dynasty of Babylon, or the Neo Babylonian Empire. New or not, it still contained the same pagan roots as old Babylon. Interestingly, the names of the four young Hebrew men mentioned in Daniel 1:6-7 all contained the Name of YHWH or the title Elohim. Once they entered into the pagan culture, they were given new names attributed to the gods of the land.

The name Daniel (דניאל) means: "El is my judge" in Hebrew. His new name Belteshazzar means: "Bel protects his life." Bel Marduk was originally the patron deity of the City of Babylon and eventually became the supreme deity of Babylonia, the sun god. Bel Marduk was credited with bringing order to an otherwise chaotic universe, and his exploits are described in the ancient text known as the Enuma Elish.

The name Haniniyah (חנניה) means: "Yah has favored" in Hebrew. His new name Shadrach means: "command of Aku." Aku was the Sumerian moon god.

The name Mishael (מישאל) means: "Who is El" in Hebrew. His new name Meshach means: "Who is Aku" and it was clearly in direct opposition to his Hebrew name.

The name Azaryah (עזריה) means: "Yah has helped" in Hebrew. His new name Abednego means: "Servent of Nego." Nego, also known as Nebo and Nabu, was the Babylonian god of wisdom, and worshipped as the son of Marduk. Thus he was the "son of god" to the Babylonians. His mother was a moon goddess Sarpanit, often depicted as being pregnant, and is considered to be the same goddess as Easter (Ishtar).

Imagine being a Torah observant Yisraelite who serves YHWH, given a name exalting an abominable pagan god. The objective was to snuff out the remembrance of the god of the captives, in this case YHWH, and enforce the worship of the victor's gods.

Despite the fact that these individuals were captives, the Scriptures record that Daniel greatly excelled in Babylon. *"17 As for these four young men, Elohim gave them knowledge and skill in all literature and wisdom; and Daniel had understanding in all visions and dreams. 18 Now at the end of the days, when the king had said that they should be brought in, the chief of the eunuchs brought them in before Nebuchadnezzar. 19 Then the king interviewed them, and among them all none was found like Daniel, Hananiah, Mishael, and Azariah; therefore they served before the king. 20 And in all matters of wisdom and understanding about which the king examined them, he found them ten times better than all the magicians and astrologers who were in all his realm. 21 Thus Daniel continued until the first year of King Cyrus."* Daniel 1:17-21.

In the tradition of Joseph, Daniel was taken to a foreign power and served in the court of the King. He also had the ability to interpret dreams and visions, although in the case of Daniel – he was also able to tell the king what he had dreamed – not just interpret the dreams.

As a result of his skills, Daniel was greatly elevated in the Babylonian Empire. He experienced great favor, esteem and power in the Babylonian Empire and was given the governorship of the province of Babylon, and the head-inspectorship of the sacerdotal caste, which consisted of the scholars, educators and scientists, including the astrologers, astronomers, magicians, sorcerers, priests and the like, also known as Magi or wise men.

Later, when the Medo-Persians conquered the Babylonians, Daniel continued his administratorship in that Empire as well. He was given the unique responsibility of being the principal administrator of two world empires - not something many people can put on their

resume.

One of the titles given to Daniel was Rab HarTumaya (חרטמיא
רב) - the Chief of the Magicians. When he continued in this role, a
Hebrew from nobility functioning in a traditional hereditary Median
priesthood, it resulted in the plot which got him thrown in the lion's
den from which he was miraculously delivered. (see Daniel 6).

As a result of his prominence in both the Babylonian and
Medo-Persian empires, Daniel likely had great riches, although he
was a eunuch with no descendants. The use of eunuchs in the king's
service was a common and barbarous custom in the oriental courts, but
it begs the question: What happened to the wealth of this man who
had no progeny? That is a question that we will investigate further, but
for now we must examine the religious culture of Babylon and Media
Persian cultures.

Daniel was immersed in a culture that worshipped gods, and
sons of gods, and he was actually in charge of the pagan priests. Again,
this is very similar to what we saw with Joseph. These patriarchs did
not try to change the cultures in which they lived, yet they stood true
to their principles.

A good example of that can be found in an incident involving
Shadrach, Meshach and Abednego. They refused to worship the idol of
gold set up by the King and were thrown into a blazing furnace. Their
testimony to the King was as follows: "*16 O Nebuchadnezzar, we do not
need to defend ourselves before you in this matter. 17 If we are thrown into the
blazing furnace, the Elohim we serve is able to save us from it, and He will
rescue us from your hand, O king. 18 But even if He does not, we want you to
know, O king, that we will not serve your gods or worship the image of gold
you have set up.*" Daniel 3:16-18.

The three were thrown in the fire, but they were not harmed. A
fourth figure appeared in the fire and the King proclaimed: "*Look . . . I
see four men loose, walking in the midst of the fire; and they are not hurt, and
the form of the fourth is like the Son of Elohim.*" Daniel 3:25.

As a result of this event, the King exalted Shadrach, Meshach
and Adednego as well as their Elohim. One cannot ignore the Messianic
implications of the statement of the King. There was no other Elohim
that could deliver from fire. While YHWH once judged the planet by
water, He will one day judge by fire. Only YHWH will be able to
deliver His people from the fiery judgment that will one day come upon
this planet. (Yeshayahu 66).

Along with the recognition and elevation of YHWH in the
Babylonian Kingdom, it must have been known that there was a

seventy (70) year judgment pronounced over the King of Babylon that was looming on the horizon. This leads to another significant event involving a Babylonian King named Belshazzar who reigned during that period of time when the punishment was scheduled to occur.

For many years scholars could not confirm the existence of any such King in the Babylonian records. "It was not until 1853 CE that archaeological evidence was unearthed which indicated that Belshazzar was a co-regent and son of Nabonidus. Until that time Nabonidus was considered to be reigning alone as the last king of Babylon by secular historians. This find, a small tablet currently located in the Yale Babylonian collection, provided archaeological evidence for the story of Belshazzar in Daniel 5:1-31.

Belshazzar was made co-regent of his father Nabonidus in the third year of Nabonidus. Father and son ruled together until Babylon was conquered by the Medo-Persian empire. Nabonidus ruled from Tema as King, while Belshazzar ruled from Babylon as a crown prince. This perfectly agrees with the account in Daniel 5:16 where Belshazzar offered to make Daniel the third highest ruler in the Kingdom if he could interpret the writing on the wall."[134]

With that understanding, let us examine the incident. *"¹ King Belshazzar gave a great banquet for a thousand of his nobles and drank wine with them. ² While Belshazzar was drinking his wine, he gave orders to bring in the gold and silver goblets that Nebuchadnezzar his father had taken from the Temple in Jerusalem, so that the king and his nobles, his wives and his concubines might drink from them. ³ So they brought in the gold goblets that had been taken from the temple of Elohim in Jerusalem, and the king and his nobles, his wives and his concubines drank from them. ⁴ As they drank the wine, they praised the gods of gold and silver, of bronze, iron, wood and stone. ⁵ Suddenly the fingers of a man's hand appeared and wrote on the plaster of the wall, near the lampstand in the royal palace. The king watched the hand as it wrote. ⁶ His face turned pale and he was so frightened that his knees knocked together and his legs gave way."* Daniel 5:1-6.

The banquet being described was a huge affair with a very specific purpose. It seems quite apparent that the purpose of this feast is in defiance of the Elohim of Yisrael. Not only were the implements of the Temple profaned, false gods were praised while the implements were being used. Interestingly, the predecessors of Belshazzar had a healthy respect for YHWH, a lesson he should have learned. This was made abundantly clear when Daniel was eventually called to interpret the handwriting after no one else in the Kingdom was able to do so. Here is what he told the King:

"*18 O king, the Most High Elah gave your father Nebuchadnezzar sovereignty and greatness and glory and splendor. 19 Because of the high position He gave him, all the peoples and nations and men of every language dreaded and feared him. Those the king wanted to put to death, he put to death; those he wanted to spare, he spared; those he wanted to promote, he promoted; and those he wanted to humble, he humbled. 20 But when his heart became arrogant and hardened with pride, he was deposed from his royal throne and stripped of his glory. 21 He was driven away from people and given the mind of an animal; he lived with the wild donkeys and ate grass like cattle; and his body was drenched with the dew of heaven, until he acknowledged that the Most High Elah is sovereign over the kingdoms of men and sets over them anyone he wishes. 22 But you his son, O Belshazzar, have not humbled yourself, though you knew all this. 23 Instead, you have set yourself up against the Master of heaven. You had the goblets from His Temple brought to you, and you and your nobles, your wives and your concubines drank wine from them. You praised the gods of silver and gold, of bronze, iron, wood and stone, which cannot see or hear or understand. But you did not honor the Elohim who holds in His Hand your life and all your ways. 24 Therefore He sent the Hand that wrote the inscription. 25 This is the inscription that was written: MENE, MENE, TEKEL, PARSIN 26 This is what these words mean: Mene: Elohim has numbered the days of your reign and brought it to an end. 27 Tekel: You have been weighed on the scales and found wanting. 28 Peres: Your kingdom is divided and given to the Medes and Persians. 29 Then at Belshazzar's command, Daniel was clothed in purple, a gold chain was placed around his neck, and he was proclaimed the third highest ruler in the kingdom. 30 That very night Belshazzar, king of the Babylonians, was slain, 31 and Darius the Mede took over the kingdom, at the age of sixty-two." Daniel 5:18-31.*

It appears that Belshazzar might have been holding this particular feast because he believed that the seventy (70) year prophecy of Yirmeyahu 29:10 had not been fulfilled. This prophecy stated that after seventy (70) years of captivity for Yahudah were accomplished, YHWH would cause Yahudah to return to Jerusalem. Belshazzar determined that this prophecy had not been fulfilled, and thereby decided there was no reason to fear YHWH.

However, YHWH never had any intention of fulfilling the prophecy of Yirmeyahu 29:10 at this time. Rather, it was the design of YHWH to fulfill the prophecy of Yirmeyahu 25:12-14 at this time in which, after seventy (70) years of Yahudah's captivity, Babylon would become a perpetual desolation.[135]

Remember, Yirmeyahu prophesied: "*12 when the seventy (70) years are fulfilled, I will punish the king of Babylon and his nation, the land of* the Babylonians, for their guilt, declares YHWH, and will make it desolate forever. [13] I will bring upon that land all the things I have spoken against it, all that are written in this book and prophesied by Yirmeyahu against all the nations. [14] They themselves will be enslaved by many nations and great kings; I will repay them according to their deeds and the work of their hands." Yirmeyahu 25:12-14.

The prophecy indicated that Yahudah would serve for seventy (70) years and the King of Babylon would then be punished. Since there were seven (7) different captivities which began in seven (7) different years over a twenty-four (24) year period, according to Daniel 1:1 and Yirmeyahu 52:30, there were many ways which YHWH could fulfill His word.

Belshazzar may have been applying an incorrect start date for the seventy (70) year prophecy of Yirmeyahu 25:12-14. That prophecy was obviously fulfilled when Belshazzar was overthrown, and his defeat was directly related to punishment by YHWH on Nabonidus.

It is important to remember that there were two different seventy (70) year prophecies. One, involving the punishment of Babylon, was fulfilled after the interpretation of the handwriting by Daniel. The second, concerning the return of Yahudah, had obviously not yet occurred. As a result, we later read how Daniel pondered the matter of the second seventy (70) year prophecy. He knew that the prophecy had been given, and therefore the matter should be discernable. He had witnessed the fulfillment of the first seventy (70) year prophecy, and he wanted to know when the second seventy (70) years would be concluded which would mark the end of the punishment of the House of Yahudah.

This is the hallmark of Daniel - time and knowledge of the occurrence of important specific events. We read about his important inquiry concerning the seventy (70) years in Chapter 9 of the Book of Daniel which begins as follows: "[1] In the first year of Darius son of Ahasuerus (a Mede by descent), who was made ruler over the Babylonian kingdom [2] in the first year of his reign, I, Daniel, understood from the Scriptures, according to the Word of YHWH given to Yirmeyahu the prophet, that the desolation of Jerusalem would last seventy years. [3] So I turned to YHWH Elohim and pleaded with Him in prayer and petition, in fasting, and in sackcloth and ashes." Daniel 9:1-3.

The Medes and the Persians were now in control of the Babylonian Kingdom, and Daniel remained powerful in that Kingdom as well. We are told that it was during the first year of Darius the Mede, son of Ahasuerus, that Daniel made this plea to YHWH.

Daniel "understood" that what he observed occur was a fulfillment of Yirmeyahu's prophecy, and he wanted to know when his people would return. Daniel proceded to confess to YHWH, and acknowledge, that the punishments which beset his people were a direct result of their failure to obey the Torah of YHWH, and because of their failure to repent. Daniel then petitioned YHWH not to delay to restore His people and Jerusalem.

Daniel recounts the following answer to his petition: "*²⁰ Now while I was speaking, praying, and confessing my sin and the sin of my people Yisrael, and presenting my supplication before YHWH my Elohay for the holy mountain of my Elohay, ²¹ yes, while I was speaking in prayer, the man Gabriel, whom I had seen in the vision at the beginning, being caused to fly swiftly, reached me <u>about the time of the evening offering</u>. ²² And he informed me, and talked with me, and said, O Daniel, <u>I have now come forth to give you skill to understand</u>. ²³ <u>At the beginning of your supplications the command went out</u>, and I have come to tell you, for you are greatly beloved; therefore consider the matter, and understand the vision: ²⁴ <u>Seventy weeks are determined for your people and for your holy city, to finish the transgression, to make an end of sins, to make reconciliation for iniquity, to bring in everlasting righteousness, to seal up vision and prophecy, and to anoint the Most Holy. ²⁵ Know therefore and understand, that from the going forth of the command to restore and build Jerusalem until Messiah the Prince, there shall be seven weeks and sixty-two weeks; the street shall be built again, and the wall, even in troublesome times. ²⁶ And after the sixty-two weeks Messiah shall be cut off, but not for Himself; and the people of the prince who is to come shall destroy the city and the sanctuary. The end of it shall be with a flood, and till the end of the war desolations are determined.</u> ²⁷ Then he shall confirm a covenant with many for one week; but in the middle of the week he shall bring an end to slaughtering and meal offering. And on the wing of abominations shall be one who makes desolate, even until the consummation, which is determined, is poured out on the desolate.*" Daniel 9:20-27.

We know that the evening offering occurred immediately after sunset, so Daniel continued to offer up prayer and praise at this important time of day despite the absence of a Temple. When the messenger Gabriel appeared, he gave Daniel skill to understand. Then he provided Daniel, not only a time frame for the appearance of the Messiah, but a detailed list of items that the Messiah was to accomplish.

He provided Daniel with a framework of seventy (70) "weeks" in which these matters would be concluded. In Hebrew we read shavuyim shavuyim (שבעים שבעים). If you took away all vowel markings these words are exactly the same. The text actually reads "seventy sevens." These periods of sevens are then further divided into seven "weeks," sixty two "weeks" and one "week" providing a total of seventy "weeks."

People have poured over these numbers for centuries wondering about their meaning. There are a variety of issues that need to be resolved to understand this passage, including the starting point. One very important question is: When was the going forth of the command or word? Was it the petition of Daniel, was it the command from heaven that resulted from Daniel's request, or was it some decree made by a ruler?

Also how do we deal with these various periods of time? Are they the same lengths or are they different? It is generally understood that the "weeks" are seven (7) year periods, but if Gabriel had wanted to give Daniel a number of years he could have simply told him 49 years, 436 years and 7 years. He was obviously telling Daniel a mystery that needed skill to understand. What takes understanding is the fact that these seven year periods were not just arbitrary seven (7) year periods – they were likely Shemitah years or rather Shemitah cycles.

The command concerning the Shemitah year is provided in the Torah. "¹⁰ For six years you are to sow your fields and harvest the crops, ¹¹ but during the seventh year let the Land lie unplowed and unused. Then the poor among your people may get food from it, and the wild animals may eat what they leave. Do the same with your vineyard and your olive grove." Shemot 23:10-11 (see also Devarim 15).

Every seventh year the Yisraelites were supposed to let the Land rest. Thus, there was a Sabbath for the Land every seven years. Just as the seven day count began at creation, so too did the seven (7) year Shemitah count. The Shemitah year would begin on the first day of the seventh month on Yom Teruah, which marks the beginning of physical Creation. From this day until the following Yom Teruah there would be no official harvest.

This cycle of sevens would occur within another cycle of sevens – The Jubilee Cycle. At the end of the seventh Shemitah year there would be a 9 day period between Yom Teruah until Yom Kippur, which would mark the beginning of the Jubilee Year – the Fiftieth year.

Amazingly, Yisrael failed to obey the command concerning the Shemitah year, and that was the reason why Yahudah was in exile for seventy (70) years. YHWH was giving His Land the rest that He commanded. (2 Chronicles 36:21).

Now it is important to recognize that these Shemitah cycles are intimately connected with the Jubilee (yovel). "¹³ For six years sow your

fields, and for six years prune your vineyards and gather their crops. ⁴ *But in the seventh year the Land is to have a Sabbath of rest, a Sabbath to YHWH. Do not sow your fields or prune your vineyards.* ⁵ *Do not reap what grows of itself or harvest the grapes of your untended vines. The Land is to have a year of rest.* ⁶ *Whatever the Land yields during the sabbath year will be food for you - for yourself, your manservant and maidservant, and the hired worker and temporary resident who live among you,* ⁷ *as well as for your livestock and the wild animals in your land. Whatever the Land produces may be eaten.* ⁸ *Count off seven Sabbaths of years - seven times seven years - so that the seven Sabbaths of years amount to a period of forty-nine years.* ⁹ *Then have the shofar sounded everywhere on the tenth day of the seventh month; on the Day of Atonement sound the shofar throughout your Land.* ¹⁰ *Consecrate the fiftieth year and proclaim liberty throughout the land to all its inhabitants. It shall be a jubilee for you; each one of you is to return to his family property and each to his own clan.* ¹¹ *The fiftieth year shall be a jubilee for you; do not sow and do not reap what grows of itself or harvest the untended vines.* ¹² *For it is a jubilee and is to be holy for you; eat only what is taken directly from the fields.*" Vayiqra 25:3-12.

The imagery of the Jubilee is reminiscent of the Feast of Shabuot, sometimes refered to as Pentecost. Shabuot involves this same count in days, and it occurs every year to remind us of the Jubilee. With that foundation being laid, let us now look at various aspects of the seventy (70) week prophecy and see if we can discern just what and when Gabriel is referring to. First we will view the information from the perspective that this is a purely Messianic prophecy then we will look at another alternative.

From the information given to Daniel by Gabriel, we discern that there is a command issued "to restore and rebuild Jerusalem." We further know that from the issuance of that command until Messiah the prince shall be seven sevens and sixty two sevens. These sevens may actually be referring to Shemitah cycles. We are further told that "*after the sixty-two weeks Messiah shall be cut off, but not for Himself.*" Sometime after the Messiah is "cut off" the city and the Temple would be destroyed.

Therefore, according to Gabriel, we should be looking at a cycle consisting of a period of time multiplied by seven (7), which should lead us either to Shabuot, a cycle of days, or the Jubilee year count, a cycle of years. We should also be focusing on a period of time consisting of sixty-two (62) multiplied by seven (7).

For the clock to begin, we need to look for the specific word or decree that was issued concerning restoring and rebuilding Jerusalem, not simply the Temple. This would obviously be linked with the end of the seventy (70) year period of exile which was the very reason why Daniel was praying in the first place. As was already discussed you might consider that Daniel's petition was that word or even the response to his petition – the answer to his prayer.

There is also very specific information in the Scriptures concerning a governmental decree which seems to meet the criteria. We read in Ezra the following account: "¹ *Now in the first year of Cyrus king of Persia, that the Word of YHWH by the mouth of Yirmeyahu might be fulfilled, YHWH stirred up the spirit of Cyrus king of Persia, so that he made a proclamation throughout all his kingdom, and also put it in writing, saying,* ² '*Thus says Cyrus king of Persia: All the kingdoms of the Earth YHWH Elohim of heaven has given me. And He has commanded me to build Him a House at Jerusalem which is in Yahudah.* ³ *Who is among you of all His people? May his Elohim be with him, and let him go up to Jerusalem which is in Yahudah, and build the House of YHWH, Elohim of Yisrael (He is Elohim), which is in Jerusalem.* ⁴ *And whoever is left in any place where he dwells, let the men of his place help him with silver and gold, with goods and livestock, besides the freewill offerings for the house of Elohim which is in Jerusalem.* ⁵ *Then the heads of the fathers' Houses of Yahudah and Benjamin, and the priests and the Levites, with all whose spirits Elohim had moved, arose to go up and build the House of YHWH which is in Jerusalem.* ⁶ *And all those who were around them encouraged them with articles of silver and gold, with goods and livestock, and with precious things, besides all that was willingly offered.* ⁷ *King Cyrus also brought out the articles of the house of YHWH, which Nebuchadnezzar had taken from Jerusalem and put in the temple of his gods;* ⁸ *and Cyrus king of Persia brought them out by the hand of Mithredath the treasurer, and counted them out to Sheshbazzar the prince of Yahudah.*" Ezra 1:1-8.*

This decree of Cyrus to return and rebuild the House was issued in the first year of his reign. What an amazing event, the King of a pagan nation declared YHWH to be Elohim. He then took on the responsibility of rebuilding the House of YHWH, returning all of the treasures which had been taken from the House and allowing the captives of Yahudah to return to their Land.

Notice that it was only those from the Tribes of Yahudah, Benjamin and the Levites who returned, because these were the Tribes that constituted the House of Yahudah which had been taken captive by the Babylonians. The other tribes from the House of Yisrael had been removed from the Land and taken by the Assyrians who moved them into the regions of the north. They were not scheduled to return

to the Land as their punishment was not completed according to the prophet Yehezqel.[136]

The issuance of the decree of Cyrus was no doubt a wonderful part of the fulfillment of the second seventy (70) year prophecy by allowing the Yahudim to return. Regardless, they still had a long and difficult road ahead of them. Over time, the decree lost its force, until it was later found by Darius, the successor of Cyrus who reissued the decree and advanced funds to finish the House.

As a result of these different decrees and because of the funding problems, the rebuilding of the Altar and the Temple experienced great delays and was fraught with difficulties. Seventy years passed from the original decree to rebuild the Second Temple by Cyrus, to its completion under Darius. It was during this period that we read certain prophets such as Haggai and Zekaryah giving encouragement and direction to those who returned.

We know from historical records that while the original decree was given in the first year of Cyrus, there were numerous subsequent decrees that followed. So the question is which one of those decrees, if any, would start the count on Daniel's seventy weeks.

The answer is none, because all of them were tied specifically with the Temple, but the decree we are looking for involved rebuilding Jerusalem. There was a decree that was issued after the Persians took control of the Medo-Persian Empire. This decree was issued by the Persian King Artaxerxes in the seventh year of his reign. Here is the decree as provided in the text of Ezra.

"*7 Some of the Yisraelites, including priests, Levites, singers, gatekeepers and Temple servants, also came up to Jerusalem in the seventh year of King Artaxerxes. 8 Ezra arrived in Jerusalem in the fifth month of the seventh year of the king. 9 He had begun his journey from Babylon on the first day of the first month, and he arrived in Jerusalem on the first day of the fifth month, for the gracious Hand of his Elohim was on him. 10 For Ezra had devoted himself to the study and observance of the Torah of YHWH, and to teaching its decrees and laws in Yisrael. 11 This is a copy of the letter King Artaxerxes had given to Ezra the priest and teacher, a man learned in matters concerning the commands and decrees of YHWH for Yisrael: 12 Artaxerxes, king of kings, To Ezra the priest, a teacher of the Law of the Elah of heaven: Greetings. 13 Now I decree that any of the Yisraelites in my kingdom, including priests and Levites, who wish to go to Jerusalem with you, may go. 14 You are sent by the king and his seven advisers to inquire about Yahudah and Jerusalem with regard to the Torah of your Elah,* which is in your hand. ¹⁵ Moreover, you are to take with you the silver and gold that the king and his advisers have freely given to the Elah of Yisrael, whose dwelling is in Jerusalem, ¹⁶ together with all the silver and gold you may obtain from the province of Babylon, as well as the freewill offerings of the people and priests for the Temple of their Elah in Jerusalem. ¹⁷ With this money be sure to buy bulls, rams and male lambs, together with their grain offerings and drink offerings, and sacrifice them on the altar of the Temple of your Elah in Jerusalem. ¹⁸ You and your brother Yahudim may then do whatever seems best with the rest of the silver and gold, in accordance with the will of your Elah. ¹⁹ Deliver to the Elah of Jerusalem all the articles entrusted to you for worship in the Temple of your Elah. ²⁰ And anything else needed for the Temple of your Elah that you may have occasion to supply, you may provide from the royal treasury. ²¹ Now I, King Artaxerxes, order all the treasurers of Trans-Euphrates to provide with diligence whatever Ezra the priest, a teacher of the Torah of the Elah of heaven, may ask of you - ²² up to a hundred talents of silver, a hundred cors of wheat, a hundred baths of wine, a hundred baths of olive oil, and salt without limit. ²³ Whatever the Elah of heaven has prescribed, let it be done with diligence for the Temple of the Elah of heaven. Why should there be wrath against the realm of the king and of his sons? ²⁴ You are also to know that you have no authority to impose taxes, tribute or duty on any of the priests, Levites, singers, gatekeepers, Temple servants or other workers at this house of Elah. ²⁵ And you, Ezra, in accordance with the wisdom of your Elah, which you possess, appoint magistrates and judges to administer justice to all the people of Trans-Euphrates - all who know the laws of your Elah. And you are to teach any who do not know them. ²⁶ Whoever does not obey the laws of your Elah and the law of the king must surely be punished by death, banishment, confiscation of property, or imprisonment." Ezra 7:12-26.

Despite this great decree given to Ezra, they still experienced problems which led to more delays and this is why we read about Nehemiah requesting help from this same king. One day the King noticed that the countenance of Nehemiah, his cup bearer, was down and he inquired regarding the problem. Nehemiah responded concerning the difficulties that his people were experiencing in Jerusalem.

"⁵ If it pleases the king and if your servant has found favor in his sight, let him send me to the city in Yahudah where my fathers are buried so that I can rebuild it. ⁶ Then the king, with the queen sitting beside him, asked me, How long will your journey take, and when will you get back? It pleased the king to send me; so I set a time. ⁷ I also said to him, If it pleases the

king, may I have letters to the governors of Trans-Euphrates, so that they will provide me safe-conduct until I arrive in Yahudah? [8] And may I have a letter to Asaph, keeper of the king's forest, so he will give me timber to make beams for the gates of the citadel by the Temple and for the city wall and for the residence I will occupy? And because the gracious hand of my Elohim was upon me, the king granted my requests. [9] So I went to the governors of Trans-Euphrates and gave them the king's letters. The king had also sent army officers and cavalry with me." Nehemiah 2:5-9.

Notice that Nehemiah specifically requested to be sent "to the city" where his fathers were buried <u>so he could rebuild it</u>. (Nehemiah 2:5). That city was Jerusalem. The king granted his request, which essentially resulted in a decree. Nehemiah was given "letters," granting him safe passage and supplies to accomplish the task of rebuilding the city of Jerusalem. This decree was made in the 20th year of Artaxerxes, and it is evident that of all the decrees previously given, this was the only decree that was issued from a man that would meet the criteria of rebuilding the City of Jerusalem. Therefore, it was this decree that would start the count.

From the decree to rebuild Jerusalem in the 20th year of Artaxerxes (Nehemiah 2:1-9) until Messiah the Prince, Daniel was told there would be seven (7) weeks and sixty-two (62) weeks (Daniel 9:25). *"[25] Know and understand this: From the issuing of the decree to restore and rebuild Jerusalem until the Messiah the Prince, there will be seven sevens and sixty two sevens. It will be rebuilt with streets and a trench, but in times of trouble. [26] After the sixty-two sevens, the Annointed One will be cut off and will have nothing."* Daniel 9:25-26.

The fact that these two divisions are mentioned separately could lead one to reasonably assume that they are different time periods. They could either be different measurements of time or they simply might not be continuous.

Daniel was looking for the restoration of the City of Jerusalem, which obviously included the House of YHWH. He was asking about a literal rebuilding of the city and he was given a literal time frame. This count historically began in the 20th year of Artaxerxes according to Nehemiah 2:1-8. The double dated Elephantine Letters place Artaxerxes ascension in 465 BCE.[137]

There have been a multitude of attempts to explain this prophecy since it was first given to Daniel. As historians and scholars have failed to perfectly understand the chronology of the medo-Persian and Persian Empires, a solid historical foundation has not been laid from which to interpret the prophecy.

What can be said with certainty is that sixty-two (62) Shemitah cycles, with eight (8) intervening Jubilee years, covers a span of 443 years. All scholars would agree that 443 years, reckoned from the 20th of Artaxerxes, would bring one to around the turn of the millennium when we would anticipate seeing the Messiah.[138]

If we look at the Prophecy in Daniel we see should note that it states "*after* the sixty-two (62) *weeks Moshiach will be* cut off." Daniel 9:26. The Hebrew text uses the word "karath" (כרת) for "cut off." The word "karath" means "cut" or "covenant." Through the Prophets, YHWH revealed His plan to restore the Kingdom by His Servant, His Right Arm - the Messiah. The Covenant made with Abraham and mediated by Mosheh at Sinai had been broken by Yisrael.

Through the Covenant made with Abraham, we see that the One that passed through the pieces was subject to the penalty of death. The death of that One would atone just as was shown through the pattern of Abraham and Yitshaq. YHWH would provide the Lamb, His only Son, who would be cut off during Passover.

Therefore, the information given to Daniel was good news coupled with bad news. It started with a decree to return and rebuild, followed by the Messiah, but then the Messiah would be cut off and the City and the Temple would be destroyed.

There is also a final time period of one additional week and other layers to this prophecy. Those will be discussed in another text.[139] For the purposes of this discussion, we are interested in the date when the Messiah would be cut off and now we have it. Using a variety of methods of calculating this great mystery we are repeatedly directed to not only the turn of a century, but also the turn of a millennium.

Armed with all of this information, we must now examine that time period described in Daniel to determine if we can discover if there was any individual that meets the requirements of the Messiah. Sadly, the Hebrew Scriptures are silent during this period of history. While we can read about the return of the House of Yahudah through the books of Ezra, Nehemiah and Esther and some of the Prophets, none reach into the time of Messiah as given to Daniel.

We can read in the texts known as the Maccabees,[140] of a time after the Persian kingdom had been defeated by another world power, but they do not shed any historical light into the time period that people would be looking for Messiah.

Interestingly, besides being told when the Messiah would come, Daniel was also shown the successive empires that would rule that region of the world – one of them being Alexander the Great.

Alexander is important because he is responsible for bringing about a transformation of the societies which he conquered through a practice referred to as Hellenism.

20

Hellenism

As was already discussed, Daniel was a unique individual. He was alive and taken captive when the House of Yahudah was conquered by the Babylonians and removed from the Land. He was also alive when the Medes and the Persians defeated the Babylonians and then permitted the House of Yahudim to return to the Land.

Like Joseph, he was forcibly brought to a great nation as a slave and rose to power in that Empire. Both Joseph and Daniel were given visions and they both were able to interpret visions of the kings which led to their success. The similarities between these two men is no coincidence and they both have deep Messianic significance. Remember that the greatest achievement in Joseph's rise was his ability to interpret dreams involving seven year periods.[141]

The life of Joseph provides many patterns for the Messiah while Daniel was unique because he was given specific dates concerning the coming of the Messiah. He also lived in the midst of the transfer of power between the Babylonian Empire and the Medo-Persian Empire. He was also given a vision concerning the powers that would reign throughout history, including the transfer of power between Babylon and Medo-Persian Empire. Those Kingdoms ruled just as Daniel was shown, and he actually provided the bad news of the demise of the Babylonian Kingdom the night that it occurred. As a result, he was evelated to the third most powerful person in the Kingdom of Babylon.

When the Babylonian Kingdom came to an end, Daniel excelled in the Medo-Persian Empire. During that time, Daniel was given a vision concerning future world powers to come. "5 . . . *suddenly a goat with a prominent horn between his eyes came from the west, crossing the whole earth without touching the ground. 6 He came toward the two-horned ram I had seen standing beside the canal and charged at him in great rage. 7 I saw him attack the ram furiously, striking the ram and shattering his two*

horns. *The ram was powerless to stand against him; the goat knocked him to the ground and trampled on him, and none could rescue the ram from his power.* [8] *The goat became very great, but at the height of his power his large horn was broken off, and in its place four prominent horns grew up toward the four winds of heaven.*" Daniel 8:5-8.

The next world power in the vision given to Daniel was described as a goat, and the interpretation of the vision was, once again, given by Gabriel as follows: "[21] *The he-goat is the king of Greece; and the great horn between his eyes is the first king.* [22] *As for the horn that was broken, in place of which four others arose, four kingdoms shall arise from his nation, but will not have the same power.*" Daniel 8:21-22.

The "he goat" was none other than Alexander the Great. Alexander was unique because of the profound impact that he had upon the cultures which he conquered. He did not simply defeat a population and dominate them, rather he merged them into the collective Grecian culture through a process called Hellenization.

As a result, a conquered people could continue to worship their own gods and they would also be introduced to foreign gods. Sometimes similar gods would be merged and what we see occurring is a sort of reversal of what happened at Babel. Mankind was reuniting under a common language and unified pagan culture.

Hellenism was the ultimate tolerant system because it embraced new and different religions and included them under the umbrella of this new Grecian culture. Prior to Alexander there was no unified Greece. Rather, in the Mediterranean region there were different city states individually known as a polis. These people were unique although they also had much in common. At times they would unify for a common purpose, such as a common enemy, while at other times they would fight among each other.

Alexander III was born at Pelia in the year 356 BCE. He was a Macedonian, the son of Philip II who was king, or rather Basileus, of

Macedon. Alexander succeeded his father to the throne in 336 BCE at the age of 20 and died in Babylon in 323 BCE at the age of 32. In his brief 12 year reign he managed to conquer and transform the civilized world as we know it.

His father, Philip, had previously succeeded in uniting most of the mainland city states of Greece under Macedonian hegemony in the League of Corinth. This set the stage for Alexander to lead the unified armies of this Grecian coalition after quelling various

internal revolts. With this experienced army under his command, Alexander was able to conquer the Persian King Darius III and the entire Persian Empire in 330 BCE.

While Alexander is considered to be one of the greatest military commanders in history, it was his impact upon culture that would have the most lasting and enduring legacy. While his father was clearly the influence on his military abilities and accomplishments, it can be strongly argued that his mother, Olympias of Epirus, was responsible for his cultural impact.

While the Epirites descended from the same Hellenic tribes, they lived in smaller rural villages rather than the polis city states of the Southern Greeks. Religion was a powerful cultural force for the Epirites with Zeus at the center of it all. The religious impact of Epirus was significant due to the presence of the shrine and the oracle of Dodona, which was regarded as second only to the oracle at Delphi.

It is important to understand that the so-called Greek gods were derived from various fables, myths and stories which were quite varied and lack any degree of uniformity. There were numerous gods and goddesses all with different origins and characteristics. One such god with varied and mixed historical accounts was Dionysus.

Olympia was "said to be a priestess of Dionysus who led her followers in orgiastic rites in which snakes apparently played a major part. One ancient author wrote of her habit of taking tame snakes out of baskets of ivy and 'allowing them to curl themselves around the thyrsis of the woman so as to terrify the men.' It is said that Phillip eventually became so nervous about his wife's religious  observances that his affection cooled, and he 'seldom came to sleep with her.'"[142]

Some believe that Dionysus was a late arrival into Greek mythology due to the minimal references by Homer, and his absence from the Olympian Pantheon. Nevertheless, his worship was quite influential in the Greek culture, especially when he became the patron god of the theater, which likely boosted his popularity and influence. Also, the fact that his worship was closely linked to wine and drunkedness did not hurt his appeal.

Dionysus was considered to be the son of Zeus. Zeus was the chief god in the Greek pantheon and his mother was a mortal woman named Semele. Thus Dionysus was a son of god, born from a mortal

woman. He was associated with fertility rites and particularly wine. He was later morphed into the Roman god Bacchus who is displayed as dying on a cross. Adherents to Dionysian worship would become intoxicated and partake in sexual orgies. "Dionysus was a savior god who . . . died and rose from the dead. The Dionysians believed in rewards in Heaven and punishments in Hell. They believed in salvation through repentance and baptism for the remission of sins. They practiced the rituals of communion and baptism."[143]

Alexander was inspired by the writings of Homer, and we see that these writings became a framework for the Hellenistic religious systems, as well as later writers such as Plutarch, who wrote about The Contendings of Horus and Seth. Many older myths were morphed and renamed into Hellenism and of course this is at the core of Hellenistic culture – "The Collective."

Thus Hellenization involved a blending of Grecian culture with other cultures in the middle and near east. A major part of the

Grecian culture which was spread included their pagan system of worship, and it was through this syncretism that the Canaanite god Baal, the Egyptian god Amon, and the Persian god Ahura Mazda became identified with the Greek sun god Zeus and the Roman sun god Jupiter.

Likewise, the Canaanite goddess Astarte (also known as Easter) and the Persian goddess Anahita (also known as Anaitis) became identified with the Greek goddess Aphrodite or the Roman goddess Venus. Through this blending process, many similarities developed between the gods and goddesses of the pagan cultures, parallels developed which led to continuity and consistency. What developed was a religious melting pot with religious tolerance and general acceptance of all gods.

Because of Alexander's affection for Homer and the popular mythologies, his invasion of Asia minor was considered to be another Trojan War. "[T]he first thing Alexander did at Troy was to pay an act of homage to Achilles, who was initially his heroic prototype. Later, Heracles, a hero who became a god in virtue of his achievements, filled this role. Alexander was also connected to Dionysus, whom the Greeks believed came from Asia and who became "the god" of the Greek expansion into the middle east, receiving the greatest amount of personal devotion in the Hellenistic kingdoms. Alexander held a

Dionysiac celebration at Nysa where, according to tradition, Dionysus was born. This religious emphasis was characteristic of Alexander. He gave his own adhesion to Zeus, and religious acts . . . were not antiquarian features for him."[144]

Thus, it could be said that the cult of Dionysus was one of the chief beneficiaries of Alexander's expansionism. As Alexander went on to conquer the Persians and expand his empire, he spread Hellenism and Dionysus worship throughout the Mediterranean and beyond, although Dionysus certainly was not the only Greek god promulgated through Hellenism.

Hellenistic cultures could aptly be described as pagan or polytheistic. They included a variety of gods who all had various personalities and "specialties" if you will. In typical pagan fashion these gods represented different aspects of the spiritual and the natural realm and had various strengths and powers, as well as weaknesses.

Greek mythology could be described as one big mythical soap opera involving love affairs, wars, feasts, triumph and tragedy all acted out by an array of gods, goddesses and some select men and women. Temples, altars and shrines were littered throughout the Greek territory as well as those lands which were conquered. Therefore, along with the Greek language and culture went their gods, which were easily adaptable to the local gods of the conquered people who were primarily polytheistic and pagan themselves.

This especially posed a problem for those from the House of Yahudah who had previously returned to the Promised Land, as we read about in the books of Nehemiah and Ezra. After all, they were considered to be "atheists" because they worshipped only one Elohim – YHWH. As a result, they were considered to be "without the gods." Polytheism, which is the belief in many gods, stands diametrically opposed to monotheism, which is the belief in a single god.

The Yahudim had only one Temple in one city, which was the House of YHWH. This stands in stark contrast to the Hellenists who had a variety of temples for a variety of gods in all of their communities, especially the larger cities. Not all of the Yahudim were able to resist the influence of Hellenism which spread into the Land through the expansionism of Alexander. Many were attracted and influenced by its allure. This was similar to how much of the modern world is currently drawn to aspects of western culture such as music, television, movies, sports and entertainment.

The typical Hellenized community would consist of an array of temples dedicated to the worship of different gods or goddesses. They

also would include a "gymnasium" where people would exercise and compete in the nude. The name comes from the Greek term *gymnos* meaning "naked." The primary purpose for being in a gymnasium was to be in the nude, and it would therefore become very apparent who was an uncircumcised Gentile and who was a circumcised Yisraelite.

The gymnasiums were directly linked to pagan temple worship which typically involved fornication, sacrifices and eating. Therefore, the gymnasiums and pagan temples in Hellenistic cultures became the center of most social activity.

We see the convergence of religion and athletics in the Olympic games which were enhanced and expanded throughout Hellenized cultures. They are rooted in paganism and their very core was religious in nature. They were held every four years, beginning on the second or third full moon after the summer solstice, not unlike those held in modern times. They were actually a religious festival held at major temple sites, and they derive their name from the most famous - Olympia.

The activities would all occur in and around pagan temples and shrines and the various athletic contests were intermixed with sacrifices and ceremonies honoring Zeus, the sun god and Pelops, the hero and mythical king of Olympia. All of the athletes trained and competed naked, offering their bodies to the glory of Zeus. Before the games began, a priest would sacrifice a bull in front of all of the participants who took an oath to Zeus. These games were so pervasive that they even affected the Temple service in Jerusalem, as priests neglected their duties to view and participate in the activities.

During the apex of Greek influence the priests of the Jerusalem Temple would sometimes leave the sacrifices half-burned on the altar to rush off to a stadium to compete in the Greek games.

We actually read about this conduct in the Book of Maccabees: ' . . . the priests were no longer intent upon their service at the altar. Despising the sanctuary and neglecting the sacrifices, they hastened to take part in the unlawful proceedings in the wrestling arena after the call to the discus, disdaining the honors prized by their fathers and putting the highest value upon Greek forms of prestige.' (2 Maccabees 4:14-15 RSV)."[145]

It should be evident that Hellenism and its accompanying

lifestyle are generally offensive to the Torah and those who follow YHWH. It is important to understand this culture which permeated the Promised Land after Alexander the Great conquered the Land. It not only influenced the Yaduhim who lived in the Land, but also the majority who did not return to the Land from exile.

As a result, despite the miraculous decrees from the Persian Kings to return and rebuild, the Yahudim, the Temple and the City of Jerusalem were in a very bad state spiritually from Hellenism. This cultural phenomenon affected and infiltrated the Yahudim throughout the Mediterranean region where they had been exiled. This occurred during the life of Alexander and beyond. While Alexander lived a very brief life, his impact was far reaching in both time and space.

On or about June 12, 323 BCE, Alexander died in the palace of Nebuchadnezzar II, in Babylon. This was quite appropriate because, one could argue, he was responsible for completing the cycle which had begun in Babylon thousands of years earlier. While sun worship had been scattered and languages had been confused originally at Babylon, Alexander had begun a process of merging these varied pagan traditions under one umbrella and one language – the Greek Language.

After the death of Alexander and the assassination of his supposed successor Perdiccas in 321 BCE, the united Maccedonean Kingdom that he had so amazingly united collapsed. This kingdom entered into a 40 year period of war between the successors, known as the *Diadochi*. This conflict eventually resulted in the Hellenistic world settling into 4 stable power blocks: 1) the Ptolemaic kingdom of Egypt, 2) the Seleucid Empire in the east, 3) the kingdom of Pergamon in Asia minor, and 4) Macedon – precisely as foretold to Daniel.

Not all of the successors continued the Hellenistic policies of Alexander, although the Seleucid Empire that ruled over the Land of Yisrael aggressively continued the Hellenization of their territory. The Seleucids experienced significant conflict with the Ptolemies to the west and the Parthians to the east as well as other tribes and surrounding powers. The Kingdom experienced a decline until a brief resurgence when Antiochus III the Great took the throne in 222 BCE.

His son, Seleucus IV Philopator reigned from 187 BCE to 176 BCE until he was assassinated. Seleucus' younger brother, Antiochus IV Epiphanes, seized the throne and reigned from 176 BCE to 166 BCE. It was during the reign of Antiochus IV Epiphanes that some dramatic events occurred in the Land. Epiphanes means: "manifest" and he claimed to be the earthly manifestation of Zeus.

By that time many of the Yahudim in the Land had become

enamored by the Grecian lifestyle to such an extent that they learned the Greek language and took on the Greek attire. This conduct would have been considered "unclean" by most followers of YHWH since both the language and the dress were so intimately associated with paganisn. Nevertheless, many "converted" to this lifestyle and were called Hellenists. While many did this voluntarily Antiochus chose to forcibly Hellenize, or rather "de-judaize" the remaining Yahudim in his kingdom.

He proceeded with his efforts through the assistance of an individual named Jason who sought the position of High Priest when Antiochus came to power. Jason was a Hellenized Yahudi who became High Priest in 176 BCE.

"He transformed Jerusalem into a Greek City, with Greek schools and gymnasiums where traditionally young athletes exercised nude (a Greek athletic practice). Even some of the young  priests at Jerusalem took up the Greek language, athletic sports, and manner of dress: ' . . . he (Jason) founded a gymnasium right under the citadel, and he induced the noblest of the young men to wear the Greek hat. There was . . . an extreme of Hellenization and increase in the adoption of foreign ways . . .' (2 Maccabees 4:12-13 RSV).[146]

Jason went so far as to send money to Antiochus to offer sacrifices to the Greek god Hercules in the city of Tyre. At that time Hercules was a popular Greek deity in the Land of Yisrael. Interestingly, Hercules was considered to be a demi-god who was the result of the union between the god Zeus and the mortal woman Alcmene. After his death, the legends teach that Hercules became a god.

"In [173 BCE]* Menelaus supplanted Jason by offering Antiochus IV more money for the position of high priest. Menelaus' original name was Onias, but, like Jason, because of his love for the Greek culture changed his name to Menelaus. Menelaus and the sons of Tobias went to King Antiochus. According to Josephus, they told the king that 'they were desirous to leave the laws of their country {the law of Moses}, and their Jewish way of living, and to follow the king's laws (ie. the religion of Dionysus), and the Greek way of living (ie. Greek philosophy).' Antiochus made Menelaus the high priest. In [170 BCE],* while Antiochus was campaigning in Egypt, Jason heard a false rumor that Antiochus had died and thus he attempted to regain by force his former position of the high priest. Jason and his supporters conquered Jerusalem, with the exception of the citadel, and murdered many supporters of his rival, the high priest Menelaus: '...Jason took no less than a thousand men and suddenly made an assault upon the city. When the troops upon the wall had been forced back and at last the city was being taken, Menelaus took refuge in the citadel.' (2 Macabees 5:5 RSV). In response to this riot, when Antiochus came back from Egypt in [170 BCE]* he took Jerusalem by storm and proceeded to enforce the Hellenization of the Jews. He forcefully established the religion of Dionysus: '... king Antiochus wrote to his whole kingdom, that all should be one people, and every one [Yahudim] should leave his laws [the Torah] ... many ... of the Israelites consented to his religion ... For the king had sent letters by messengers to Jerusalem and the cities of Judah that they should ... forbid burnt offerings, and sacrifice [to Elohim] ... set up altars, and groves, and chapels of (Dionysian) idols, and sacrifice swine's flesh, and unclean beasts: That they should also leave their children uncircumcised ... forget the law (of Moses), and change all the (religious) ordinances ... And he appointed inspectors over all the people and commanded the cities of Judah to offer sacrifices, city by city. Many of the people, everyone who forsook the law, joined them ...' (1 Maccabees 1:41-49, 51-51 RSV) Many people forsook the law of Moses and joined the mysteries of Dionysus."[147]

From this point on we see that those in the Land needed to make a choice – obey the King or obey the Torah of YHWH. Worship the son of god Dionysus or worship YHWH. Things continued to escalate until Antiochus raised a statue of Zeus above the Altar in the Temple of YHWH – the Temple that had been rebuilt by Zerubabbel after the return of the Yahudim from Persia.

He then proceeded to slaughter a pig on the Altar which is an outright abomination. The slaughter of pigs was a Dionysian practice and we can see the influence that Dionysus worship had upon this flagrant act. Antiochus then commanded that the Yahudim offer worship there.

According to 1 Maccabees 1:54, Antiochus set up a horrible thing on the Altar in year 145 of the Syrian Kingdom. This date equates with the year 170 BCE.* 1 Maccabees 4:52-54 clearly indicates that this event occurred on Day 25 of Month 9, which equates with Sunday, December 21, 170 BCE* on the proleptic Julian Calendar.

This was more than the faithful Yahudim could take. The Yahudim revolted under the leadership of the Mattathias Maccabee and his sons. The Yahudim regained control of the City of Jerusalem in 164 BCE* and the Temple was thereafter cleansed, which is where the celebration of Hanukah derives.

After three years of fighting with the Seleucids, the Yahudim were granted freedom of religion and political autonomy by Antiochus V in 165 BCE.* This condition continued for 27 years until Antiochus VII Sidetes invaded Judea in 138 BCE.* During this period of Hasmonean rule, the Kingdom and priesthood remained very political in nature, and rivalry developed between two factions known as the Sadduceess and the Pharisees.

Roman influence in the region came about as a result of the conquests of a military commander of the Roman Republic known as Pompey the Great. In 64 BCE, the Yahudim were suffering from internal power struggles after the death of King Alexander Jannaeus which threatened the stability of their kingdom. The King's sons, Hyrcanus and Aristobulus, as well as other political and religious factions, all vied for the crown, and eventually sought mediation from Pompey.

Pompey endorsed Hyrcanus, but Aristobulus and his followers waited to resist the decision. While Pompey was busy in a minor campaign against the Nabataeans, Aristobulus seized Jerusalem. This resulted in Pompey conquering Jerusalem in the spring of 64 BCE, whereupon he made Hyrcanus the high priest and established Judaea as a client state of Rome.

Despite this new status, Judaea remained independent of Roman authority as long as they maintained order and allegiance to Rome. In 47 BCE, Julius Caesar arrived in Judea and the Yahudim were granted various benefits owing to the uniqueness of their monotheistic religion, and Hyrcanus was officially made the King or Ethnarch. In 45/44 BCE,* Julius Caesar even respected the Yahudim enough that he decreed they did not have to pay tribute because it was a Sabbath Year. (Josephus, *Antiquities*, 14/10/5/200-201).

Antipater Idumean was granted the first Roman title of the area. He was appointed as procurator. It was his responsibility to see to the day to day management of Roman interests and oversee the province. He was assassinated soon after his appointment and his son, Herod, took his place. Parthian invasions from Syria then set up Aristobulus II on the throne, but Herod garnered the intervention of the Roman Senate and was confirmed as Ethnarch in 37 BCE.

Herod was a brutal man who, upon taking power, executed forty-five of the Sanhedrin (the governing body of the Yahudim) and arrested Antigonus, the King of the Yahudim who was later beheaded. Herod maintained a disdain for the Yahudim descendents having royal blood, but despite his brutality and disinterest in customs of the

Yahudim he was careful not to infringe too far upon the traditions of the people.

He found it vital to his own survival to seek the approval of the masses, but the overwhelming reason for his success was the administration of force to suppress open opposition. The Yahudim exercised limited self-rule as it related to their religious practices. The Sanhedrin was maintained under Herod as a sort of religious council to oversee the affairs of faith and religious law.

Upon the death of Herod, the Roman emperor, Augustus, was faced with a difficult decision. He initially appointed Herod's sons as rulers of smaller districts within the larger kingdom, but was eventually forced to place Judaea under the direct control of Roman Prefects, who were in turn responsible to the Governor of Syria. Pontius Pilate was the Prefect between the years 26 CE and 36 CE.[148]

Things were quite tenuous under Roman rule. The "King" was not really a king at all but a ruler who derived his power from the Roman Empire, and shared power with other Roman authorities. Herod and his sons were Idumean, which means that they were not from the tribe of Yahudah. Rather, the "Kingly" line was now established with descendants of Edom who were, in turn, descended from Esau - Yaakov's brother.

The High Priesthood had become a political position which could be bought. The Temple service had fallen into the hands of a sect of Yahudim referred to as the Sadducees, who claimed their descendency from the Zadokites. There were two other primary sects known as the Pharisees and the Essenes. All of these sects had different interpretations of the Torah, as well as unique traditions and customs which each developed to adapt to their very precarious existence in the Land. There were also many other smaller factions with varying practices and customs.

Up to this point, despite the corruption in the Priesthood and the Throne, Yahudah had maintained a ruling body known as the Sanhedrin. This body consisted of elders from the Land who may or may not have belonged to one of the differing sects. It was through the Sanhedrin that matters of Torah were discussed and ruled upon. It was the religious Court and deciding body of the Yahudim.

An interesting and important event occurred prior to the time when the Prefect Pontious Pilate was appointed. "According to Josephus (Antiquities 17:13) around the year [CE] 6-7, the son and successor to King Herod, a man named Herod Archelaus, was dethroned and banished to Vienna, a city of Gaul. He was replaced, not by a Jewish king, but by a Roman Procurator named Caponius. The legal power of the Sanhedrin was then immediately restricted. With the ascension of Caponius, the Sanhedrin lost their ability to adjudicate capital cases. This was the normal policy toward all the nations under the yoke of the Romans. The province of Judea had, however, been spared from this policy up to this point. However, Caesar Augustus had had enough of the [Yahudim] and finally removed the judicial authority from them at the ascension of Caponius. This transfer of power was recorded by Josephus. 'And now Archelaus' part of Judea was reduced into a province, and Caponius, one of the equestrian order of the Romans, was sent as a procurator, having the power of life and death put into his hands by Caesar!' The power of the Sanhedrin to adjudicate capital cases was immediately removed. In the minds of the . . . leadership, this event signified the removal of the scepter or national identity of the tribe of [Yahudah]!"[149]

This directly impacts the prophecy given by Yaakov in Beresheet 49:10 which states: *"The scepter shall not depart from Yahudah, nor a lawgiver from between his feet, until Shiloh comes; and to Him shall be the obedience of the people."* If Shiloh, in fact, referred to the Messiah, then that would mean that the Messiah must have been born before this event occurred, before 6 CE.

We already had an outside date provided by Daniel that the Messiah would be cut off after sixty-two (62) Shemitah cycles or 443 years which points to around 1 BCE. The Roman Empire was also prophesied to have a significant impact upon the Land and Jerusalem. (Daniel 2:40-43 see also Daniel 9:26).

This simply adds to the fact that those who remained faithful to YHWH around the turn of the millennium would be anxiously anticipating their Messiah. The Messiah was now at the forefront of people's minds. There was a very narrow and focused window when the Messiah was expected to appear.

During this period, the Yahudim were a divided and conquered people living under the control and in the midst of a pagan culture. Their own leadership was corrupted and dysfunctional. This was the environment into which the Messiah would come and be cut off, as foretold by Gabriel.

Some, like the Essenes, apparently were preparing for the Messiah and they likely took the writings of Daniel seriously. In fact, there were various Scrolls of Daniel found around Qumran, which many believe to be an Essene settlement.

The information contained in this chapter is a very condensed

version of history, but necessary to understand the time and environment into which the Messiah was predicted to come. This information has come from a variety of historical records as well as the Books of the Maccabees, none of which are found in the Tanak, and none of which are found in "canonized" Old Testament Scriptures.

Interestingly, the historical writings in the Tanak leave off in Persia, and the Maccabees, being pseudo-pygryphia leave off in the Second Century BCE. At first glance, there appear to be no Hebrew Scriptures that would show us whether or not the Messiah came as foretold by Gabriel. So how could someone in this day and age know whether or not the Messiah actually appeared?

Thankfully, there are Hebrew and Aramaic texts which have been included in a compilation of texts called the New Testament. Many believe that these texts were originally written in Greek, but there is ample evidence to show that they were first written in Hebrew and Aramaic, which was the language used by the Yahudim at that time.[150]

Therefore, it is appropriate to look and see if we can find information regarding the Messiah of Yisrael in those texts called The New Testament.

21

The New Testament

As stated previously, I dislike the label "The New Testament" because right from the beginning it prejudices the reader and taints the text. It must be understood that the contents of "The New Testament" were written by Yahudim. These writings were intended to compliment, and show the fulfillment of The Torah, The Prophets and The Writings.

Sadly, as they began to be collected and "canonized," certain individuals, such as Marcion of Sinope, made a distinction between these texts and those found in the Tanak. History reveals that Marcion had an agenda to promote his dualistic theology. He not only rejected the Hebrew Scriptures, he also promoted the notion that there were two gods – the strict, harsh god of the tribes of Yisrael, and the kind, benevolent god promoted by Jesus.

Marcion was deemed a heretic, but the effects of his division remain to this day. Most "Bibles" include a clear separation between "The Old Testament" and "The New Testament." By continuing to label these texts as "old" and "new," it gives the distinctive impression that the new is better than the old. In essence, it perpetuates the heretical dualistic scheme advocated by Marcion.

This is why I refer to "The Old Testament" Scriptures as the Tanak. I refer to "The New Testament" Scriptures as the "Messianic writings," because that is what they are about, the Messiah of Yisrael.

If you set aside the labels and view the Messianic writings as a continuation of the Tanak you will see an amazing thing happen – the fulfillment of the patterns and prophecies contained within the Hebrew Scriptures. It turns out that the Messianic writings fill in the missing information concerning the Messiah which we do not find in the Tanak.

This has not always been easy to see, for a number of reasons that will be discussed throughout the remainder of this book. It is important to recognize that the Tanak is really a living work in progress. While it had a beginning, it did not necessarily have an end. As long as there were Covenants and promises left unfulfilled, there was surely more to the story.

The Tanak is a collection of texts which detail the work of YHWH through time. As long as time continues and He remains active with mankind, there is surely more information beyond the text of the Tanak. Therefore, we all should be willing to seek out the fulfillment of this, so far, unfinished work.

After all, the Tanak does not describe the fulfillment of the many prophecies given concerning the Messiah, but we do have texts which provide that information. It is therefore important to set aside prejudices and predispositions and take a critical look to see what those texts contain.

As with the Tanak, the Messianic writings are divided into various groups. The first is referred to as "The Gospels" or better yet, "The Good News." These consist of four writings known as Matthew, Mark, Luke and John. Named after their purported authors, these texts describe a portion of the life and teachings of Yahushua son of Joseph and Miryam - not one who the world presently calls Jesus. The name Jesus will be discussed in the following chapter.

These four texts were not just a haphazard compilation of information. Rather, they were each written to highlight a specifc aspect of Yahushua as the Messiah of Yisrael. For instance, Matthew was written to reveal Messiah the King, the Branch of David (Yirmeyahu 23:5-6; Yeshayahu 11:1). Mark was written to reveal Messiah the Servant, "My servant the Branch" (Zekaryah 3:8). Luke was written to reveal Messiah as the Son of Man, The Man called the Branch (Zekaryah 6:12). John (Yahanan) was written to reveal the Messiah as the Son of Elohim, The Branch of YHWH (Yeshayahu 4:2).

The Messianic writings contain the Book of Acts which is a history of the early followers of Yahushua. They also include numerous letters, known as Epistles, which detail various communications addressing some specific issues that arose within the called out Assembly. The Writings conclude with the Revelation given to Yahanan, which describes the return of Yahushua in the end. That Revelation actually describes the regathering and restoration of Yisrael, as well as the judgment of YHWH upon the world.

The Messianic writings fill in the missing information from that all important time period given to Daniel when the Messiah was prophesied to appear. The Messianic writings begin describing a time

period just before the turn of the millenium around 4 BCE during the reign of King Herod.

At that period in time, the only "official" Scriptural texts that existed for Yisrael were those found in the Tanak. There were a number of religious texts which were not included in the Tanak, all carrying different weight and authority, but that is a subject for another book.[151]

We now have a book called "The Bible" which has merged the Tanak with a collection of these Messianic writings. The Bible contains a portion of Scriptures collectively referred to as "The New Testament" which was compiled by the Christian religion, although these texts were written by Hebrews. They specifically focused on the appearance of the Messiah, His life, His ministry, His death and His resurrection.

They were not officially compiled as Scriptures until they were collected by adherents of the Christian religion, which was officially formed in the Third Century CE as the Roman Catholic Church. Just exactly which Messianic writings were included was a subject of great debate. It was not always agreed which particular writings would be "canonized" and included in the "official" Scriptures of Roman Christianity.

The newly created religion of Christianity essentially developed its own set of Scriptures and added them to the Tanak. This new compilation has come to represent the foundation of the Christian faith, and as previously mentioned, it has been divided into two primary sections: 1) The Old Testament and 2) The New Testament.

Interestingly, this division is consistent with the languages of the current source texts used for these texts. Hebrew is the primary language of the texts in the Tanak while Greek is generally considered to be the source language of the New Testament texts.[152] Hebrew is an eastern language, while Greek is a western language, which poses some challenges when attempting to synchronize the Scriptural texts.

Hebrew reads from right to left and Greek reads from left to right. The languages are in many ways opposite. While Hebrew is considered to be a "holy" language, Greek is considered to be "unclean." Hebrew was the language used by YHWH to reveal Himself, while Greek was a language used by pagans to spread the destructive Hellenistic culture. Therefore, this newly created text called the Bible has some very interesting and profound contrasts.

The fact that those who translate and publish the Bible repeatedly place a division between the Tanak and the Messianic writings, and then place "old" versus "new" labels upon them is a real

problem. Instead of aiding the reader in seeing the perfect harmony between Mosheh, the Prophets, the Writings and the Messiah, these labels do the exact opposite. They actually contrast one against the other, rather than demonstrating the "fulfillment" and the continuity brought by the Messiah.

This division has nothing to do with the content of the texts, and everything to do with the predispositions of the translators and those who compiled the text.

I often encourage people to tear out the page which separates the Book of Malachi with the Good News of Matthew. You know, that page which states "The New Testament." I can assure you that this page was not inspired by YHWH, and it causes more confusion for people than I could possibly describe.

Therefore, over the centuries, the Christian faith has made it clear that their Scriptures are "new" and the Hebrew Scriptures are "old." This gives the impression that the new is also different and better than the old. After all, wouldn't you rather have a new house than an old house, new clothes rather than old clothes, a new car, etc.

So before we look at what these "new" texts say about the Messiah, it may first help to see how they developed and examine how the New Testament has impacted the teaching and understanding concerning the Messiah.

First, it is important to note that there are no original texts known as "autographs" for the Tanak or the Messianic writings. Any Scripture that anyone has in their hands today results from a process of transmitting information from the original autographs. This process is called textual transmission. The issue of inspiration of Scripture, the canonicity of the Scriptures, and the transmission of the Scriptures is a field to which some scholars have devoted a lifetime of study. That being said, there are a few points that can be quickly made concerning the transmission of the Scriptures.

The Tanak that we have today derives from a very small number of manuscripts, which are essentially descended from one basic text type established around 100 CE. As a result, there are very few variants in the texts of the Tanak. The Aleppo Codex is considered to be about 1,000 years old. With the discovery of the Dead Sea Scrolls, which are dated to the time of Yahushua, there were texts found which were 1,000 years older

than the Aleppo Codex. There is a very good correspondence between the text in the Aleppo Codex and the Dead Sea Scrolls.

With the Messianic writings there are around 5,000 manuscripts, and therefore a larger number of variants. Some scholars have tabulated that there are 200,000 variants in the Messianic writings.[153] However, this number cannot be compared to the number of variants in the Tanak, due to the large number of manuscripts.

"There is an ambiguity in saying that there are some 200,000 variants in the existing manuscripts of the New Testament, since these represent only 10,000 places in the New Testament. If one single word is misspelled in 3,000 different manuscripts, this is counted as 3,000 variants or readings. Once this counting procedure is understood, and the mechanical (orthographic) variants have been eliminated, the remaining variants are surprisingly few in number."

"Textual criticism is the art and science of reconstructing the original text from a multitude of variants contained in the manuscripts."[154] There is no original "Gospel According to Matthew" that we know of - if there were one it would probably be written in Hebrew.[155] In fact, there are also accounts that Paul (Shaul) wrote his letters in Hebrew and they were thereafter translated into Greek.[156]

This is entirely possible and very probable because the writers of the New Testament text were Yisraelite converts,[157] telling about the Hebrew Messiah. The language spoken by the Yahudim around the turn of the millennium was Aramaic. Because of the pagan influence of Hellenism, the Yahudim, aside from the Hellenists, considered Koine Greek to be an "unclean" language and they would have stayed away from it as much as possible – especially the devout Yisraelites who were anticipating the Messiah.

Although some people believe that their particular modern translation of the Scriptures is infallible, the truth is that certain translation errors have occurred when the Hebrew or Aramaic text was translated into Greek. There are also certain errors that have occurred in the translation of the Greek to English, or other modern languages. However, the truth is always available to those who are willing to search for it.

With that understanding, let us take a look at some of these issues, and see how the development and translation of the Scriptures has impacted our perception of the Messiah.

If you perform a word search in most modern English translations of the Bible you will rarely, if ever, find the word Messiah. In fact, the only consistent location is in the Messianic writings - in the Good News according to Yahanan.

In the New International Version we read the following: "⁴⁰ *Andrew, Simon Peter's brother, was one of the two who heard what John had said and who had followed Jesus. ⁴¹ The first thing Andrew did was to find his brother Simon and tell him, "We have found the Messiah" (that is, the Christ). ⁴² And he brought him to Jesus."* John 1:40-42 NIV.

On the surface this seems to state that the early followers of Jesus were called disciples. The word "disciple" is not a very accurate translation of what they really were – talmidim. The text also seems to indicate that these talmidim recognized the Messiah as Jesus and called him "the Christ."

In another passage involving a Samaritan woman at a well we read the following in a popular English translation: *"The woman said, I know that Messiah (called Christ) is coming. When He comes, He will explain everything to us."* John 4:25 NIV. Notice that in each instance there is a note in parenthesis, this is an annotation – it is not in the original texts.

Therefore, the talmidim only said, "We have found the Messiah." They did not use the word "Christ" and as we shall later see, they did not call Him Jesus. Likewise, the woman at the well did not use the word "Christ." She simply stated: *"I know that Messiah is coming. When He comes, He will explain everything to us."* Her statement was accurate and holds true to this day. The problem is that somewhere along the way, someone inserted the word "Christ" into the text which is both confusing and erroneous.

This begs the question: Did anybody ever call the Messiah the Christ? One thing is certain – it was not the early Hebrew talmidim. It was more likely pagans who later became Christians, and then transmitted these texts with their own comments and additions. Since "christ" was a common title used by pagans to refer to their gods, they may not have understood the gravity of their actions.

Some might argue that there is no difference, and it is really just a matter of semantics. My response is that there is a big difference. While there were many who were "anointed" in the Scriptures, the title "Messiah" belongs to only One, and there are very specific prophecies and attributes associated with The Messiah of Yisrael.

There are numerous pagan christs, and if you start applying pagan titles to the Messiah of Yisrael there is a danger of confusion and blending other pagan elements. This is exactly what has occurred through the ages by the continuing influence of Hellenism.

So far, we have looked at additions to the text, but at least they are contained in parenthesis so we know they were added. What I find more problematic is when changes and alterations are made which are not so easily discernable. It is a well known fact that certain names in early compilations of Scriptures were altered or "Hellenized." In other words, they were changed to ascribe the attributes or reflect the names of pagan deities.

One striking example was that of Elijah (Eliyahu) whose name means "YHWH is Elohim." In an act of unbelievable ignorance and audacity, his name was replaced in Greek texts with the name of the sun god Helios. They apparently did this because Helios is often depicted as riding a chariot, and Eliyahu was swept away in a whirlwind at the appearance of a "chariot of fire." (2 Kings 2:11).

This is no small mistake. By replacing the name of Eliyahu with a pagan god, the Name of YHWH was removed from the Scriptures as well as the declaration that YHWH was Elohim. It was founded upon pure ignorance, but is not difficult to understand when viewed in the proper historical context. Many ancient synagogues in the land of Israel actually contain mosaics in their floors with the Zodiac and a depiction of Helios in the center. This demonstrates the strength of the Hellenistic influence on the  Yahudim. It was not just Christianity that allowed pagan influences to penetrate their faith, the religion of Judaism is guilty of the same errors.

If you view a Greek manuscript of Matthew 17:11 you will read: *"Helias surely shall come and restore all things."* I count at least 30 instances where the name of Helios is found in the Textus Receptus. So then, the source texts for the New Testament still contain this grievous mistake which I would hope would raise some eyebrows. Interestingly, the Hebrew versions of Matthew that I have inspected do not contain the Hellenization.[158]

 Sadly, this was not the only instance where names were Hellenized in the New Testament. To this day you will still find the name "Easter" in the King James Version of the Bible at Acts 12:4 instead of the proper Appointed Time of Passover. In this case, the source text contains the Greek word Pascha, which corresponds to the Hebrew word Pesach. Regardless, the English translators chose to replace the Scriptural Appointed Time with the name of a pagan

goddess.

Easter is the pagan fertility goddess also known as "The Goddess of the Dawn" who is worshipped around the vernal equinox. Through the process of syncretism, many Christians have unknowingly participated in her worship by holding Easter sunrise services.

Easter has nothing to do with the Appointed Time of Passover, except for the fact that they typically both occur around the same time in the spring. The celebration of Easter is a pagan fertility rite rooted in sun worship. Instead of the blood of the Passover Lamb being celebrated, Easter festivities involved shedding the blood of infants, dipping (coloring) eggs red in the blood of those infants, along with other perverse sexual rites.[159]

This translation error clearly reveals that the Christian faith had been sufficiently Hellenized by the time that the English translation was developed, so that a pagan tradition actually superceded a proper rendering of the text. In other words, a pagan tradition had replaced a Scriptural Appointed Time, to the extent that the translators chose their traditions over the truth.

There are many other problems with the Messianic writings – none too great to resolve but nevertheless critical to recognize and resolve. While many modern translations have corrected some of those mistakes, much of the damage has already been done throughout the centuries. Sun worship was introduced through the Hellenization process early on, which has not only impacted the texts, but also traditions and even core beliefs in the Christian religion.

Sometimes tradition overpowers truth, as with the Easter example. That leads us to one of the most grievous issues concerning the One claimed to be the Messiah through the Messianic Writings – the name Jesus Christ.

22

Jesus Christ

Most of Christianity, and the world for that matter, currently believes that a man once lived 2,000 years ago with long brown hair, beard and fair complexion named Jesus – more formally known as Jesus Christ. This belief is reinforced by untold numbers of English Bibles and other texts which contain accounts of his life and clearly state that his name was Jesus. That would appear to settle the matter, but that is not the case. All of these writings are misrepresenting the name of the one they purportedly represent.

While there was a man who actually lived and breathed as described in the Messianic writings, he likely looked much different than the traditional depictions and his name was definitely not Jesus. Here is a sample of what some religious scholars have written concerning the Name of the Messiah: "In Hebrew it is the same as Joshua. In two places [Acts 7:45 and Hebrews 4:8] in the New Testament it is used where it means Joshua, the leader of the Jews into Canaan, and in our translation the name Joshua should have been retained."[160]

"Jesus - This is the regular Greek translation of the Hebrew Joshua."[161] "Jesus Christ - The name Jesus means Savior, and was a common name, derived from the ancient Hebrew Jehoshua."[162] "Jesus - The Greek form of the name Joshua or Jeshua. Jeshua – [YHWH] is Salvation or [YHWH] is opulence."[163] "Jesus - The same name as Joshua, the former deliverer of Israel."[164]

Now take a look at some secular references: "Jesus Christ - Although Matthew (1:21) interprets the name originally Joshua, that is, 'Yahweh [YHWH] is Salvation,' and finds it specially appropriate for Jesus of Nazareth, it was a common one at that time."[165] "Jesus Christ - . . . the customary Greek form for the common Hebrew name Joshua."[166]

The scholars, both religious and secular, are in agreement that the name of the man commonly referred to as Joshua, son of Nun, is the same Name as the Hebrew Messiah, traditionally called Jesus. This begs the question: If Joshua is the English equivalent to the Hebrew name Yahushua why didn't translators use Joshua when referring to the Messiah?

This is very significant, and not a simple translation mistake. It has been done knowingly and intentionally for centuries. While scholars of the Scriptures have known the truth, they have allowed the true Name of the Messiah to be hidden from the masses.

So how is it that such a well known fact is so unknown to the general public - even from those who claim to be devout adherents to the teachings of this individual. To understand the answer to this question it is important to look at some history concerning this name.

You see the name "Jesus" is the English version of the Hellenized Greek name "Iesous" or "Iesus" in Latin. Some say that this name has no specific meaning, while others indicate that it refers to different pagan deities. One thing is for certain, Jesus was not a Hebrew name, nor is it a translation of the Hebrew Name Yahushua. The English name Jesus is not even a transliteration of the Greek or Latin names because it starts with a "J" sound.

Whether in English, Greek or Latin, it bears little resemblance to the correct Hebrew Name. On the other hand, the Greek name Iesous is strikingly similar to the name Iaso, also spelled Ieso, which is the name of a Greek goddess of healing. Ieso is directly related to sun god worship. In fact, according to Greek mythology, the father of Ieso was Asclepius, the deity of healing. His father was Apollo, the sun god.

"Iaso is Ieso in the Ionic dialect of the Greeks, Iesous being the contracted genitive form. In David Kravitz's, *Dictionary of Greek and Roman Mythology*, we find a similar form, namely Iasus. There are four different Greek deities with the name Iasus, one of them being the son of Rhea."[167]

There is significant proof that Iesus is linked to the mystery cult of the pagan god Dionysus, a savior god, whose father was Zeus, the Greek sun god. According to mythology Zeus also had sons named Iasus, Iasion and Iasius - all considered to be "sons of god." There is also a relationship to the Egyptian goddess Isis and her son Isu.

"According to Reallexikon der Agpyptischen Religionsgeschichte, the name of Isis appears in hieroglyphic

inscriptions as ESU or ES. Isu and Esu sound exactly like "Jesu" that the Savior is called in the translated Scriptures of many languages. Esus was a Gallic deity comparable to the Scandinavian Odin. The Greek abbreviation for Iesous is IHS, which is found on many inscriptions made by the "Church" during the Middle Ages. IHS was the mystery name for Bacchus (Tammuz) [Dionysus] another sun-deity."[168]

It appears quite evident that the name Jesus derives from pagan sun god worship. It could not have been the name of the Messiah of Yisrael nor was that name ever spoken while Yahushua was alive. We know this because there was no letter "J" in either the Hebrew or Aramaic languages, nor was there a letter "J" in the Greek alphabet. None of these languages even contain the "J" sound in their vocabulary.

Any time you see a "J" in an English translation of a Hebrew or Aramaic transcript it should be given the "Y" sound and any time you see a "J" in an English translation of a Greek manuscript it should be given an "I" sound. In fact, the letter "J" with the unique and specific "J" sound is a fairly new addition to the linguistic world. According to Miriam Webster the letter "J" did not exist until after the mid 1500's. The name Jesus has only been in existence since the year 1559 CE. In fact, the first edition of the King James Bible in 1611 used "Iesus" as "J" was not in regular use at that time.

We first see the Name of the Messiah in the Messianic Writings of Matthew (Mattityahu)[169] as follows: "[18] *Now the birth of Yahushua Messiah was as follows: After His mother Miriam was betrothed to Yoseph, before they came together, she was found with child of the Holy Spirit.* [19] *Then Yoseph her husband, being a just man, and not wanting to make her a public example, was minded to put her away secretly.* [20] *But while he thought about these things, behold, a messenger of YHWH appeared to him in a dream, saying, 'Yoseph, son of David, do not be afraid to take to you Miriam your wife, for that which is conceived in her is of the Set Apart Spirit.* [21] *And she will bring forth a Son, and you shall call His Name Yahushua, for He will save His people from their transgressions.'* [22] *So all this was done that it might be fulfilled which was spoken by YHWH through the prophet, saying:* [23] *'Behold, the virgin shall be with child, and bear a Son, and they shall call His name Immanuel,' which is translated, 'El with us.'* [24] *Then Yoseph, being aroused from sleep, did as the angel of YHWH commanded him and took to him his wife,* [25] *and did not know her till she had brought forth her firstborn Son. And he called His name Yahushua."* Mattityahu 1:18-25.

Of course if you read this passage in most English Bibles you will find the name Jesus and if you look in the Greek you will find Iesous. Regardless, there is no source that I am aware of which gives the name Jesus or Iesous as the original name of the Messiah described in this text. To the contrary, they all validate the fact that the name derives from Yahushua, spelled יהושע in Hebrew, and rendered Joshua in English.

The Scriptures record that Mosheh changed the name of Joshua, son of Nun, from Hoshea to Yahushua. (Bemidbar 13:16). This is a very important event, because whenever you see someone get a name change in the Scriptures, it is a red flag that there is an important teaching. In the case of Joshua [Yahushua] son of Nun we read that his name was originally Hoshea (הושע) which simply means "salvation" or "deliverer."

"He was Hoshea only ("he will save") up to his noble witness of spying Canaan. Henceforth, [YHWH's] Name is prefixed, '[YHWH] by him would save Israel' [Bemidbar 13:16]. Son of Nun, of Ephraim (1 Chronicles 7:27). This forms the contrast in the Antitype found in the Messiah (Matthew 1:21), 'you shall call His name Yahushua, for He shall save His people from their trespasses.'"[170]

It is also interesting to note that in the Hebrew text of Bemidbar 13:16-17 where we read about this name change there are three instances of the Aleph Taw (את). This is another clear indication and affirmation concerning the Name of the Messiah.

According to Brown-Driver-Briggs Hebrew and English Lexicon the Name Yahushua (יהושע, יהושע), later Yahshua (ישוע) means "YHWH is salvation." The Hebrew word for "salvation" is ישע (yashua). The Name of the Father is YHWH (יהוה). You will notice that both the Name of the Father and the Name of the Son start with the same three consonant roots - yud ('י), hey (ה), vav (ו) - YHW (יהו).

This is significant, because in the Hebrew language when words share a root it signifies a connection between them. The Scriptures tell us that the Name of Messiah the Son means "He saves His people" and they further reveal that He is Emmanuel, "El with us." Since we know that it is Yah that saves His people it only makes sense that we pronounce the Name as Yahushua.

Therefore, the true name of the One described as the Messiah in the Messianic Writings is spelled יהושע in Modern Hebrew. The most common English transliteration spellings used today are: Yeshua, Yahshua, Yahushua and Yahusha. We know that names had a tendency

to change and sometimes varied with time, so it is not precisely known how this name was pronounced 2,000 years ago.

As a result, there is no sure way of knowing how to transliterate the name into English. This is why you will see variances in the English spellings. It is important not to get too caught up in the exact English spelling since it is only a transliteration to assist us in pronouncing His Hebrew Name correctly in our own language. For consistency, I usually spell the Name as follows: Yahushua.[171]

The important point to recognize is that Jesus Christ is not, and cannot be, the name of the Messiah. Christ is simply a title and Jesus is a name which derives from pagan sun worship. Regrettably, this is another example of the Hellenization of the Greek manuscripts used as the source texts for the New Testament. It is a fact well known in scholarship, yet the Christian religion has continued to perpetrate a lie which has deceived millions, if not billions over time.

It is difficult to know someone when you do not even know their name. Names have always been important in the Scriptures, and they often revealed a person's purpose and identity. If the names of prophets and other significant Hebrew Patriarchs contained the Name of the Father, it would make sense that the Name of the Messiah also would contain the Name. In fact, the Messianic prophesy provided by King David in Tehillim 118:26 specifically states: *"Blessed is He who is coming in the Name of YHWH!"*

In fact, it was already demonstrated through the Prophets that the Messiah would indeed contain the Name of the Father and would be Yahushua. This was clearly revealed in Chapter 18. So we see that over the centuries the Yahudim would have been waiting for the Messiah known as "YHWH their Salvation" – Yahushua. In the meantime, the Christian Church has been trying to present to the world a Hellenized Greek messiah named Jesus, which is untrue.

This is not to say that the One described in the New Testament was not the Messiah, only that Jesus was not His Name. When examined closely, those texts actually affirm the fact that His real Name was Yahushua, which perfectly matches with the prophesied Name of the Messiah. That matter having been rectified, it is now essential to look further to see if this Yahushua fits the other criteria set forth in the Tanak concerning the Messiah.

23

The Birth

As we have examined, the New Testament texts describe a candidate for the Messiah of Yisrael. The English translations call Him Jesus, but His actual name was Yahushua. Once you understand that the name of Yahushua has been misrepresented throughout the centuries, you should probably ask, as I did, if there is anything else about this individual that has been changed.

With a little investigation, it is easy to discern that there are many more errors which must be corrected in order to accurately understand the life of Yahushua. It turns out that it is not just his name that has been changed. His teachings, and even the chronology of his life, have been filtered through multiple lenses of tradition, history and linguistics.

As a result, we will now turn our discussion to the life of Yahushua and where better to start then at the beginning – His birth. While most of the world celebrates his birth on December 25, no one seriously believes that was when He was actually born. After all, December 25 was the traditional pagan date for the birth and rebirth of sun gods long before the birth of Yahushua.

The date of December 25 was attributed to such savior gods as Tammuz, Bacchus, and of course, Dionysus because that was the ancient date for the winter solstice by 405 BCE.* The winter solstice is the shortest day of the year, after which the sun is "resurrected" from death to new life. Therefore, to pagans, it represents the birth and rebirth of their sun deities.

The tradition of attributing December 25 to the birth of Yahushua, is another example of how the Christian religion has adopted pagan concepts and traditions. While most recognize December 25 as a fictitious birth date, there is great debate over the actual time of Yahushua's birth. Any investigation into the correct date must logically

begin in the New Testament although, at first glance, there appear to be conflicts between those texts.

The Book of Mattityahu places the birth "during the time of King Herod" who has traditionally been thought to have died in 4 BCE. We know that Herod ordered the death of children two years old and younger after learning of the birth of Yahushua. This was apparently because when he heard about the birth from the wise men it was possible that Yahushua had been alive for up to two years prior. So, based upon the information in Mattityahu, the birth of Yahushua would be around 6 BCE.

The Book of Luke ties the birth of Yahushua with the census of Quirinius which is traditionally thought to have occurred in 6 CE. This would seem to create an eleven year difference between the two accounts, which is certainly a problem. As it turns out, neither Mattityahu nor Luke are wrong, rather the commonly accepted dates of the events that they refer to are incorrect. The date of Herod's death was not 4 BCE, but more probably 1 BCE, and the census of Quirinius was likely not in 6 CE. Both of these dates will be discussed further in this examination.

With that understanding, let us begin our investigation by looking at Luke 2:1 which provides that Yahushua's birth was during the reign of Augustus Caesar. Augustus Caesar reigned from 44 BCE to his death in 15 CE. The method of measuring time in the ancient Roman world was based on the reigns of the Emperors. Thus the early "Church fathers" of Christianity dated the birth of Yahushua according to the accepted method used by the Romans, arriving at the following figures: Irenius: states that it was in the 41st year of Augustus's reign, which would place it at 4/3 BCE depending on how you date the beginning of Augustus's reign. Clement of Alexandria: dates it November 18, 3 BCE. Tertullian provides the date: 3/2 BCE. Julius Africanus provides the date: 3/2 BCE. Eusebius of Caesarea provides the date: 3/2 BCE. Hypolotus of Rome provides the date: 3/2 BCE. Epiphanius provides the date: 3/2 BCE.[172]

Due to the above, there appears to be agreement from earlier historical records that Yahushua was born around 3 BCE, although this is widely disputed, again, largely because of the accepted dating of Herod's death and the census of Quirinius. So how do we reconcile these matters?

There is actually another way, besides historical accounts, that we can make this determination from the Scriptures, but first we need a little background regarding time and the calendar. In Beresheet 1:14

we read: *"And Elohim said, Let there be lights in the expanse of the sky to separate the day from the night, and let them serve as signs to mark seasons and days and years."* Days and years are clear but what exactly is meant by "signs" and "seasons."

A sign is something which is visibly observable – a signal. The Hebrew word for sign is owt (אות) and is used to describe the signs or marks of the Covenants made with YHWH. For instance, the rainbow, circumcision and the Sabbath are all signs of YHWH's Covenants and they are all visible.

The Hebrew word for "seasons" is moadim (מועדים) and refers more accurately to "Appointed Times." These moadim are set forth throughout the Torah. They are often erroneously referred to as Jewish Holidays, because the religion of Judaism celebrates them along with various other days not set forth in the Scriptures. Interestingly, YHWH specifically stated that they were His days and they belonged to Him, not Yisrael or any particular group or religion. (Vayiqra 23:2,4).

The moadim are considered to be rehearsals, and they all teach about the plan that YHWH has to restore His Creation, and get His chosen people back into a right relationship with Him. So the moadim are there to teach about things which were to come in the future. In fact, they are critical to our understanding of the life and ministry of the Messiah, and you cannot fully recognize the Messiah without understanding the moadim.

As the restoration of all things is centered around the Messiah, it should not be any surprise that The Appointed Times are intimately related to the Messiah. The first moed is the weekly sabbath. It relies upon the seven day count that began on creation week. The remaining seven moadim occur on an annual cycle and rely on the sun and the moon. They are specifically enumerated in order in the text of Vayiqra 23 as follows: 1) Passover; 2) The Feast of Unleavened Bread; 3) Shabuot; 4) Yom Teruah; 5) Yom Kippur; 6) Succot; and 7) Shemini Atzeret.

Remember the discussion regarding the difference between eastern and western thought. Hebrew is an eastern language and culture. These Appointed Times provide a continuous loop which repeats, and when a people enter into the life and faith expressed in the Hebrew Scriptures, they need to join this cycle of life and participate in the moadim. Through this process we synchronize with creation and the Creator.

According to the Creator's Calendar, the months of the year are numbered "one" through "twelve." It is believed that creation of the physical universe actually began at what is now considered month seven. When YHWH called Yisrael out of Egypt YHWH told Mosheh, prior to the Passover – *"This month shall be your beginning of months; it shall be the first month of the year to you."* Shemot 12:2. In other words, YHWH wanted to teach Yisrael to number their months from the season of spring. It is possible that they had been numbering their months from the season of fall. This may be because Adam was believed to have been created in the season of fall.

We see here that a sort of dimensional shift occurred, and at that moment a significant change took place. At that new moon (rosh chodesh) when Yisrael left Egypt, the numbering of the months changed and time, in essence, shifted. The seventh month effectively became the first month. (Shemoth 12:2). Those of the Jewish faith now operate on two different calendars to recognize this change, and they designate them the civil calendar and the religious calendar.

The civil calendar begins on the first day of the seventh month – marking the beginning of creation and the original calendar. The religious calendar, on the other hand, begins on the first day of the first month as it was changed at the time of the Exodus.

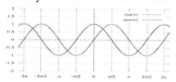

Therefore, Judaism operates with two calendars, flowing on parallel courses, likened to the shifted phases of the sine and cosine functions common in advanced electronics. This is not just a Jewish thing, this shift was ordained by YHWH, and it is an important concept to understand as we look at the birth of Yahushua.

With a better understanding of the Calendar, we can look at the Messianic Writings and recognize certain information that directs us to the birth date of Yahushua. Our investigation continues with a comment in the Book of Luke which helps us discern what year Yahushua was born. The passage indicates that Yahushua began His ministry "about 30 years of age."

According to Luke *"¹ In the fifteenth year of the reign of Tiberius Caesar - when Pontius Pilate was governor of Judea, Herod tetrarch of Galilee, his brother Philip tetrarch of Iturea and Traconitis, and Lysanias tetrarch of Abilene - ² during the high priesthood of Annas and Caiaphas, the Word of Elohim came to Yahanan son of Zekaryah in the desert."* We are also told around this time that Yahushua *"was about thirty years old when he began his ministry."* Luke 3:1-2, 23.

Luke provides an incredible amount of historical data when "The Word of Elohim" came to Yahanan . . . in the desert." Remember the connection between "The Word" and the Aleph Taw (את). The text is not only giving us a way to date the event, it is also linking Yahushua with the Aleph Taw (את) as The Word going to Yahanan when he was "about thirty years old."

The fifteenth year of Tiberius Caesar has been much debated by modern scholars, and many theories have been advanced. We know that Tiberius became Emperor of Rome on August 19 in the year 14 CE. Since the Romans were pagans, they did not use the Creator's Calendar which operated on a lunar system. They worshipped the sun and therefore they used a solar calendar.

Roman scholars who lived when Luke was writing, such as Tacitus or Suetonius, generally dated the first regnal year of a Roman ruler from January 1 of the year following the date of accession. It is most probable that Luke would have reckoned the years of Tiberius Caesar in this manner. The first year of Tiberius would therefore be reckoned from January 1 to December 31, 15 CE and his fifteenth year would have been reckoned between January 1 to December 31, 29 CE.[173]

Yahushua would have been 30 ½ years old in the spring of 29 CE. If we count back 30 years we see that Yahushua was likely born in the fall of 3 BCE, just as was stated by the early Christians. This year can be further confirmed by some additional information contained in the Messianic Writings. The account of Luke provides the following dating at the time of His birth: *"¹ In those days Caesar Augustus issued a decree that a census should be taken of the entire Roman world. ² (This was the first census that took place while Quirinius was governor of Syria.) ³ And everyone went to his own town to register."* Luke 2:1-3.

"Caesar Augustus" reigned as emperor of the Roman empire from 27 [BCE] to 14 [CE] . . . 41 years in all. The grandnephew of Julius Caesar (100 - 44 [BCE]), his real name was Gaius Octavius and he lived from 63 [BCE] to 14 [CE] Because Julius Caesar had legally adopted Octavius as his son, Octavius took the name "Caesar" from Julius, which in later years became a name almost equivalent to "emperor." "Augustus" is a Latin term that means "worthy of reverence." Caesar Augustus's reign was marked by peace and security - the famous Pax Romana - as well as by lavish building projects throughout the empire. In addition, according to Paul Maier, Augustus had such an intense interest in religion within his realm that, if not for his other great achievements, he might have gone down in history as a religious reformer. In his day, belief in the traditional Greco-Roman pantheon had decreased dramatically as philosophical skepticism grew and a growing number joined the foreign mystery religions. Augustus was convinced that belief in the old gods had made Rome great so he set

out to encourage his subjects to return to the worship of these gods. He restored eighty-two temples in Rome alone! He became the pontifex maximus (highest priest) in the state cult."[174]

So we see that Augustus revived the pagan religious systems in the Empire. While he was not technically an emperor, he was highly esteemed and after his death in 14 CE, the Roman senate declared him a god. We know that Augustus issued a decree for a census on three different occasions during his reign, namely 28 BCE, 8 BCE and 14 CE. Since these were empire-wide decrees, they likely took time to implement, so Luke was probably referring to the second decree in 8 BCE.

This appears to pose a problem by the fact that Quirinius was governor of Syria in the years 6 CE to 7 CE. How could the comment in Luke be correct which states: "This was the first census that took place while Quirinius was governor of Syria." There are various plausible explanations for this apparent discrepancy. The Greek word that has been translated as "first" is *prote* which can mean "prior to" or "before." Therefore, Luke was likely referring to the second census of Augustus (8 BCE) which occurred "before" Quirinius was Governor rather than the third census of Augustus which occurred after he was governor.

There is also evidence that Quirinius served an earlier tour of duty in Syria, and that this census was actually from a later tour of duty, when the people of the Roman Empire were required to take an oath when Augustus was being named Pater Patriae. The oath would likely have been obtained in 3 BCE as the honor was bestowed upon Augustus in 2 BCE.[175]

All of this information seems to confirm that 3 BCE was indeed the year of the birth of Yahushua. Later in this chapter we will see a final proof that makes it an absolute certainty, but for now we will continue to look at the further proofs in the Messianic Writings to see if they provide detail concerning the day and month, if possible.

For that we must start with the birth of the man commonly known as John the Baptist. I like to use his proper Hebrew name of Yahanan. Since there were no Christians, let alone Baptists, during the time of his ministry he is more accurately described as Yahanan the Immerser.

The Book of Luke provides the following account. "*[5] In the time of Herod king of Yudea there was a priest named <u>Zekaryah, who belonged to the priestly division of Abijah</u>; his wife Elizabeth was also a descendant of Aaron. [6] Both of them were upright in the sight of Elohim, observing all YHWH's commandments and regulations blamelessly. [7] But they had no children, because*

Elizabeth was barren; and they were both well along in years. ^{8} Once when Zekaryah's division was on duty and he was serving as priest before Elohim, ^{9} he was chosen by lot, according to the custom of the priesthood, to go into the House of YHWH and burn incense. ^{10} And when the time for the burning of incense came, all the assembled worshipers were praying outside. ^{11} Then a messenger of YHWH appeared to him, standing at the right side of the altar of incense. ^{12} When Zekaryah saw him, he was startled and was gripped with fear. ^{13} But the angel said to him: 'Do not be afraid, Zekaryah; your prayer has been heard. Your wife Elizabeth will bear you a son, and you are to give him the name Yahanan. ^{14} He will be a joy and delight to you, and many will rejoice because of his birth, ^{15} for he will be great in the sight of YHWH. He is never to take wine or other fermented drink, and he will be filled with the Set Apart Spirit even from birth. ^{16} Many of the people of Yisrael will he bring back to YHWH their Elohim. ^{17} <u>And he will go on before YHWH, in the spirit and power of Eliyahu, to turn the hearts of the fathers to their children and the disobedient to the wisdom of the righteous - to make ready a people prepared for YHWH</u>. ^{18} Zekaryah asked the angel, "How can I be sure of this? I am an old man and my wife is well along in years. ^{19} The messenger answered, I am Gabriel. I stand in the presence of Elohim, and I have been sent to speak to you and to tell you this good news. ^{20} And now you will be silent and not able to speak until the day this happens, because you did not believe my words, which will come true at their proper time." Luke 1:5-20.

This passage gives an incredible amount of information. First we know that it had to occur before 1 BCE because Herod was still the King of Judea. Here we see Gabriel appearing before Zekaryah in answer to prayer, just as had occurred with Daniel. It is also interesting to note that this event occurred right around the time period that Gabriel told Daniel the Messiah would arrive, so the presence of Gabriel confirms that this has to do with the Messiah.

We know from this text that Zekaryah was a priest, and his service was in the division of Abijah. It is important to understand that the priests from the Tribe of Levi lived throughout the Land. They were divided into 24 divisions, or courses, which determined when they were required to travel to Jerusalem and serve in the House of YHWH.

Since all males were required to go up to Jerusalem for the Feast of Passover, Shabuot and Sukkot (Shemot 23:14; Devarim 16:16) all priests would be in Jerusalem to serve at the Temple for these busy events. (II Chronicles 5:11). They would be required to serve two additional non-consecutive weeks throughout the year. According to 1 Chronicles 24:10 the course of Abijah was the eighth division. Each division ran from Shabbat to Shabbat and the count of the divisions

began in the first month. (II Chronicles 23:8; II Kings 11:5).

According to the best evidence available, the first course of Jehoiarib always began on the Sabbath on or before Day 1 of Month 7.[176] According to the Creation Calendar, the first course of Jehoiarib would have begun on Day 29 of Month 6 in 5 BCE. The eighth course of Abijah would have therefore occurred on Day 10 of Month 1 in 4 BCE which is equivalent to April 7, 4 BCE on the proleptic Julian calendar.[177]

Zekaryah would have been serving from Day 10 of Month 1 to Day 17 of Month 1, or April 7 to April 14 of 4 BCE.[178] It was a great honor to be chosen to burn incense and Zekaryah had obviously waited a long time for this privilege. Apparently, a priest might perform this particular duty only once in his life. He was probably anxious and excited as he concentrated on the task at hand.

When Gabriel appeared to him, it must have been quite a shock, and instead of simply believing and thanking the messenger for the good news, he questioned the promise since both he and his wife were old. This sounds a bit like the story of Abraham and Sarah. As a result of his response, Zekaryah lost his ability to speak until the promise came to pass.

It is highly probable that people watched and waited to see what became of this promised son. Since they were in the time frame described by Daniel and since we have Gabriel bringing this message it is possible that the people thought Yahanan was The Messiah.

Zekaryah would have returned home to the hill country in Judea to his wife, on Day 18 of Month 1, "when his time of service was completed." (Luke 1:23). Since he was promised a child he knew how that was accomplished so he likely set about the business of accomplishing that work. If we believe that the promise of a son was true, we can safely assume that his wife, Elizabeth, conceived shortly thereafter, possibly on Day 18 of Month 1 or April 15, 4 BCE on the proleptic Julian calendar.[179]

The gestation period of an individual is around 280 days or 40 weeks. We can therefore establish an approximate birth date for Yahanan as Day 18 of Month 10 or January 6, 3 BCE on the proleptic Julian calendar.[180]

The question might be posed: What about the first term of Zekaryah's service on Day 18 of Month 8? While it is certainly possible that all of the events described thus far occurred in the first term of Zekaryah's service in the Temple, none of the dates work. While the reader is welcome to calculate those dates, it has been done and you will soon see why the dates discussed to this point are the correct ones.

With that said let us now look to the mother of Yahushua, the younger relative of Elizabeth, Miryam.

"²⁶ *In the sixth month, Elohim sent the messenger Gabriel to Nazareth, a town in Galilee,* ²⁷ *to a virgin pledged to be married to a man named Joseph, a descendant of David. The virgin's name was Miryam.* ²⁸ *The messenger went to her and said, Greetings, you who are highly favored! YHWH is with you.* ²⁹ *Miryam was greatly troubled at his words and wondered what kind of greeting this might be.* ³⁰ *But the messenger said to her, Do not be afraid, Miryam, you have found favor with Elohim.* ³¹ *You will be with child and give birth to a son, and you are to give him the name Yahushua.* ³² <u>*He will be great and will be called the Son of the Most High. YHWH Elohim will give Him the throne of his father David,*</u> ³³ <u>*and He will reign over the House of Yaakov forever; His kingdom will never end.*</u> ³⁴ *How will this be, Miryam asked the messenger, since I am a virgin?* ³⁵ *The messenger answered, The Set Apart Spirit will come upon you, and the power of the Most High will overshadow you.* <u>*So the Set Apart One to be born will be called the Son of Elohim.*</u> ³⁶ <u>*Even Elizabeth your relative is going to have a child in her old age, and she who was said to be barren is in her sixth month.*</u> ³⁷ *For nothing is impossible with Elohim.* ³⁸ *I am YHWH's servant, Miryam answered. May it be to me as you have said. Then the messenger left her.* ³⁹ *At that time Miryam got ready and hurried to a town in the hill country of Judea,* ⁴⁰ *where she entered Zekaryah's home and greeted Elizabeth.* ⁴¹ *When Elizabeth heard Miryam's greeting, the baby leaped in her womb, and Elizabeth was filled with the Set Apart Spirit.* ⁴² *In a loud voice she exclaimed: Blessed are you among women, and blessed is the child you will bear!* ⁴³ *But why am I so favored, that the mother of my Master should come to me?* ⁴⁴ *As soon as the sound of your greeting reached my ears, the baby in my womb leaped for joy.* ⁴⁵ *Blessed is she who has believed that what YHWH has said to her will be accomplished!* ⁴⁶ *And Miryam said: My soul glorifies YHWH* ⁴⁷ *and my spirit rejoices in Elohim my Savior,* ⁴⁸ *for He has been mindful of the humble state of His servant. From now on all generations will call me blessed,* ⁴⁹ *for the Mighty One has done great things for me – Set Apart is His Name.* ⁵⁰ *His mercy extends to those who fear Him, from generation to generation.* ⁵¹ *He has performed mighty deeds with His Arm; He has scattered those who are proud in their inmost thoughts.* ⁵² *He has brought down rulers from their thrones but has lifted up the humble.* ⁵³ *He has filled the hungry with good things but has sent the rich away empty.* ⁵⁴ *He has helped His servant Yisrael, remembering to be merciful* ⁵⁵ *to Abraham*

and his descendants forever, even as he said to our fathers. ⁵⁶ Miryam stayed with Elizabeth for about three months and then returned home. ⁵⁷ When it was time for Elizabeth to have her baby, she gave birth to a son. ⁵⁸ Her neighbors and relatives heard that YHWH had shown her great mercy, and they shared her joy. ⁵⁹ On the eighth day they came to circumcise the child, and they were going to name him after his father Zekaryah, ⁶⁰ but his mother spoke up and said, No! He is to be called Yahanan. ⁶¹ They said to her, There is no one among your relatives who has that name. ⁶² Then they made signs to his father, to find out what he would like to name the child. ⁶³ He asked for a writing tablet, and to everyone's astonishment he wrote: His name is Yahanan. ⁶⁴ Immediately his mouth was opened and his tongue was loosed, and he began to speak, praising Elohim. ⁶⁵ The neighbors were all filled with awe, and throughout the hill country of Judea people were talking about all these things. ⁶⁶ Everyone who heard this wondered about it, asking, What then is this child going to be? For YHWH's Hand was with him. ⁶⁷ His father Zekaryah was filled with the Set Apart Spirit and prophesied: ⁶⁸ Praise be to YHWH, the Elohim of Yisrael, because he has come and has redeemed his people. ⁶⁹ He has raised up a horn of salvation for us in the house of his servant David ⁷⁰ (as He said through His set apart prophets of long ago), ⁷¹ salvation from our enemies and from the hand of all who hate us - ⁷² to show mercy to our fathers and to remember His Set Apart Covenant, ⁷³ the oath He swore to our father Abraham: ⁷⁴ to rescue us from the hand of our enemies, and to enable us to serve Him without fear ⁷⁵ in set apartness and righteousness before Him all our days. ⁷⁶ And you, my child, will be called a prophet of the Most High; for you will go on before YHWH to prepare the way for Him, ⁷⁷ to give His people the knowledge of salvation through the forgiveness of their sins, ⁷⁸ because of the tender mercy of our Elohim, by which the rising sun will come to us from heaven ⁷⁹ to shine on those living in darkness and in the shadow of death, to guide our feet into the path of peace. ⁸⁰ And the child grew and became strong in spirit; and he lived in the desert until he appeared publicly to Yisrael." Luke 1:26-80.

From Luke we read that Miryam, who was a virgin, went to see Elizabeth when she was in her sixth month of pregnancy with Yahanan. She went after being visited by a Messenger of YHWH and told that she would bear a child, even though she was a virgin. It is assumed that she then conceived shortly thereafter, thus we can calculate the birth of Yahushua as being at least six months after Yahanan.

The conception of the Messiah happened around Hannukah in

the year 4 BCE. Hannukah is not an Appointed Time prescribed in the Torah, but was a relatively new celebration at that time, which recalled the rededication of the Temple after the Maccabean Revolt. Some hold that this eight (8) day celebration was actually also a remembrance of Succot and Shemini Atzeret, two Appointed Times which had been missed during the original revolt.

Miryam is recorded as staying with Elizabeth for three months, presumably until Yahanan was born. This was ample time away from her fiancé Joseph to assure that there could be no question that he was the actual father of her child.

By the spring of 3 BCE, Joseph had discovered the pregnancy of Myriam. Under normal circumstances this would have been sufficient reason to call off the wedding, but that did not occur.

"*18 This is how the birth of Messiah Yahushua came about: His mother Miryam was pledged to be married to Joseph, but before they came together, she was found to be with child through the Set Apart Spirit. 19 Because Joseph her husband was a righteous man and did not want to expose her to public disgrace, he had in mind to divorce her quietly. 20 But after he had considered this, a messenger of YHWH appeared to him in a dream and said, Joseph son of David, do not be afraid to take Miryam home as your wife, because what is conceived in her is from the Set Apart Spirit. 21 She will give birth to a son, and you are to give him the name Yahushua, because He will save His people from their sins. 22 All this took place to fulfill what YHWH had said through the prophet: 23 The virgin will be with child and will give birth to a son, and they will call Him Immanuel which means: 'El with us.' 24 When Joseph woke up, he did what the messenger of YHWH had commanded him and took Miryam home as his wife. 25 But he had no union with her until she gave birth to a son. And he gave Him the name Yahushua.*" Mattityahu 1:18-25.

This brings us back to the census that was discussed earlier. We know that Joseph and Miryam were both descendants of David and were of royal lineage. As a result, they both would have been required to swear allegiance to Augustus and would have been mandated to participate in the "census." This meant that they both needed to go to Bethlehem., their town of origin – the birth place of David in the region of Judea. They were, after all, from the tribe of Yahudah.

If you had to go to Bethlehem and you lived in the Galilee this was no small trip. If you knew that you were going to an obligatory Feast in Jerusalem three times a year, which was extremely close to Bethlehem you would probably try to combine these trips. Only males were required to make the trek to Jerusalem three times a year for the Appointed Times, and why would a pregnant woman otherwise travel

such a distance?

All Yisraelite women would have surely remembered the travails of Rachel as she gave birth to Benjamin while traveling from Bethel to Ephratah. Ephratah was the name for Bethlehem in Yaakov's time. Rachel died on her way to Bethlehem which was likely on the mind of Miryam the entire trip. Miryam likely would not have gone on such a journey under normal circumstances.

Thus, we see both Joseph and Miryam traveling to Bethlehem around the seventh month of the year, right before the birth of Yahushua. Interestingly, Luke says that they were "betrothed" or "engaged" but there is no mention that they were married at this time. This is because they did not actually "know" one another until after the birth of Yahushua, and it is that sexual union which ultimately seals the marriage. Up until that time they were still "engaged."

This was surely a very awkward situation for both of them. Traveling together in such a fashion while not being married was not typical, and with Miryam so far along in her pregnancy, the appearance of impropriety must have been enormous. They probably did not bother explaining themselves since the story of the conception would have been a bit more than most people were prepared to accept.

Yahushua was born while they were in Bethlehem. The following is the account of his birth: "⁴ *So Joseph also went up from the town of Nazareth in Galilee to Judea, to Bethlehem the town of David, because he belonged to the house and line of David. ⁵ He went there to register with Miryam, who was pledged to be married to him and was expecting a child. ⁶ While they were there, the time came for the baby to be born, ⁷ and she gave birth to her firstborn, a son. She wrapped him in cloths and placed him in a manger, because there was no room for them in the Inn.*" Luke 2:4-7.

So Yahushua was born while his mother was unmarried and her husband was not his father. If this fact would have been known, it would put the status of Yahushua in a difficult state. Some may have deemed him a "mamzer" as a result. In other words, he would have been treated as a bastard, which would have made him an outsider in the community.

Interestingly, the text states that there was no room at the Inn. The "Inn" was not a motel or a bed and breakfast, but more likely a guestroom in the home of a family member or friend. We do not know why it was occupied, but we can deduce that this was likely one of the three times that males were commanded to travel to Jerusalem to celebrate a festival to YHWH.

It has been taught by some that Yahushua was born around

the time of the Feast of Succot, which occurs in the seventh month during what is commonly referred to as the fall season. The book of Luke describes the infant being placed in a "manger" which can refer to a feeding trough although some refer to it as a stall or a tabernacle.

This seems to work well with the phrase from Yahanan 1:14 which declares that he "tabernacled with us." This could also be styled that he "pitched his tent" with us. As a result, some people believe that Yahushua was actually born in a succa during the Feast of Succot, also known as the Feast of Tabernacles. It is important to recognize that Succot is not the only Appointed Time to occur in the seventh month. Within the two week period preceding Succot there is Yom Teruah and Yom Kippur.

It would probably not be uncommon for those coming to Jerusalem for Succot to come early and celebrate all of the Appointed Times of the seventh month namely: Yom Teruah, Yom Kippur, Succot and Shemini Atzeret. Since there was no room in the "Inn" and people were supposed to be living outside in succas during the Feast of Succot, then there is a distinct possibility that the birth occurred earlier in the seventh month.

There is no commandment to be in Jerusalem during Yom Teruah or Yom Kippur and it is also important to point out that Yahushua was born in Bethlehem - not Jerusalem. While the two are both geographically close in proximity, they are not the same, and it would not have been appropriate to build a succa and celebrate Succot in Bethlehem rather than Jerusalem. If Yahushua was born during Succot, then he would have been in Jerusalem.

In fact, it would be highly unlikely for Yahushua to have been born at Succot according to the Scriptures. Luke 2:3 states that "all went to be registered, everyone to his own city." This means that every Yahudite went to the town of their birth, to be registered for a Roman census. It must be understood that the relationship between the Judeans and the Romans was tenuous and volatile at this time. It is unthinkable that the Romans would schedule a census for the Yahudim at Succot when all of the males were to be in Jerusalem.

In the year 3 BCE Yom Teruah, also known as the Feast of Trumpets, occurred on the First Day of the Seventh month at the sighting of the New Moon on September 11. This is an extremely significant day because Yom Teruah was traditionally considered to be the birthday of Creation. It is the day that Elohim said: "Let there be light." It was also the day that the ancient kings of Yahudah reckoned their regnal years from. This procedure was followed consistently in

the time of Solomon, Yirmeyahu and Ezra.[181]

Therefore, Yom Teruah in 3 BCE appears to be the definitive date for the birth of Yahushua – the Annointed King of Yahudah. This brings us to a very interesting and often misunderstood event involving "wise men." According to the Book of Mattityahu there were "wise men" who knew about this birth by looking at the stars – one star in particular. We know from modern technology that prior to September 11, 3 BCE there were spectacular "signs" in the sky.

Remember that the constellations and the planets were created for specific purposes. The Sages were well aware of this fact and Job clearly spoke of certain constellations in his writings. While the occult and pagans have taken these concepts and twisted them, it is important to remember that the Creator of the Universe also created these things for His glory and His purpose.

One of these purposes is to provide a "sign" for the coming of the Messiah. The Book of Mattityahu speaks of "wise men" or "magi" from the East who came because they saw "the star."

"[1] Now <u>after Yahushua was born in Bethlehem of Judea</u> in the days of Herod the king, behold, wise men from the East came to Jerusalem, [2] saying, Where is He who has been born King of the Yahudim? <u>For we have seen His star in the East and have come to worship Him</u>. [3] When Herod the king heard this, he was troubled, and all Jerusalem with him. [4] And when he had gathered all the chief priests and scribes of the people together, he inquired of them where the Messiah was to be born. [5] So they said to him, In Bethlehem of Judea, for thus it is written by the prophet: [6] But you, Bethlehem, in the Land of Yahudah, are not the least among the rulers of Yahudah; for out of you shall come a Ruler Who will shepherd My people Yisrael. [7] Then Herod, when he had secretly called the wise men, determined from them what time the star appeared. [8] And he sent them to Bethlehem and said, go and search carefully for the young Child, and when you have found Him, bring back word to me, that I may come and worship Him also. [9] When they heard the king, they departed; and behold, the star which they had seen in the East went before them, till it came and stood over where the young Child was. [10] When they saw the star, they rejoiced with exceedingly great joy. [11] And when they had come into the house, they saw the young Child with Miryam His mother, and fell down and worshiped Him. And when they had opened their treasures, they presented gifts to Him: gold, frankincense, and myrrh. [12] Then, being divinely warned in a dream that they should not return to Herod, they departed for their own country another way." Mattityahu 2:1-12

The wise men appeared after Yahushua was born, they did not appear the night that he was born. Their appearance was really quite an amazing event because we have these "wise men" approaching Herod, the supposed "king" of Yahudah, telling him that they have come to see the real King of Yahudah. It was a blatant assertion that the kingship of Herod was illegitimate, but notice how he played along. They said that they saw "His Star" meaning the "King of the Yahudim's star."

This would have certainly brought remembrance to the word spoken from Balaam to Balak: "*¹⁷ I see Him, but not now; I behold Him, but not near. A star will come out of Yaakov; a scepter will rise out of Yisrael. He will crush the foreheads of Moab, the skulls of all the sons of Sheth. ¹⁸ Edom will be conquered; Seir, his enemy, will be conquered, but Yisrael will grow strong. ¹⁹ A ruler will come out of Yaakov and destroy the survivors of the city.*" Bemidbar 24:17-19.

Herod was an Edomite, and the word indicated that a ruler would come out of Yisrael and Edom would be conquered. He took this event "deadly" serious because it was an affront to his reign. He took it so serious that he later ordered the death of all children two years and younger (Mattityahu 2:16). Why two years and younger? Because the wisemen came to Yahushua after a significant period of time from when they first saw the star.

Contrary to popular belief these wise men, called Magi, did not come to the baby while he was in the manger - they came much later. Most manger scenes are inaccurate when they show the baby Jesus in a manger with the "Three Wise Men" looking over him.

In fact, the Scriptures do not mention three wise men, but rather three gifts: gold, frankincense, and myrrh. There were most likely many more than three of them, and they probably would have had a large entourage to carry and protect the gifts and supplies necessary for such a long journey which would have taken time to assemble. The only witnesses to the birth of the infant, according to the Scriptures, were the shepherds. (Luke 2:12).

There is considerable evidence to support the fact that the "wise men" found Yahushua in the Galilee - not in Bethlehem. One significant reason is because after Yahushua was circumcised on the eighth day in accordance with the Torah and after the days of purification were completed, Yoseph and Miryam took him to Jerusalem to present him before YHWH and "*to offer a sacrifice according to what is said in the Torah of YHWH, a pair of turtledoves or two young pigeons.*" Luke 2:34.

What Luke is telling us is that they presented a sacrifice which a *poor person* would bring to the Temple. According to the Torah: "*⁶ When the days of her purification are fulfilled, whether for a son or a daughter, she shall bring to the priest a lamb of the first year as a burnt offering, and a*

young pigeon or a turtledove as a sin offering, to the door of the tabernacle of meeting.⁷ Then he shall offer it before YHWH, and make atonement for her. And she shall be clean from the flow of her blood. This is the Torah for her who has born a male or a female. ⁸ <u>And if she is not able to bring a lamb, then she may bring two turtledoves or two young pigeons</u> - one as a burnt offering and the other as a sin offering. So the priest shall make atonement for her, and she will be clean." Vayiqra 12:6-8.

Since they did not bring a lamb, they must have been poor. This is inconsistent with the myth that Yahushua and his family were loaded up with gold and other gifts on the night he was born. The wise men were nowhere near the manger in Bethlehem because the Scriptures later record: "**And coming into the House**, *they saw the Child with Miryam His mother, and fell down and did reverence Him . . .*" Mattityahu 2:11.

The wise men appeared at the "House" - not at the manger when Yahushua was a "child" - not a baby. They actually found Yahushua around a year after his birth. It was only then that they worshiped him and gave him gifts. It was after that point that they were warned in a dream not to return to Herod. (Mattityahu 2:12).

Herod had already learned from the wise men exactly what time the star appeared. That is why, when he learned that he had been duped by them he ordered all children two years old and younger to be killed. Yoseph was also warned in a dream to flee to Egypt and he now could afford the trip because he had just been given the resources necessary for the journey. (Mattityahu 2:13).

Just who were these "wise men" seems to be the mystery of the ages, although it is possible to piece together their identity through a historical analysis. At the time of the birth of Yahushua, the Roman Empire and the Parthian Empire were experiencing somewhat of a détente. While the Roman Empire ruled the west, the Parthian Empire ruled the east.

The wise men described in the Scriptures were likely Parthians from Persia, members of the Megistanes, who were very high officials in the Parthian Empire.[182] The historian Josephus strongly implies that these Parthians may have been Yisraelites formerly deported by the Assyrian Empire, which was later replaced by the Parthian Empire.[183]

It is important to remember that Daniel was a "wise man" and was placed in charge of the "wise men" in the Babylonian Kingdom. He was no doubt a wealthy and powerful man with no known heir due to the fact that he was a eunuch. He also happened to have incredible insight into the coming of the Messiah. It is highly probable that these "wise men" from the East brought with them the wealth of Daniel.

One of the titles given to Daniel was Rab HarTumaya (חרטמיא רב) - the Chief of the Magicians. As a result of his prominence in both the Babylonian and Medo-Persian empires, Daniel likely had great riches. What happened to the wealth of this man who had no progeny?

Being a Prophet of the Most High he was given wisdom, knowledge and revelation beyond any man of his time which he was told to *"close up and seal the words of the scroll until the time of the end."* (Daniel 12:4). Daniel likely knew when the Messiah would come, or at least the signs to look for, since he was one prophet that was given very specific time frames for prophetic events.

As such, it is believed by some that he passed on his riches through his eventual successors, the Parthian Magi, with instructions to bring his wealth to the Messiah when the sign of his birth was seen in the Heavens. Since the Magi were a priestly line they may have actually been priests of Yisrael. When the Magi saw the sign, they knew that it signaled the birth of the Hebrew Messiah. Since the prophecies indicated where the Messiah would be born (Micha 5:2-5) and where He would dwell (Yeshayahu 9), they knew where to look for Him.

Their entourage would have been enormous, in the hundreds, if not thousands. They would have brought a small army with them since they were Parthian dignitaries traveling within the Roman Empire carrying great riches. This is why Herod and all of the inhabitants of Jerusalem were *"disturbed"* and *"troubled"* by their arrival. (Mattityahu 2:3). It is a scene which most people will not be presented with in Sunday School, but it is supported by history and the Scriptures.

Their journey likely took many months and they did not arrive to see the infant, which is "brephos" in the Greek, but rather a toddler "paidion," indicating that the birth itself had been some months before. When they finally located *"the Child"* Yahushua in the Galilee, they anointed Him King of Yahudah and gave him the riches of his Kingdom. This could have very possibly occurred on his first birthday, Yom Teruah in the year 2 BCE, a date from which Kings of Yahudah would reckon their reigns.[184]

It is important to understand that Yahushua was not some theoretical or self-proclaimed king. He was actually the King of Yahudah, and that was the context within which we must view his time on Earth in order to properly understand his actions and teachings. This is why the Messianic Scriptures provide the lineage of both the mother and the adoptive father of Yahushua. (see Mattityahu 1:1-16; Luke 3:23-38). In either case, Yahushua was a descendant of David and

an heir to the throne of Yahudah. Joseph was a direct descendant of Solomon who was the fifth son of David and Bathsheba. Miryam was a direct descendant of Nathan who was the fourth son of David and Bathsheba.

The rulership of the Northern Kingdom had been taken away from David's line. Therefore, if Yahushua was the Messiah, son of David, he would be able to lead the House of Yahudah, but that was only part of the work to be accomplished. There was still the issue of the Northern Kingdom which will be treated later in this book.

The specific purpose of the "wise men" was to find the King of Yahudah because they saw his Star. So what was this star, this sign that made them come looking for the King of the Yahudim. Incredibly, with the advent of computers and technology we can now see what they saw.

They first indicated that they saw the star in the east. In other words, they first saw it when they were at their home in the east. This star first appeared at a certain time. (Mattityahu 2:7). After conferring with Herod we read the following account. "⁹ After they had heard the king, they went on their way, and the star they had seen in the east went ahead of them until it stopped over the place where the child was. ¹⁰ When they saw the star, they were overjoyed." Mattityahu 2:9-11.

Many people believe that this was some sort of light bobbing around in the sky like tinker bell in a Disney movie, but that is not the case. This was clearly a heavenly body which was moving in such a way as to provide them with directions.

There were numerous celestial events which occurred prior to and after the birth of Yahushua, including nine major conjunctions which occurred between May 19, 3 BCE and August 26, 2 BCE.¹⁸⁵ One particular event occurred which would have certainly attracted attention on August 12, 3 BCE. On that day Jupiter rose as a morning star in conjunction with Venus.

Astronomically, Jupiter was said to represent the father of the gods. When we talk about the planets and the stars as signs it is important to remember that the pagans took creation and twisted it to fit their own myths – thus the name Jupiter. The Hebrew name for this planet is Tzedeq, which means "righteousness." Therefore, we see the planet Jupiter representing the King of Righteousness or The Righteous Ruler.

Astronomically, Venus is symbolic of the Virgin. So the King Planet coming into conjunction with the Virgin signaled a royal birth. The Hebrew name for this planet is Nogah, which indicates brightness, illumination and splendor. Twenty days later, Mercury, which was deemed the Messenger of the gods, came into conjunction with Venus.

Known as Kochav, in Hebrew it actually means: "star." Thus this "star" left its position with the Sun and positioned itself into close conjunction with Venus. This took place when the sun had just entered the constellation of Virgo – The Virgin.

Mercury and Venus were then in the constellation of Leo, which represents the Lion – Yahudah. Jupiter was just then entering Leo. This would certainly lead one to the final words of Malachi referring to the Messiah as "the sun of righteousness."

Throughout this period Jupiter was also moving above Regulus, known as the King Star, and actually made a loop or crowning motion over Regulus. Regulus is the brightest star in the constellation of Leo. The track of Jupiter appeared to move in its normal path, then it appeared to stop and move in the opposite direction. Astronomers call this backwards movement retrograde movement. After a certain amount of retrograde motion of Jupiter around Regulus, Jupiter then stopped a second time and continued to proceed on its original course. In this way Jupiter appeared to circle around Regulus, symbolizing the birth of a King to the Magi. This event is likely what the magi were referring to when they talked about his star.[186]

All of these celestial events culminated with the great sign that occurred in the heavens on September 11, 3 BCE shown below.

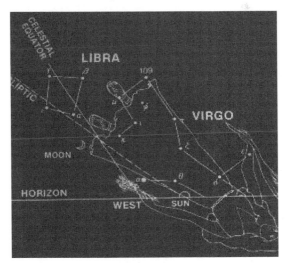

Amazingly, this is the sign which was specifically provided in the Book of Revelation as follows: "[1] *Now a great sign appeared in heaven: a woman clothed with the sun, with the moon under her feet, and on her head*

a garland of twelve stars. ² *Then being with child, she cried out in labor and in pain to give birth."* Revelation 12:1-2.

This has long been a mystery to those who did not realize that a celestial event was being described. The woman is obviously Yisrael, represented through the constellation of the Virgin, known as Bethula, in Hebrew.

Thanks to the precision afforded by technology we can discern the moment that the sign in Revelation 12 occurred. Up to this point we could approximate from the text of the Messianic writings the date of Yahushua's birth and now we know that the sign confirms the fact that Yahushua was born at sunset, the beginning of September 11, 3 BCE Yom Teruah – The Feast of Trumpets. At the moment of his birth, trumpets and ram's horns, known as shofars, were blasting throughout the Land of Yisrael. It was the fulfillment of a rehearsal that had occurred for centuries in anticipation of this very moment – to announce the birth of the Messiah.

So Yahushua was born on Yom Teruah 3 BCE, and anointed by the wise men in 2 BCE exactly as provided through Daniel. He also "came" and was anointed before 6 CE, the time when the Scepter departed from Yahudah. He descended from the line of David on his maternal side, and legally through Joseph on his paternal side.

Based simply upon the timing of his birth, Yahushua is a genuine contender for the Messiah. In fact, I know of no other historical figure who meets the criterion established by Gabriel in the Book of Daniel and the prophecy given by Yaakov that the Scepter would not depart from Yahudah until Shiloh (Messiah) comes. (Beresheet 49:10). This should certainly peak anyone's interest, and now we will look to his teachings to see what he said and did, which is another test to confirm whether he actually was the Messiah.

24

The Life

While the Messianic writings, particularly Matthew and Luke, speak to the birth of Yahushua – not much is known about his early years. The texts detail how he returned to the Galilee region with his parents after his circumcision on the 8th day, and after Miryam had offered the required sacrifices after the completion of her cleansing period.

The text in Luke indicates that Joseph and Miryam did everything required by the Torah, but it does not specifically mention whether they redeemed Yahushua according to Shemot 13:13. This was to be done of all firstborn in remembrance of the Passover. If Yahushua was not redeemed then that would mean he belonged to YHWH.

After returning to Galilee, the child Yahushua remained there with his parents until the wise men anointed him around the age of one. He then proceeded to Egypt, and we know that He returned at some point after the death of Herod. While traditionally the death of Herod was thought to be in 4 BCE, this has been determined to be an erroneous date by many, and the actual date is likely 1 BCE.[187]

The Book of Luke tells us that his parents went to the Passover every year (Luke 2:41). We know that when Yahushua was twelve he was brought to Jerusalem. (Luke 2:42). Other than that particular event, the Scriptural record is scant concerning his childhood. If you travel to Egypt there is significant Coptic tradition surrounding Yahushua's time in Egypt.

In fact, there are a number of traditions throughout the world which maintain the idea that Yahushua was away from the Land for a long time while he was growing up. This may be supported by various incidents in the Scriptures which seem to indicate that he returned to the Land at a much later date.

One particular event involving Yahanan seems to confirm the

fact that Yahushua was away for a while, and suddenly returned later in his life. Yahanan was immersing people in the Jordan River in preparation for the coming Messiah. During this time, when Yahanan first encountered Yahushua, he apparently did not even know

him. Here is what Yahanan stated: *"³¹ I myself did not know him, but the reason I came immersing with water was that he might be revealed to Yisrael . . . ³³ I would not have known him, except that the one who sent me to immerse with water told me."* Yahanan 1:31, 33.

These two were cousins yet Yahanan spoke as if he did not recognize Yahushua. This could be the result of Yahanan living in the desert, but it seems more consistent with the thought that Yahushua had been absent from the Land. This notion is later endorsed when certain talmidim from the Galilee do not seem to know who Yahushua was, and even questioned whether anything good could come from Nazareth. (Yahanan 1:46).

We know that Yahushua made a profound impact on the religious leaders during his previous encounter in Jerusalem when he was twelve. (Luke 2:46). The account provided in Luke then leaps forward to when Yahushua was an adult, around the age of thirty. Clearly if Yahushua had been present in the Land all of those years he would have, no doubt, been very well known. To the contrary, even those from the Galilee do not seem to know him, although they acknowledged knowing his father and mother. (Yahanan 6:42).

In any event, we read about a time when Yahushua encountered Yahanan at the Jordan River, apparently after an extended absence from the Land. It is generally understood that this would have been around the year 29 CE. ¹⁸⁸ We know that both Yahanan and Yahushua had attained the age of thirty years old, so the year 29 CE would be consistent with the text.

Their ages are significant because thirty (30) was the accepted age when a priest would begin his service. Since Yahanan was older than Yahushua, and since he was of the priestly line, he probably would have begun his service at the age of thirty. This would have occurred around the seventh month in 28 CE. In fact, he may have begun his ministry on Yahushua's birthday – the first day of the seventh month. Since 28 CE was a leap year we see Yahushua beginning his ministry seven (7) months later on the first day of the first month. These are both very significant dates on the Scriptural Calendar.

We do not know if Yahanan ever actually served in the Temple, which had been corrupted and politicized. As was the case with the Essenes, Yahanan rejected the Temple and the corrupted religious establishment in Jerusalem.

The Essenes, the purported authors of the Dead Sea Scrolls, went into the desert because that is what the prophecy said to do. "*In the desert prepare the way for YHWH. Make straight in the wilderness a highway for our Elohim.*" Yeshayahu 40:3. According to the Community Rule Scroll, as well as others, they were anticipating two messiahs: The Messiah of Aharon and The Messiah of Yisrael.

They understood the need for a righteous king and a righteous priest, neither of which existed at that time. They were in the desert preparing the way for The Messiah. Yahanan had been in the desert much of his life and there is speculation that Yahanan was intimately associated with The Essenes. Yahanan was in the desert making the path straight so that all flesh would see the salvation of Elohim. (Yeshayahu 40:4).

Therefore we see this priest, Yahanan, performing his duties in the desert, well away from the corrupted Temple in Jerusalem. Instead of shedding blood, he was cleansing people with water. He is traditionally called John the Baptist, but there was no Baptist denomination at that time and he was certainly not a Christian.

Yahanan was not doing anything new or unusual. He was not instituting some new religious rite. He was simply immersing people, which is often called "mikvah." The mikvah is the ritual cleansing that a person performs before entering the House of YHWH or the service of YHWH. It is required throughout the Torah when a person is in a state of uncleanness. The mikvah is a very important step for someone transitioning from an unclean state to a clean state. Of course, you need to know and understand the Torah, which distinguished between clean and unclean.

While there is obviously a physical aspect to this bathing process, the meaning is much more spiritual. It is symbolic of a person being completely washed inside and out. It represents a spiritual renewal wherein all of the sin and filth in a person's life is washed away by the living waters.

In this particular case, the physical location is profound. Yahanan was just north of the Dead Sea which is literally a dead body of water. The fresh "living waters" of the Jordan flow into the Sea and

are deposited into a lifeless body of water which was likened to Hell. In fact, the Dead Sea was called The Lake of Fire due to the tar and pitch which would float and burn on the surface.

This was also a very strategic geographical location because it was at an intersection for pilgrims travelling to and from Jerusalem to celebrate the Appointed Times.[189] While it might have been faster for Galileans to travel through Samaria to get to Jerusalem, it was much more precarious and dangerous. As a result, most Galileans followed the Jordan River Valley to Jericho and then traveled west to Jerusalem.

While Yahanan was immersing people he was specifically questioned about his role. Obviously what was happening peaked people's attention. There was an excitement in the air as people anxiously looked for the Messiah. In fact, Yahanan was asked if he was the Messiah, Eliyahu or the Prophet. (Yahanan 1:19-21).

It is clear that there were different expectations concerning the Messiah, and people wanted to know if Yahanan fit into their understanding. Yahanan denied falling into any of these categories stating: "*I am the voice of one calling 'In the desert make straight the way of YHWH.'*" Yahanan 1:23.

In the midst of it all, there came a time when Yahushua asked Yahanan to immerse him. Here is the account as provided in the Book of Mattityahu. "*[11] I immerse you with water for repentance. But after me will come one who is more powerful than I, whose sandals I am not fit to carry. He will immerse you with the Set Apart Spirit and with fire. [12] His winnowing fork is in his hand, and he will clear his threshing floor, gathering his wheat into the barn and burning up the chaff with unquenchable fire. [13] Then Yahushua came from Galilee to the Jordan to be immersed by Yahanan. [14] But Yahanan tried to deter him, saying, 'I need to be immersed by you, and do you come to me?' [15] Yahushua replied, 'Let it be so now; it is proper for us to do this to fulfill all righteousness.' Then Yahanan consented. [16] As soon as Yahushua was immersed, he went up out of the water. At that moment heaven was opened, and he saw the Spirit of Elohim descending like a dove and lighting on him. [17] And a voice from heaven said, 'This is My Son, whom I love; with him I am well pleased.'*" Mattityahu 3:11-17.

Notice that Yahanan said Yahushua would immerse with the Spirit and with fire. After Yahushua was immersed with water the heavens opened and the Spirit of Elohim descended upon him like a dove and lightning. A voice from heaven testified that Yahushua was the Son of Elohim

As a result of what Yahanan witnessed he testified that Yahushua was the Son of Elohim (Yahanan 1:34) and that he was

the Lamb of Elohim (Yahanan 1:36). Yahanan, being of the priestly line, was authorized to declare a sacrifice acceptable before it could be sacrificed. In fact, this was required for all sacrifices before they could be offered to YHWH.

Further, lambs chosen for slaughter would be washed before they were presented. Thus we see the Lamb of Elohim being prepared for slaughter. It is important to realize that this was no arbitrary act performed by Yahanan. He was a Levite priest performing a priestly duty concerning the Lamb of Elohim.

Interestingly, since Yahanan was immersing on the eastern side of the Jordan, Yahushua likely crossed the Jordan into the Land just as had been done by His predecessor – Yahushua (Joshua) who led Yisrael into the Promised Land immediately prior to Passover.

He was fulfilling patterns and as such, he went in the wilderness for forty (40) days and forty (40) nights fasting. This forty (40) day period marked the beginning phase of his ministry, and in the tradition of Mosheh, it pointed to him being the Prophet like Mosheh – the Messiah. After his period of fasting He was tempted, just as his predecessors were tempted in the wilderness for forty (40) years.

Where his predecessors failed, he succeeded and in each instance, his method of overcoming the temptation was to quote the Torah. Of course, the Torah was at the center of his entire ministry. When he began his ministry one of the first things that he proclaimed was: *"Repent for the Kingdom of Heaven is at hand."* Mattityahu 4:17. This is the same exact message that Yahanan was preaching. (see Mattityahu 3:2).

The word "repent" in Hebrew is "teshuva" which means "to return." It is intimately connected with the Torah and the instructions of the Torah show us how to return to YHWH. Therefore, repentance always involves the Torah. All of Yisrael was supposed to be obeying the Torah if they wanted to dwell in the Land and be blessed. The Land, after all, represented the Kingdom of YHWH. It was a place where YHWH would dwell with His people if they obeyed – just as it was in the Garden.

Yisrael had already been punished for their disobedience. The House of Yahudah had been expelled for seventy (70) years and the House of Yisrael was still in exile. Sadly, Yahudah had once again fallen away, and they were going to be punished again if they did not repent.

So Yahushua, as the anointed King of the Yahudim, was telling the people that the Kingdom was in their face – their King had arrived.

They had better repent of their disobedience and get right before YHWH, which involved obedience to His commandments. One cannot ignore the parallel between Yahushua and David who began his reign over the House of Yahudah at the age of thirty.

When Yahushua began his ministry, which could be described as his reign since he was functioning as the righteous King (Melchizedek), he began assembling talmidim. Interestingly, he did not find them in the religious center of Jerusalem, rather, he gathered them in the region of the Sea of Galilee.

After the immersion of Yahushua, Yahanan had been imprisoned and some speculate that Yahushua was also a marked man. The Galilee was a zealot stronghold and an ideal place to find cover from Herod Antipas and the Roman authorities. Yahanan had talmidim, and it was from these talmidim that Yahushua gathered his first talmid, even before Yahanan was imprisoned.

"*35 The next day Yahanan was there again with two of his talmidim. 36 When he saw Yahushua passing by, he said, Look, the Lamb of Elohim! 37 When the two talmidim heard him say this, they followed Yahushua. 38 Turning around, Yahushua saw them following and asked, What do you want? They said, Rabbi, where are you staying? 39 Come, he replied, and you will see. So they went and saw where he was staying, and spent that day with him. It was about the tenth hour. 40 Andrew, Simon Peter's brother, was one of the two who heard what Yahanan had said and who had followed Yahushua. 41 The first thing Andrew did was to find his brother Simon and tell him, We have found the Messiah. 42 And he brought him to Yahushua. Yahushua looked at him and said, You are Simon son of Yahanan. You will be called Cephas. 43 The next day Yahushua decided to leave for Galilee. Finding Philip, He said to him, Follow me. 44 Philip, like Andrew and Peter, was from the town of Bethsaida. 45 Philip found Nathanael and told him, We have found the one Mosheh wrote about in the Torah, and about whom the Prophets also wrote - Yahushua of Nazareth, the son of Joseph.*" Yahanan 1:35-45.

It is important to recognize that these individuals were not the ignorant, simple men as they are often portrayed. They were clearly spiritual men intent on serving YHWH and anticipating the Messiah. This is confirmed by the statement from Philip "*we have found the One Mosheh wrote about in the Torah and about Whom the Prophets also wrote.*" They knew the Scriptures and the promises found therein concerning the Messiah.

One of the trademark phrases used by Yahushua in gathering the talmidim was: "Follow me." Yahushua was on the move and if you wanted to be with him you needed to move with him. This was

reminiscent of the Children of Yisrael in the desert. When the cloud moved they had to pack up their tents and follow the cloud, otherwise they would be left behind.

He was like a shepherd gathering sheep. The fact that he called twelve talmidim clearly reveals that his purpose revolved around the twelve tribes – Yisrael. Interestingly, five of those talmidim were fishermen, which should have sent a resounding message that he came to fulfill what was prophesied by Yirmeyahu concerning the restoration of Yisrael. It was, after all, Yirmeyahu who said YHWH would send fishers to fish for men. (Yirmeyahu 16:16).

We know that right away, certain talmidim of Yahanan followed Yahushua, because they heard his testimony and therefore believed that Yahushua was the Messiah. After arriving in the Galilee, we read of a fairly peculiar incident at a wedding feast in Cana. How interesting that the first major story attributed to the Hebrew Messiah involves a wedding. And of all things, the focus is a miracle involving turning water into wine.

This event has been so obscured over time that the true significance has been seemingly lost. Actually, the event at Cana was the ideal beginning for the ministry of the Messiah.

"*¹ On the third day a wedding took place at Cana in Galilee. Yahushua's mother was there, ² and Yahushua and His talmidim had also been invited to the wedding. ³ When the wine was gone, Yahushua's mother said to him, They have no more wine. ⁴ Dear woman, why do you involve me? Yahushua replied. My time has not yet come. ⁵ His mother said to the servants, Do whatever he tells you. ⁶ Nearby stood six stone water jars, the kind used by the Yahudim for ceremonial washing, each holding from twenty to thirty gallons. ⁷ Yahushua said to the servants, Fill the jars with water, so they filled them to the brim. ⁸ Then he told them, Now draw some out and take it to the master of the banquet. They did so, ⁹ and the master of the banquet tasted the water that had been turned into wine. He did not realize where it had come from, though the servants who had drawn the water knew. Then he called the bridegroom aside ¹⁰ and said, Everyone brings out the choice wine first and then the cheaper wine after the guests have had too much to drink; but you have saved the best till now.*" Yahanan 2:1-10.

Now this wedding occurred after a sequence of daily events in the text, which is preceded with the statement "On the third day." You could interpret this as being three days after the preceeding event or simply a reference to the third day of the week, commonly known as Tuesday. So we really do not know for sure when this event happened and there could have been a significant lapse of time.

At a minimum, it shows that Yahushua knew the difference between good wine and bad wine. For wine enthusiasts, this is certainly good news, but there is so much more. It was certainly a miracle to turn water into wine, so we see that Yahushua operated with power, but this same power was something claimed to belong to the god Dionysus.

Remember that Dionysus was the pagan god of wine, and turning water into wine was something that allegedly occurred at certain Dionysian feasts. Dionysus was worshipped in the Galilee, especially in the nearby city of Sepphoris, which was also the traditional birth place of Miryam, the mother of Yahushua.

Dionysus was also likely worshipped in the decapolis cities of Hippos and Sythopolis as well, which were near the Sea of Galilee. As a result, one must speculate whether this miracle was a direct affront to that pagan savior diety Dionysus who people claimed to be the son of god? Most likely it was, but there was even more.

The fact that this miracle occurred at a wedding is also quite significant. There are those who believe that it occurred on the first day of the first month when the Tabernacle was set up.[190] If so, was Yahushua emphasizing that his purpose was all about a wedding? During the traditional Hebrew wedding a Chuppah, which is symbolic of the Tabernacle, is set up over the bride and the groom. The symbolism cannot be ignored.

There was also another element to this miracle which often gets overlooked. This miracle of turning water into wine may also have been a direct affront to the Yahudim's tradition concerning ceremonially purified water. For those familiar with the mikvah, it is clear why people would have large quantities of water for ritual immersions in their home, although it is questionable whether an immersion pool in a home actually qualifies as "living water."

Since most people used liquid containers to store either wine or water, it would have been important to thoroughly wash the containers to remove any remnant of wine if they were going to hold ritually purified water. According to tradition, this water was not to have any vinegar taste or evidence of wine, otherwise it would not be considered pure. By using these designated water jugs, which were filled with water that was then turned into wine, Yahushua was sending a powerful message concerning the customs of the Yahudim. (Yahanan 2:6).[191]

This entire tradition was man-made and not found within the Torah. Yahushua actually spent much of his ministry coming against the customs and traditions which were not founded on pure Torah. In fact, early in his ministry he made it a point to declare his intentions

concerning the Torah.

"*17 Do not think that I have come to abolish the Torah or the Prophets; I have not come to abolish them but to fulfill them. *18 I tell you the truth, until heaven and earth disappear, not the smallest letter, not the least stroke of a pen, will by any means disappear from the Torah until everything is accomplished. *19 Anyone who breaks one of the least of these commandments and teaches others to do the same will be called least in the kingdom of heaven, but whoever practices and teaches these commands will be called great in the kingdom of heaven. *20 For I tell you that unless your righteousness surpasses that of the Pharisees and the teachers of the Torah, you will certainly not enter the kingdom of heaven."* Mattityahu 5:17-20

The Pharisees were thought to be righteous, but their righteousness needed to be exceeded in order to enter into the Kingdom. This statement would have highly offended the Pharisees, because it meant that the Pharisees were not in the Kingdom. You see, the Pharisees had violated a critical command not to add to or take away from the Torah. (Devarim 12:32).

They had created a myriad of traditions and man-made commandments which did just that. Because they were not following the Torah, they were not walking in purity and righteousness. They were adding to the Torah and taking away from the Torah, which was specifically prohibited.

Interestingly, the final words of the "Old Testament" found in most English translations of the Scriptures come from the Prophet Malachi which reads: "*4 Remember the Torah of Mosheh, My servant, which I commanded him in Horeb for all Yisrael, with the statutes and judgments."* Malachi 4:4. Christians, who claim to follow the teachings of Yahushua, often struggle with this passage, because it does not synchronize with their understanding of "the Law" and Grace.

The popular Christian mantra that "we are under Grace and not under the Law" has been useful in justifying the notion that Christians do not need to obey the instructions of YHWH found in the Torah, despite the fact that a contextual examination of the Scriptures clearly reveals otherwise.

As a result, a critical test of whether or not Yahushua is the Messiah revolves around his treatment of the Torah. Christianity promotes a messiah named Jesus who allegedly did away with the Torah, which they call "the Law." This position is diametrically opposed to the Scriptures and actually makes no sense if you claim to follow YHWH. In this respect and others, Christianity has more in common with Dionysian worship than it does with the worship of

YHWH.

The Torah was a gift given by YHWH to His Bride - Yisrael. It was given to show her the righteous conduct which would allow her to draw close to YHWH. This is when true intimacy and knowledge can take place. The Torah and the Messiah are therefore closely connected - not opposed.

One of the reasons for the confusion surrounding Yahushua's statement is that people often think of "fulfilling" as completing or bringing something to an end. What Yahushua meant was that he came "to make perfect" or "to fill up, to give meaning" and to show the heart of the Torah. Essentially, the written Torah was incomplete without the Messiah – the Living Torah. Thus Yahushua did not come to do away with the Torah, but rather to fill it up with meaning. He showed us what it was really like to live and walk according to the instructions of YHWH – He became our living, breathing example – the Torah in the flesh.

David H. Stern in his commentary on Mattityahu 5:17 states: "[t]he Greek word for 'to complete' is 'plerosai,' literally, 'to fill;' the usual rendering here, however, is 'to fulfill.' Replacement theology, which wrongly teaches that the Church has replaced the Jews as [Elohim's] people, understands this verse wrongly . . . [Yahushua's] 'fulfilling' the Torah is thought to mean that it is unnecessary for people to fulfill it now. But there is no logic to the presupposition that [Yahushua's] obeying the Torah does away with our need to obey it . . . [Yahushua] did not come to abolish but 'to make full' (plerosai) the meaning of what the Torah and the ethical demands of the Prophets require. Thus he came to complete our understanding of the Torah and the Prophets so that we can try more effectively to be and do what they say to be and do."[192]

Mr. Stern is quite correct when he links Replacement Theology with the teaching that Yahushua's fulfillment of the Torah resulted in the abolition of the Torah. The text in Mattityahu very clearly and succinctly says the exact opposite. Only when you try to apply a preconceived theology that the "Church" has replaced Yisrael, and that grace has replaced the Torah would you ever even attempt to construe the text in such a fashion.

It is important to note that twice in verse 17 Yahushua states that he *did not come to destroy the Torah*. He then goes on to state the converse - that he came to fill up or fulfill the Torah - these are clearly different objectives. Destroy means to "do away with," and he specifically said that he did not come to do that. The word plerosai (πληρωσαι)

which is often translated as "fulfill" in that particular passage does not, and cannot, mean to do away with. Otherwise Yahushua would be contradicting himself. Therefore, when Yahushua said that he came to fulfill the Torah, he did not mean that he came to do away with the Torah.

Further, when Yahushua said that *"till heaven and earth pass away not one jot or one tittle"* of the Torah would pass away, he was making a very precise and definitive statement. First of all he gave a time frame, which is the passing of heaven and earth. Since heaven and earth are still here, it is very safe to say that the Torah has not passed away. Second, he said that not one jot or tittle would pass from the Torah till <u>all</u> is fulfilled. As a result, according to Yahushua all of the Torah is still relevant and applicable to this day.

It is commonly taught that the jot is meant to signify the "iota" (ι) and the "yud" (י) which are the smallest letters in the Greek and Hebrew alphabets. A tittle is a stroke, a dot or other marking made on the Torah scroll such as the decorative spurs added to Hebrew characters. This is certainly an accurate understanding, but there is another interpretation regarding the jots and the tittles which is a little more profound.

Aside from the observable Hebrew characters written on a Torah Scroll, there are other messages imbedded within the text which are not discernable unless you examine a Hebrew Scroll. This is because there are many untranslated markings which were allegedly written by Mosheh and included in every Torah Scroll written thereafter. These are not necessarily as apparent as the "jots" and "tittles" and could easily be missed by the casual reader. These markings include such things as dots, enlarged letters, reduced letters, inverted letters, reversed letters, elongated letters and gaps, all with special meaning, but none of them are ever translated. An example of these are the untranslated Aleph Taw (את) and the enlarged bet (ב) that we saw in Beresheet 1:1.

Therefore, if you only review an English translation of the Torah you will never see these things. Thus, the jots and the tittles can be interpreted to mean, not only the Hebrew characters and the strokes and spurs added to them, but also the dots and the markings which are not even spoken or translated such as the inverted nun depicted in the picture above.

With either interpretation, the resounding point being made is that nothing in the Torah, not even the smallest mark or letter – whether translated or not - will change or pass away as long as heaven and earth are still in existence.

No rabbi in the first century would have ever contemplated "destroying" the Torah. The life of a rabbi and the entire people of Yahudah revolved around every word of the Torah. The meaning of the word "destroying" in context has to do with destroying the intended meaning of the text through faulty interpretation. It is only after centuries of false teaching that any person could possibly imagine that the promised Messiah of Yisrael came to destroy the word of YHWH.

This seems profound and is certainly contrary to accepted Christian theology, even though it was spoken by Yahushua at the beginning of the Messianic Scriptures, and despite the fact that Mosheh specifically provided that there would come a Prophet like him.

A close examination of the Scriptures reveals many striking similarities between Yahushua and Mosheh, and this should be of no surprise since Mosheh provided a vivid description of the Messiah in the Book of Devarim as follows: "¹⁵ _YHWH your Elohim will raise up for you a Prophet like me_ from your midst, from your brethren. _Him you shall hear,_ ¹⁶ _according to all you desired of YHWH your Elohim in Horeb in the day of the assembly, saying, 'Let me not hear again the voice of YHWH my Elohim, nor let me see this great fire anymore, lest I die.' ¹⁷ And YHWH said to me: 'What they have spoken is good. ¹⁸ I will raise up for them a Prophet like you from among their brethren, and will put My words in His mouth, and He shall speak to them all that I command Him. ¹⁹ And it shall be that whoever will not hear My words, which He speaks in My Name, I will require it of him.'"_ Devarim 18:15-19.

Those anticipating the Messiah would therefore be looking for someone "like Mosheh" – someone Who would speak in the Name of YHWH and follow His commands. That is why they asked Yahanan if he was "The Prophet." The Yahudim in the first century CE did not necessarily realize that the Prophet and the Messiah were the same.

One of the most significant roles of Mosheh was the fact that he was the mediator of the Covenant between YHWH and Yisrael. That Covenant was a continuation of the Covenant previously made with Abraham. It was a marriage Covenant between YHWH and Yisrael, and because Yisrael sinned and broke the Covenant, it needed to be renewed.

The Messiah would not come to do away with the former Covenant and mediate a brand new Covenant with the Bride – Yisrael.

Rather, He needed to restore and mediate the Renewed Covenant as prophesied by the Prophet Yirmeyahu. (Yirmeyahu 31:31). Therefore, if Yahushua was the Messiah, he would be in the business of restoring and renewing, not abolishing and replacing.

Remember that YHWH only uttered the Ten Commandments to Yisrael. The people could not listen to the voice of YHWH, and asked if Mosheh would meet with YHWH and relate His words to the Assembly. Therefore, although the Torah was from YHWH, it came through Mosheh.

Once you get past the false traditions and bad translations, it is clear to see that Yahushua was indeed like Mosheh in that he instructed people concerning the Torah with authority. Many times people marveled about how he spoke with authority which is "smikah" in Hebrew. Authority was something that was typically passed on from one to another. Just like the pattern shown in the Torah of Mosheh passing on his authority to, none other than, a man named Yahushua

According to Yahushua, his authority came from YHWH – just like with Mosheh. This is why Yahanan gave his testimony regarding Yahushua. As a result, Yahushua fit the description of "The Prophet" foretold by Mosheh, and people were supposed to listen to him and heed his words.

While speaking of his authority through parables, Yahushua also made it clear that he was the Son of Elohim.*[1] Now it happened on one of those days, as he taught the people in the Temple and preached the good news, that the chief priests and the scribes, together with the elders, confronted him [2] and spoke to him, saying, Tell us, by what authority are you doing these things? Or who is he who gave you this authority? [3] But he answered and said to them, I also will ask you one thing, and answer me: [4] The immersion of Yahanan - was it from heaven or from men? [5] And they reasoned among themselves, saying, If we say, From heaven, he will say, Why then did you not believe him? [6] But if we say, From men, all the people will stone us, for they are persuaded that Yahanan was a prophet. [7] So they answered that they did not know where it was from. [8] And Yahushua said to them, Neither will I tell you by what authority I do these things. [9] Then he began to tell the people this parable: A certain man planted a vineyard, leased it to vinedressers, and went into a far country for a long time. [10] Now at vintage-time he sent a servant to the vinedressers, that they might give him some of the fruit of the vineyard. But the vinedressers beat him and sent him away empty-handed. [11] Again he sent another servant; and they beat him also, treated him shamefully, and sent him away empty-handed. [12] And again he sent a third; and they wounded him also and cast him out. [13] Then the owner of the vineyard said, What shall I do? I will *send my beloved son. Probably they will respect him when they see him.* ¹⁴ *But when the vinedressers saw him, they reasoned among themselves, saying, This is the heir. Come, let us kill him, that the inheritance may be ours.* ¹⁵ *So they cast him out of the vineyard and killed him.* Therefore what will the owner of the vineyard do to them? ¹⁶ He will come and destroy those vinedressers and give the vineyard to others. And when they heard it they said, Certainly not! ¹⁷ Then he looked at them and said, What then is this that is written: The stone which the builders rejected has become the Chief capstone? ¹⁸ Whoever falls on that stone will be broken; but on whomever it falls, it will grind him to powder. ¹⁹ And the chief priests and the scribes that very hour sought to lay hands on him, but they feared the people - for they knew he had spoken this parable against them." Luke 20:1-19 (See also Mattityahu 21:33-46; Mark 12:1-12).

There is an enormous amount of information contained in this one parable. While we will not discuss every point here, it appears to show that he was sent, or rather born, during the grape harvest (Vintage time), which is around the seventh month. He was also predicting His death at the hands of the Yahudim.

By mentioning the source of Yahanan's authority, Yahushua was referring back to what happened when he was immersed, and the testimony from Yahanan that Yahushua was the Lamb of Elohim and the Son of Elohim. In typical Hebrew fashion, he was stating that his authority came from YHWH. The religious leaders knew the answer, but they would not say it because by doing so they would inevitably diminish their own authority, which was derived from man.

They did not want to listen to Yahushua because they had not been following Mosheh – the Torah. That is why Yahushua proclaimed: "⁴⁶ *If you believed Mosheh, you would believe me, for he wrote about me. ⁴⁷ But since you do not believe what he wrote, how are you going to believe what I say?"* Yahanan 5:46-47.

Interestingly, Yahushua stated that Mosheh wrote about him, which is an affirmation that he was The Prophet foretold by Mosheh. The people were told to listen to The Prophet. (Devarim 18:18). When Yisrael listened to Mosheh they were delivered from death and bondage. When they did not listen, they were punished in the wilderness.

Yahushua spent much time teaching Mosheh to the people as he ascended and descended in the style of Mosheh. Interestingly, Yahushua is often portrayed as opposing or contradicting Mosheh although nothing could be further from the truth. The general belief is that Mosheh taught *"eye for an eye"* and Yahushua taught *"turn the other cheek"* – Mosheh taught *"hate your enemy"* while Yahushua taught to *"love your enemy."*

We shall soon see that these seeming contradictions are not contradictions at all. It must be clearly understood that Yahushua was unambiguous about the fact that He and Mosheh agreed. Yahushua always taught the Torah, and he came against those who taught otherwise.

The following account makes his position very clear. "*¹⁷ Now as he was going out on the road, one came running, knelt before him, and asked him, Good Teacher, what shall I do that I may inherit eternal life?" ¹⁸ So Yahushua said to him, Why do you call Me good? No one is good but One, that is, Elohim. ¹⁹ You know the commandments: Do not commit adultery, Do not murder, Do not steal, Do not bear false witness, Do not defraud, Honor your father and your mother. ²⁰ And he answered and said to Him, Teacher, all these things I have kept from my youth. ²¹ Then Yahushua, looking at him, loved him, and said to him, One thing you lack: Go your way, sell whatever you have and give to the poor, and you will have treasure in heaven; and come, take up your stake, and follow me. ²² But he was sad at this word, and went away sorrowful, for he had great possessions.*" Mark 10:17-22.

When asked how one could enter into the kingdom and inherit eternal life Yahushua responded – Obey the commandments. He answered in typical Hebrew fashion by listing six specific commandments, but by doing so he was referring to the entire Torah.

This particular individual claimed that he had obeyed the Torah since he was young so he believed that he was set, but he probably would not have asked the question if that were truly the case. It turns out that this man was rich and his wealth had become an idol to him. Yahushua knew this and therefore advised him to sell all that he had. The man was very sad because he had made money his idol and Yahushua had revealed that matter.

This is what Yahushua came to teach - YHWH wants us to have circumcised hearts, not just circumcised flesh. That, of course is what Mosheh had taught Yisrael long ago when he proclaimed: "*Circumcise your hearts, therefore, and do not be stiff-necked any longer.*" Devarim 10:16. It was not just about obeying the Torah on the exterior where men could see, but more importantly it was about obeying in your heart which was the intimate place that belonged to YHWH.

Does this mean that wealthy people will not be in the Kingdom – Certainly not. It is simply harder for them if they are placing their trust and faith in their riches. Yahushua emphasized this point with a parable. "*²⁴ . . . Children, how hard it is for those who trust in riches to enter the Kingdom of Elohim! ²⁵ It is easier for a camel to go through the eye of a needle than for a rich man to enter the Kingdom of Elohim.*" Mark 10:24-25.

There are various ways to translate this text since the Aramaic could actually mean "cord" rather than "camel." If you look at that translation it would be difficult to force a "thick rope" or "cable" through the eye of a needle. Better yet, the eye of the needle traditionally represented a small door built into a gate which was used after the gates were closed. It was small so that it could be easily defended and controlled. A camel laden with goods could never squeeze through this door. The goods must first be removed before it could enter in.

This is the same with the Kingdom of YHWH. We cannot enter in with our baggage – we need to leave it outside the gates. Yahushua was demonstrating that although the man thought that he was obeying all of the commandments, he had a serious problem with his wealth. His wealth had become an idol and he had placed it before YHWH. He was unable to give it up. This is why Yahushua encouraged people to "store up treasures in heaven" (Mark 6:20).

This was a typical part of the ministry of Yahushua. He was able to reveal deep issues of the heart. He taught Mosheh, but he taught the heart of the Torah. So while the Pharisees were asserting their authority to interpret the Torah of Mosheh, Yahushua directly challenged that authority. He also clearly stated that he in no way intended on destroying the Torah and, until heaven and earth pass away, not the smallest part of the Torah will pass away.

He taught people to do as Mosheh told them to do, not follow the Pharisees when they deviated from the Torah. With that understanding now we can properly view the teachings of Yahushua.

There is not enough room in this book to discuss all of the teachings of Yahushua in light of the Torah, although it can be unequivovally stated that all of His teachings were about the Torah.

Some people believe that Yahushua changed the commandments or reduced them to just two. They use the following passage to support their position. "³⁴ But the Pharisees having heard that he had silenced the Sadducees, were gathered together, ³⁵ and one of them, one learned in the Torah, did question, trying him and saying ³⁶ 'Teacher, which is the greatest commandment in the Torah?' ³⁷ Yahushua replied: 'Love YHWH your Elohim with all your heart and with all your soul and with all your mind.' ³⁸ This is the first and greatest commandment. ³⁹ And the second is like it: 'Love your neighbor as yourself.' ⁴⁰All the Torah and the Prophets hang on these two commandments." Mattityahu 22:36-40 (see also Mark 12:29-31).

Many often miss the fact that Yahushua quoted "The Shema" which is arguably the most important prayer and Scripture to the people of Yisrael - "⁴ Hear, O Yisrael: YHWH our Elohim, YHWH is One! ⁵ You

shall love YHWH your Elohim with all your heart, with all your soul, and with all your strength." Devarim 6:4-5.

He also quoted Vayiqra 19:18: *"You shall not take vengeance, nor bear any grudge against the children of your people, but you shall love your neighbor as yourself: I am YHWH."* As we can plainly see - He was teaching from the Torah. He did not say that these were the <u>only</u> commandments and that he was abolishing the rest - He simply revealed that love was at the very heart of the Torah and he showed us the priority of our love and relationships.

Still others quote passages such as Mattityahu 5:38-45 to prove that Yahushua changed the Torah. The portion reads as follows: *"³⁸ You have heard that it was said, 'An eye for an eye and a tooth for a tooth.' ³⁹ But I tell you not to resist an evil person. But whoever slaps you on your right cheek, turn the other to him also. ⁴⁰ If anyone wants to sue you and take away your tunic, let him have your cloak also. ⁴¹ And whoever compels you to go one mile, go with him two. ⁴² Give to him who asks you, and from him who wants to borrow from you do not turn away. ⁴³ You have heard that it was said, 'You shall love your neighbor and hate your enemy.' ⁴⁴ But I say to you, love your enemies, bless those who curse you, do good to those who hate you, and pray for those who spitefully use you and persecute you, ⁴⁵ that you may be sons of your Father in heaven; for He makes His sun rise on the evil and on the good, and sends rain on the just and on the unjust."* Mattityahu 5:38-45.

This is a greatly misunderstood passage because you must know and appreciate the Torah to comprehend the teaching. First of all, when Yahushua refers to *"an eye for an eye and a tooth for a tooth"* he is specifically referencing the Torah, in particular Shemot 21:20-27 which refers to the treatment of people who were considered the property of others.

The allusion that Yahushua was making concerned the maltreatment of a bondservant. (see Shemot 21:1-11). He was declaring that if you belong to YHWH, then you look to Him for justice - you do not need to pursue the justice of a freeman which seeks retribution or compensation. Bondservants are to look to their Master for justice.[193] Yahushua was not changing the Torah, rather He was teaching something that was always in the Torah. He was simply elaborating on the heart of the Torah and went beyond the letter of the Torah.

As an innocent and blameless man, he did not deserve to be judged and mistreated by men – let alone killed. He had the right to seek justice for himself, but he came as a bondservant (Yeshayahu 42) and in that capacity he did not seek his own will, but that of his Master. With that understanding we then read Yahushua making a

rather peculiar statement: "*You have heard that it was said, 'You shall love your neighbor and hate your enemy.'*" The problem with this passage is that the Torah never instructed anyone to hate their enemy.

This begs the question: Did Yahushua misquote the Torah? While this was not a direct quote from the Torah it was a common teaching of the Essene Sect.[194] The Torah always taught that an individual should show kindness to an enemy when the opportunity presented itself (Shemot 23:4-5), and Yahushua taught his talmidim, as bondservants, to love their enemies and let their Master take care of the rest.

It is clear then that Yahushua was never changing, adding or taking away from the Torah – He was always explaining and revealing the depth of the Torah – the heart of the Torah or as He described them – "*the weightier matters of the Torah.*" Often times the religious leaders were so caught up in the minutia that they forgot what was really important.

Yahushua revealed how the Pharisees confused things by imposing their traditions and customs which resulted in Torah observance becaming a burden rather than a joy. They attempted to achieve righteousness through their man-made customs, traditions and laws and by doing so lost sight of the pure Torah. Yahushua was distinguishing between the traditions and laws of the Pharisees, referred to as their takanot (enactments) and ma'asim (precedents), and the unadulterated instructions of YHWH found in the Torah.

Yahushua aptly demonstrated this point to the Pharisees in an account recorded in Mattityahu 23:23 as follows: "*Woe to you, Scribes and Pharisees, hypocrites! For you pay tithe of mint and anise and cummin, and have neglected the weightier matters of the Torah: justice and mercy and faith. These you ought to have done, without leaving the others undone.*"

To properly understand this statement it is important to understand the tithe. For the purposes of this discussion we will look at one of the primary passages in the Torah concerning the tithe found in Sefer Devarim. "*[22] You shall truly tithe all the increase of your grain that the field produces year by year. [23] And you shall eat before YHWH your Elohom, in the place where He chooses to make His name abide, the tithe of your grain and your new wine and your oil, of the firstborn of your herds and your flocks, that you may learn to fear YHWH your Elohim always.*" Devarim 14:22-23.

The tithe revolved around the Scriptural Appointed Times described in Vayiqra 23 which are intimately connected to the major harvests in the Land. The object was that after the harvest, people would bring their offerings up to the place where YHWH designated and enjoy a celebration. For a long time it was located at Shiloh and later, under the reign of King David, it was moved to Jerusalem. (1 Kings 11:36). When Yisrael obeyed, it was a demonstration of the perfect harmony intended to exist between the Creator

and all of His Creation – mankind, the fruit of the soil and the beasts of the field.

The tithe was on the increase, and the Scriptures refer to the first fruits of grain, grapes, olives and flocks. There is no mention of herbs or the need to tithe herbs although if you want to, you are free to tithe them.

The point that Yahushua was making was that the Pharisees did things which were not even specifically prescribed in the Torah - yet at the same time – they missed the most important things that they were supposed to learn: justice, mercy and faith. In a similar passage in Luke 11:42 it refers to "*justice and the love of Elohim.*"

These are the "weightier matters" that we are supposed to be learning through the Torah, and these are the things that Yahushua came to teach. This was not a new teaching. In fact YHWH gave these same words to Zekaryah centuries earlier when Yahudah was returning from their exile in Babylon. (Zekaryah 7:8-10).

With that understanding we can look to other teachings and see how Yahuhsua was revealing the depth of the commandments. "*21Have you not heard what was said to those of old: 'You shall not murder and whoever murders is guilty of a judgment of death?' 22 But I say to you, he who angers his companion is guilty of judgment; he who calls his brother inferior shall be guilty of judgment before the congregation; (he) who calls him a fool is guilty of the fire of Gehenna.*" Mattityahu 5:21-22.

We see here that Yahushua is instructing people not only to obey the letter of the Torah, but the Spirit of the Torah. In other words, he is explaining that YHWH is concerned with matters of the heart, not just outward acts and appearances.

He taught in a similar fashion concerning another commandment. "*27 You have heard that it was said, 'Do not commit adultery.' 28 But I tell you that anyone who looks at a woman lustfully has already committed adultery with her in his heart.*" Mattityahu 5:27-28. Once again he is expecting more than the written Torah requires - he is talking

about our hearts. This is what Mosheh instructed (Devarim 10:16; 30:6) and it was prophesied concerning the Renewed Covenant – that our hearts would be circumcised. (Yehezqel 36:22-38; see also Yehezqel 44:6-9). This was not a new concept, but one that had been lost by the religious teachers.

Yahushua was distinguishing between obedience from the heart and external obedience for the benefit of men. YHWH desires obedience from the heart, not just superficial observances. This is why Yahushua told the Pharisees to: "*first cleanse the inside of the cup and dish, that the outside of them may be clean also.*" Mattityahu 23:26. He actually called them white washed tombs filled with dead mens bones (Mattityahu 23:27). They were more concerned with obeying the "letter of the law" to prove their righteousness externally, for the sake of others, but they were unclean inside. Yahushua was teaching that we first need to get our hearts right and obey internally for the sake of YHWH.

This notion is directly linked to his proclamation quoted previously: "*For I tell you that unless your righteousness surpasses that of the Pharisees and the teachers of the Torah, you will certainly not enter the kingdom of heaven.*" Mattityahu 5:20.

This is a powerful and profound statement since the Pharisees and Scribes were the teachers of the Torah, and they were the ones who were supposed to be righteous. Yahushua was teaching that they were not in the Kingdom, and this sheds light on his many confrontations with them. Since they were not in the Kingdom, they had no right to instruct the people concerning the rules of the Kingdom – the Torah.

So what do we make of the following statement attributed to Yahushua: "*2 The Scribes and the Pharisees sit in Mosheh's seat. 3 Therefore whatever they tell you to observe, that observe and do, but do not do according to their works; for they say, and do not do. 4 For they bind heavy burdens, hard to bear, and lay them on men's shoulders; but they themselves will not move them with one of their fingers.*" Mattityahu 23:2-4 NKJV.

This may at first appear to conflict with other teachings of Yahushua where he consistently corrects the Scribes and Pharisees and challenges their authority. In this passage he seems to be telling people to follow the Scribes and the Pharisees by doing what they tell people to do, but not follow their example in how they act.

It is important to recognize that Yahushua spoke of the seat of Mosheh. The seat of Mosheh can refer to either a chair, or a raised platform in a synagogue. Yahushua's instructions become perfectly clear when it is understood that the seat of Mosheh refers to the place where the written Torah is read. His instructions are as valid today as they were when he first gave them. Yahushua was saying that when someone stands in the synagogue and reads the Torah of Mosheh, do what they say, but not necessarily do what they do.

Yahushua was telling people to do what Mosheh says, not what the Pharisees do. In other words, what Mosheh said and what the Pharisees did were not always the same, therefore defer to Mosheh and do what he instructed.

Yahushua also made an interesting comment which is often overlooked. He stated in verse 5: "*But their works they do to be seen by men. They make broad straps for their teffilin and enlarge the tzitzit of their mantles.*" This statement will seem quite foreign for anyone unfamiliar with the commandments concerning teffilin and tzitzit.

Teffilin are worn to fulfill the commandments found in Shemot 13:9 as well as Devarim 6:8 and 11:18 which provide direction concerning the instructions to "*bind them as a sign on your hand, and they shall be as frontlets between your eyes.*" The Pharisees, instead of wearing modest Teffilin wore large Teffilin to impress men.

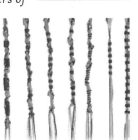

Likewise, the tzitzit (צִיצִת), often called tassels or fringes, are commanded to be worn on two separate instances in the Torah. In Devarim 22:12 YHWH commands: "*Make tzitzit on the four corners of the garment with which you cover yourself.*" According to Bemidbar 15:37-41: "*37 YHWH spoke to Mosheh, saying, 38 Speak to the children of Yisrael, and you shall say to them to make tzitziyot on the corners of their garments throughout their generations, and to put a blue cord in the tzitzit of the corners. 39 And it shall be to you for a tzitzit, and you shall see it, and shall remember all the commands of YHWH and shall do them, and not search after your own heart and your own eyes after which you went whoring, 40 so that you remember, and shall do all My commands, and be set apart unto your Elohim. 41 I am YHWH your Elohim, Who brought you out of the land of Egypt, to be your Elohim. I am YHWH your Elohim.*"

The Pharisees did not just wear simple phylacteries, they wore very large ones. They did not just wear modest tzitzit, they wore *very long* tzitzit, as if the size of their phylacteries or tzitzit demonstrated their degree of piousness. Their obedience became a show and was mere

pageantry. This was not the result intended by the very commandments which they were supposed to be obeying. The tzitzit and the phylacteries are supposed to remind us of the commandments so that we walk in obedience, but the Pharisees had turned them into religious badges.

Their hearts were not right and their intentions were misplaced. The point here is that Yahushua was not criticizing the fact that they obeyed the Torah but rather the manner in which they obeyed.

Clearly Yahushua himself obeyed the commandments. He wore tzitzit on his garment and was not against teffilin. In fact, we can see an incredible fulfillment of prophecy in and through his Torah observance. A prophecy in the Tanak speaks of the Messiah as follows: *"The Sun of Righteousness shall arise with healing in His wings."* Malachi 4:2 NKJV. These "wings" are kanaph (כנף) in Hebrew and refer to the edge of a garment, which is where the tzitzit are placed. In fact one of the commandments concerning the wearing of tzitzit specifies that they are to be placed in the "wings" (כנף) of the garment. (see Bemidbar 15:38). So the prophecy is stating that the Messiah will come with healing in His tzitzit.

We read in the book of Luke the following: *"[43] Now a woman, having a flow of blood for twelve years, who had spent all her livelihood on physicians and could not be healed by any, [44] came from behind and touched the border of his garment. And immediately her flow of blood stopped."* Luke 8:43-44 NKJV. The Greek word used to describe a "border" is kraspedon (κρασπεδον) which means a fringe or tassel - tzitzit. Therefore, the woman grabbed Yahushua's tzitzit, which he was wearing in obedience to the Torah, and she was instantly healed just as the Prophet Malachi foretold.

Also, in Mattityahu 14:35-36 we read: *"[35] And when the men of that place (Gennesar) recognized him, they sent out into all that surrounding country, and brought to him all who were sick, [36] and begged him to let them only touch the tzitzit of his garment. And as many as touched it were completely healed."*

We see in these passages not only a beautiful fulfillment of prophecy, but also an example of the Torah observance of Yahushua which has been obscured due to translation inconsistencies and ignorance on the part of translators. By taking hold of the tztizit - which represent the commandments, the terms of the Covenant - people were shown that healing and blessings come through the Torah which is what Messiah came to teach and fulfill.

Once it is understood that Yahushua affirmed the Torah and its continuing validity, *"until all is fulfilled and as long as Heaven and*

Earth remain," it is easy to see that all of his teachings were in absolute agreement with the Torah.

While the religious leaders were adding to the Torah and taking away from the Torah, Yahushua was restoring the Torah. Much of what we read about in the Messianic writings revolved around the issue of who had the authority to interpret and teach the Torah.

Yahushua claimed that he was the Son of Elohim and His authority derived from Heaven. The religious leaders were not willing to submit to his authority, nor the Torah of Mosheh. They wanted to keep their authority which involved building a fence around the Torah by adding to the Torah.

This, of course, was provided in the riddle concerning the Name of the Son that was previously discussed. "*4 . . . What is His Name, and the Name of His Son? Tell me if you know! 5 Every word of Elohim is flawless; He is a shield to those who take refuge in Him. 6 Do not add to His words, or He will rebuke you and prove you a liar."* Proverbs 30:4-6. This is exactly what the Son did, he rebuked those who added to the words of YHWH.

At times we read about Yahushua doing some rather peculiar things which do not necessarily make sense, because we fail to understand the essence of this conflict. When he confronted the religious leadership he would often provoke them by intentionally violating their man made laws. By doing so, he was knocking down the fence that they had build around the Torah.

He often used healing as a way to demonstrate this point. On one occasion, using saliva, Yahushua made clay and placed it into a man's eyes to heal him which was in direct contradiction to the man-made laws regarding what could be done on the Sabbath. According to tradition, it was a violation to make anything on the Sabbath and, believe it or not, it was prohibited to put saliva in a person's eyes to heal them on the Sabbath. (Talmud – Mas. Shabbath 108b). There were also those who considered it a violation to heal on the Sabbath. Therefore in this one instance, he violated three of the man made laws, but none of the Torah commandments. (Yahanan 9:1).

Another example can be seen when Yahushua healed a paralyzed man on the Sabbath who was waiting by the pool at the Sheep Gate called Beit Zatha. *"8 Then Yahushua said to him, Get up! Pick up your mat and walk. 9 At once the man was cured; he picked up his mat and walked. The day on which this took place was a Sabbath, 10 and so the Yahudim said to the man who had*

been healed, It is the Sabbath; the law forbids you to carry your mat. " But he replied, The man who made me well said to me, Pick up your mat and walk." Yahanan 5:8-11.

Yahushua healed a man and specifically told him to pick up his mat and walk. The Torah does not prohibit a person from picking up their mat and walking on the Sabbath, especially when they have just been miraculously healed. It was only the tradition of men which forbid such a thing.

As already mentioned, the Scribes and Pharisees even argued that it was unlawful to heal on the Sabbath. "⁶ Now it happened on another Sabbath, also, that he entered the synagogue and taught. And a man was there whose right hand was withered.⁷ So the Scribes and Pharisees watched him closely, whether he would heal on the Sabbath, that they might find an accusation against him ⁸ But he knew their thoughts, and said to the man who had the withered hand, Arise and stand here. And he arose and stood. ⁹ Then Yahushua said to them, I will ask you one thing: Is it lawful on the Sabbath to do good or to do evil, to save life or to destroy? ¹⁰ And when he had looked around at them all, he said to the man, Stretch out your hand. And he did so, and his hand was restored as whole as the other. ¹¹ But they were filled with rage, and discussed with one another what they might do to Yahushua." Luke 6:6-11.

Imagine that! The religious leaders were so blinded by their own unhealthy legalistic mindset, that they failed to recognize the miracles which were occurring before their eyes. Instead of rejoicing that they had just witnessed a miracle they were filled with rage.

The Sabbath which YHWH created for good was meant to be an easy commandment for His people to bear. Sadly, it had been turned into a heavy weight around men's necks by the religious leaders. (Acts 15:10). The Sabbath was meant to give needed rest and refreshment to YHWH's creation, and what better time to heal His people than on this blessed, set apart day.

It seems utterly absurd that anyone would ever believe YHWH would prohibit healing on the Sabbath. The reason that this is so bizarre is that all true healing comes from YHWH, so if a person gets healed on the Sabbath, then it surely must be acceptable. This demonstrates how far Yisrael had strayed from the truth by the time Yahushua came.

It clearly angered him to see how men had twisted the commands which were meant to liberate and bless people. Instead of providing rest, the traditions of men were enslaving people. He was bringing people back to the freedom and simplicity of the Torah, and showing the blessings and rest that the commandments actually provided.

There are really very few commandments concerning the Sabbath in the Torah, but the Pharisees had developed hundreds. Again, it is apparent that Yahushua calculated his actions to challenge the authority of the Pharisees, including their takanot and ma'asim, although he always observed the Torah.

In fact, in another instance of healing, Yahushua specifically instructed a leper to obey the Torah after he had been healed. Here is a description of the event taken from a modern translation *"¹² And it happened when he was in a certain city, that behold, a man who was full of leprosy saw Yahushua; and he fell on his face and implored him, saying, 'Master, if you are willing, you can make me clean.' ¹³ Then he put out his hand and touched him, saying, 'I am willing; be cleansed.' Immediately the leprosy left him.¹⁴ And he charged him to tell no one, 'But go and show yourself to the priest, and make an offering for your cleansing, as a testimony to them, just as Mosheh commanded.'"* Luke 5:12-14.

In this case, the man recognized he was diseased and unclean, just as we need to recognize that our transgressions make us unclean. He had faith that Yahushua could heal him and, in fact, Yahushua demonstrated that he was willing to heal him. The man was touched by Yahushua and he was healed.

Instead of avoiding the leper, as most people would do, Yahushua touched him which was a wonderful demonstration of his love and compassion. He then instructed the man to obey the Torah concerning the healing of leprosy which is found in Vayiqra 4:1-32.

This particular command is very detailed and I suspect was not done very often, if ever. Notice that Yahushua instructed the man to obey the Torah *"as a testimony to them"* - meaning the priests. This is often true with our obedience to the Torah - it is for our blessing, but it is also a testimony to others. Surely this must have amazed the priests to see a man healed from leprosy, for this was a well understood and accepted sign of the Messiah.

The incident described in Luke is likely the same incident described in Mark 1:41, but in this text it adds a little more flavor. It reads as follows: *"⁴¹ Then Yahushua, moved with compassion, stretched out his hand and touched him, and said to him, I am willing; be cleansed. ⁴² As soon as he had spoken, immediately the leprosy left him, and he was cleansed. ⁴³ And he strictly warned him and sent him away at once, ⁴⁴ and said to him, See that you say nothing to anyone; but go your way, show yourself to the priest, and offer for your cleansing those things which Mosheh commanded, as a testimony to them."* Mark 1:41-44.

Notice that he healed the man then he *"strictly warned him and sent him away.*" There are some translations which state that Yahushua "*rebuked the man.*" This has been an interesting passage for many because Yahushua first has "compassion" and then "rebukes" the man.

This is an example of the oldest manuscript not necessarily being the accepted version. The surviving manuscripts of Mark preserve verse 41 in two different forms. The most common and accepted version, which is found in many modern translations, has Yahushua "moved with compassion" and later rebuking the man.

The Greek word for feeling compassion is "splangnistheis" and this is found in most of the existing manuscripts. Another version found in one of the oldest witnesses called Codex Bezae which is supported by three Latin manuscripts has the word "orgistheis" instead of "splangnistheis."

Orgistheis means: "becoming angry." Because of the agreement between Greek and Latin witnesses, orgistheis is generally conceded by textual specialists to go back at least to the second century making it the oldest witness of this text.

While Yahushua becoming angry does not fit within our accepted understanding, it certainly fits the context. To begin – Mark on several occasions describes Yahushua as becoming angry, so it would not be unusual for him to describe an angry Yahushua. (see Mark 3:5 and 11:15). It is also important to remember that this man, being a leper, was in a place where he was not supposed to be.

The passage clearly states that Yahuhsua was in a certain city. This is important because lepers were not supposed to be in cities. They were considered to be tamei (טמא) or unclean. In fact, a leper was required to tear their clothing, shave their head and cry out "Unclean! Unclean!" so that people would not go near them. (Vayiqra 13:45-46). This is what we call being quarantined.

Therefore, it is very possible that Yahushua did, in fact, become angry at the man who was blatantly disobeying the commandments. It is consistent with the facts that after Yahushua healed the man, he sharply rebuked him and told him to go and obey the commandments.[195] While Yahushua was clearly willing to heal the man, he may have been angered by the circumstances, which is entirely consistent with the fact that he came teaching the fullness of the Torah.

As mentioned, this was not the only time that Yahushua is recorded as becoming angry. Most people are aware of an instance when he made whips and overturned the tables of the money changers in the Temple complex. This is often viewed as an isolated event, but it did not happen just once.

The synoptic Gospels describe him cleansing the Temple after his Triumphal Entry and prior to the last Passover before he was killed. (Mattityahu 21:12-16; Mark 11:15-17; Luke 19:45-47). This event occurred at the end of his ministry. Yahanan refers to a time when he cleansed the Temple during his first recorded Passover in Jerusalem. This occurred when he initially began his ministry. (Yahanan 2:14-16). I believe that he likely did it every time he went to Jerusalem, or that he was bracketing his ministry with these two events at Passover which is a very Hebraic thing to do.

Read about one encounter according to Mark: *"¹⁵ So they came to Jerusalem. Then Yahushua went into the House of YHWH and began to drive out those who bought and sold in the House of YHWH, and overturned the tables of the money changers and the seats of those who sold doves. ¹⁶ And he would not allow anyone to carry wares through the House of YHWH.¹⁷ Then he taught, saying to them, Is it not written, 'My house shall be called a House of Prayer for all nations?' But you have made it a den of thieves."* Mark 11:15-17.

Yahanan actually describes Yahushua as making a *"whip of cords"* and driving the merchants away. (Yahanan 2:15). The question in most people's mind when they read this passage is usually: "What exactly was going on here?" This does not sound like Yahushua, The Suffering Servant (Yeshayahu 53:3) found in the rest of the Scriptures.

He clearly showed how zealous he was for the House of YHWH (Tehillim 69:9). To fully understand the passage you must realize, in that day, there was a custom that people would use the Court of the Gentiles, which was part of the House of YHWH, as a venue in which they would sell their goods at excessive prices.

The Scriptures record that all of this was taking place *"in the House of YHWH."* (Yahanan 2:14). Also, it is believed that the money changers and the merchants were selling to the Gentiles on the Sabbath, because it was falsely believed that the Sabbath was not applicable to the Gentiles, who were sometimes referred to as dogs.

In that day, Gentiles were treated as unclean and were restricted

in their worship of YHWH. They were not permitted beyond the Court of the Gentiles under penalty of death. In other words, they were not permitted to enter into the House of YHWH as far as the native Yisraelites, which sent a resounding message that they were inferior or not as "special" as a native born Yisraelite.

Even to this day, the descendents of the Pharisees, the Rabbinic Jews, make no bones about the fact that the Western Wall in Jerusalem, known as the kotel, is their turf and they can be quite rude to a person who they do not want worshipping near their wall, which they consider to be a set apart place. This type of religious elitism is wrong and not supported by the Torah. It appears that once again, a wall is creating an obstacle between the Yahudim and the Nations.

The problem is that this conduct is diametrically opposed to the will of YHWH, so these Pharasaic religious systems have placed themselves in direct opposition to YHWH. Instead of being a Light to the Nations, and drawing the Nations to YHWH, they have been pushing the Nations away.

Yahushua was clearly upset when he saw the condition of the City, the House of YHWH and the people. Instead of being a "Light to the Nations" they were dark. Instead of revealing the truth of the Torah, they had hidden it from men behind their customs and traditions. Much of the blame fell on the shoulders of the "shepherds" – the religious leaders.

Because the system had failed and there were no shepherds for the sheep, Yahushua, acting as the Great Shepherd, gathered his talmidim and was training them to fulfill the Torah. An important part of restoring the Kingdom was to regather the lost sheep of the House of Yisrael. Although the House of Yisrael was in exile, and no longer a kingdom or a people, the prophecies spoke of a time when they would be regathered and joined together with the House of Yahudah.

Therefore, we see Yahushua, as the King of the Yahudim, teaching the rules of the Kingdom and preparing for the prophesied regathering. He clearly stated: *"for the Son of Adam has come to seek and to save that which was lost."* Luke 19:10. The House of Yisrael was

lost. They had been scattered into the nations and were like lost sheep waiting for a shepherd. The fact that he spent most of his ministry in the Galilee, also known as the Galilee of the Nations, or the Galilee of the Gentiles, (Yeshayahu 9:1) is indicative of the fact that he came for the lost sheep which had been scattered amongst the nations. The Galilee was surrounded by pagan nations.

He clearly stated that he came for these lost sheep. "*I was sent only to the lost sheep of Yisrael.*" Mattityahu 15:24. The regathering of the lost sheep of Yisrael was an integral part of the Torah. Mosheh set forth the terms of the Covenant very clearly as well as the curses associated with disobeying the Covenant. Their disobedience would cause them to be thrown out of the Land, but they would eventually be regathered and once again obey the commandments!

Read the words of the Torah: "*⁹ Carefully follow the terms of this Covenant, so that you may prosper in everything you do. ¹⁰ All of you are standing today in the presence of YHWH your Elohim - your leaders and chief men, your elders and officials, and all the other men of Yisrael, ¹¹ together with your children and your wives, and the aliens living in your camps who chop your wood and carry your water. ¹² You are standing here in order to enter into a Covenant with YHWH your Elohim, a Covenant YHWH is making with you this day and sealing with an oath, ¹³ to confirm you this day as his people, that he may be your Elohim as he promised you and as he swore to your fathers, Abraham, Yitshaq and Yaakov. ¹⁴ I am making this Covenant, with its oath, not only with you ¹⁵ who are standing here with us today in the presence of YHWH our Elohim but also with those who are not here today. ¹⁶ You yourselves know how we lived in Egypt and how we passed through the countries on the way here. ¹⁷ You saw among them their detestable images and idols of wood and stone, of silver and gold. ¹⁸ Make sure there is no man or woman, clan or tribe among you today whose heart turns away from YHWH our Elohim to go and worship the gods of those nations; make sure there is no root among you that produces such bitter poison. ¹⁹ When such a person hears the words of this oath, he invokes a blessing on himself and therefore thinks, 'I will be safe, even though I persist in going my own way.' This will bring disaster on the watered land as well as the dry. ²⁰ YHWH will never be willing to forgive him; his wrath and zeal will burn against that man. <u>All the curses written in this Scroll will fall upon him, and YHWH will blot out his name from under heaven.</u> ²¹ YHWH will single him out from all the tribes of Yisrael for disaster, according to all the curses of the Covenant written in this Scroll of the Torah.*

²² Your children who follow you in later generations and foreigners who come from distant lands will see the calamities that have fallen on the Land and the diseases with which YHWH has afflicted it. ²³ The whole Land will be a burning waste of salt and sulfur - nothing planted, nothing sprouting, no vegetation growing on it. It will be like the destruction of Sodom and Gomorrah, Admah and Zeboiim, which YHWH overthrew in fierce anger. ²⁴ All the nations will ask: Why has YHWH done this to this Land? Why this fierce, burning anger? ²⁵ And the answer will be: It is because this people abandoned the Covenant of YHWH, the Elohim of their fathers, the Covenant He made with them when He brought them out of Egypt. ²⁶ They went off and worshiped other gods and bowed down to them, gods they did not know, gods He had not given them. ²⁷ Therefore YHWH's anger burned against this Land, so that He brought on it all the curses written in this Scroll. ²⁸ In furious anger and in great wrath YHWH uprooted them from their Land and thrust them into another land, as it is now. ²⁹ The secret things belong to YHWH our Elohim, but the things revealed belong to us and to our children forever, that we may follow all the words of this Torah. ³⁰:¹ _When all these blessings and curses I have set before you come upon you and you take them to heart wherever YHWH your Elohim disperses you among the nations,_ ² _and when you and your children return to YHWH your Elohim and obey Him with all your heart and with all your soul according to everything I command you today,_ ³ _then YHWH your Elohim will restore your fortunes and have compassion on you and gather you again from all the nations where He scattered you._ ⁴ _Even if you have been banished to the most distant land under the heavens, from there YHWH your Elohim will gather you and bring you back._ ⁵ _He will bring you to the Land that belonged to your fathers, and you will take possession of it._ He will make you more prosperous and numerous than your fathers. ⁶ _YHWH your Elohim will circumcise your hearts and the hearts of your descendants, so that you may love Him with all your heart and with all your soul, and live._ ⁷ YHWH your Elohim will put all these curses on your enemies who hate and persecute you. ⁸ _You will again obey YHWH and follow all his commands I am giving you today._ ⁹ Then YHWH your Elohim will make you most prosperous in all the work of your hands and in the fruit of your womb, the young of your livestock and the crops of your Land. YHWH will again delight in you and make you prosperous, just as he delighted in your fathers, ¹⁰ if you obey YHWH your Elohim and keep His commands and decrees that are written in this Scroll of the Torah and

turn to YHWH your Elohim with all your heart and with all your soul. [11] Now what I am commanding you today is not too difficult for you or beyond your reach. [12] It is not up in heaven, so that you have to ask: Who will ascend into heaven to get it and proclaim it to us so we may obey it? [13] Nor is it beyond the sea, so that you have to ask: Who will cross the sea to get it and proclaim it to us so we may obey it? [14] No, the word is very near you; it is in your mouth and in your heart so you may obey it. [15] See, I set before you today life and prosperity, death and destruction. [16] For I command you today to love YHWH your Elohim, to walk in His ways, and to keep His commands, decrees and laws; then you will live and increase, and YHWH your Elohim will bless you in the Land you are entering to possess. [17] But if your heart turns away and you are not obedient, and if you are drawn away to bow down to other gods and worship them, [18] I declare to you this day that you will certainly be destroyed. You will not live long in the Land you are crossing the Jordan to enter and possess. [19] This day I call heaven and earth as witnesses against you that I have set before you life and death, blessings and curses. Now choose life, so that you and your children may live [20] and that you may love YHWH your Elohim, listen to His voice, and hold fast to him. For YHWH is your life, and He will give you many years in the Land He swore to give to your fathers, Abraham, Yitshaq and Yaakov." Devarim 29:9 - 30:20.

These words from Mosheh summarize the Covenant. Obey and be blessed in the Land. Disobey and you will be cursed and expelled. There was also a promise of return if they turned back to YHWH after being expelled. The words spoken by Mosheh had become a reality as both Houses had suffered the punishment of expulsion for their failure to obey the commands which were *"not too difficult."*

The Yahudim were back in the Land, but the House of Yisrael was still lost. Their punishment still had a long way to go until they could be returned to the Land, but once they were found, they needed to be restored to the Covenant and live lives of obedience according to the Torah.

The problem was that few were looking for the lost sheep and even if they were, they were not leading them into the truth of the Torah. Read what Yahushua said about the Pharisees. *"Woe to you teachers of the Torah and Pharisees – You hypocrites! You travel over land and sea to win a single convert and when he becomes one you make him twice as much a son of hell as you are."* Mattityahu 23:15. He clearly was not impressed with their evangelist outreach efforts.

The religious leaders had developed traditions and laws beyond

the Torah. They were controlling the people and diverting them away from YHWH and toward their man made religious system. YHWH had become a figurehead in this system, no different than the lifeless statues found in the pagan temples which were run by powerful priesthoods.

In fact, the House of YHWH was empty in the sense that there was no Ark of the Covenant, which represented the Throne of YHWH. The Temple in Jerusalem had been rebuilt and adorned by Herod, a tyrant with blood on his hands. YHWH was not pleased with the condition of things and He was not present in their religious system.

This is why we see many examples of Yahushua being sarcastic and critical of the religious leaders. He was not a pacifist by any means nor was he timid. He was confrontational and opinionated, bold and aggressive – not the picture that is typically portrayed by Christianity. He was challenging the religious leaders and exposing them before the people.

There is one particular confrontation which reveals the dynamics of the conflict between Yahushua and the religious leaders involving the washing of hands. "*¹ Then the Scribes and Pharisees who were from Jerusalem came to Yahushua, saying, ² 'Why do your talmidim transgress the tradition of the elders? For they do not wash their hands when they eat bread.' ³ He answered and said to them, 'Why do you also transgress the commandment of Elohim because of your tradition?' ⁴ For Elohim commanded, saying, 'Honor your father and your mother' and, 'He who curses father or mother, let him be put to death.' ⁵ But you say, 'Whoever says to his father or mother, 'Whatever profit you might have received from me is a gift to Elohim' - ⁶ then he need not honor his father or mother.' Thus you have made the commandment of Elohim of no effect by your tradition. ⁷ Hypocrites! Well did Yeshayahu prophesy about you, saying: ⁸ 'These people draw near to Me with their mouth, and honor Me with their lips, but their heart is far from Me. ⁹ And in vain they worship Me, teaching as doctrines the commandments of men.'*" Mattityahu 15:1-9.

To fully understand what is going on in this text, it is helpful to understand the historical background as well as to go beyond the English text. As discussed, the Pharisees had developed their own religious traditions apart from the Torah, one of them being the commandment concerning the washing of the hands. While many who read this passage believe that there is actually a commandment concerning the washing of hands in the Torah - they are wrong. This is really nothing more than a man-made tradition – you will not find this commandment anywhere in the Torah.

Regardless, the tradition exists to this day known as Netilat Yadaim. The following is a sample liturgy commonly used by those in Judaism to fulfill their inherited takanot. This one is done before making bread.

<u>Washing the Hands for Challah</u>
- Make sure your hands are clean and dry.
- Grasp the washing cup with your right hand.
- Transfer the washing cup to your left hand.
- Make a loose fist of your right hand.
- Pour water over your right hand -- enough to wet both the inside and outside of your right fist.
- Repeat.
- Transfer the washing cup to your right hand.
- Pour water over your left hand -- enough to wet both the inside and outside of your left fist.
- Repeat.
- Loosely cup your hands, palms upwards, as if to "accept" the purity, raise your hands and recite:
  Ba-rooch Attah A-doy-noy,
  E-lo-hay-noo Melech ha-olam,
  asher ki-di-sha-noo bi-mi-tz-vo-sav,
  vi-tzee-va-noo al ni-tee-las ya-da-yim.
  (Blessed are You Hashem (the Master) our G-d (Source of our strength) Ruler of the universe, Who has made us holy (special to Him) through His commandments, and commanded us concerning washing (our) hands.)
  Dry your hands perfectly.[196]

While the Pharisees may not have followed this exact procedure, this is the end result of the takanot which they were referencing. Notice that in their prayer they state that YHWH commanded us concerning washing our hands – which He did not. While it is certainly not a bad idea to wash your hands before you cook or eat, it is not a commandment.

If you examine the Hebrew text of Mattityahu, the essence of the conflict is crystal clear. The Pharisees first confront Yahushua by asking Him: "*Why do your talmidim transgress the takanot of antiquity by not washing their hands before eating?*" Amazingly, they considered it a transgression to disobey a takanot – one of their rules. Yahushua responded to them by asking: "*Why do you transgress the Words of Elohim because of your takanot?*" Notice He calls it <u>their</u> takanot which

is absolutely correct. It is not in the Torah and the takanot is not from YHWH - it is from men.

Yahushua was giving the religious elite a lesson in the Torah. He was also rebuking them for placing their own traditions above the Torah and, in fact, replacing the Torah and making it of no effect. A remarkable aspect of this passage is that Yahushua quotes the Prophet Yeshayahu during part of the rebuke which goes to show that the conduct of the Pharisees was nothing new - it had been prophesied centuries earlier. Because of this, Yahushua specifically provoked the Pharisees to prove his point.

Yahushua clearly instructed people to obey the Torah and I believe He often instructed his talmidim and others to disobey the takanot intentionally so that He could point out the error of the Pharisees. A good example of this fact is when the talmidim were walking through grain fields on the Sabbath (Luke 6:1-2).

As they walked, they plucked heads of grain, rubbed them in their hands and ate them. Seeing this, some of the Pharisees asked Yahushua why they were doing something which was not permitted on the Sabbath. Again, you can search the Torah high and low and you will not find any commandment prohibiting such conduct on the Sabbath, although it was prohibited by the traditions of men.

His actions were often a direct affront to the takanot of the religious leaders, and unless you understand the dynamics of what was going on you will miss much of the flavor of his ministry. Armed with this insight, it is my hope that the reader can now study the Messianic writings in a new light and see that Yahushua kept his word. He did not come to add to or take away from the Torah, but to show us the fullness of the Torah.

The religious leaders had hidden the Torah from most people and Yahushua came to reveal the Torah and expose the Pharisees – He was right in their face. In Mattityahu 23:27-28 we read as Messiah proclaims: "²⁷ *Woe to you, Scribes and Pharisees, hypocrites! For you are like whitewashed tombs which indeed appear beautiful outwardly, but inside are full of dead men's bones and all uncleanness.* ²⁸ *Even so you also outwardly appear righteous to men, but inside you are full of hypocrisy and lawlessness.*"

The word lawlessness comes from the Greek word anomias (ανομιασ) which specifically means without Torah. Therefore, the very people who were supposed to be teaching the Torah are accused of not having the Torah in them. Through their takanot and ma'asim they added to and took away from the Torah which was specifically prohibited. They placed heavy burdens upon men which was the exact opposite of what the Torah was intended to do.

The Torah was given to a redeemed people who were former slaves. It was not intended to put them back into bondage – it was meant for a free people. This is why Yahushua specifically stated that His yoke – which is the Torah – is light and easy. (Mattityahu 11:30).[197]

A yoke is meant to provide guidance and direction, and Yahushua came teaching, correcting and healing. Through his teaching of the Torah he was redirecting people away from the traditions of men and their religious systems back to YHWH. He also came seeking and gathering the lost. Everything Yahushua did was about the Torah and if you fail to understand this critical fact, then you will never understand Yahushua. He was actually a walking, talking, living example of how man was meant to live righteously before YHWH.

This could not be any clearer. The Torah has been described as: the Way, the Truth, the Light and Life (Tehillim 119:142, Proverbs 6:23; Tehillim 119:92). There is no coincidence that Yahushua uses these same words to refer to himself since he was the very embodiment of the Torah. His teachings were always consistent with the written Torah and his life was a fulfillment of the Torah.

According to the Book of Yahanan, Yahushua did many more things than could possibly be written down. *"If every one of them were written down, I suppose that even the whole world would not have room for the books that would be written."* Yahanan 21:25. As a result, it is not possible to deal with all of the actions and teachings of Yahushua in one chapter, or an entire book for that matter.

Through this chapter, it should be clear that Yahushua came teaching the Torah. He acted as both Priest and King to the flock of Yisrael until his death. He not only fed people's spirits through his teaching, he fed them physically. He healed the sick, cast out demons and raised the dead. While none of these signs proved that he was the Messiah, they certainly draw attention to him as one with authority from YHWH.

He was, in fact, the rightful King of the Yahudim with authority from YHWH. He was a King laying out the rules of the Kingdom and he inevitably challenged the authority of those who opposed him. He confronted the Pharisees on doctrinal issues and the Sadducees on financial matters. He was bad for their business because he kept exposing their defilement of the Temple system.

The religious "leaders" had only man-made authority and it was corrupted. This clash over authority inevitably led to their conspiring to kill the Son, just as Yahushua had foretold. The Messianic Writings

do not provide a complete, itemized chronological record of the length and duration of his reign. As a result, it is not immediately clear how long he ministered before he was killed. To find the answer to that question we will look at the final days of the life of Yahushua and the circumstances surrounding his death.

25

The Death

The Messianic writings detail the death of Yahushua around the Feast of Passover and Unleavened Bread although interestingly, they do not provide the year. In order to determine the timing and events surrounding the death of Yahushua it is imperative to understand the relationship between the Feast of Passover and the Feast of Unleavened Bread, both of which occur in the first month, commonly referred to as the month of the Abib.

As we saw from the teachings of Yahushua, he spent considerable time correcting the religious leaders who had added to and taken away from the Torah. They had strayed from the Torah through their traditions and the Passover was no exception.

The original commandment concerning the Passover directed the Children of Yisrael as follows: "*2 This month is to be for you the first month, the first month of your year. 3 Tell the whole community of Yisrael that on the tenth day of this month each man is to take a lamb for his family, one for each household. 4 If any household is too small for a whole lamb, they must share one with their nearest neighbor, having taken into account the number of people there are. You are to determine the amount of lamb needed in accordance with what each person will eat. 5 The animals you choose must be year old males without defect, and you may take them from the sheep or the goats. 6 Take care of them until the fourteenth day of the month, when all the people of the community of Yisrael must slaughter them at twilight. 7 Then they are to take some of the blood and put it on the sides and tops of the doorframes of the houses where they eat the lambs. 8 That same night they are to eat the meat roasted over the fire, along with bitter herbs, and bread made without yeast. 9 Do not eat the meat raw or cooked in water, but roast it over the fire - head, legs and inner parts. 10 Do not leave any of it till morning; if some is left till morning, you must burn it. 11 This is how you are to eat it: with your cloak tucked into your belt, your sandals on your feet and your staff in your hand.*

Eat it in haste; it is YHWH's Passover." Shemot 12:2-11.

This was the commandment concerning the first Passover which was a bit unique, since it occurred while the Children of Yisrael were still in Egypt – still slaves. Basically, it provided that there should be a lamb for a household and the blood of that lamb would provide a covering for the occupants of the household while other houses, which were not covered by the blood of a lamb, would suffer the death of the first born.

All those who trusted in YHWH and desired to obey His command were to select a lamb without defect on the 10th day of the month. They were to take care of it for four days, all the while inspecting it to assure that it was without blemish – an acceptable sacrifice to YHWH. For all practical purposes this adorable, soft, fluffy little lamb became a member of the family until it was killed on behalf of the occupants of the house.

The blood of this former "family member" then covered the inhabitants and protected the firstborn from death. It was to be eaten in haste as the household was prepared to leave.

There was no altar set up in Egypt nor was there a Levitic priesthood. Each family would kill their own lamb and sprinkle the blood on their doorposts themselves. In the future, they would take their lambs to the House of YHWH and kill their lambs where a priest would sprinkle the blood on the Altar.

There are other commandments concerning the Passover found in the Torah. "*YHWH's Passover begins at twilight on the fourteenth day of the first month.*" Vayiqra 23:5. Also we read "*On the fourteenth day of the first month YHWH's Passover is to be held.*" Bemidbar 28:16.

It is clear that the Passover was always commanded to occur on the fourteenth day at "twilight." Twilight in the modern understanding is similar as in ancient days. The Hebrew for twilight is: "beyn ha'arbayim" (בין הערבים) which is often described as meaning "between the evenings."

This phrase has been the subject of controversy from ancient times until this very day. The Pharisees taught that the "evening" and "between the two evenings" was any time from after noon to sunset. The Samaritans, Karaites, and Sadduceans, all taught that it was the time after sunset and before complete darkness.[198]

I believe that the most accurate definition of the Hebrew phrase describes the time between when the sun set below the horizon and total darkness. Remember that the command concerning the Passover in Egypt required the slaughter "between the evenings" on the 14th day,

not the 13th day.

In fact, the Torah specifically states that all the rites and ceremonies of the Passover were to take place on the 14th day of the first month. This requires the Hebrew phrase "beyn ha'arbayim" to be interpreted as beginning after sunset, as a Hebrew day begins at sunset. So the Torah was correctly interpreted by the ancient Samaritans, Karaites and Sadduceeans on this particular point.[199]

After the lambs were slaughtered they needed to be cooked and eaten in haste. The time after the meal was traditionally considered a vigil when the Yisraelites would stay awake and watch.

It was still the Passover when the sun arose the following morning and it was during this time that Yisrael plundered the Egyptians before they departed. Finally, at sunset, when the 14th day ended and the 15th day began, they left Ramses boldly, by divisions, as a victorious army. This was now the first day of the Feast of Unleavened Bread. (Bemidbar 33:3).

Therefore, Passover occurred on the 14th day of the first month, a full day before the Feast of Unleavened Bread, which began on the fifteenth day of the month. "*5 YHWH's Passover begins at twilight on the fourteenth day of the first month. 6 On the fifteenth day of that month YHWH's Feast of Unleavened Bread begins; for seven days you must eat bread made without yeast. 7 On the first day hold a sacred assembly and do no regular work. 8 For seven days present an offering made to YHWH by fire. And on the seventh day hold a sacred assembly and do no regular work.*" Vayiqra 23:5-8.

So the Passover was a meal that was commanded to occur after sunset, beginning on the 14th day of the first month. It was more than just a meal – it was an event. When the Yisraelites first celebrated the Passover in Egypt they did not eat the meal, clean up and go to sleep. There were thousands of the firstborn of Egypt being slaughtered throughout the land.

The Yisraelites did exactly as they were told, they had their staffs in their hands, they were fully dressed with their sandals on their feet. They were ready to leave and so the Passover continued through the full day of the 14th on to the Feast of Unleavened Bread which occurred on the 15th day.

This was how Mosheh and the Yisraelites kept the Passover in the year of the Exodus. The Passover was on the 14th day of the first month, and Unleavened Bread went another seven days from the 15th day to the 21st day of the first month. However, somewhere in Yisrael's history, the Passover was merged into the Feast of Unleavened Bread.[200]

As a result, the adherants of Rabbinic Judaism, Karaite Judaism and even Messianic Judaism have adopted this error in their practice.

With that knowledge and understanding, let us look at the final days of the life of Yahushua. We must remember that Yahushua always observed the Torah of Mosheh, not the traditions of men. As a result, he would have been going to Jerusalem at the proper time, and as the Lamb of Elohim he needed to arrive four days prior to the Passover to be inspected.

"*¹ As they approached Jerusalem and came to Bethphage on the Mount of Olives, Yahushua sent two talmidim, ² saying to them, Go to the village ahead of you, and at once you will find a donkey tied there, with her colt by her. Untie them and bring them to me. ³ If anyone says anything to you, tell him that YHWH needs them, and he will send them right away. ⁴ This took place to fulfill what was spoken through the prophet.*" Mattityahu 21:1-4.

The prophet being referred to was Zekaryah and reads as follows: "*Rejoice greatly, O Daughter of Zion! Shout, Daughter of Jerusalem! See, your King comes to you, righteous and having salvation, gentle and riding on a donkey, on a colt, the foal of a donkey.*" Zekaryah 9:9.

Yahushua surely knew this prophecy. It is not as if a donkey and a colt just happened to appear so he got on them and rode them into Jerusalem. Nor is it likely that he just came up with the idea at that moment. Rather, he was intentionally carrying out this act to fulfill the prophecy. This even becomes more pronounced by the fact that he did not ride them all the way from the Galilee, but only as he entered into the boundaries of Jerusalem.

By doing so he was declaring that he was King and he was arriving with the fanfare deserving of a King. This event should bring back the memory of David and it surely did for many at the time. The Messianic writings record people referring to Yahushua as the Son of David.

Here is the account of His arrival into the city. "*⁶ The talmidim went and did as Yahushua had instructed them. ⁷ They brought the donkey and the colt, placed their cloaks on them, and Yahushua sat on them. ⁸ A very large crowd spread their cloaks on the road, while others cut branches from the trees and spread them on the road. ⁹ The crowds that went ahead of him and those that followed shouted, Hosanna to the Son of David! Blessed is he who comes in the Name of YHWH! Hosanna in the highest! ¹⁰ When Yahushua entered Jerusalem, the whole city was stirred and asked, Who is this? ¹¹ The crowds answered, <u>This is Yahushua, the prophet from Nazareth in Galilee.</u> ¹² Yahushua entered the Temple area and drove out all who were buying and selling there. He overturned the tables of the money changers and the benches* *of those selling doves.*" Mattityahu 21:6-12.

The people were well aware of the prophecy, and their instinct was that the King was coming to deliver them from their Roman oppressors. The palm branch was the symbol of the Zealots and this waving of the palms was an act of defiance against Rome. The people cried out "Hosheana" which means: "save now!" Their cries were not about eternal life or about going to heaven when they died in the future. This cry was referring to an immediate need to be freed from the Roman oppression. They wanted Yahushua to kick out the Romans and take up his throne then and there. It was a battle cry and it was steeped in violence – it was about revolution! Sadly, the people did not understand what was happening.

Notice that the first thing Yahushua does upon His arrival is to drive out the merchants and the money changers from the Temple. He was directly confronting the Sadducees, not the Romans. He was attacking the profiteering that was going on in the House of YHWH. This apparently caused some confusion because people thought He was a prophet, not necessarily the Messiah. On the other hand they thought that Yahanan was the Messiah.

It may be that Yahanan was in the Land his entire life and had built a reputation while Yahushua was away and a fairly new comer to the scene. Yahanan had died and they might have thought Him to be the Messiah, the Suffering Servant. Most likely it is because they were simply confused, just as people are still confused to this day concerning the Messiah. They did not understand that The Prophet and The Messiah were actually the same person.

In any event, after his arrival into the city Yahushua, as the Lamb of Elohim underwent the four day inspection as required by the Torah. He had already been declared to be an acceptable sacrifice by Yahanan, who was a priest authorized to make such a declaration. The Scriptures record that Yahushua was in the House of YHWH daily and was inspected by the religious leaders, although He would depart to Bethany at night.

While in Bethany, Yahushua was anointed by a woman when "*the Passover and the Feast of Unleavened Bread were only two days away.*" Mark 14:1. She apparently took a very expensive alabaster jar of perfume, genuine nard, sometimes referred to as Spikenard. She poured this expensive nard on his head which apparently made some people upset, because they thought it should have been sold and given to the poor. Yahushua indicated that it was a good deed and he was being prepared for burial. How sad that the people witnessing these profound events

did not even recognize what was happening before their very eyes.

At the end of the inspection, after silencing the religious leaders from their attempts to trick him, he asked them a final question: "⁴² *What do you think about the Messiah? Whose Son is He? The Son of David, they replied.* ⁴³ *He said to them, How is it then that David, speaking by the Spirit, calls Him 'Master'? For he says,* ⁴⁴ <u>*YHWH said to my Master: Sit at My right hand until I put your enemies under Your feet.*</u> ⁴⁵ *If then David calls Him 'Master' how can He be his Son?"* ⁴⁶ *No one could say a word in reply, and from that day on no one dared to ask him any more questions."* Mattityahu 22:42-46.

This passage emphasizes the fact that the people did not understand the Messiah as the Son of Elohim, only the Son of David – the Son of Adam. In other words, they were looking for a man who would be their king, deliver them from the Romans and bring them unity and autonomy, but they were short sighted. They were looking at the here and now – the physical. They failed to see the greater work of the Messiah that only the Son – the Lamb of Elohim could accomplish.

This was such an important concept that the teachers of the people – the shepherds of the flock failed to understand. After silencing the religious leaders, Yahushua was clearly disgusted. He then proceeded to detail how pathetic these "teachers of the Torah" really were in what is popularly referred to as the seven woes.

"¹³ <u>*Woe to you, Scribes and Pharisees, you hypocrites! You shut the kingdom of heaven in men's faces. You yourselves do not enter, nor will you let those enter who are trying to.*</u> ¹⁵ <u>*Woe to you, Scribes and Pharisees, you hypocrites*</u>! *You travel over land and sea to win a single convert, and when he becomes one, you make him twice as much a son of hell as you are.* ¹⁶ <u>*Woe to you, blind guides!*</u> *You say, If anyone swears by the temple, it means nothing; but if anyone swears by the gold of the temple, he is bound by his oath.* ¹⁷ <u>*You blind fools!*</u> *Which is greater: the gold, or the temple that makes the gold sacred?* ¹⁸ *You also say, If anyone swears by the Altar, it means nothing; but if anyone swears by the gift on it, he is bound by his oath.* ¹⁹ <u>*You blind men!*</u> *Which is greater: the gift, or the altar that makes the gift sacred?* ²⁰ *Therefore, he who swears by the Altar swears by it and by everything on it.* ²¹ *And he who swears by the Temple swears by it and by the one who dwells in it.* ²² *And he who swears by heaven swears by Elohim's throne and by the one who sits on it.* ²³ <u>*Woe to you, Scribes and Pharisees, you hypocrites*</u>! *You give a tenth of your spices - mint, dill and cummin. But you have neglected the weightier matters of the Torah - justice, mercy and faithfulness. You should have practiced the latter, without neglecting the former.* ²⁴ <u>*You blind guides! You strain out a gnat but swallow a camel.*</u> ²⁵ <u>*Woe to you, Scribes and Pharisees, you hypocrites!*</u>

You clean the outside of the cup and dish, but inside they are full of greed and self-indulgence. ²⁶ *Blind Pharisee! First clean the inside of the cup and dish, and then the outside also will be clean.* ²⁷ *Woe to you, Scribes and Pharisees, you hypocrites! You are like whitewashed tombs, which look beautiful on the outside but on the inside are full of dead men's bones and everything unclean.* ²⁸ *In the same way, on the outside you appear to people as righteous but on the inside you are full of hypocrisy and wickedness.* ²⁹ *Woe to you, Scribes and Pharisees, you hypocrites! You build tombs for the prophets and decorate the graves of the righteous.* ³⁰ *And you say, If we had lived in the days of our forefathers, we would not have taken part with them in shedding the blood of the prophets.* ³¹ *So you testify against yourselves that you are the descendants of those who murdered the prophets.* ³² *Fill up, then, the measure of the sin of your forefathers!* ³³ *You snakes! You brood of vipers! How will you escape being condemned to hell?* ³⁴ *Therefore I am sending you prophets and wise men and teachers. Some of them you will kill and crucify; others you will flog in your synagogues and pursue from town to town.* ³⁵ *And so upon you will come all the righteous blood that has been shed on earth, from the blood of righteous Abel to the blood of Zekaryah son of Berekiah, whom you murdered between the temple and the altar.* ³⁶ *I tell you the truth, all this will come upon this generation.* ³⁷ *O Jerusalem, Jerusalem, you who kill the prophets and stone those sent to you, how often I have longed to gather your children together, as a hen gathers her chicks under her wings, but you were not willing.* ³⁸ *Look, your house is left to you desolate.* ³⁹ *For I tell you, you will not see me again until you say, Blessed is He who comes in the Name of YHWH."* Mattityahu 23:13-39

These were strong words which could only be spoken with authority from Heaven. Yahushua was full of righteous indignation, and after these statements, it is easy to see how the Scribes and Pharisees hated him to the point that they wanted him dead and out of the way. They were blinded to the fact that he was instructing them in righteousness and they needed to heed his words. This is because the truth was not in them. Once again, it is the condition of the heart which is most important. Outward acts are meaningless to YHWH if your heart is not circumcised.

We know that they did, in fact, conspire to kill Yahushua. Yahudah from Qerioth, commonly referred to as Judas Iscariot, joined with them for a payment of 30 pieces of silver, the price prophesied to be paid for the Messiah. (Zekaryah 11:12). His betrayal would not occur until after the Passover meal had occurred.

Judas was an interesting character because he was from Qerioth, which was a known Zealot enclave in the region of Judea. Therefore, he was likely a Zealot, or influenced by the Zealot philosophy. He later

"hung himself" on a sword which seems to reinforce the notion that he was armed and ready for conflict. (Mattityahu 27:5). Hanging oneself on a sword was a common form of suicide for a soldier.

Yahushua had another talmid who was also a Zealot, known as Simon the Zealot. Zealots subscribed to the notion of civil disobedience and were terrorists in the eyes of the Romans. The fact that Yahushua had "terrorists" as talmidim creates a very interesting scenario, and may be part of the reason why people expected him to conquer the Romans using violence.

Judas may have betrayed Yahushua to speed up the process of revolution. He may have intended to force the hand of Yahushua and get him to act. No one knows for sure what motivated Judas to betray Yahushua, but it is likely that the Zealot influence may have been a central factor.

The Book of Luke describes the following: "*7 Then came the day of Unleavened Bread on which the Passover lamb had to be sacrificed. 8 Yahushua sent Kepha and Yahanan, saying, Go and make preparations for us to eat the Passover. 9 Where do you want us to prepare for it? They asked. 10 He replied, As you enter the city, a man carrying a jar of water will meet you. Follow him to the house that he enters, 11 and say to the owner of the house, The Teacher asks: Where is the guest room, where I may eat the Passover with my talmidim? 12 He will show you a large upper room, all furnished. Make preparations there. 13 They left and found things just as Yahushua had told them. So they prepared the Passover.*" Luke 22:7-13.

The Book of Mark records the following concerning the same event: "*12 On the first day of the Feast of Unleavened Bread, when it was customary to sacrifice the Passover lamb, Yahushua's talmidim asked him, Where do you want us to go and make preparations for you to eat the Passover? 13 So He sent two of His talmidim, telling them, Go into the city, and a man carrying a jar of water will meet you. Follow him. 14 Say to the owner of the house he enters, The Teacher asks: Where is my guest room, where I may eat the Passover with my talmidim? 15 He will show you a large upper room, furnished and ready. Make preparations for us there. 16 The talmidim left, went into the city and found things just as Yahushua had told them. So they prepared the Passover. 17 When evening came, Yahushua arrived with the Twelve. 18 While they were reclining at the table eating, He said, I tell you the truth, one of you will betray me - one who is eating with me.*" Mark 14:12-18.

At first glance, these passages seem simple and straight forward. Interestingly, both of these events describe a man carrying water. For anyone familiar with eastern customs, the gathering of water was the exclusive role of women with one exception – the Essenes. Many

believe that this is a specific clue that Yahushua celebrated the Passover meal in the Essene Quarter of Jerusalem.

There is also great speculation that the Essene Sect was the source of many of the early talmidim. We know that the Essenes were particularly interested in the Messiah, and they rejected the religious leadership and the Temple system, so it makes sense that Yahushua would have attracted many from that sect.

Luke sets the day as *"the day of Unleavened Bread on which the Passover lamb had to be sacrificed."* Mark describes the time as "on <u>the first day of the Feast of Unleavened Bread</u>, *when it was customary to sacrifice the Passover lamb."* It is important to remember that the Passover meal had not yet occurred, because they were still making preparations for the meal.

It was a Passover meal held at the time prescribed by Mosheh. Remember that according to Mosheh, the slaughter of the lamb or goat would occur "between the evenings" on the 14th day. The animal would be roasted and the meal would be eaten thereafter.

So the Passover meal attended by Yahushua and His talmidim would have been in the evening of the 14th day, which was the beginning of the day. This was not a weekly Sabbath, nor was it considered to be a High Sabbath. The High Sabbath did not occur until the sundown the next day when the 15th day began, marking the first day of the Feast of Unleavened Bread. The Feast of Unleavened Bread would then last for a period of seven days. (Vayiqra 23:6-7).

As mentioned previously, some of the confusion lies in the fact that the two different times – Passover and Unleavened Bread – are often looked upon as one and the same Feast. The Messianic writings refer to the entire eight day period as either the Passover or Unleavened Bread, but the two Feasts are really quite separate and unique.

A similar mistake is made with the Festival of Sukkot in Messianic Judaism today. Shemini Atzeret is an Appointed Time – a High Sabbath. It occurs on the 22nd day of the seventh month, immediately following the seven days of Succot, which occur between the 15th day and the 21st day of the seventh month. Shemini Atzeret is separate from the Feast of Succot and not part of it, as the Feast of Succot lasts seven days. (Vayiqra 23:34-42; Devarim 16:13-15).

Again, modern followers of Rabbinic Judaism, Karaite Judaism and Messianic Judaism have merged the events of the Passover (14th) with the events of the First Day of the Feast of Unleavened Bread (15th) and treat the Passover meal as a High Sabbath, or at least a meal that merged into the High Sabbath.

The talmidim were not preparing to slaughter the lamb on the First Day of Unleavened Bread because that began on the 15th day – after the Passover meal. They were preparing for the Passover on what was commonly known as Preparation Day, the 14th day of the first month.

The previously quoted texts from Mark and Luke make sense when you understand that the Preparation Day was considered an important day in the general time known as "Unleavened Bread." So *"the day of Unleavened Bread on which the Passover lamb had to be sacrificed"* referred to in Luke was the Preparation Day.

The text in Mark, as is commonly translated, seems a little confusing. As already stated, the Preparation Day could not be the First Day of the Feast of Unleavened Bread although it could be referred to as the first day of the general eight day period. If viewed in that context it does not conflict with Luke.

There is also another simple explanation which synchronizes the texts. In Mark, the word translated as "first" is protos (πρώτη) in the Greek which means: "before, beginning, foremost in time, place, order or importance." Therefore it is understood that the events described in Mark occurred "on the foremost day before" the First Day of Unleavened Bread.

So two of Yahushua's talmidim prepared the Passover seder on the evening beginning the 14th, and several hours later, Yahushua ate the Passover meal with all twelve of his talmidim. There are some who speculate whether they were eating a Passover meal, or simply a meal before the arrival of Passover. All of the Scriptures unequivically state that they prepared and ate a Passover meal at the proper time. (Mattityahu 26:19-20; Mark 14:16-17; Luke 22:13-16; Yahanan 13:1-2).

One of the primary arguments presented in support of the fact that it was not a Passover meal is based upon the type of bread described at the meal. The Greek word used to describe the bread is arton (αρτον). (Mattityahu 26:26; Mark 14:22; Luke 22:19). Arton is a general word for bread, distinguished from the uniquely flat unleavened bread, known as matzah (מצה) in Hebrew and azumon (αζύμων) in Greek. Since arton is used instead of azumon, it is argued that they ate leavened bread, thus disqualifying the meal as a Passover meal, which must include unleavened bread. (Shemot 12:8).

What many fail to recognize is that the Greek word arton (αρτον) was also used to describe the showbread. (Mattityahu 12:3-4). The showbread refers to the twelve loaves of unleavened bread kept in the Set Apart Place in the House of YHWH (Vayiqra 24:5-8). The showbread is baked as loaves, rather than flat. According to the

Mishnah, it was considered lawful for the showbread to be prepared in Bethpage, where Yahushua and his talmidim had just been. (Menachoth 11:2). Therefore, it is very likely that Yahushua and his talmidim ate showbread in the pattern provided by David. (1 Shemuel 21:4-6). The use of unleavened showbread instead of the typical flat matzah makes this meal even more profound.[201]

As a result, there is no evidence that the meal described in the Messianic writings was anything but a Passover meal held at the proper time. It is important to recognize this fact, because it was Yisrael's participation in the Passover meal, specifically kept in accordance with the instructions provided by Mosheh which saved them. In Egypt, if they had applied the blood to their doorposts and kept the meal a day after Mosheh prescribed, it would have been too late – their firstborn would have been dead.

The Passover meal was not only a remembrance of the time when Yisrael was delivered from Egypt, but it was a shadow of a future event. In fact, up to that point it was kept as a rehearsal for this very Passover meal, when the Lamb of Elohim – the firstborn of YHWH – would take away the sins of the world. The Appointed Times are specific points in YHWH's plan when, in certain specific years, He initiates certain aspects of His Covenant with mankind. All of the Appointed Times are still extremely significant and important rehearsals, especially for those who believe that Yahushua is the Messiah.

The deliverance from Egypt was not a complete deliverance. While the people were physically redeemed and delivered from bondage, mankind still was under the curse of death inherited from their father Adam. In the first Passover the Yisraelites, along with a mixed multitude, entered into a Covenant with YHWH. That Covenant, which originated with Abraham, was written on stone and had been broken by the Yisraelites.

The punishment for breaking that Covenant must be born by the one who originally passed through the cuttings of the Covenant – YHWH. The Covenant could then be renewed as prophesied by Yirmeyahu. This time, instead of being written on stone, the Torah would be written on the hearts and in the minds of Yisrael. (Yirmeyahu 31:33).

The Passover meal, conducted by Yahushua, was the execution of the Renewed Covenant with the Lamb of Elohim present. The Book of Luke describes that renewal as follows: *"14 When the hour had come, he sat down, and the twelve talmidim with him. 15 Then he said to them, With*

fervent desire I have desired to eat this Passover with you before I suffer; [16] *for I say to you, I will no longer eat of it until it is fulfilled in the kingdom of Elohim.* [17] *Then he took the cup, and gave thanks, and said, Take this and divide it among yourselves;* [18] *for I say to you, I will not drink of the fruit of the vine until the kingdom of Elohim comes.* [19] *And he took bread, gave thanks and broke it, and gave it to them, saying, This is my body which is given for you; do this in remembrance of me.* [20] *Likewise he also took the cup after supper, saying: This cup is the Renewed Covenant in my blood, which is shed for you.*" Luke 22:14-21.

As with every blood covenant, there was a meal, typically following the sacrifice. In this case, since Yahushua was the sacrifice, the meal came first and the bread represented his body which would later be broken. The wine represented his blood which would later be shed. Notice it was the cup <u>after</u> supper which represented his blood and the Renewal of the Covenant.

This is significant because in the traditional Passover Seder, the fifth and last cup is the cup of Elijah, and it is all about the Messianic expectation. At the time of Yahushua, the Passover seder was not fully developed into the 15 step ritual that we now see in Rabbinic Judaism. That did not occur until the Talmudic Era after the destruction of the Second Temple.

At the Passover attended by Yahushua the final cup would not have been the cup of Elijah. The cup of Elijah was a rabbinic compromise that occurred when it could not be decided whether there should be four or five cups at the Passover Seder. The cup of Elijah was instituted to indicate that when Elijah came, he would settle the argument.

In fact, the cup of Elijah may have actually been inserted by Rabbinic Judaism to emphasize their belief that the Messiah <u>had not yet come</u>, and they were still expecting Elijah to herald the coming of the Messiah. As a result, the final cup in the traditional Jewish seder may stand in direct opposition to Yahushua.

However, the final cup in the Passover seder held by Yahushua showed the fulfillment of the Passover Feast by commemorating the renewal of the Covenant with Yisrael. This has been referred to as "the cup of thanksgiving" or "the cup of blessing." (1 Corinthians 10:16).

A letter from Paul, included in the Messianic writings, gives the following account of this Passover seder: "[23] *For I received from the Master what I also passed on to you: The Master Yahushua, on the night he was betrayed, took bread,* [24] *and when he had given thanks, he broke it and said, This is my body, which is for you; do this in remembrance of me.* [25] *In the same way, after supper he took the cup, saying, This cup is the Renewed*

Covenant in my blood; do this, whenever you drink it, in remembrance of me. [26] For whenever you eat this bread and drink this cup, you proclaim the Master's death until he comes." 1 Corinthians 11:23-26.

In other words, the emphasis of the Passover seder would no longer only be about the deliverance from Egypt. The remembrance would be the greater fulfillment of the Feast by Yahushua which was the Renewal of the Covenant. Many people believe that Yahushua was instituting a brand new Covenant, but that was not the case. It was the same marriage Covenant made with Yisrael at Sinai that was subsequently renewed. Only this time, according to the prophets, the Torah would be in the minds and written on the hearts of Yisrael. (Yirmeyahu 31:33).

Just as Mosheh was Mediator of the Passover in Egypt and the Covenant at Sinai during Shabuot, so Yahushua was fulfilling the Passover and mediating the Renewed Covenant later at Shabuot. The twelve talmidim represented the twelve Tribes of Yisrael. Yahushua was acting in the capacity of both King and Priest – not a priest according to the Tribe of Levi, although we know that his mother had Levite blood. Instead, Yahushua was acting in the role of a Priest according to the Order of Melchizedek. That fact was aptly expressed in the Book of Hebrews (see Hebrews 6:13-7:17).

Remember that the Passover was all about the judgment of the first born sons of Egypt. It was the firstborn that were killed and it is no coincidence that this was the time when the firstborn of Creation - the Son of Elohim - would die for the transgressions of the world. This was the culmination of so many patterns in the Torah. Yahushua's last Passover was the specific event that all of those patterns pointed to. Yisrael had been rehearsing for this particular Passover for over 14 centuries.

After the meal, this King and Priest spent time giving final teachings to his talmidim. (Yahanan 13 – 17). He was prepared to stay up all night long and commemorate the Passover vigil. After teaching, he walked to the Mount of Olives to finish what he started. He went to a place called Gethsemane to pray. Gethsemane means: "oil press" and how appropriate that this was the place where Yahushua was pressed before his death. It is through pressing that we receive oil and oil represents the Spirit in Hebraic thought.

As the Son of Adam, Yahushua needed to succeed where Adam was unsuccessful. Adam disobeyed by failing to "watch." Yahushua kept vigil all night while his talmidim kept falling asleep. The Tehillim allude to this event. "'I will lift up mine eyes unto the hills, from whence *cometh my help. ² My help cometh from YHWH, which made heaven and earth. ³ He will not suffer thy foot to be moved: he that keepeth thee will not slumber. ⁴ Behold, He that keepeth Yisrael shall neither slumber nor sleep. ⁵ YHWH is thy keeper: YHWH is thy shade upon thy right hand. ⁶ The sun shall not smite thee by day, nor the moon by night. ⁷ YHWH shall preserve thee from all evil: He shall preserve thy soul. ⁸ YHWH shall preserve thy going out and thy coming in from this time forth, and even for evermore."* Tehillim 121:1-8.

Yahushua stayed up keeping vigil – watching over Yisrael. He did not sleep nor did he slumber. Through the betrayal of Judas the Zealot, he was taken by an armed crowd arranged by the priests and elders. His response to them was essentially: *"Am I a Zealot that you come out with swords and clubs to take me?"* (Mattityahu 26:55).

Even though his entourage contained Zealots and he had been popular amongst the Zealots, he was making it clear that he was not one of them. He made this clear only days earlier when he declared *"Give unto Caesar what is Caesar's and to Elohim what is Elohim's."* (Mattityahu 22:21). Some speculate that he outraged the Zealots when he did not come out in opposition to Roman taxation. Through this response he lost the support of the Zealots which may have been a factor in the betrayal of his Zealot talmid, Judas.[202]

After being taken into custody, he was first taken before the former High Priest Annas, who was deposed by the Romans in 15 C.E., although he still wielded considerable power. He was then sent to the High Priest Caiaphas, and an examination was held before the ruling body of the Yahudim known as the Sanhedrin.

The Yahudim conducted a trial and the best charge that they could come up with was blasphemy. During this trial the High Priest asked Yahushua whether he was "the Messiah, the Son of Elohim." Here is his response and what followed thereafter: *"⁶⁴ Yes, it is as you say, Yahushua replied. But I say to all of you: In the future you will see the Son of Man sitting at the Right Hand of the Mighty One and coming on the clouds of heaven. ⁶⁵ Then the High Priest tore his clothes and said, He has spoken blasphemy! Why do we need any more witnesses? Look, now you have heard the blasphemy. ⁶⁶ What do you think? He is worthy of death, they answered. ⁶⁷ Then they spit in his face and struck him with their fists. Others slapped him ⁶⁸ and said, Prophesy to us, Messiah. Who hit you?"* (Mattityahu 26:64-68 see also Mark 14:61-65).

This conduct sounds more like a gang of schoolyard punks than a group of elders who were supposed to be Torah observant leaders of Yisrael. They were, in fact, frustrated and impotent men because they

did not even have the power to execute the sentence they had rendered.

Yahushua told them point blank that he was the Messiah – He answered their question. Apparently, declaring one self to be the Messiah was blasphemous according to these men. This demonstrates that they were never really prepared to receive or submit to the Messiah.

As if to drive the point home, Yahushua's brief response sent a powerful message. He was, in fact, referencing Tehillim 110 which reads as follows: "¹ YHWH says to my Master: 'Sit at My Right Hand until I make your enemies a footstool for your feet.' ² YHWH will extend your mighty scepter from Zion; you will rule in the midst of your enemies. ³ Your troops will be willing on your day of battle. Arrayed in set apart majesty, from the womb of the dawn (the dawning of the day) you will receive the dew of your youth. ⁴ YHWH has sworn and will not change His mind: 'You are a priest forever, in the order of Melchizedek.' ⁵ YHWH is at Your Right Hand; He will crush kings on the day of His wrath. ⁶ He will judge the nations, heaping up the dead and crushing the rulers of the whole earth. ⁷ He will drink from a brook beside the way; therefore he will lift up his head." Tehillim 110:1-7.

We have already discussed the Messianic implications of this passage. By quoting this Mizmor. Yahushua was proclaiming that he now had the scepter and that he would sit at the Right Hand of YHWH. He was a priest forever according to the Order of Melchizedek. He was proclaiming that he had all authority and they had been stripped of their authority.

Apparently, something worthy of death had occurred in this brief interchange that constituted blasphemy. It was determined by the Sanhedrin that Yahushua should suffer the death penalty, but this posed a problem.

Remember that the Scepter had departed from Yahudah. They did not have the power or authority to convict Yahushua of a capital crime, nor did they have the power to sentence him to death. This is why they went to Pontius Pilate, the Roman Curator.

Pontius Pilate examined Yahushua and originally found no fault in him, which was an interesting declaration for him to make. Yahushua as the Lamb of Elohim had gone through the four day inspection period and none, not even the pagan Roman ruler could find any real fault in him.

Regardless, the religious leaders were anxious to kill him before the Feast of Unleavened Bread began. They were in a hurry because it was their Preparation Day, and they wanted to get this deed over so that they could get on with their religious celebrations. It is quite astonishing that these religious men, so pious and righteous in their

own eyes, were plotting to murder an innocent man that offended them.

Apparently, it was important for these religious men to kill this nuisance so they could get on with their celebrations and enjoy their feast. They were supposed to be preparing their hearts to meet with YHWH, at His Appointed Time. Sadly, they did not even realize that he had come to meet with them through His Son who they were scheming to kill.

They were pawning off their problem on the Romans so that they could remain "clean." It was important for them to be clean so that they could participate in one of the most set apart Feasts established by YHWH. They were blinded, and while they were hurriedly preparing for their religious rituals, they could not recognize the Lamb of Elohim in their midst. This was the hypocrisy which Yahushua repeatedly confronted them with during His ministry. While they were trying so hard to be clean on the outside, they were rotten to the core.

So their religious rituals and observances, which were held on the wrong day, were of no value since they failed to understand the true spiritual significance. They were not following the Torah of Mosheh and therefore were "dead."

The Scriptures provide significant detail concerning the charges and the procedures followed throughout that Passover night into the early morning hours – the very night that the firstborn of Egypt were being killed centuries earlier. On this night it was the Firstborn of YHWH that was being sentenced to death.

There is a statement in the Book of Yahanan that has caused some confusion. "*13 When Pilate heard this, he brought Yahushua out and sat down on the judge's seat at a place known as the Stone Pavement (which in Aramaic is Gabbatha). 14 It was the day of Preparation of Passover Week, about the sixth hour.*" Yahanan 19:13-14.

It is very hard to synchronize the synoptic accounts in Mattityahu, Mark and Luke with this account in Yahanan. This is because the synoptic authors used Hebraic reckoning to designate the hours of the day, and Yahanan employs Roman reckoning to designate the hours of the day. Once this is understood, the accounts mesh perfectly.

Pilate brought Yahushua out before the judge's seat at around 6:00 am Roman reckoning. It was the morning of the Preparation Day, and final preparations were being made for the High Sabbath – the first day of Unleavened Bread which began at sunset. As it was 6:00 am Roman reckoning, it would have been just after sunrise – the exact moment that the morning sacrifice was being offered.

The Scriptures recount that Pilate found no fault in Yahushua and sought to release Him, but the people insisted that he be impaled. Pilate presented Yahushua to the people as their Sovereign – their King. They rejected Yahushua as their King and stated that they had no sovereign but Caesar.

Now Pilate had the authority to release Yahushua. He knew that Yahushua was innocent and not deserving of death. He did not apply justice, but rather political expediency. He was pressured by the religious leaders and he succumbed to that pressure.

The Book of Yahanan provides the following account: "[16] *Then he delivered him to them to be impaled. Then they took Yahushua and led him away.* [17] *And he, bearing his stake, went out to a place called the Place of a Skull, which is called in Hebrew, Golgotha,* [18] *where they crucified him, and two others with him, one on either side, and Yahushua in the center.* [19] *Now Pilate wrote a title and put it on the stake. And the writing was:* YAHUSHUA OF NAZARETH, THE KING OF THE YAHUDIM. [20] *Then many of the Yahudim read this title, for the place where Yahushua was impaled was near the city; and it was written in Hebrew, Greek, and Latin.* [21] *Therefore the chief priests of the Yahudim said to Pilate, Do not write: The King of the Yahudim, but, He said: I am the King of the Yahudim.* [22] *Pilate answered, What I have written, I have written.* [23] *Then the soldiers, when they had impaled Yahushua, took his garments and made four parts, to each soldier a part, and also the tunic. Now the tunic was without seam, woven from the top in one piece.* [24] *They said therefore among themselves, Let us not tear it, but cast lots for it, whose it shall be, that the Scripture might be fulfilled which says: They divided My garments among them, and for My clothing they cast lots. Therefore the soldiers did these things.* [25] *Now there stood by the stake of Yahushua his mother, and his mother's sister, Miryam the wife of Clopas, and Miryam Magdalene.* [26] *When Yahushua therefore saw his mother, and the talmid whom he loved standing by, he said to his mother, Woman, behold your son!* [27] *Then he said to the talmid, Behold your mother! And from that hour that talmid took her to his own home.* [28] *After this, Yahushua, knowing that all things were now accomplished, that the Scripture might be fulfilled, said, I thirst!* [29] *Now a vessel full of sour wine was sitting there; and they filled a sponge with sour wine, put it on hyssop, and put it to his mouth.* [30] *So when Yahushua had received the sour wine, he said: It is finished! And bowing his head, he gave up his spirit.* [31] *Therefore, because it was the Preparation Day, that the bodies should not remain on the stake on the Sabbath (for that Sabbath was a high day), the Yahudim asked Pilate that their legs might be broken, and that they might be taken away.* [32] *Then the soldiers came and broke the legs of the first and of the other who was impaled with him.* [33] *But when they came to Yahushua and saw that he was already*

dead, they did not break his legs. ³⁴ *But one of the soldiers pierced his side with a spear, and immediately blood and water came out.* ³⁵ *And he who has seen has testified, and his testimony is true; and he knows that he is telling the truth, so that you may believe.* ³⁶ *For these things were done that the Scripture should be fulfilled, not one of his bones shall be broken.* ³⁷ *And again another Scripture says, They shall look on him whom they pierced.*" Yahanan 19:16-37.

Yahanan indicates that he was present and witnessed all of these events personally, which is not necessarily the case with the other accounts of this event found at Mattityahu 27:32-56, Mark 15:21-41 and Luke 23:26-49. Interestingly, all of the accounts describe the mistreatment of Yahushua before He was impaled.

All three describe how the soldiers dressed him up as royalty by clothing him with a scarlet robe, placing a crown of thorns on his head and a reed in his hand. The soldiers then mocked him as the "King of the Yahudim." Mattityahu and Mark detail that he was whipped and beaten.

Typically, this treatment would suffice for a common criminal, but for some reason Yahushua was subjected to the penalty of death. The implication, which apparently prompted Pilate to pass this judgment, was that the Kingship of Yahushua was somehow an act of insurrection against the authority of Caesar. (See Luke 23:1-2; Yahanan 19:12).

This would appear to be supported by the charges which were posted on the stake of Yahushua. The Romans typically placed the criminal charges on the execution stake of the one being executed so that people could read and understand the reason for the execution. This was part of their method of deterrence. On the stake of Yahushua was posted the accusation that He was "The King of the Yahudim."

Interestingly, this accusation was more like a finding and a proclaimation made by Rome. When Pilate sat in his judgment seat and passed sentence, it was with all of the authority of Rome that he was making that judgment. So while Rome was declaring that Yahushua was the King of the Yahudim, the leaders of the Yahudim rejected Him as their King. Interestingly, there was more to this proclamation than meets the eye and you will never see it in the English language.

The proclaimation made by Pilate was written in three languages: Hebrew, Greek and Latin. This proclamation written in Hebrew would have read as follows: "Y̲ahushua H̲aNatzri V̲'Melech H̲aYahudim" or "יֵ̲הוֹשֻׁעַ הַ̲נִּצְרִי וַ̲מֶלֶךְ הַ̲יְּהוֹדִם". Therefore what would have been clearly seen by the Hebrews written above the head of Yahushua was יהוה which is the Hebrew spelling for the Name of YHWH, also known as YHVH.

While the Hebrew letter (ו) is often called "vav" and given a "v" sound it is believed to have had a "w" sound in ancient times and can also be called "waw." Thus the difference in transliterations of YHWH and YHVH. In any event, that is only an issue in English, the Hebrew would still be spelled the same.

As a result, the proclamation made by Pilate not only declared him King - it also declared that he was YHWH. This was probably part of the reason why the priests were so upset and wanted Pilate to change the wording, which he refused to do.

Yahushua was crucified between two "lestai" in the Greek, which were Zealots. So this King was crucified for sedition between two Zealots, who were considered to be terrorists by the Romans. According to the Book of Mark, Yahushua was impaled on the third hour, which would have been 9:00 o'clock in the morning. Mattityahu, Mark and Luke all describe that there was darkness over the Land from the sixth hour (noon) until the ninth hour (3:00 pm) when Yahushua gave up his Spirit.

He cried out "Eli, Eli lemah zabtani" (אלי אלי למה עזבתני). This was the beginning line of Tehillim 22:1 which aptly describes in great detail the event that was occurring. By making this declaration, Yahushua was confirming the fact that His suffering and death was fulfilling this prophecy. He then aptly declared: "*It is finished.*" Yahanan 19:30.

The reader may notice the use of the word "impale" instead of "crucify." I have also used the word "stake" instead of "cross." Not only is this the more accurate rendering of the word "stauros" in Greek, it also emphasizes an important point that is often overlooked or ignored by Christianity – Yahushua did not necessarily die on a crucifix.

Impaling a person was a terrible form of death that involved complete humiliation and suffering. Traditions have not always accurately depicted this event. To begin, the person being impaled was not raised very high off the ground and they were certainly not executed on remote hills, off the beaten path. Those being executed were typically placed at eye level on busy streets or roads so that each person passing by could look into their suffering face. This was, after all, supposed to have a deterrent effect.

The person was hung naked, which was a powerful part of the humiliation process. There was no loin cloth wrapped around Yahushua – He hung naked on the stake before all of mankind and the Creator.

There are three likely possibilities for the method of his impaling. He was either: 1) Hung on a single vertical stake placed in

the ground which was carried to the site of the execution. In this case his arms would have been stretched over his head and nails would have been placed through his hands and feet to affix his body to this single stake; or 2) his arms would have been stretched outward on a horizontal stake which was then affixed to a vertical pole. His feet would have then been nailed to the vertical pole; or 3) His arms would have been stretched outward on a horizontal stake which was then affixed to a tree.

Any one of these methods would have been consistent with the Scriptures which record that Yahushua carried his "stake" to his execution. The first method would have appeared similar to the way the Passover sacrifice was prepared on a single pomegranate spit. The notion that Yahushua carried an actual crucifix does not fit with the descriptions given, nor is it likely Yahushua would have had the strength to carry such a cross any distance at all.

The accounts in the Messianic writings found in Acts 5:30, 10:39, 13:29, Galatians 3:13 and 1 Peter 2:24 indicate that Yahushua was hung on a "tree" which is the Greek word "xylon." The combined accounts seem to indicate the third method: Yahushua's arms were stretched out on a horizontal "stauros" which was affixed to a living "xylon."

The Christian tradition surrounding the crucifix poses even more of a problem when you understand the mythology involving the pagan savior gods Dionysus and Bacchus. These pagan gods are one and the same with some variations as they were translated from the Greek into the Roman culture. They both predate the death of Yahushua, although there are some interesting similarities between Christian tradition and pagan tradition. Archaeological evidence has been found, predating the impaling of Yahushua by centuries, which depicts the crucifixion of Bacchus, also known as Dionysus.

Some try to use this as proof that the life and death of Yahushua were just another pagan fabrication, but that proposition is absurd. What this evidence does demonstrate is the fact that the Christian religion incorporated many pagan traditions throughout the centuries, particularly those associated with Dionysus. That is a very provable historical fact and will be discussed in more detail in this text.

Yahushua himself described his death as the fulfillment of the pattern provided by Mosheh. Read His words: "*14 Just as Mosheh lifted up the snake in the desert, so the Son of Man must be lifted up, 15 that*

everyone who believes in Him may have eternal life." Yahanan 3:14-15.

This was a profound statement by Yahushua because the event in the wilderness had always been a mystery. As it turns out, it was a picture of the Messiah and it symbolized the idea that faith in the Messiah would deliver from death. Based upon the foregoing evidence, I believe that Yahushua was nailed to a single stake or pole with His arms raised above His head, like the "seraph" (שׂרף) on the pole raised up by Mosheh. (Bemidbar 21:8).

The Romans were efficient executioners and needed the process to be as fast and easy as possible. Nailing a person to a single stake and placing it in the ground was just that – expedient. Most of us are used to seeing movie depictions of the Romans using crane mechanisms to raise an enormous cross on the top of a hill, but that simply makes no sense. It is very dramatic, but it is far from reality. While this event is very important to followers of Yahushua, it was not considered unique or important by the Romans at that time.

The cross has become a powerful tradition that is just that - a tradition borrowed from the cult of Dionysus. Dionysus, later known as Bacchus, was crucified on a "<u>T</u>ammuz cross". It was only after Christianity began blending pagan traditions that this became so important.

I mention this issue because there is considerable controversy regarding the similarity of Jesus with pagan deities such as Dionysus, Bacchus and Horus. Those who oppose the fact that Yahushua was the Messiah attempt to categorize him as simply another pagan diety in a long history of pagan savior gods. It is important to recognize that many of the similarities exist because they were later borrowed by Christianity and incorporated into the Christian religion.

I am not trying to assert that I know exactly how the execution occurred – no one knows that for sure. I simply believe that the method of death has taken up far too much attention. The emphasis on the cross and the crucifix as a symbol is dangerous and distracting. That the crucifix has actually become the symbol of the Christian religion is quite profound, because it places the emphasis on death rather than life – in particular the method of death which is probably not even accurate.

It is important that Yahushua died as prophesied, if he is to be considered the Messiah, although his death alone is not the most important part of his ministry. Everyone dies, and if the story ended there, he would have been just another prophet killed in Jerusalem by

those he offended. This was nothing new in Yisrael, and if that were the case, it is possible that history would never even have remembered him. It is the continuation of the story that leads us further into the examination of Yahushua as the Messiah, particularly the fact that he was resurrected.

26

The Resurrection

We know that Yahushua died on Passover day on a stake. To this day, the Samaritans on Mount Gerezim slaughter their Passover lambs and bind them to stakes. This is likely the closest example that we can see in modern times to the ancient practice of slaughtering and roasting the Passover lamb. Interestingly, after the lambs are killed and placed on a stake, they are lowered into fiery pits, which could be likened to Sheol, also known as hell.

The Messianic writings record that once Yahushua had died, around 3:00 pm in the afternoon, it became necessary to get him off the stake and into the ground. We know from the text that a High Sabbath was approaching - the First Day of the Feast of Unleavened Bread which occurred on the 15th day of the first month.

This is where the Torah and the tradition came back into synch. After sunset, the 15th day began which was, according to all reckonings, the First Day of the Feast of Unleavened Bread. It is considered a High Sabbath because it is a "no work day" and a set apart gathering, regardless of whether or not it falls on the seventh day of the week. (Vayiqra 23:7).

It is important to understand that impaling, also known as crucifixion, was a grissly ordeal and the Romans were capable of delaying death for a long time if they so desired – some say up to a week. They could also hasten death by breaking the legs of the one being punished. If the legs were broken, the person hanging could no longer push up, which means they could no longer breathe. In essence, the one being hung would suffocate to death.

Yahushua died around 3:00 pm without having his legs broken.

His body was then hastily placed in a tomb in a garden before sunset. The objective was to get him into the ground before the sun went down and a new day began – which was a High Sabbath. This was in accordance with the commandment in the Torah which states: "*²² If a man guilty of a capital offense is put to death and his body is hung on a tree, ²³ you must not leave his body on the tree overnight. Be sure to bury him that same day, because anyone who is hung on a tree is under Elohim's curse. You must not desecrate the Land YHWH your Elohim is giving you as an inheritance.*" Devarim 21:22-23.

Now this commandment is quite profound and calls for some special attention. To begin, it follows a commandment concerning the firstborn status of sons born when a man has two wives, one which is loved and one which is unloved. The conclusion is that the man "*must acknowledge the son of his unloved wife as the firstborn by giving him a double share of all he has.*" Devarim 21:17.

The parallels to the House of Yisrael and the House of Yahudah are profound. Even though the House of Yisrael was still in exile, her firstborn Joseph was still entitled to the double portion of the firstborn.

The text then proceeds to deal with the issue of a rebellious son – the son who will not obey and is a glutton and a drunkard. If his parents, acting as two witnesses against him, bring him to the elders then all of the men of the city are to stone the son. (Devarim 21:18-21). The fact that Yahushua was accused of being a glutton and a drunkard cannot be ignored. (Mattityahu 11:19; Luke 7:34). Also, there were occasions in his life when the people tried to stone him. Stoning, after all, was the customary method of punishment in Yisrael.

That is what makes the verse about a person hung on a tree particularly interesting. The Torah speaks about stoning as the method of punishment for the rebellious son and then prescribes what to do with a body that has been hanged on a tree. It does not seem to fit until you understand the prophetic nature of the verse. It is even more amazing when you realize that Yahushua, while hated by the Yahudim who used stoning as a method of punishment, was killed by the Romans who used hanging on a tree/stake as their accepted form of execution. As a result, the Torah specifically required that in this instance, his body not remain hanging overnight so it had to come down before sunset. It is this command which then gives us a precise understanding of when Yahushua was placed in the tomb – the 14th day before sunset.

Here is an account of his burial: "*³⁸ After this, Joseph of Arimathea, being a talmid of Yahushua, but secretly, for fear of the Yahudim, asked Pilate that he might take away the body of Yahushua; and Pilate gave him permission.*

So he came and took the body of Yahushua. *39* *And Nicodemus, who at first came to Yahushua by night, also came, bringing a mixture of myrrh and aloes, about a hundred pounds.* *40* *Then they took the body of Yahushua, and bound it in strips of linen with the spices, as the custom of the Yahudim is to bury.* *41* <u>*Now in the place where He was impaled there was a garden, and in the garden a new tomb in which no one had yet been laid.*</u> *42* *So there they laid Yahushua, because of* <u>*the Yahudims' Preparation Day,*</u> *for the tomb was nearby." Yahanan 19:38-42, see also Mattityahu 27:57-61; Mark 15:42-47; Luke 23:50-56.*

Anyone touching his dead body would have been unclean which reminds us of the red heifer sacrifice. This is another intriguing and mysterious commandment in the Torah. The Yisraelites were to take a red heifer without defect or blemish to the High Priest. The heifer would be slaughtered "outside the camp" in his presence. This was the one and only sacrifice which did not occur on the bronze Altar.

The blood of the red heifer would be sprinkled at the front of the Tabernacle and the ashes would be used in the waters of cleansing for the purification from sin. Those who were involved in this process, in particular the priest that offered the sacrifice and the one who gathered the ashes after the heifer was killed, became unclean. (Bemidbar 19:2-10).

This is unique from any other sacrifice and was always a mystery to the Yisraelites because it was about the Messiah. The fact that it was a red heifer is, of course, not an arbitrary matter. The word for red in Hebrew is adom (אדם) which is the same word for man - adam (אדם). Interestingly though, a heifer is a female cow which has not yet given birth.

So a "man-heifer" is the symbol provided for the Messiah which is a picture of Adam, the man who "gave birth" to Hawah and all of mankind. This red heifer sacrifice was pointing to another man, the Messiah, Who was the Last Adam being slaughtered for the transgression of the First Adam outside the camp or rather - the gates. The blood of the heifer is then sprinkled seven times at the door of the Tabernacle which shows how YHWH will cleanse the way for man to re-enter His House, which is representative of the Garden.

Just as those involved in the red heifer sacrifice were made unclean, so too were those involved in the fulfillment of the red heifer sacrifice of the Messiah. Those that took care of the body of Yahushua were not simply unclean for one day, they became unclean for seven days.

Incredibly, this particular commandment concerning uncleanness from a dead body immediately follows the commandment

concerning the red heifer in Bemidbar 19:11 which states: "*¹¹ Whoever touches the dead body of anyone will be unclean for seven days. ¹² He must purify himself with the water on the third day and on the seventh day; then he will be clean. But if he does not purify himself on the third and seventh days, he will not be clean. ¹³ Whoever touches the dead body of anyone and fails to purify himself defiles YHWH's Tabernacle. That person must be cut off from Yisrael. Because the water of cleansing has not been sprinkled on him, he is unclean; his uncleanness remains on him.*" Bemidbar 19:11-13.

The connection between the red heifer and the death of a man are intimately tied together, and as the Torah states, the person who became unclean must be cleansed with the waters of purification derived from the red heifer. These are deep mysteries revealed through the death of Yahushua.

As a result of their handling the body of Yahushua, they needed to wash on the "third day" and the "seventh day." It just so happens that at the time of Yahushua's death, these days were very significant days. Yahushua stated: "*The Son of Adam is going to be betrayed into the hands of men. They will kill him, and after three days he will rise.*" Mark 9:31. When asked what miraculous sign he could show to prove his authority he proclaimed: "*Destroy this Temple, and I will raise it again in three days.*" Yahanan 2:19.

Yahushua indicated that he would be resurrected on the third day. The third day after his death would have been the first day of cleansing for those who handled his body. It was also a weekly Sabbath. The second day of cleansing occurred on the seventh day of the Feast of Unleavened Bread – a High Sabbath. Each day of cleansing occurred on a Sabbath which has profound implications when examining the Messiah, especially when you consider that the final cleansing occurred at the conclusion or fulfillment of a Feast.

Because of their state of uncleanness they would have been precluded from participating in the activities of the entire Feast. Interestingly, YHWH had already made special provision for them, through Mosheh. It happens that there is another unique portion in the Torah allowing anyone who is unclean from touching a dead body to participate in the Passover in the second month beginning on the 14th day, if they miss the regular Passover because of their uncleanness. (Bemidbar 9:6-13).

This too is no coincidence and no doubt prophetic. As a result of this provision, the Passover season did not technically end for every Yisraelite until around 40 days after the first Passover held in the first month.

We know that Yahushua was placed in a tomb before sunset on the 14th day in accordance with the Torah. The Scriptures do not end with his death. They continue to speak of his resurrection three days later. Despite the many statements made by Yahushua concerning his rising on the third day, the talmidim were apparently not thinking about such a thing. This is despite the fact that the religious leaders had the tomb sealed so that people could not steal the body and claim that he was resurrected. (Mattityahu 27:66)

It seems that his followers were more concerned with finishing the preparations over his body, which had not been completed due to the necessitated haste of his burial. They were focused on his death when they should have been focused on his life. They were not even thinking about the possibility that he had been resurrected – despite the fact that he had told them he would arise on the third day.

"¹ _Now on the first of the Sabbaths, very early in the morning_, they, and certain other women with them, came to the tomb bringing the spices which they had prepared. ² But they found the stone rolled away from the tomb. ³ Then they went in and did not find the body of the Master Yahushua. ⁴ And it happened, as they were greatly perplexed about this, that behold, two men stood by them in shining garments. ⁵ Then, as they were afraid and bowed their faces to the earth, they said to them, "Why do you seek the living among the dead? ⁶ _He is not here, but is risen! Remember how he spoke to you when he was still in Galilee,_ ⁷ _saying, The Son of Adam must be delivered into the hands of sinful men, and be crucified, and the third day rise again._ ⁸ _And they remembered his words._ ⁹ Then they returned from the tomb and told all these things to the eleven and to all the rest. ¹⁰ It was Miryam Magdalene, Joanna, Miryam the mother of Yaakov, and the other women with them, who told these things to the talmidim. ¹¹ And their words seemed to them like idle tales, and they did not believe them. ¹² But Peter arose and ran to the tomb; and stooping down, he saw the linen cloths lying by themselves; and he departed, marveling to himself at what had happened." Luke 24:1-12.

Matthew and Mark describe similar accounts and the important point is that they describe this event at dawn, "on the first of the Sabbaths." Many translations provide "The first day of the week," but the Greek is mia ton shabbaton (μια των σαββτων). This was the first of seven weekly Sabbaths in the counting of the Omer to Shabuot. We know that the Tomb was empty when they arrived so Yahushua must have been raised before that time.

Modern Christianity celebrates the death of Jesus on "Good Friday" and the resurrection on "Easter Sunday." While, at first glance, this may appear to satisfy the sign of rising on the third day, it does not

adequately fulfill the sign provided by Jonah.

Before his death he clearly indicated: "*39 An evil and adulterous generation seeks after a sign, and no sign will be given to it except the sign of the prophet Jonah. 40 For as Jonah was three days and three nights in the belly of the great fish, so will the Son of Adam be three days and three nights in the heart of the earth. 41 The men of Nineveh will rise up in the judgment with this generation and condemn it, because they repented at the preaching of Jonah; and indeed a greater than Jonah is here. 42 The queen of the South will rise up in the judgment with this generation and condemn it, for she came from the ends of the earth to hear the wisdom of Solomon; and indeed a greater than Solomon is here.*" Mattityahu 12:39-42 (see also Luke 11:29-32). He reiterated this sign again when they asked him for a sign from Heaven. (Mattityahu 16:40).

Because of this statement, we expect that Yahushua would die and be in the ground for three days and three nights until he was raised back to life. The reason for the three days and three nights was to assure that he was actually dead. Only after a person was dead for three days were they determined to be "officially" dead. (See The Companion Bible, E.W. Bullinger, Appendix 148.)

The tradition of crucifixion on Good Friday and resurrection on Easter Sunday is centered around pagan customs, not the Scriptures. The Friday to Sunday period does not fit the one sign provided by Yahushua, because it does not constitute three days and three nights.[203]

This begs the question? When was Yahushua impaled and when was He resurrected? To make that determination we need to go back to the beginning of his life. We know that Yahushua was born in 3 BCE and began his ministry around the age of 30 years old which puts us at 29 CE when he began his ministry.

The Messianic writings do not give us a chronological, day by day or even year by year account of his life. As a result, there is much speculation concerning the length of his ministry which then brings into question the date of his death.

Thankfully, we are able to discern that event by a process of elimination. First of all, we know that Pontius Pilate was the fifth governor of the Roman province of Judea and served between 26 CE until early in the year 37 CE when he was called to Rome by Vitellius, the legate of Syria to provide an account to Tiberias for his actions in quelling an incident involving the Samaritans on Mt. Gerezim.[204]

Since Pilate was recalled prior to the death of Tiberias, which occurred on March 16 of 37 CE, we know that he left for Rome prior to Passover in 37 CE. Thus Yahushua could not have been crucified in 37

CE or any year thereafter. As a result we are left with a window from 29 CE to 36 CE.

Yahushua was clearly not killed during the first year of his ministry, and the Book of Yahanan speaks of at least three different Passover Feasts in Yahushua's adult life, so we are left with six potential Passovers between 31 CE and 36 CE in which he could possibly have been killed.

There is significant evidence that the Passover meal, often referred to as the Last Supper, occurred on a Tuesday evening when Yahushua celebrated his last Passover. This is confirmed by several early sources such as The Didascalia in Syria, Epiphanius of Salamis and Victorinus of Pettua, and most importantly the internal evidence in the Scriptures.

That being the case, then the 14th day of the first month would have begun on Tuesday evening at sunset. Yahushua would have then been killed on Wednesday afternoon at around 3:00 pm and hurriedly placed in a tomb nearby before sunset. He was in the tomb 3 days – Day 14, Day 15 and Day 16. He was in the tomb 3 nights – Night 15, Night 16 and Night 17. This leads to a resurrection on Saturday - Shabbat - which would have fallen on the 17th day of the month. I believe that Yahushua was resurrected at "the dawning of the day" on Shabbat.

The following chart helps to illustrate the timing.

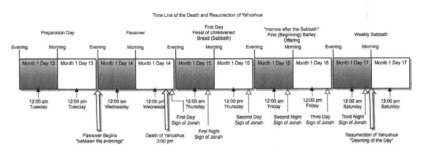

Examining the years within our range, there is only one year that this sequence of events could have taken place – 34 CE. Thus, Yahushua was likely killed on Wednesday, March 24, 34 CE at 3:00 pm. Yahushua ate the Passover at the beginning of the 14th day of the first month, and died as the Passover Lamb as the 14th day was coming to an end.

Some attempt to capture the date using lunar and solar eclipse models. They do this because of the accounts of the darkened sky when Yahushua was on the stake. (Mattityahu 27:45; Mark 15:33; Luke 23: 45-

48). This would be nice if it were actually relevant, but you can never have a solar eclipse in the middle of a lunar month.

Passover and the Feast of Unleavened Bread always occur when the moon is in its full phase. As a result, it is astronomically impossible to have a lunar eclipse during this period of time. Therefore, if you are selecting a date based upon eclipse data you are selecting an incorrect date. This is clearly known in the scientific community.

There are certainly other phenomena which might have accounted for this event. Around Passover it is not uncommon to experience large sandstorms known as al-Khamasin, which interestingly means: "fifty" in Arabic. The name refers to the number of days on which they occur, and they are common to Israel, Egypt and Syria in the spring. These storms can block out the sun and reduce visibility drastically. They can also change the color of the sun to red.

Therefore, if we recognize that Yahushua was killed on Wednesday, March 24, 34 CE at 3:00 pm, we can calculate, based upon

the one sign given, that he was resurrected before sunrise on Saturday, March 27, 34 CE. There is a strong belief by many that Yahushua was resurrected on the barley resheet offering that occurs within the Feast of Unleavened Bread. However, this would be impossible.

Here is what the Torah provides:
"*¹⁰ Speak to the Yisraelites and say to them: When you enter the Land I am going to give you and you reap its harvest, bring to the priest a sheaf of the first (resheet) grain you harvest. ¹¹ He is to wave the sheaf before YHWH so it will be accepted on your behalf; the priest is to wave it on the day after the Sabbath.*" Vayiqra 23:10-12.

The debate rests in the meaning of the words "the day after the Sabbath." The question is whether the Sabbath referred to is the High Sabbath (ie. the First Day of Unleavened Bread) or the weekly Sabbath. If you believe that the commandment is referring to the High Sabbath, which is always on Day 15 of the first month, then the resheet offering would always be on Day 16 of the first month. If you believe that the commandment is referring to the weekly Sabbath, then the resheet offering is always going to occur on a Sunday.

Yahushua could not have risen on the day of the offering under either scenario. If "the day after the Sabbath" is counted from Day 15, the offering occurs on Day 16 which is not the day of the resurrection on Day 17. If "the day after the Sabbath" is counted from the weekly

Sabbath, the offering occurs on Day 18, which is not the day of the resurrection on Day 17. Although these facts in no way settle the issue on how to count the Omer, it should be clear that although Yahushua is the first (resheet) of the resurrection, he was not resurrected on the first day of the Omer count. It should also be evident that he was not resurrected on Sunday.

Through this text it should be clear that Yahushua died during the period of time that Daniel said the Messiah would be cut off. By his resurrection he demonstrated that he was the promised Moshiach. The Messianic writings claim that he ascended and will be returning, which should not be a surprise.

According to Yeshayahu "*¹⁰ In that day the Root of Jesse will stand as a banner for the peoples; the nations will rally to him, and his place of rest will be glorious. ¹¹ In that day* <u>*YHWH will reach out His Hand a second time*</u> *to reclaim the remnant that is left of his people from Assyria, from Lower Egypt, from Upper Egypt, from Cush, from Elam, from Babylonia, from Hamath and from the islands of the sea. ¹² He will raise a banner for the nations and gather the exiles of Yisrael; he will assemble the scattered people of Yahudah from the four quarters of the earth.*" Yeshayahu 11:10-12.

As of the writing of this book, the House of Yisrael is still scattered and in exile. Yahushua came first as the King of Yahudah and as the Suffering Servant. As the Lamb of Elohim, his death was required to redeem Yisrael and satisfy the punishment for Yisrael breaking the Covenant. As the Root of Jesse, hanging on a stake, he was a banner to the nations. Those who looked upon him and believed in his death and resurrection would be healed and spared from death.

The day will soon come when "YHWH will reach out His Hand a second time" and regather the Lost Sheep of Yisrael and Yahudah. He will restore the divided Kingdom and rule as One King over a reunited Kingdom of Yisrael. This is what the prophets foretold, and this is what Yahushua did and is expected to accomplish in the future.

27

Yahushua the Messiah

Immediately following His resurrection, we read an interesting story about Yahushua appearing with two individuals on the road to Emmaus. These two were His talmidim, but they did not recognize Him. They knew that His body was no longer in the tomb, but they were depressed. They apparently did not realize that He was resurrected.

Yahushua walked with these individuals and listened to their sad account of the past week. They had thought that Yahushua would be the One to Redeem Yisrael, but their hopes were shattered.

There finally came a time when Yahushua grew tired of their moaning. "*25 He said to them, How foolish you are, and how slow of heart to believe all that the Prophets have spoken! 26 Did not the Messiah have to suffer these things and then enter His glory? 27 And beginning with Mosheh and all the Prophets, He explained to them what was said in all the Scriptures concerning Himself.*" Luke 24:25-27.

After hearing all that He had to say they later sat down to eat and finally recognized Him when He broke the bread. They returned to Jerusalem and reported their encounter. While there were many instances when He appeared to people after the resurrection, one in particular stands out because of the hidden message found within the passage. The incident is described by Yahanan as follows:

"*1 Afterward Yahushua appeared again to His talmidim, by the Sea of Tiberias. It happened this way: 2 Simon Peter, Thomas (called Didymus), Nathanael from Cana in Galilee, the sons of Zebedee, and two other talmidim were together. 3 I'm going out to fish, Simon Peter told them, and they said, We'll go with you. So they went out and got into the boat, but that night they caught nothing. 4 Early in the morning, Yahushua stood on the shore, but the talmidim did not realize that it was Yahushua. 5 He called out to them, Friends, haven't you any fish? No, they answered. 6 He said, Throw your net on the right* side of the boat and you will find some. When they did, they were unable to haul the net in because of the large number of fish. ⁷ Then the talmid whom Yahushua loved said to Peter, It is the Master! As soon as Simon Peter heard him say, It is the Master, he wrapped his outer garment around him (for he had taken it off) and jumped into the water. ⁸ The other talmidim followed in the boat, towing the net full of fish, for they were not far from shore, about a hundred yards. ⁹ When they landed, they saw a fire of burning coals there with fish on it, and some bread. ¹⁰ Yahushua said to them, Bring some of the fish you have just caught. ¹¹ Simon Peter climbed aboard and dragged the net ashore. *It was full of large fish, 153, but even with so many the net was not torn.* ¹² Yahushua said to them, Come and have breakfast. None of the talmidim dared ask Him, Who are you? They knew it was the Master. ¹³ Yahushua came, took the bread and gave it to them, and did the same with the fish. ¹⁴ This was now the third time Yahushua appeared to His talmidim after He was raised from the dead. ¹⁵ When they had finished eating, Yahushua said to Simon Peter, Simon son of Yahanan, do you truly love Me more than these? Yes, Master, he said, you know that I love You. Yahushua said, Feed My lambs. ¹⁶ Again Yahushua said, Simon son of Yahanan, do you truly love Me? He answered, Yes, Master, You know that I love You. Yahushua said, Take care of My sheep. ¹⁷ The third time He said to him, Simon son of Yahanan, do you love Me? Peter was hurt because Yahushua asked him the third time, Do you love me? He said, Master, you know all things; you know that I love you. Yahushua said, Feed My sheep." Yahanan 21:1 – 17.

How interesting that there were 153 fish in the net. Remember that when Yahushua first called these talmidim He said that He would make them fishers of men. Instead, these talmidim were still fishing for fish. The fact that they caught large fish is of particular interest because based upon the time, location and method of fishing, they were looking for small fish – sardines.

They caught large fish that they were not looking for, and the quantity – 153 – is of particular interest. It directly leads to the prophecy in Hoshea which spoke of the House of Yisrael becoming the sons of Elohim. Yahushua was clearly showing that they were supposed to be fishing for men – "the sons of Elohim" which equals 153 in Hebrew gematria.

Remember, Beni Ha-Elohim (בְּנֵי הָאֱלֹהִים) is broken down as follows: (ב = 2), (נ = 50), (י = 10), (ה = 5), (א = 1), (ל = 30), (ה = 5), (י = 10), (ם = 40). Therefore, 2 + 50 + 10 + 5 + 1 + 30 + 5 + 10 + 40 = 153. This would be the fulfillment of the prophecy given by Yirmeyahu concerning the great regathering of Yisrael. (Yirmeyahu 16:16).

Of course we already know that Yahushua previously sent His talmidim to the "lost sheep of the House of Yisrael," and we see that this would be an ongoing mission. This was the purpose that He had prepared His talmidim to accomplish. He specifically instructed them to: "*Go into all the world and preach the good news to all creation.*" Mark 16:15. He did not send them out to spread a new religion called Christianity. Rather, He sent them out to find the lost sheep.

After helping them catch the 153 fish, He prepared a meal and fed them. This was not the only time that Yahushua met and ate with His talmidim after the resurrection. There is testimony that Yahushua appeared to His talmidim and over 500 people after His resurrection. (1 Corinthians 15:6).

According to the Book of Acts: "*3 After His suffering, He showed Himself to these men and gave many convincing proofs that He was alive. He appeared to them over a period of forty days and spoke about the Kingdom of Elohim. 4 On one occasion, while He was eating with them, He gave them this command: Do not leave Jerusalem, but wait for the gift my Father promised, which you have heard Me speak about. 5 For Yahanan immersed with water, but in a few days you will be immersed with the Set Apart Spirit.*" Acts 1:3-5.

The Messianic writings indicate that Yahushua ascended forty (40) days after His resurrection. Notice that His ministry was bracketed within forty (40) day intervals. The first forty (40) days at the beginning involved suffering and temptation. This final forty (40) days was a sort of "victory lap."

Paul in his letter to the Colossians said that Yahushua "*disarmed principalities and powers . . . He made a public spectacle of them, triumphing over them in it.*" Colossians 2:15. The Greek word used to describe Yahushua's victory over death is "apekduomai." This word had a specific meaning to people living in the Roman Empire.

When a Roman Emperor achieved a victory in the ancient world, he rode in an open chariot in front of his conquered foes. The captives would be stripped of their armour and their hands would be tied behind their backs while they were exposed in public disgrace.[205] This is the picture of Yahushua's victory over death. There would be no more suffering – no more temptation. He had conquered the power of sin and death.

He was taken up from the Mount of Olives after the final forty (40) day period. Here is the account provided from the Books of Acts. "*6 So when they met together, they asked Him, Master, are You at this time*

going to restore the Kingdom to Yisrael? [7] He said to them: It is not for you to know the times or dates the Father has set by His own authority. [8] But you will receive power when the Set Apart Spirit comes on you; and you will be My witnesses in Jerusalem, and in all Judea and Samaria, and to the ends of the earth. [9] After He said this, He was taken up before their very eyes, and a cloud hid Him from their sight. [10] They were looking intently up into the sky as He was going, when suddenly two men dressed in white stood beside them. [11] Men of Galilee, they said, Why do you stand here looking into the sky? This same Yahushua, who has been taken from you into heaven, will come back in the same way you have seen Him go into heaven." Acts 1:6-11.

Notice that the primary question the talmidim wanted answered before Yahushua departed was, "When the Kingdom of Yisrael would be restored?" This was the continuing expectation, and the response from Yahushua revealed that it was a valid and critically important question. Yahushua was thereafter taken up into the sky, and the talmidim were told by two men dressed in white that He would return in that same fashion. Before His return there was work to be done. They needed to start fishing, and they were promised power to assist them on their world-wide mission.

The ascension of Yahushua would have been toward the end of the Omer Count and nearing the Appointed Time of Shabuot. Shabuot, sometimes referred to as Pentecost, was one of three Appointed Times when males were to gather together at the place where YHWH chose to place His Name. At that time it was, of course, Jerusalem.

As instructed, the talmidim were present for that Appointed Time and we can read about what happened on that special day. "[2] When the day of Shabuot came, they were all together in one place. [2] Suddenly a sound like the blowing of a violent wind came from heaven and filled the whole house where they were sitting. [3] They saw what seemed to be tongues of fire that separated and came to rest on each of them. [4] All of them were filled with the Set Apart Spirit and began to speak in other tongues as the Spirit enabled them. [5] Now there were staying in Jerusalem Elohim-fearing Yahudim from every nation under heaven. [6] When they heard this sound, a crowd came together in bewilderment, because each one heard them speaking in his own language. [7] Utterly amazed, they asked: Are not all these men who are speaking Galileans? [8] Then how is it that each of us hears them in his own native language? [9] Parthians, Medes and Elamites; residents of Mesopotamia, Yudea and Cappadocia, Pontus and Asia, [10] Phrygia and Pamphylia, Egypt and the parts of Libya near Cyrene; visitors from Rome [11] (both Yahudim and converts); Cretans and Arabs — we hear them declaring the wonders of Elohim in our own tongues!" Acts 2:1-12.

This event occurred on the traditional date when the Torah was given to Yisrael at Mt. Sinai. Often called the Baptism of fire, or Baptism of the Spirit, this was the infilling that was needed to fulfill the Renewed Covenant. Just as the Torah was written on stone tablets for Yisrael at Sinai, the promise was that the Covenant would be renewed by having the Torah placed in their minds and written on their hearts.

This is how the Covenant was renewed. Water can only clean the outside, it takes the fire of the Spirit of YHWH to clean the inside of a man. YHWH was now preparing people as living Tabernacles within which He could set up His throne. This was the pattern provided by the Tabernacle. By His fire He wrote the Torah on the hearts and in the minds of these Yisraelites.

Imagine if the talmidim had not been obeying the Torah – they would have missed this incredible event. This is why it is so important to know and obey the Commandments concerning the Appointed Times precisely. The plan of YHWH revolves around these times, which are of His choosing. They are literally appointments with the Creator.

Aa a result, the life and ministry of Yahushua also revolved around the Torah and the Appointed Times. This is not generally understood, but Yahushua could not have made it any clearer. One of the first things that Yahushua stated in His ministry was that He did not come to destroy the Torah, but to fulfill it. The Messianic writings commonly referred to as "The Gospels," describe how He fulfilled the Torah by filling it full of meaning. His life was a visible demonstration of the purpose and meaning of the Torah. As He walked and taught, the Torah came alive through Him. He lived the Torah for everyone to see how it was done. He was the Torah in the flesh.

The Messianic writings record that Yahushua was born from a virgin. Some skeptics charge that this is a pagan concept and not Scriptural. It is important to recognize that many things deemed pagan are often distortions of the truth. While it is true that many pagan traditions involve god-men being born from a virgin, the concept can be traced straight back from the Garden when Hawah proclaimed: "*I have acquired a man from YHWH*." Beresheet 4:1.

The virgin birth has also been proclaimed through the constellations in the sky, better known as Mazzaroth. This is another truth which has been considered pagan because of the twisted practice of astrology. In reality, the constellations show how the Redeemer will come from a virgin, and there there is nothing pagan about these signs placed in the heavens by the Creator.

YHWH proclaimed that He would do nothing without first revealing it through His servants the prophets. (Amos 3:7). This was understood by the Yahudim as we read in the Talmud: "All the prophets prophesied only the days of the Messiah" (Sanhedrin 99a), and "The world was created only for the Messiah" (Sanhedrin 98b). It has long been understood that the Messiah is the entire focus of history.

We already saw that the sign provided through Jonah was about how the Messiah would die and be resurrected in three days and three nights. YHWH also revealed the sign of the birth of Messiah through the prophet Yeshayahu. The prophet declared: *"Therefore YHWH Himself will give you a sign: Behold, the almah, shall conceive, and bear a Son, and shall call His Name Immanuel."* Yeshayahu 7:14.

According to Yeshayahu, YHWH Himself would provide a sign. The Hebrew word for sign is owt (אות) and it is something visible - it is "a sign, a mark, a miracle." The text provides that a Son will be born from an "almah" and this Son shall be called Immanuel, which means "El with us." Notice that I have kept the Hebrew word "almah" intact because this is the main point of controversy concerning the passage.

The word "almah" (עלמה) is often translated as "virgin," but it is argued by some that it should simply be translated as "young woman." I disagree with that argument for several reasons. To begin, whenever you read the word "Behold" it means that something important is about to follow. The question is whether the birth of a son from a young woman is a miracle or some sort of sign. Obviously not.

Those who insist upon translating almah as "young woman" typically have an agenda, which is to avoid the truth that The Messiah would be Elohim in flesh, and that He would come from the closed womb of a virgin.

Two hundred years prior to the birth of Yahushua, the word almah was translated in The Greek Septuagint as parthenos (παρθένος) which means: "virgin." This is the same word in the Messianic writings used to describe Miryam, the mother of Yahushua. The Aramaic Peshitta also referenced a virgin. In fact, in the Yisraelite culture all young women were expected to be virgins so the argument lacks merit on every level.

Therefore, before the virgin birth of Yahushua, the sign in this passage was traditionally considered to be a virgin birth. It appears that the insistence on retranslating this passage in Judasim is simply in response to the fact that Yahushua was born of a virgin. This is typical in Judaism as it attempts to distance itself from Christianity, even if it means reinterpreting the plain meaning of their Scriptures.

There is ample precedence in the Scriptures that "almah" would refer to a "virgin." (Beresheet 24:43). The word 'almah" is used seven (7) times in the Tanak and there is no instance where almah is used to refer to a young woman who is married or has known a man.

As if it could not be any clearer, the Prophet Yeshayahu later describes this Son, born from a almah, as follows: "*6 For to us a Child is born, to us a Son is given, and the government will be on His shoulders. And He will be called Wonderful Counselor, Mighty Elohim, Everlasting Father, Prince of Peace. 7 Of the increase (l'marbah) of His government and peace there will be no end. He will reign on David's throne and over His kingdom, establishing and upholding it with justice and righteousness from that time on and forever. The zeal of YHWH Almighty will accomplish this.*" Yeshayahu 9:6-7.

This is no mere mortal man being described here. He sits on the throne of David, which is consistent since there is another Messianic prophecy which refers to the Messiah as the Branch - the root or shoot of Jesse. (Yeshayahu 11:10). This offspring of Jesse in the Davidic line will rule forever.

There is something deeper in this passage which can only be seen in the Hebrew text. In Hebrew, the word l'marbah (לםרבה), which means "increase," contains something quite profound. The mem (מ) in this word is a closed mem (ם) which is only used as a final mem - when the mem is at the end of the word. In this case, the closed mem (ם) is found in the middle of the word, which is grammatically incorrect, but many see it as confirmation of the sign of the virgin birth.

The letter mem (מ) signifies water and the womb. The closed mem (ם) has been seen to symbolize the closed womb of a virgin. In fact, the Rabbis have taught that when it is time for the Redemption, the closed mem of Yeshayahu's *l'marbeh* will open for the coming of the Messiah. (Radak, Yeshayau 9:6). Further, "The Zohar . . . decides that the closed 'm' refers to the fact that the Messiah will be born from a 'closed womb.'"[206]

The notion of the Promised Seed coming from a closed womb is found throughout the Torah. Think back to all of the matriarchs in the Scriptures – Sarai, Rivkah and Rachel. All of them were barren until YHWH opened their wombs. The most miraculous of these was no doubt Sarai who bore the Promised Son when she was very old – beyond the age of bearing children.

It is interesting to note the presence of an "almah" in the life of Mosheh – one of the greatest Messianic figures in the Tanak. This

sister of Mosheh, aptly named Miryam, was described as an almah. (Shemot 2:8). The virgin Miryam was told by Pharaoh's daughter to find a Hebrew woman to nurse Mosheh whose name means: "out of water," and points to the fact that the Messiah would come out of water – the water of a womb.

Even the name Miryam has incredible significance. This, of course was the true Hebrew name of the mother of Yahushua – not Mary. In Hebrew it is spelled (מרים) and it means: "rebellion." So out of the rebellion of man would come the One that would redeem mankind. Also note that the name begins with the open mem (מ) and ends with the closed mem (ם).

Remember that in Hebrew Gematria the letter mem (מ) has the numerical equivalent of forty (40) – a number repeatedly attributed to the Messiah. The name Miryam begins and ends with forty (40), just as the ministry of Yahushua began and ended with periods of forty (40) days.

So we see that Yeshayahu provided some interesting information regarding the Messiah. He would be a Son, born from a virgin and He would be "El with us." He would be the Son of Elohim representing the Creator. This could not be any clearer from the incredible titles attributed to Him – *Wonderful Counselor, Mighty Elohim, Everlasting Father, Prince of Peace*.

The Messiah had to come from a virgin in order to be in the Image of YHWH, rather than in the image of Adam. He had to be born from a virgin so that He did not share the tainted blood of Adam. He was not in the Image of Adam, rather He was in the Image of YHWH. He could not come from the seed of a man and correct the transgression that occurred in the Garden.

Only YHWH could solve the problem created by man, but ironically it had to be done through flesh and blood. Blood had to be shed to solve this problem as was aptly demonstrated after the fall. Remember that YHWH passed through the cuttings of the blood Covenant as a smoking furnace and a blazing lamp. He had to pay the price for Abraham's descendents breaking the Covenant, so He took on flesh by planting His Seed in the womb of a virgin. From that womb was born Yahushua – the Son of Adam.

Yahushua was born in Bethlehem which means: "The House Bread," because He was the Bread of Life. The manna which fed Yisrael while they were in the desert was symbolic of the Messiah. Bethlehem was the city where they traditionally raised the lambs that were slaughtered in the Temple, and how appropriate that this is where

The Lamb of Elohim was born.

Bethlehem was also the city where David was born. Both Miryam and Joseph were descended from David, and therefore Yahushua was legitimately entitled to the throne of David, and to be King of the Yahudim.

After His virgin birth, Yahushua was brought to the Temple to be circumcised on the eighth day, and two witnesses testified regarding the fact that He was the Messiah. "²⁵ *Now there was a man in Jerusalem called Simeon, who was righteous and devout. He was waiting for the consolation of Yisrael, and the Set Apart Spirit was upon him.* ²⁶ *It had been revealed to him by the Set Apart Spirit that he would not die before he had seen YHWH's Moshiach.* ²⁷ *Moved by the Spirit, he went into the Temple courts. When the parents brought in the child Yahushua to do for Him what the custom of the Torah required,* ²⁸ *Simeon took Him in his arms and praised Elohim, saying:* ²⁹ *Sovereign YHWH, as You have promised, You now dismiss Your servant in peace.* ³⁰ *For my eyes have seen Your salvation,* ³¹ *which You have prepared in the sight of all people,* ³² *a light for revelation to the Gentiles and for glory to Your people Yisrael.* ³³ *The child's father and mother marveled at what was said about Him.* ³⁴ *Then Simeon blessed them and said to Miryam, his mother:* This child is destined to cause the falling and rising of many in Yisrael, and to be a sign that will be spoken against, ³⁵ *so that the thoughts of many hearts will be revealed. And a sword will pierce Your own soul too.* ³⁶ *There was also a prophetess, Anna, the daughter of Phanuel, of the tribe of Asher. She was very old; she had lived with her husband seven years after her marriage,* ³⁷ *and then had been a widow for eight-four years. She never left the Temple but worshiped night and day, fasting and praying.* ³⁸ *Coming up to them at that very moment, she gave thanks to Elohim and spoke about the Child to all who were looking forward to the redemption of Jerusalem.*" Luke 2:25-38.

These prophetic witnesses were given when Yahushua became a Son of the Covenant – through the shedding of His blood. Thereafter, His parents brought Him to the Galilee where this "shoot" or "root" of Jesse lived in a town called Nazareth, which literally means: "Shootville." It was while He was a Child in Nazareth, likely around the age of one, that He was anointed and given the riches of a King.

Even though Yahushua was anointed, He was forced to flee from the Land because a tryant King tried to kill Him, just as David was forced to flee for his life from Shaul. Yahushua later began to reign over Yahudah when He was 30 years old. He came first as the King of the House of Yahudah, and once the House of Yisrael is restored, He will be anointed King over all of the Kingdom of Yisrael. This is all in accordance with the pattern of David.

While Yahushua was operating in His role as King of Yahudah, He was acting as both King and Priest. He was feeding the people and saving them. He was also healing the deaf, the dumb, the blind, the lepers and the paralytic. He was casting out demons and teaching people the Torah.

He spoke with authority because He had the authority. He taught in parables and He rebuked and corrected the false teachers. By operating as a King and Priest, He was functioning in the role of Melchizedek.

He did not meet the expectations that people had for the coming Messiah. People wanted a King to come and free them from the Roman oppression. They wanted Him to regather the House of Yisrael and restore the divided Kingdom then and there.

While He clearly indicated that He came for the lost sheep of the House of Yisrael, there was other work that He needed to accomplish. He first came as the Suffering Servant – the Son of Joseph. As the Suffering Servant He became a guilt offering. The Pattern of Abraham and Yitshaq clearly showed that YHWH would offer up His only Son at the place where YHWH provides - the mountains of Moriah - Jerusalem.

Yahushua as the only Son of YHWH demonstrated, through the renewal of the Covenant at the Passover meal, that He was the promised Lamb of Elohim. This was the fulfillment of the Passover Feast, and the reason why Yisrael had been rehearsing the meal for centuries.

In contrast to the first Adam who sinned at the tree and covered his nakedness in shame, Yahushua hung on a tree – naked and unashamed. As the Son of Adam, the Last Adam, He repaired the breach in the wall of the Garden that Adam allowed to be opened by his sin. Yahushua paid the price for that sin by the shedding of His blood which was the renewal of the Covenant.

Through the renewal of the Covenant with Yisrael, and His life of walking out the Torah, we see that Yahushua was the Prophet like Mosheh. His ministry was even bracketed by periods of forty (40) days, just like the life of Mosheh involved repeated patterns of forty (40). His entire life was patterned around the Torah because He was the fulfillment of the Torah – the Word of Elohim. This is the critical issue which has divided men since Yahushua was taken up.

He was killed near a garden and entombed in a garden. How appropriate that the Son of Adam was victorious in the garden and he paid the penalty of mankind in a garden. As a result, those who looked

upon this "seraph" (שָׂרָף) hanging on a pole and believed would be saved from death and enter into the Garden of YHWH - paradise. This was the fulfillment of the pattern provided by Mosheh when he placed the serpent on the pole. Those who looked upon it and believed were saved from the burning death that these "fiery serpents" would inflict.

Beyond all of the fulfilled patterns, His birth, death and resurrection fell within the time period provided through the various Messianic prophecies found in the Tanak, and there is no other person who fulfilled those prophecies. The statistical probability in and of itself is compelling and conclusive.[207]

While some claim that Yahushua was a great man, a man of peace or even a prophet - just as the Yahudim in the past - they do not follow through with the belief that He is the Messiah. Those who cling to the opinion that He was a good man, a great teacher or even a prophet, have obviously not studied His teachings. Yahushua, by His own words, left no doubt about Who He was. He specifically claimed to be the Son of YHWH and the Messiah.

Therefore, if He was a great teacher, and He claimed to be the Messiah, then He must be the Messiah. Ultimately, He was either Who He said He was or He was deluded.

His actions and His teachings all align with the Torah, the Prophets and the Writings. The perfection and purity of His life and teachings, and the synchronicity that He demonstrated with the Torah and the Appointed Times, essentially prove that He is the Messiah and there is no other figure in the history of mankind who even comes close. In fact, based upon the timing given to Daniel by Gabriel, there is no one else who could possibly be the Messiah other than Yahushua.

It should be quite evident that Yahushua was the One described in the Torah, the Prophets and the Writings. He was and is the Messiah of Yisrael. Sadly, the religion which promotes Him as the Messiah has seriously misrepresented His Name, His teachings and His purpose. As a result, most of those in Judaism fail to recognize Him as the Messiah of Yisrael.

Therefore, the two religions that share the common heritage of Yisrael, as well as the Scriptures containing the Torah, the Prophets and the Writings, disagree on the critical issue concerning the Messiah. We will now briefly discuss how this division occurred between Christianity and Judaism.

28

Christianity and Judaism

There currently exists a religion called Christianity which worships a "christ" named Jesus. It has been demonstrated that the Christian religion is promoting an incorrect name for their christ, but it is now necessary to examine whether the name is the only error perpetuated by this religion.

Sadly, it goes far beyond semantics. As has been intimated, there are clearly similarities between Jesus and other pagan deities such as Dionysus, Bacchus, Horus and others. This is no coincidence, since the religion that worships the god-man named Jesus, has actually morphed into a pagan religion by adopting many pagan practices over past centuries. This was done intentionally through the process known as syncretism.

What began as a group of Torah observant Yisraelites following the teachings of Yahushua, grew into a religious system separate and apart from Yisrael. In fact, Christianity now promotes a doctrine known as Replacement Theology, which advocates the notion that an entity called "The Church" has replaced Yisrael, which was and remains the only Set Apart Assembly of YHWH.[208]

The Christian religion was actually established by the Roman Empire, and its world headquarters has always been in Rome. After the Set Apart Spirit fell upon the Yisraelites gathered in Jerusalem on Shabuot, the followers of Messiah began to gather together and form a community within Yisrael.

They were considered a sect of Yisraelites separate and distinct from the other sects, although obviously still part of Yisrael. They did not create a new religion. Instead, they remained Torah observant Yisraelites who were walking out a pure path as displayed by their Teacher and Messiah - Yahushua. They were originally refered to as followers of The Way and Natzrim which means: "shoots." This

was based upon the recognition that Yahushua was the Shoot of Jesse prophesied by Yeshayahu (Yeshayahu 11:10).

They continued to live, work and worship with their fellow Yisraelites, but this was destined for problems because of their differences. The Pharisees and Sadducees had, after all, conspired to kill Yahushua. The Temple system was still corrupted, Yisrael was still subject to the Roman Empire and various sects continued to vye for power over the people.

While the Messianic writings indicate that there were some Pharisees who believed that Yahushua was the Messiah, there were many others who did not, and they vehemently opposed the new sect. Paul of Tarsus was one those Pharisees who originally set out to persecute and root out these alleged "heretics."

The Book of Acts describes some of this conflict, but amazingly there is scant detail in the Messianic writings concerning some important historical occurrences of the first century.

After the death and resurrection of Yahushua, there were still those who violently opposed the Roman occupation. The Zealots eventually began what is commonly referred to as the First Jewish-Roman War that resulted in the destruction of Jerusalem in 70 CE.

It was during this period of time, prior to the fall of Jerusalem, that a certain Pharisee made an arrangement with the Romans. Rabbi Yohanan ben Zakkai is credited with negotiating with Vespasian to allow the Pharisees to set up a community in Yavneh. This request was granted, and Jerusalem was thereafter razed by Titus and the Roman Army. The Temple was completely destroyed and many Yisraelites were slaughtered.

The Pharisees who survived under the leadership of Rabbi Yohanan ben Zakkai established their new headquarters at Yavneh, where Rabbinic Judaism developed into what we see today as a very different religion from what existed over 2,000 years ago.[209] This religion continued and expanded the Pharasaic teachings, which included the oral law and traditions that Yahushua opposed.

The eventual destruction of Jerusalem and the Temple had a major impact upon the religious life of Yisrael. While the Pharisees survived and regrouped their sect in Yavneh, the other sects were scattered and some nearly vanished. The Natzrim were already expanding their teachings away from Jerusalem. They were, after all, searching out the scattered and lost sheep of the House of Yisrael. So while the Pharisees consolidated power in Yavneh, the Natzrim spread their message concerning the Messiah throughout the world. Thus we

see the Pharisaic and the Natzrim sects separating even further, both with very different goals.

Another clear point of contention between the sects came with the Bar Kokhba revolt which occurred between 132-135 CE. The revolt started when Emperor Hadrian constructed a pagan temple in Jerusalem on the site where the House of YHWH once stood. He renamed Jerusalem, Aelia Capitolina, and forbade Torah observance.

Rabbi Akiva ben Yoseph (alternatively Akiba) convinced the Sanhedrin to support the impending revolt, and regarded the chosen commander Simon Bar Kokhba to be the Messiah, according to the verse from Bemidbar 24:17: *"There shall come a star out of Jacob."* "Bar Kokhba" means "son of a star" in the Aramaic language.[210]

Sadly Akiba changed this so-called messiah's name to fit within the prophecy in Bemidbar. His original name was actually Bar Kosiba which can mean "son of a lie" which was really quite appropriate. A close examination reveals that much of what Akiba did to contrive the messiahship of Kokhba was a distortion of the truth. Akiba likely knew that the time for Messiah had come and gone and it appears that he took the actions out of desparation. Despite these well known facts, Akiba is still highly revered and considered to be one of the great Rabbis of Judaism.

The messianic claim in favor of Bar Kokhba clearly alienated the Natzrim, who believed that the true Messiah was Yahushua. Because the Pharasaic "Jews" rallied around the leaders of their particular religion as well as a false messiah, the Natzrim were excluded from joining the revolt - it was really not their fight. They were thus viewed with disdain by the Pharisees which created further separation and deeper division.

This was particularly a problem for the Natzrim who were native Yisraelites. The "gentile converts"[211] coming into the sect did not necessarily share any of the loyalties of their native Yisraelite brethren, whose failure to stand arm in arm with the Yisraelites who followed bar Kokhba and the rabbis made them appear disloyal.

As a result, the Pharasaic Sect came to dominate the faith of the Yisraelites. They continued to perpetuate their newly created religious system. They developed the Mishnah, and a calendar which operates on a man-made mathematical calculation still in use to this day. This new religion is aptly called Judaism, since it consisted primarily of those

from the House of Judah – Yahudah. It was and remains a continuation of the Pharasaic sect traditions and oral law. They developed their own new power structure and vested authority in Rabbis, instead of Priests, Prophets and Kings

The Pharisees continued their fierce opposition to Yahushua and The Natzrim. Obviously, their chosen messiah, Bar Kokhba, was not the Messiah and they had lost serious credibility. The Natzrim and their Messiah were a real threat to the Rabbis who actively promoted further separation between the sects. The Rabbis even added a curse directed toward The Natzrim into their daily prayers. This was called the Birkat ha-Minim which translates to "The Heretic Benediction." It is the Twelfth Benediction of the set daily prayer commonly referred to as the Shemoneh Esreh (the Eighteen Benedictions) or Amidah.

The Twelfth Benediction of the Genizah text reads: "For meshumaddim [apostates] let there be no hope, and the dominion of arrogance do Thou speedily root out in our days; and let the Natzrim and minim perish in a moment, let them be blotted out of the book of the living and let them not be written with the righteous." This was not a blessing as is the purpose of a benediction. Thus many have considered this to be a malediction or curse.[212]

The Shemoneh Esreh was one of the most important rabbinic prayers, and was to be recited three times every day in the Synagogue. Obviously, the Natzrim would not say this prayer. It would also be difficult, if not impossible, for the Natzrim to gather and pray with people who were cursing them three times a day.

Centuries later, another prominent Jewish Rabbi developed what are known as the 13 Principles of Faith. Rabbi Mosheh Maimonides, also known as Rambam, lived in the Middle Ages and developed these principles as a guide or framework. While some of the principles are in accordance with the Torah, there are a few which seem aimed at continuing the division with those who believe that Yahushua is Messiah.

For instance, Principle 3 deals with Elohim's spirituality and incorporeality. It essentially states that Elohim does not have a body. Physical concepts do not apply to Him. Nothing resembles Him at all. This completely contradicts the Scriptures which state that Elohim made man in His Image. Accordingly, YHWH has an Image and Messiah Yahushua came representing that Image as the Last Adam.

Principle 7 proclaims that the prophecy of Mosheh is absolutely true. It states that he was the chief of all prophets, both before and after him. This principle diminishes the prophecy in Devarim which states:

"¹⁸ I will raise up for them a Prophet like you from among their brothers; I will put My words in His mouth, and He will tell them everything I command Him. ¹⁹ If anyone does not listen to My words that the Prophet speaks in My Name, I Myself will <u>call him to account</u>." Devarim 18:18-19.

The Messianic writings interpret this prophecy in this way: *"²² For Mosheh said, 'YHWH your Elohim will raise up for you a Prophet like me from among your own people. You will hear Him in all things, whatever He says to you. ²³ And it shall be that every soul who will not hear that Prophet shall be <u>utterly destroyed</u> from among the people."* Acts 3:22-23. Principle 7 is in error for esteeming Mosheh as greater than Mesiah.

Principle 12 deals specifically with the Messiah and acknowledges the coming of the Messiah no matter how long it takes. Again, this principle implies that the Messiah has not yet come, and seems to indicate that we do not know when the Messiah will come. This Principle is also contrary to the Torah and the Prophets, and actually contradicts Principle 6 which states that all of the words of the prophets are true.

Thus we see a series of events which, over time, hastened the division between the sects of Yisrael until the Pharisees ultimately became the self proclaimed representatives of Yisrael. These are only a few examples in a conflict which continued, until eventually there was a complete separation between these two groups of Yisraelites, which eventually "evolved" into two separate and distinct religions known as Judaism and Christianity.

While Judaism was set on separating themselves, and establishing their own religious system, which could function without a priesthood and without a Temple, the followers of Yahushua were on a very different journey. We read in the Book of Acts how they began to include "converts" from the nations. Pagans from the nations, commonly referred to as Gentiles or Heathens began to repent, convert and join with this sect of Yisraelites in the worship of YHWH.

This, of course, was one of the reasons that the Pharisees were so angered by the Natzrim. It ultimately came down to power and authority, as do most problems between men. The issue regarding converts was particularly interesting because it struck an important nerve. The Pharisees and the Sadducees had turned Yisrael into a "members only" club. They were not particularly interested in converts and they tended to look upon Gentiles with disdain. Some commonly referred to them as "unclean" and "dogs."

There was a conversion process, but it was intentionally made difficult. The Gentiles who were converting and joining with the

Natzrim were not joining Yisrael under the authority of the Sadducees or the Pharisees. They were not undergoing the traditional conversion process, they were simply repenting and being immersed in the name (authority) of Yahushua. The leaders of this fledgling community determined how a former Gentile could become "grafted in" to Yisrael which was an affront to the authority of the other Yisraelite sects who generally refrained from contact with Gentiles.

We read about a very interesting dispute raised in the Messianic writings at Acts 15. It shows how the new sect dealt with this issue in their Council at Jerusalem, which was their "headquarters." They clearly intended for these Gentile converts to obey the Torah, and the prescription set forth was to have them immediately observe the commandments known as the "heart of the Torah." They were then expected to assemble each Shabbat where the Torah was read. The convert could then progress in their walk by learning and obeying the rest of the Torah as they grew into their new faith.

These early converts were originally joining with Yisrael, but after centuries of division the Natzrim sect also divided and morphed into a separate and distinct religion. Since the Pharisees won the power struggle to dominate the identity of Yisrael, the Natzrim eventually found a new identity with the help of the Roman Empire.

As the separation from the Pharisees continued to widen, the Natzrim grew at an astounding rate. It was actually considered to be a threat to the Roman Empire under certain Emperors. As a result, the followers of Yahushua, who were later tagged with the label "Christians," were persecuted severely. Despite the persecution, they flourished until one particular Emperor changed the accepted response to this perceived threat.

Rather than persecuting the "Christians" he decided to merge some of their beliefs into Roman culture, and by doing so he ended up founding the religion of Christianity. Through this process the separation became complete as adherents to this new synchretistic religion called Christianity became identified with an entity called "The Church."

The Christian religion was officially established as the state religion of the Roman Empire by Caesar Flavius Valerius Aurelius Constantinus Augustus, commonly known as Constantine I or Constantine the Great.

Emperor Constantine reversed the persecutions of his predecessor Diocletian, and issued the Edict of Milan in 313 CE which promoted religious tolerance throughout the Empire. He is considered

to be the first Christian Emperor, and Christianity often takes solace in that fact, but history indicates that Constantine's motives were purely political.

Emperor Constantine did worship a christ, although it was not the Hebrew Messiah. He was a worshipper of the sun god Mithras, and remained one after his alleged conversion to Christianity. All you have to do is look at his works to see which god he worshiped.

Constantine called Mithras the "Unconquered Sun, my companion." He issued coins proclaiming "Sol Invictus" - The Unconquered Sun, and in 331 C.E. he issued a coin to commemorate the founding of Rome by none other than Romulus and Remus, the mythical twin brothers who were the sons of the pagan god Mars and the Vestal Virgin. The coin displays the she-wolf that allegedly suckled the twins when they were children on one side, and the goddess Roma on the other side. This sounds like something a pagan would do - not someone who worshipped the Elohim of Yisrael.

As it turns out, Constantine was "a wolf in sheep's clothing." He was, after all, Pontifex Maximus – the High Priest of Paganism. He maintained that role to the day of his death. In that capacity he continued to extol pagan gods. After his victory in the Battle of the Milvian Bridge, he ordered the building of a triumphal arch, known as the Arch of Constantine. The arch is decorated with images of the goddess Victoria, and sacrifices to gods like Apollo, Diana, or Hercules were offered. In 321 CE, Constantine instructed that Christians and non-Christians should be united in observing the "venerable day of the sun" – thus the beginning of Sunday worship in Christianity.

While Constantine supposedly made a profession with his mouth that he was a Christian, his actions demonstrated how he defined the term Christian. This is exactly why James (Yaakov)[201] said "show me your works," because your actions reveal what you really believe.

"14 What does it profit, my brethren, if someone says he has faith but does not have works? Can faith save him? 15 If a brother or sister is naked and destitute of daily food, 16 and one of you says to them, Depart in peace, be warmed and filled, but you do not give them the things which are needed for the body, what does it profit? 17 Thus also faith by itself, if it does not have works, is dead. 18 But someone will say, You have faith, and I have works. Show me your faith without your works, and I will show you my faith by my works. 19

You believe that there is one Elohim. You do well. Even the demons believe - and tremble! [20] But do you want to know, O foolish man, that faith without works is dead? [21] Was not Abraham our father justified by works when he offered Yitshaq his son on the altar? [22] <u>Do you see that faith was working together with his works, and by works faith was made perfect?</u> [23] And the Scripture was fulfilled which says, Abraham believed Elohim, and it was accounted to him for righteousness. And he was called the friend of Elohim. [24] You see then that a man is justified by works, and not by faith only. [25] Likewise, was not Rahab the harlot also justified by works when she received the messengers, and sent them out another way? [26] For as the body without the spirit is dead, so faith without works is dead also." Yaakov 2:14-26.

History is clear that the Christian religion had tremendous pagan influences from its inception. Over the centuries, it continued on

a steady course of merging pagan practices with this newly formed religion. As a result, we see that most of Christianity has adopted pagan concepts and practices, and the Christian savior is more akin to a pagan deity than the prophesied Messiah described throughout the Tanak.

Several years ago I recall seeing a popular Christian worship program on television. It was filled with exciting music, dancing, large video screens with visual effects and a light show. The crowd was facing the stage with arms outstretched and directing their worship toward the band which consisted of a number of young, good looking hip musicians.

The mood was very similar to a modern pop concert, and it struck me how similar Christianity is mirroring the entertainment systems of the world. They sound and look almost identical, although the words of Christian music are usually more "positive" and "encouraging." In my opinion, YHWH does not need amplifiers, light shows and the like to promote His truth. In fact, He often speaks in a "still small voice" or "a gentle whisper." 1 Kings 19:12.

I fear that many are unable to hear YHWH in all the noise, and I wonder if people are confusing the mood that technology provides with the presence of YHWH. Although this is something to consider, it was not the most profound thing that I observed. What especially intrigued me were the words of the song that they were singing – "There is no one else for me – none but Jesus."

Aside from the fact that they are using the wrong name to refer to the Messiah, I could not believe what I was hearing, and it struck me that Christianity was actually a religion primarily centered upon the worship of their christ named Jesus. Yahushua always directed people to the Father, yet Christians seem to have forgotten YHWH, or at least relegated Him to one of the "three persons" in their godhead which they call the Trinity. We have already seen that the concept of the Trinity originated in Babylonian sun worship and the Scriptures clearly describe YHWH as One - Echad.

The fact that Christianity has adopted Babylonian concepts should be no surprise when you recognize that sun worship was consistent with Christianity from its inception. It was, after all, founded by a sun worshipper and always was a religion which, at the very core, involved sun worship.

Christians now worship a christ that bears little resemblance to Yahushua the Messiah. By changing His Name, His teachings and even His appearance, they have misrepresented the true Messiah and are actually promoting a false messiah. To the uninformed, the Christian Jesus appears to be just another savior figure in a long line of pagan sun worship that traces back to Babylon. In one sense they are correct, but it is imperative that they see the truth hidden beneath the traditions set in place by Christianity.

It is partially due to the existence of these pagan elements that Judaism has justified their rejection of the Christian messiah. Sadly, they have failed to fully examine this Messiah and see the truth that lies underneath the surface. This is not simply a failure to investigate though - the division runs far deeper than mere ignorance or mistake. Some argue that it has been a planned and continuous rejection of the One named Yahushua since the very days of Yahushua.

It appears that the founders of Judaism have set themselves, and their religion, in direct opposition to the Messiah from its inception. The problems of Christianity simply provide a convenient justification for this rejection.

The Talmud has a number of derogatory references to Yahushua and His mother Miryam. Some of these statements are disputed, but there are others which quite obviously referred to Miryam as a whore and Yahushua the result of her alleged adultery. (Sanhedrin 106a,b).

This would make Him a mamzer, which is a bastard child. (Yabbamoth 49b). He is also called a magician and a fool. (Shabbat 104b).

Even the name that the rabbis use to refer to Yahushua is derogatory. They call Him Yesu or Yeshu, which is actually an acronym – YSU (ישו). In Hebrew it stands for Yemach Shmo v'zikro" (וזכרו ימח שמו) which means: "may his name and memory be blotted out."

This derogatory treatment has likely tainted every student of the Talmud, and thus kept them away from considering the possibility that Yahushua is their Messiah. If this were not bad enough, the leaders of Judaism have purposefully kept the people in ignorance. They have altered and reinterpreted texts which might point people to Yahushua as the Messiah. They have also kept clear Messianic passages which were fulfilled by Yahushua out of the synagogue liturgy, so that no connection is made with Yahushua.[214]

In short, they have purposefully hidden Yahushua from their flock. Is it any wonder that of all of the religions, Judaism has the most vague, arbitrary and confusing understanding of the Messiah? This is due to the fact that the rabbis of Judaism have tried so hard to distance their Messianic understanding from that of Christianity, they have nothing left. If they are truly honest about what the Scriptures show about the Messiah, they must ultimately admit that it points, not to the Christian Jesus, but to the real Hebrew Messiah – Yahushua.

So then we see these two religions, Judaism and Christianity, which at one point shared a common root in Yisrael. Over time, both have taken very separate journeys away from the Torah and away from the true Messiah.

29

In the End

Despite all of their differences, the one thing that Christianity and Judaism currently share in common is the belief that Messiah is coming. In fact, we are living in a time when adherents to all of the three so-called monotheistic religions, Christianity, Judaism and Islam, are anxiously awaiting the coming of a Messiah.

Christians believe that Jesus Christ is returning for a second time to marry his bride identified as The Church. The religion of Islam also believes that Jesus will be returning, only not as the Messiah.[215]

Sadly, the religion of Judaism, which supposedly has the Torah, the Prophets and the Writings as its essential Scriptures, has no cohesive or specific expectation, save some smaller groups such as the Lubavitchers. Otherwise, the Messianic beliefs in Judaism are vague, sometimes esoteric, and generally not founded on any real Scriptural authority.

The reason for this is because they have clearly missed the Messiah. Their Scriptures provide very specific patterns and promises, which have been detailed in this book, and they must admit that they have no Messiah that meets those criteria. Now this is not for lack of trying, by some counts they have had at least 50 potential Messianic candidates in the past.[216]

Interestingly, there is a great resistance on the part of most Jews to even consider the possibility that Yahushua is the Messiah. This is certainly understandable based upon history. Even though there have been many Christians who have risked their lives to help Jewish individuals, Roman Catholic popes, and Protestant reformers such as Martin Luther, have generally been more of an enemy to the Jews than a friend. But this is not the only reason.

As was previously discussed, when early followers of Yahushua were a fledgling sect of Yisrael, they too were met with hostility and

hatred by the Pharisees - the forerunners of Rabbinic Judaism. Both of these sects pushed away from the other, and it is known that the Pharisees took very direct and intentional steps to distance themselves from the followers of Yahushua.

Later, when Christians overtook the sect of the followers of Yahushua, they did the same by distancing themselves from many of the original core beliefs of their predecessors and largely rejecting the Torah – which to them was "Jewish."

Christianity now teaches and follows a false messiah, one with a fabricated name and teachings which are in direct opposition to the One that they claim to follow. This is a continuing and legitimate objection offered by Jews. Christianity is now presenting a pagan, lawless messiah to the world – one who does not qualify according to the Scriptures.

One of the main arguments that Judaism presently has against Yahushua is that He did not restore the Kingdom of Yisrael. While Christianity has represented Jesus as the Messiah building a Church separate and apart from Yisrael, they have completely ignored this important function of Messiah. Accordingly, they have made their messiah irrelevant to most Jews anticipating the restoration of the Kingdom of Yisrael.

After all, why would a Jew consider a messiah that failed to fix a significant problem that called for a Messiah – the division and exile of Yisrael? Why would a Jew accept a messiah with a name attributed to a pagan sun god and supposedly born on the traditional date that pagan sun gods were born? Why would a Jew recognize or partake in festivities such as Easter and Christmas which clearly originated as pagan fertility celebrations? Why would a Jew consider a messiah that apparently did away with the Torah and the Sabbath, and supposedly replaced the Sabbath with Sunday worship – a day traditionally commemorated by sun worshippers?

The fact is, I do not blame modern adherents of Judaism for rejecting the Christian messiah. After all, the Messiah, as presented by Christianity, is a false messiah and they have every right to reject Jesus. Not until they see Yahushua the Messiah will their eyes truly be opened, and they will not be converting to Christianity when that happens.

As previously stated, Christianity has developed a subversive doctrine, known as Replacement Theology, which promotes the notion that The Church has become Spiritual Yisrael, thus replacing Yisrael. They then perform doctrinal backflips to explain and deal with

the physical descendants of Yaakov, who are incorrectly referred to collectively as "Jews." Christianity desperately needs to correct their erroneous views taught concerning the Messiah and Yisrael.

At the same time, we see the religion of Islam which claims to believe the Hebrew Scriptures as well as the Koran (Qu'ran). One of the pillars of the Islamic faith is that "There is no God but Allah and Mohammed is his prophet." This is a clear contradiction with the Hebrew Scriptures, which profess that YHWH is Elohim.

This is not the only contradiction in Islam. Mohammed actually contradicted himself as he progressed through his life. Early on he was friendly toward the Jews and the Christians, and this is reflected in his writings when he was in Mecca. He actually referred to Jews and Christians as "People of the Book." Later in his life, when he failed to convert the Jews and the Christians, he grew more hostile toward them, and we see that hostility reflected in his writings from Medina.

This is why we currently see Muslims claiming that Islam is a religion of peace – they are quoting from Mohammed in Mecca. At the same time we see Muslims declaring jihad and justifying every sort of killing of infidels – they are quoting from Mohammed in Medina. Since his words from Medina were spoken later in his life, they are considered to supercede his earlier statements. Therefore, it is difficult to consider Islam a religion of peace, when the later words of Mohammed promote violence.

Interestingly, Muslims believe that Jesus will return in the future at Damascus.[217] They believe when he returns he will perform all of the prayers of a faithful Muslim, he will institute Islamic Law according to the Qur'an, and he will abolish all other religions and tell Christians to convert to Islam. He will deny that he was Elohim or the Son of Elohim. He will simply be Allah's slave and messenger. He will kill the Muslim antichrist, get married, have children and die. He will then be buried next to the Prophet Muhammad.[218]

So while Muslims believe in Jesus, and his return to Earth, they do not see him as The Messiah. In fact they believe that he will submit to Imam Mahdi, the Muslim Messiah.

There is no question that the stage is set for very interesting times ahead, and things will prove to be quite confusing for those who are not firm in their knowledge and understanding of the Scriptures. The focus will likely be about the Messiah, and those who fail to know and understand the true Messiah will surely be deceived.

It is clear that when Yahushua first came there was a strong Messianic expectation, but people did not fully understand how the

Scriptures would be fulfilled. We already saw that some were expecting two different Messiahs – the Son of Joseph (The Suffering Servant) and the Son of David (The Conquering and Uniting King). They also knew that Elijah was to come (Malachi 4:5-6) and they did not know what to make of The Prophet like Mosheh (Devarim 18).

Their confusion is evident when we read about their interrogation of Yahanan the Immerser. Yahanan clearly stated that he was not The Messiah. They asked him, "²¹ . . . Then who are you? Are you Elijah? He said, 'I am not.' 'Are you the Prophet?' He answered, 'No.' ²² Finally they said, 'Who are you? Give us an answer to take back to those who sent us. What do you say about yourself?' ²³ Yahanan replied in the words of Yeshayahu the prophet, 'I am the voice of one calling in the desert, Make straight the way for YHWH.' ²⁴ Now some Pharisees who had been sent ²⁵ questioned him, 'Why then do you baptize if you are not the Messiah, nor Elijah, nor the Prophet?'" Yahanan 1:19-27.

Yahanan did not identify himself with any of the individuals that the people were expecting, although Yahushua later identified him with Elijah. This is a very important subject relative to the Messiah and it is helpful to, once again, review what Malachi prophesied concerning Elijah.

"⁵ See, I will send you את the prophet Elijah before that great and dreadful day of YHWH comes. ⁶ He will turn the hearts of the fathers to their children, and the hearts of the children to their fathers; or else I will come and strike את the land with a curse." Malachi 4:5-6. Notice the appearance of the Aleph Taw (את) twice, which hints to the appearance of not only the Messiah, but also Elijah, on two occasions. According to this prophecy, "the prophet Elijah" would come and do two things before the day of YHWH. He would turn 1) the hearts of the fathers to their children; and 2) the hearts of the children to their fathers.

When the Messenger Gabriel appeared to Yahanan's father, Zekaryah, he stated: "¹⁶ And many of the children of Yisrael shall he turn to YHWH their Elohim. ¹⁷ And he (Yahanan) shall go before Him in the spirit and power of Elijah, to turn the hearts of the fathers to the children, and the disobedient to the wisdom of the just; to make ready a people prepared for YHWH." Luke 1:16-17.

Notice that this was only half of the prophecy given through Malachi - "to turn the hearts of the fathers to the children." Yahanan was not Elijah the prophet, but he came "in the spirit and power of Elijah."

Yahanan functioned as the Breaker prophesied by Micah. "¹² I will surely gather all of you, O Yaakov; I will surely bring together the remnant of Yisrael. I will bring them together like sheep in a pen, like a flock *in its pasture; the place will throng with people. ¹³ One who breaks open the way will go up before them; they will break through the gate and go out. Their King will pass through before them, YHWH at their head."* Micah 2:12-13.

According to Micah, the Breaker must come before the King. "Ancient Jewish commentators were keenly aware of the two outstanding figures in the verse, the breaker and the king . . . [Rabbi David Kimchi known as Radak] comments upon the interpretation of Micah 2:13 by quoting an earlier Jewish source. 'In the words of our teachers of blessed memory and in the Midrash, it is taught that "the breaker" is Elijah and "their king" is the branch of the son of David."²¹⁹

This is important to understand because in the first appearance of Yahushua, Yahanan the Immerser was the Breaker. He opened the way for the sheep to break forth out of the restraints of the religious system that entangled them. He spiritually broke down "the fence" around the Torah and the wall around the House of YHWH so that the Kingdom could go forth.

This is the precise imagery used by Yahushua when referring to Yahanan. Here is a modern translation of an often misunderstood statement. *"¹¹ Truly, I say to you, among those born of women there has not arisen anyone greater than Yahanan the Immerser; yet he who is least in the kingdom of heaven is greater than he. ¹² <u>And from the days of Yahanan the Immerser until now the kingdom of heaven suffers violence, and violent men take it by force</u>. ¹³ For all the prophets and the Torah prophesied until Yahanan. ¹⁴ And if you care to accept it, he himself is Elijah, who was to come."* Mattityahu 11:11-14.

Yahushua refered to Yahanan as Elijah, because he was The Breaker. The meaning of the passage becomes even clearer when we clarify the text. The Greek word often translated as "suffers violence" is "biazo," which is active, not passive. Thus, "biazo" is more likened to the active Hebrew word "peretz" which means: "break forth." As a result, the statement of Yahushua would more likely be rendered *"the Kingdom of Heaven breaks forth (peretz) and those breaking forth are pursuing [seeking] it."*²²⁰

Yahanan is "haperetz" – the Breaker, and he came before the King – Yahushua. This should direct us back to the Messianic pattern seen in the birth of Yahudah's twins – Zerah and Peretz. At first, only the hand of Zerah was seen, then Peretz broke forth followed by Zerah. (Beresheet 38:27-30). In His first appearance we saw Yahushua – the Hand of YHWH. In His second coming we will fully see Him in all of His fullness and interestingly, the meaning of Zerah is "rising light."

When asked about Elijah coming first, Yahushua replied: *"¹² To* be sure, Elijah does come first and restores all things. Why then is it written that the Son of Man must suffer much and be rejected? [13] But I tell you, Elijah has come, and they have done to him what they wished, just as it is written about him." Mark 9:12-13. In other words, if the Son of Man must suffer, then why would it be any different for Elijah. And if they killed Elijah (Yahanan) then they are going to kill the king. Yahushua was giving them the sense that these prophecies were multi-layered.

In the first partial fulfillment, Yahanan as Elijah, The Breaker, was killed as was Yahushua the King. In their next appearance, things will be much different. The prophecy of Malachi has not been completely fulfilled. Elijah must still come and turn the hearts of the children to the fathers. Let us be clear, this is not the Spirit of Elijah, it is "the prophet Elijah." There are many who talk about the spirit of Elijah, but that is not what Malachi prophesied. Therefore those anticipating the Messiah should also be anticipating Elijah.

Unless people clearly understand the prophets and how the prophecies will be fulfilled in the end, they are susceptible to being deceived. Thankfully we are able to sift through all of these religions, denominations, doctrines and traditions. The evidence is clear, and the truth is there to be found.

Yahushua taught and lived the Torah of YHWH. He did not change anything that Mosheh taught. Instead, He embodied and personified the Torah as the Way, the Truth and the Life. All those who follow Him are instructed to walk as He walked – totally submitted to Elohim – loving Elohim with all one's heart, soul, mind and strength and loving one's neighbor as oneself.

Despite the many proofs provided concerning the Messiahship of Yahushua, some continue their objections, because they claim Yahushua has not fulfilled all of the prophecies. It is true that all of the prophecies have not been fulfilled and that is because we have not yet seen The Day of YHWH.

There are still things which need to occur, such as the regathering of the outcasts of Yisrael and the restoration of the Kingdom of Yisrael – not to be confused with the modern State of Israel.[221] That is why Yahushua gave the revelation of the end to His talmid Yahanan. While some in Judaism refer to the Book of Revelation as a "stolen book," because it shares much in common with various texts in the Tanak, The Book of Revelation actually "reveals" how Yahushua will fulfill the remaining prophecies and restore the Kingdom of Yisrael.

The Revelation given to Yahanan is a prophetic vision of how Yahushua the Messiah will reveal Himself to those who keep the commandments of Elohim, and have the testimony of Yahushua. (Revelation 14:12). In order to comprehend this mysterious text, it is imperative that you understand the Torah and particularly the Appointed Times. Without this foundation, the book will lack cohesiveness and the things described in the text will not make sense.

This discussion is about the identity and purpose of the Messiah, and is not meant to be an analysis of the Book of Revelation - that is for another discussion.[222] The important thing to recognize is that the Book of Revelation describes Yahushua returning to fulfill the Covenant that is established in the Torah. Yahushua is returning to keep the Millennial Sabbath with all of those who have believed and obeyed Him. (Revelation 22:14).

A popular misconception is that things concerning the end have been and will remain a mystery. When approached with the subject of the end of the ages and the return of Yahushua, many Christians instinctively parrot the response that "No man knows the day or the hour of His return." Many also claim that He could return at anytime. Both of these statements ignore the fact that the Scriptures provided very specific information concerning His first coming. Should it be any different with His return?

The reason for this attitude of accepted ignorance is consistent with the continuing failure to understand YHWH and His plan for His people. YHWH declared through the prophet Yeshayahu "*I make known the end from the beginning, from ancient times, what is still to come.*" Yeshayahu 46:10. The prophet Amos clearly stated that: "*Surely the Sovereign YHWH does nothing without revealing His plan to His servants the prophets.*" Amos 3:7.

Yahushua has provided significant information regarding His return, and amazingly, this information was made known from the beginning. Consistent with this promise of revealing His plan to His prophets, the Book of Revelation indicates that there will be two particular prophets who will prophesy to the world for three and a half years prior to the return of Yahushua. (Revelation 11:3).

Before His departure, Yahushua said that He was going to prepare a place for His Bride, but would return. We saw at Sinai that the Bride was Yisrael and the Bride is still Yisrael – not "The Church." Yahushua provided many parables which were intended to inform the Bride about His return.

When Yahushua told His talmidim: "*I go to prepare a place for you*" the intent was clear. This is what a Hebrew bridegroom would say to his bride before he left her to prepare the bridal chamber in his

father's house. This is the context of the passage found in the Good News according to Yahanan when Yahushua stated "² *In My Father's House are many mansions; if it were not so, I would have told you. I go to prepare a place for you. ³ And if I go and prepare a place for you, I will come again and receive you to Myself; that where I am, there you may be also.⁴ And where I go you know, and the way you know.*" Yahanan 14:2-4.

In a traditional eastern marriage arrangement, the deal is struck and the groom departs to prepare the dwelling place for his bride. Notice, once again, the patterns from the Torah. Yitshaq was offered at Moriah before a bride was provided to him sometime later. Yahushua, as the Lamb of YHWH, had to be offered up before He could receive His Bride.

Since He was taken up after the resurrection, Yahushua has been preparing for His Bride and the Bride, in turn, is being prepared to live with her Husband. Once the home is completed and the preparations are complete, the groom returns for his bride "as a thief in the night." In a traditional eastern marriage, this is a joyous occasion when the groom comes and takes his bride to the bridal chamber and consummates the marriage. It is a time full of suspense and excitement which is followed by a wedding feast.

Prior to the groom's arrival, the bride must attend to some necessary preparations. She must ready herself and her trousseau - the possessions, such as clothing and linens which a bride assembles for her marriage. Thus there are preparations which must be performed by both the bride and the groom. If one of them is not ready, then the wedding cannot take place.

The interesting thing about the ancient Hebrew wedding ritual is that the bride was not necessarily ignorant as to when her groom would be appearing. A loving groom wants his bride to be ready - he wants to get married. The last thing that he wants is to appear and find his bride unprepared. Therefore, he might send friends or messengers to communicate to the bride the day and the hour of his future coming.

This is definitely the case with Yahushua. He has told us that He will be returning as a thief in the night and warns: "*Therefore if you will not watch, I will come upon you as a thief, and you will not know what hour I will come upon you.*" Revelation 3:3. Later in the book of Revelation He states: "*Behold, I am coming as a thief. Blessed is he who watches, and keeps his garments, lest he walk naked and they see his shame.*" Revelation 16:15 NKJV.

Both of these passages share the common theme of watching. They are likely referring to the role of the priest who tended the fires of the Altar throughout the night in preparation for the morning sacrifices. Tradition holds that the High Priest would come stealthily into the Court of the Priests like "a thief in the night" to see if the priest tending the fire on the Great Altar was awake or sleeping. If he was sleeping, the High Priest would take some of the fire and set the clothing of the sleeping priest ablaze. Those linen priestly garments would quickly burn, leaving the priest naked and ashamed.

The texts reveal the need to watch and be ready as diligent priests – each of us tending the fire on our altars. The message is clear that if we watch, we will not be taken by surprise. If we do not watch, we may miss the wedding. When Yahushua was speaking concerning the end times and His return He spoke of the ten virgins.

"¹ _At that time_ the kingdom of heaven will be like ten virgins who took their lamps and went out to meet the bridegroom. ² Five of them were foolish and five were wise. ³ The foolish ones took their lamps but did not take any oil with them. ⁴ The wise, however, took oil in jars along with their lamps. ⁵ The bridegroom was a long time in coming, and they all became drowsy and fell asleep. ⁶ At midnight the cry rang out: Here's the bridegroom! Come out to meet him! ⁷ Then all the virgins woke up and trimmed their lamps. ⁸ The foolish ones said to the wise, Give us some of your oil; our lamps are going out. ⁹ No, they replied, there may not be enough for both us and you. Instead, go to those who sell oil and buy some for yourselves. ¹⁰ But while they were on their way to buy the oil, the bridegroom arrived. The virgins who were ready went in with him to the wedding banquet. And the door was shut. ¹¹ Later the others also came. Sir! Sir! they said. Open the door for us! ¹² But he replied, I tell you the truth, I don't know you. ¹³ Therefore keep watch, because you do not know the day or the hour." Mattityahu 25:1-13.

Notice that the ten virgins all wanted to get married, but they were not all prepared. Five were foolish and unprepared while five were wise and prepared. As with the diligent priest, the wise virgins who were tending their lamps - their fires - were ready. (see also Luke 12:35-37). As a watchful Bride anxiously awaits her Groom, Yahushua wants us to be ready and He has given us information to help us be ready for His return.

Interestingly the text states that we should keep watch because we do not know (oida) the day or the hour. This does not mean that we are completely ignorant of when He will return. Read how the Groom warns His Bride: "⁴² Watch therefore, for you do not know (oida) what hour your Master is coming. ⁴³ But know (ginosko) this, that if the Master of the house had known what hour the thief would come, he would have watched and not allowed his house to be broken into. ⁴⁴ Therefore,

<u>you also be ready</u>, for the Son of Man is coming at an hour you do not expect." Mattityahu 24:42-44.

The Greek word "oida" means: "intuitive knowledge" while the Greek word "ginosko" means: "objective knowledge" or "acquired knowledge with effort."[223] In other words, you had better watch and figure it out, because you do not know "intuitively" what hour the Son of Man is coming. It is not impossible to know when a thief is coming, they are stealthy, but if you are watchful and diligent you can figure it out.

Remember, the Master wants us to know when He is coming, and the wise servant will be ready for the Master's return. The wicked servant, on the other hand, is the one who will be surprised and caught off guard. The faithful and wise servant is the one found doing what he is supposed to be doing when his Master returns. The wicked servant will be caught doing what he is not supposed to be doing. "*The Master of that (wicked) servant will come on a day when he does not expect Him and at an hour he is not aware of.*" Mattityahu 24:50.

The Book of Revelation has been given to reveal the day and the hour to the bondservants of Yahushua who are watching for His return. That is why Yahushua said that it was the wicked servant who would be unaware of the day and hour of the Master's return. It is also why Paul said that this day would not come on the sons of light like a thief. (1 Thessalonians 5:4-5).

Yahushua the Messiah is returning at a specific time – an Appointed Time from the Torah. As a result, it is very important to learn all about the Appointed Times. The notion that He can return at any time is a false teaching, and misrepresents the Creator and His intentions. He is not playing games with His servants, He simply wants them to diligently seek out His Ways.

Can you imagine how a groom would feel after spending months or even years of preparation and planning, his heart aching with anxious anticipation to retrieve his bride, only to show up and find his bride filthy, unkempt, sleeping and unprepared. Her state of preparedness reveals her heart. She obviously does not love the groom as much as he loves her. The groom wants to find his bride as ready and prepared as himself. So it is with our Messiah, the Bridegroom. (Mattityahu 25:1-13).

Messiah is preparing a home for His Bride – the set apart congregation of Yisrael. The home that He is building is the new Jerusalem. "*[11] Indeed YHWH has proclaimed to the end of the world: Say to the daughter of Zion, Surely your salvation is coming; Behold, His reward is* with Him and His work before Him. ¹² And they shall call them The Set Apart People, The Redeemed of YHWH; and you shall be called Sought Out, A City Not Forsaken." Yeshayahu 62:10-12.

In a clear Messianic Scripture we see how the Prophet Yeshayahu describes the people of Elohim as the Redeemed – A City not Forsaken. The word translated as "city" is ayer (עיר) which can mean a guarded place – just as Adam was to guard – shamar – the garden. This city, after all, is the restored Eden – the new Jerusalem. A place where renewed man, made in the image of YHWH can dwell in His presence.

Yahanan, a talmid of Yahushua, was also a Prophet of Yisrael who described in detail this City – the Bride as she will appear at the end of history and the beginning of the Eternal State: "⁹ Then one of the seven angels who had the seven bowls filled with the seven last plagues came to me and talked with me, saying, 'Come, I will show you the Bride, the Lamb's wife.' ¹⁰ And he carried me away in the Spirit to a great and high mountain, and showed me the great city, the set apart Jerusalem, descending out of heaven from Elohim, ¹¹ having the glory of Elohim. Her light was like a most precious stone, like a jasper stone, clear as crystal. ¹² Also <u>she had a great and high wall with twelve gates, and twelve angels at the gates, and names written on them, which are the names of the twelve tribes of the children of Yisrael</u>: ¹³ three gates on the east, three gates on the north, three gates on the south, and three gates on the west. ¹⁴ Now the wall of the city had twelve foundations, and on them were the names of the twelve apostles of the Lamb. ¹⁵ And he who talked with me had a gold reed to measure the city, its gates, and its wall. ¹⁶ The city is laid out as a square; its length is as great as its breadth. And he measured the city with the reed: twelve thousand furlongs. Its length, breadth, and height are equal. ¹⁷ Then he measured its wall: one hundred and forty-four cubits, according to the measure of a man, that is, of an angel. ¹⁸ The construction of its wall was of jasper; and the city was pure gold, like clear glass. ¹⁹ The foundations of the wall of the city were adorned with all kinds of precious stones: the first foundation was jasper, the second sapphire, the third chalcedony, the fourth emerald, ²⁰ the fifth sardonyx, the sixth sardius, the seventh chrysolite, the eighth beryl, the ninth topaz, the tenth chrysoprase, the eleventh jacinth, and the twelfth amethyst. ²¹ The twelve gates were twelve pearls: each individual gate was of one pearl. And the street of the city was pure gold, like transparent glass." Revelation 21:9-21.

The new Jerusalem will have twelve gates which are guarded, and notice the twelve gates have the names of the twelve tribes of Yisrael. There is no gate of "The Gentiles" or gate of "The Christians." You must be joined with a tribe and be part of Yisrael to enter. In fact,

we were already provided a pattern for the layout of the City through the encampment of Yisrael in the wilderness, and the gates will be named according to the location of the various tribes.

This is made clear by the following: "² *I saw the set apart City, the new Jerusalem, coming down out of heaven from Elohim, prepared as a bride beautifully dressed for her husband. ³ And I heard a loud voice from the throne saying, 'Now the dwelling of Elohim is with men, and He will live with them. They will be His people, and Elohim Himself will be with them and be their Elohim.*" Revelation 21:2-4. Can you hear the prophecy of Hoshea echoing from the past? This is the very fulfillment of his words – the restoration of Yisrael that Messiah will accomplish.

As the Garden contained the Tree of Life – so too does the new Jerusalem. "*In the middle of its street, and on either side of the river, was the tree of life, which bore twelve fruits, each tree yielding its fruit every month. The leaves of the tree were for the healing of the nations.*" Revelation 22:2. Again, you must pass through a gate to partake of the Tree and notice the number of fruits – twelve. This Tree is for Yisrael and only those who partake of the Tree will have everlasting life.

The regathering and remarriage will occur according to the patterns established from the beginning. YHWH previously made a Covenant with Abraham which involved the shedding of blood. It was continued by a later generation through Mosheh when Yisrael was in bondage in Egypt. The Covenant was broken and Yahushua renewed that Covenant through the shedding of His blood. It is vital to understand that the Renewed Covenant has yet to be completely fulfilled.

We currently see the "Lost Sheep of Yisrael" still scattered throughout the world and enslaved in Egypt – the world system. Just as YHWH sent Mosheh the shepherd, mediator and deliverer to Yisrael, so He will send Yahushua, His Right Hand, a second time to deliver and regather Yisrael from the world. Yahushua already mediated the Renewed Covenant, and in the end, He will fulfill that Renewed Covenant. Just as those who heard Mosheh and obeyed were saved from death and delivered from Egypt, the same will hold true for those who hear and obey Yahushua in the end.

Just as YHWH sent Mosheh and Aharon to the Children of Yisrael enslaved in Egypt, in the end YHWH will send two witnesses. Just as YHWH sent great plagues against Egypt, so He will soon do to the entire planet. Just as He once judged Egypt, He will soon judge the nations of the world. These judgments are specifically described in the Book of Revelation, and they will occur according to the patterns found in the Appointed Times. The patterns in the Torah are there for us to learn, so we know how to live and respond to future events. The people of YHWH should not be ignorant.

Those who Hear and Obey (shema) YHWH and remain set apart will once again be saved and delivered through and from His judgment. The Book of Revelation clearly describes this process. "*4 Then I heard another voice from heaven say: Come out of her, My people, so that you will not share in her sins, so that you will not receive any of her plagues; 5 for her sins are piled up to heaven, and Elohim has remembered her crimes. 6 Give back to her as she has given; pay her back double for what she has done. Mix her a double portion from her own cup. 7 Give her as much torture and grief as the glory and luxury she gave herself. In her heart she boasts, I sit as queen; I am not a widow, and I will never mourn. 8 Therefore in one day her plagues will overtake her: death, mourning and famine. She will be consumed by fire, for mighty is YHWH Elohim who judges her.*" Revelation 18:4-8.

This text should lead people back to the prophecy given by Yirmeyahu concerning Babylon. (Yirmeyahu 51). Yisrael must come out of Babylon and remain set apart as the nations of the world are being judged. Through this process there will be a great regathering of Yisrael and a great Exodus.[224] YHWH will regather His people – not simply from one nation, but from the entire planet.

This has been clearly foretold through the Prophets and this is what the Book of Revelation is all about – the final regathering and the punishment of the world. Just as YHWH warned His people and set them apart from the plagues of the Egyptians, YHWH has warned His people and they must be set apart when the final judgments come.

Many Christians believe that they will simply be removed from the planet through the Rapture before any trouble strikes. That is not how the future Exodus will take place. Just as in the first Exodus, the miraculous deliverance of Yisrael coincided with the destruction of Egypt, so in the second Exodus the miraculous deliverance of Yisrael will coincide with the destruction of the entire system of false worship summarized in Scriptures as "Babylon."

The miracle is that in the midst of it all YHWH will shepherd His flock and protect them while those around them are suffering. This will be a testimony to the world as they see His Mighty Hand. All the world will then know His Name. Therefore, it is not about being taken out before any trouble strikes. Rather it is about being set apart when the trouble strikes and persevering until the deliverance.

These are all patterns provided in the Torah, and those patterns are for a future generation. Yisrael was not "raptured" from Egypt –

they were set apart through obedience, covered by the blood of the lamb and saved. They were then delivered from slavery, not in a panic, but as a conquering army. It was then that they were immersed through the waters of the Red Sea and prepared for the wedding at Sinai. This is a very important pattern for understanding what will happen in the end.

Just as Yahushua (Joshua) and Caleb were allowed to enter the Promised Land because they followed YHWH wholeheartedly, so it will be with those who persevere to the end. Those who do not fear the giants, those who keep the faith and give a good report will enter in. As we saw the pattern of Yahushua (Joshua) leading Yisrael across the Jordan and the mystery of the Jubilee associated with that event, we understand that this was a pattern that gives us insight into the return of Messiah Yahushua described in Revelation.

In fact, it is in the Book of Revelation, the last book in the Messianic writings, that one of the greatest mysteries in the Torah was revealed – that of the Aleph and the Taw (את). As we saw this mystery in the beginning we now see the answer in the end.

In the beginning of the Book of Revelation YHWH Elohim declares: "*I Am the Aleph (א) and the Taw (ת) Who is, and Who was, and Who is to come, the Almighty.*" Revelation 1:8. Later, at the end of the Book Yahushua also declares: "*I Am the Aleph (א) and the Taw (ת), the First and the Last, the Beginning and the End.*" Revelation 22:13.

The statement by Yahushua that He is "the Beginning and the End" is a direct reference to the prophecy found in Yeshayahu and is very telling. "*6 This is what YHWH says - Yisrael's King and Redeemer, YHWH Almighty; I Am the first and I Am the last; apart from Me there is no Elohim. 7 Who then is like Me? Let him proclaim it. Let him declare and lay out before Me what has happened since I established My ancient people, and what is yet to come - yes, let him foretell what will come. 8 Do not tremble, do not be afraid. Did I not proclaim this and foretell it long ago? You are My witnesses. Is there any Elohim besides Me? No, there is no other Rock, I know not one.*" Yeshayahu 44:6-8.

Yahushua is proclaiming that He was at the Beginning of Creation and He is at the End. Remember that we are not talking about two points on a line that are at opposite ends of the spectrum, we are looking at one point, the beginning and completion of a cycle. Yahushua is declaring that He is the King and Redeemer of Yisrael, the Rock – YHWH Almighty. Yahushua and The Father are united as One - Echad. This is the mystery of Elohim which has been declared by the Shema for centuries. (Devarim 6:4). This is when YHWH will be King over the Earth and His Name is One. (Zekaryah 14:9).

YHWH through His Son Yahushua - His Right Arm - has Redeemed Yisrael. He is gathering His Sheep and preparing His Bride and will soon return to deliver them and attend the climax of history – The Wedding and the Feast of the Lamb at the beginning of the Age of Life.[225]

There are many who find it hard to comprehend that the Messiah is more than a mortal man, but is this really so hard to believe? Yahushua said, *"Before Abraham was – I Am."* (Yahanan 8:58). When asked to show the Father, Yahushua said, *"If you have seen Me you have seen the Father."* (Yahanan 14:9). If we have learned anything from the Torah, it is that all men have fallen short. Only the Son of Elohim, the Last Adam could restore that which was lost. Only He could atone for the sin that had corrupted all of Creation, and make a way back into the Garden - back into the presence of Elohim – where we can once again partake of the Tree of Life.

This was the pattern provided by the Temple service – which represented the House of YHWH. At the entrance of the House was the Laver where we must wash before entering. We then approach the Altar where we atone for sin by the shedding of innocent blood from an unblemished sacrifice. We can then enter into the Set Apart Place and partake of the Feast at the Table of YHWH. There we partake of the Bread of Life and are lit by the Menorah, which represents the Spirits of YHWH (Yeshayahu 11:1). There we offer up prayers and praise to Him which is represented by the Table of Incense.

Only at the culmination of history, at the end of the Age of Life and at the beginning of the World to Come, is the Bride permitted beyond the veil into the Bridal Chamber to become One (Echad) with Her Husband in the Most Set Apart Place. She may then join with YHWH Who sits upon the throne - represented by the Ark of the Covenant. Within the Ark of the Covenant is the Testimony – the Commandments, which is the marriage contract. There we also find the manna, which is the Bread of Life. Beside the Ark is the Rod of Aharon – the almond tree - which represents the Tree of Life. The House of YHWH represented the Garden, the new Jerusalem – the marital residence of YHWH and His Bride.

As it was in the beginning, so it will be in the end. YHWH will complete His cycle – His plan to build an eternal House and fill it with His family. The Messiah allows us entrance into this House through a restored relationship with our Creator. In the role of the Son of David, He will soon appear to deliver His people from the world as described in the Revelation given to Yahanan. It is Yisrael that will be delivered,

not specific groups called Christians or Jews. Only the Redeemed who are part of Yisrael will enter the House – those who are in Covenant with YHWH – the Family of Elohim.

There will come a day when all eyes will be opened – they will see the One Who was pierced. Just as the Messianic figure Joseph was living in a pagan culture, married to a pagan woman, looking like a pagan and even given a pagan name – the same has occurred with Yahushua who is Messiah ben Joseph.

Yahushua has had the pagan name Jesus applied to Him. His teachings have been altered to the point where He appears to be a pagan, married to a pagan bride called The Church. Just as the eyes of Joseph's brothers were opened during their period of famine and hardship, the same will occur in the future concerning the true identity of Yahushua.

"¹ . . . Thus says YHWH, Who stretches out the heavens, lays the foundation of the earth, and forms the spirit of man within him: ² 'Behold, I will make Jerusalem a cup of drunkenness to all the surrounding peoples, when they lay siege against Yahudah and Jerusalem. ³ And it shall happen in that day that I will make Jerusalem a very heavy stone for all peoples; all who would heave it away will surely be cut in pieces, though all nations of the earth are gathered against it. ⁴ In that day, says YHWH, I will strike every horse with confusion, and its rider with madness; I will open My eyes on the House of Yahudah, and will strike every horse of the peoples with blindness. ⁵ And the governors of Yahudah shall say in their heart, The inhabitants of Jerusalem are my strength in YHWH of hosts, their Elohim. ⁶ In that day I will make the governors of Yahudah like a firepan in the woodpile, and like a fiery torch in the sheaves; they shall devour all the surrounding peoples on the right hand and on the left, but Jerusalem shall be inhabited again in her own place - Jerusalem. ⁷ YHWH will save the tents of Yahudah first, so that the glory of the House of David and the glory of the inhabitants of Jerusalem shall not become greater than that of Yahudah. ⁸ In that day YHWH will defend the inhabitants of Jerusalem; the one who is feeble among them in that day shall be like David, and the house of David shall be like Elohim, like the Angel of YHWH before them. ⁹ It shall be in that day that I will seek to destroy all the nations that come against Jerusalem. ¹⁰ And I will pour on the House of David and on the inhabitants of Jerusalem the Spirit of grace and supplication; then they will look on את Whom they pierced. Yes, they will mourn for Him as one mourns for his only son, and grieve for Him as one grieves for a firstborn." Zekaryah 12:1-10.

This text clearly states that there will come a time of tribulation and hardship when the nations will come against Jerusalem – which is inhabited by the House of David. When this occurs, they will look upon את Whom they pierced and they will mourn. Their eyes will be opened to Yahushua the Messiah.

Whether Christian or Jew, once their eyes are opened to the True Messiah, it is then necessary to receive the atonement which He provided and enter into the Renewed Covenant. An essential part of joining the Renewed Covenant is to live according to the teachings of Yahushua and the terms of the Covenant – The Torah.

The Book of Revelation states: "¹⁴ _Blessed are those who do His commandments, that they may have the right to the Tree of Life, and may enter through the gates into the city._ ¹⁵ _But outside are dogs and sorcerers and sexually immoral and murderers and idolaters, and whoever loves and practices a lie._" Revelation 22:14-15.

The city is the new Jerusalem - paradise restored. Only those who obey the commandments can get in through the gates and enter into life. You must be part of Yisrael to enter and as a result, you must be a part of the Renewed Covenant. As we have repeatedly seen, the critical element to remaining in Covenant with YHWH is obedience to the commandments - which are the instructions for life found within the Torah.

Adam and Hawah were ejected from the Garden due to their disobedience. "_So He drove out the man; and He placed cherubim at the east of the garden of Eden, and a flaming sword which turned every way, to guard the way to the Tree of Life._" Beresheet 3:24. They could not get back into the Garden because of their sin. Paradise was now guarded and restricted to sinful man.

The same holds true with the new Jerusalem, which is described as a fortress City. There are twelve gates leading into the new Jerusalem and they are all guarded. (Revelation 21:12). You can only get in if you obey. The amazing thing is that the gates are now open, thanks to the work of Messiah. Only those who have been cleansed from the sin of the garden can get in - only those who have been washed by the blood of the Lamb of Elohim. Those who are without spot or blemish and have on their wedding garments – the Bride. Your name must be found in The Lamb's Book of Life because He owns it. He paid for it with His blood.

You cannot become part of the Bride and live unless death has passed over you - His blood must be sprinkled on the doorposts of your tabernacle - which is your body. Unless you are covered by this Blood you will not live, and you must be alive to attend the wedding.

This is why Yahushua continually used the wedding as a parable and warned people to get ready. He told the following parable: "² _The kingdom of heaven is like a certain king who arranged a marriage for his_

son, ³ and sent out his servants to call those who were invited to the wedding; and they were not willing to come. ⁴ Again, he sent out other servants, saying, 'Tell those who are invited, See, I have prepared my dinner; my oxen and fatted cattle are killed, and all things are ready. Come to the wedding. ⁵ But they made light of it and went their ways, one to his own farm, another to his business. ⁶ And the rest seized his servants, treated them spitefully, and killed them. ⁷ But when the king heard about it, he was furious. And he sent out his armies, destroyed those murderers, and burned up their city. ⁸ Then he said to his servants, The wedding is ready, but those who were invited were not worthy. ⁹ Therefore go into the highways, and as many as you find, invite to the wedding. ¹⁰ So those servants went out into the highways and gathered together all whom they found, both bad and good. And the wedding hall was filled with guests. ¹¹ But when the king came in to see the guests, he saw a man there who did not have on a wedding garment. ¹² So he said to him, 'Friend, how did you come in here without a wedding garment?' And he was speechless. ¹³ Then the king said to the servants, Bind him hand and foot, take him away, and cast him into outer darkness; there will be weeping and gnashing of teeth. ¹⁴ <u>For many are called, but few are chosen</u>." Mattityahu 22:2-14.

The choice is yours – a great wedding feast which is paradise, or the outer darkness which is sheol. It is really not complicated, but religious systems and traditions have clouded the simple truth from the masses. We now find many in a confused state, following false and dangerous doctrines which are leading people away from the great wedding feast toward that place of darkness. They need to see the Light of Messiah – the Light of Truth and then walk in that Light.

This world is headed into very complex and difficult times. There are many proclaiming the end of the world and there is much fear and trepidation concerning the future. The Scriptures also tell of difficult times ahead, but they provide hope and a great promise for those who hold to the Torah and have the testimony of the true Messiah.

My desire is that through this text, all can now see the true Savior of the world, the Lamb of Elohim, the Redeemer of Yisrael who came as the Son of Joseph and will some day return as the Son of David, our King and High Priest - Yahushua The Messiah!

Endnotes

¹   Time is not only a dimension, it is the very framework within which the Creator
    has placed His Creation. Time is not arbitrary nor is it insignificant in the
    Creation Plan outlined in the Scriptures. It is imperative that anyone seeking
    truth understand time as well as the Creator's reckoning of time. Once you know
    how to tell time you can determine where you are in time and you can begin to
    synchronize with the Creator and His purpose for Creation. Understanding time
    plays an integral part in this study of the Messiah and in this text we will challenge
    some accepted methods of reckoning time as well as some accepted historical
    dates. The subject of time is discussed further in the Walk in the Light series book
    entitled "The Appointed Times."

²   Beresheet is the transliteration of the Hebrew word בראשית which is often
    translated as Genesis. It means "in the beginning" and it is the name of the first
    book in the Scriptures as well as the first word in that book. Keep in mind that I
    use the word book very loosely because in this modern day we use books in codex
    form which are bound by a spine and generally have writing on both pages. By
    using the word "book" we create a mental image regarding manuscripts which
    may not be accurate. Manuscripts such as the Torah and other writings in the
    Tanakh were written on scrolls, so instead of the word book, it is more accurate to
    refer to the scroll or the sefer (ספר) when referring to these ancient manuscripts.
    Therefore "book" of Beresheet would be more accurately described as Sefer
    Beresheet ספר בראשית since it originally came as a scroll.

³   The term "Old Testament" is often used to describe the Scriptures, commonly
    known as the "Jewish Bible," or the Tanak which was originally written in Hebrew.
    I believe that the term "Old Testament" is terribly misleading because it gives the
    impression that everything contained therein is old or outdated. While growing
    up in a mainline Christian denomination I was given the distinct impression that
    it was full of great stories, but it applied to "The Jews" and it was replaced by
    the "New Testament" which contained the important Scriptures for Christians.
    While this may or may not have been done intentionally, I believe that it is a
    notion which is pervasive throughout much of Christianity. Without a doubt, the
    Tanak is essential to the faith, and these are the Scriptures which must be at the
    core of our belief system. If these truths are not at the foundation and considered
    completely relevant for today, then people are prone to be misled and follow false
    and twisted doctrines. This problem is amplified by the fact that most of the source
    texts for the "New Testament" derive from copies of Greek or Latin manuscripts
    which are western languages and have often been translated in such a fashion that
    the Eastern concepts of the faith are lost or distorted. While it is possible that some
    or all of the texts of the "New Testament" were originally written in Hebrew or
    Aramaic, the Bible as we know it, exclusively uses western language source texts.
    In this book we will examine this point as it relates to the Messiah, but the issue is
    discussed at length in The Walk in the Light Series book entitled "Scriptures."

⁴   Without a doubt the most popular and well known Psalm is Psalm 23. A portion

of that Psalm reads *"He leads me in paths of righteousness for His Name's sake."* The Hebrew word for paths is "magal" (מעגל) and depicts a revolution or a circular motion. Therefore a more accurate translation would read: *"He leads me in cycles of righteousness for His Name's sake."* These cycles of righteousness are the Appointed Times that the Creator established for those who desire to learn about Him and walk in righteousness. These times are detailed further in the Walk in the Light series entitles "The Appointed Times."

5   Benner, Jeff A., Learn to Read Biblical Hebrew, Virtualbookworm.com 2004 Page 41.

6   The problems which are found in many English translations is a topic of the Walk in the Light series book entitled "Scriptures." It is important to make the distinction between the inerrancy of the Word and the inerrancy of a particular translation. In the present context I am only referring to errors made by translators.

7   Elohim (אלהים) is technically plural, but that does not designate more than one Creator. The singular form is El (אל) and could refer to any "mighty one," but because the plural is used to describe the Creator, it means that Elohim is qualitatively stronger or more powerful than any singular El (אל). In Hebrew, the plural form can mean that something or someone is qualitatively greater not just quantitatively greater. We see in the first sentence of the Scriptures that "In the Beginning Elohim created" the Hebrew for "created" is bara (ברא) which literally is "He created." It is masculine singular showing that while Elohim is plural He is masculine singular. For an excellent discussion of the Hebrew Etymology of the Name of Elohim I recommend His Name is One written by Jeff A. Benner, Virtualbookworm.com Publishing 2002.

8   The term "god" is a generic term which can be attached to any number of powerful beings described in mythology and worshipped in pagan religions. Some use a capital "G" to refer to "the God of the Bible" but I find it a disservice to apply this label to the Creator of the Universe when the Hebrew Scriptures clearly refer to Him as Elohim. The pagan origins of the word "god" are discussed in the Walk in the Light series book entitled "Names."

9   Yahuhanan (יהותנן) is a Hebrew name which means "YHWH has given." Many pronounce his Hebrew name as Yochanan (יוחנן) but that pronunciation loses the Name of YHWH. According to McClintock and Strong it is "a contracted form of the name Jehohanan." Therefore, in an effort to keep the original flavor of the name I use the Yahonatan, Yahuhanan or Yahanan when referring to Yahanan the Immerser or the New Testament individual commonly called John.

10   It is important to read and study the Scriptures in their proper context. To begin, the majority of the Scriptures were originally written in Hebrew and later translated into different languages. The translation process is not perfect and sometimes the full meaning of a passage gets "lost in translation." Therefore understanding the original language is extremely helpful and important if we are to fully grasp the meaning of some of the texts. Many people refer to the entire Bible as "The Word of God" but the Scriptures contain many other words than just the Word of Elohim. The Scriptures are record of the history of mankind which has been written by men who were inspired by Elohim. The Scriptures must always be interpreted in the context in which they were written. The intended purpose of the

Scriptures is to instruct mankind on Elohim's plans and purposes for His creation.

11   *What the Rabbis Know About the Messiah*, Rachmiel Frydland, Messianic Publishing Company 2001 Page 6. The term God changed to Elohim by author for consistency.

12   The book of Revelation is actually the revelation of the Messiah. It provides a depiction of how the Messiah will return to the Earth and take dominion of the planet.

13   The Alpha and the Omega is a Greek phrase which has been retained in the Greek language in English translations of the Bible. If you were to look at this statement as one made by a Hebrew Messiah to a Hebrew disciple (talmid), it would be more accurately rendered as Aleph Taw in the Hebrew language.

14   Tanak is an acronym and stands for: Torah, Nebiim (Prophets) and Kethubim (Writings) T-N-K = Tanak. The use of this acronym describes the contents, but does not categorize them as "Old." Therefore, I prefer using Tanak to refer to the entire collection of Scriptures commonly referred to as The Old Testament.

15   Most people entering the Christian faith for the first time are presented with a 4 step prayer also known as "The Four Spiritual Laws" as the entry point to the faith. The typical prayer essentially recognizes that God loves you, that man is sinful, that Jesus Christ is God's only provision for man's sin, and finally we must receive Jesus Christ as our Lord and Savior in order to be saved. The problem is that many believe and profess that this simple prayer provides a ticket to paradise, and this is incredibly deceptive. The Scriptures do not support such an interpretation, and one of the primary purposes of this book, and the entire Walk in the Light Series, is to expose this fallacy.

16   These statements are very general and are not meant to minimize any spiritual experience that many experience while entering into the Christian faith. Since there is not enough space in this text to detail the many different doctrinal varieties of the Christian Denominations, I must out of necessity paint with broad brush strokes to make the point as quickly and simply as possible.

17   The early disciples (talmidim) described in The New Testament were likely raised with significant knowledge of the Scriptures. They lived in a region of the Galilee sometimes referred to as the Orthodox Triangle. In this region there were communities of devotedly faithful Israelites who studied and obeyed the Scriptures as a lifestyle. When they followed the Messiah, they did not convert to any new religion, rather they recognized the appearance of Messiah as a fulfillment of the Scriptures and their faith.

18   The Torah (תורה) is the first five books of the Hebrew and Christian Scriptures. It was written by Moses (Mosheh) and is often referred to as "The Law" in many modern English Bibles . Law is a very harsh, cold word which often results in the Torah being confused with the laws, customs and traditions of the religious leaders as well as the laws of particular countries. The Torah is more accurately defined as the "instruction" of YHWH for His set apart people. The Torah contains instruction for those who desire to live righteous, set apart lives in accordance with the will of YHWH. Contrary to popular belief, people can obey the Torah. (Devarim 30:11-14). It is the myriads of regulations, customs and traditions which men attach to the Torah that make it impossible and burdensome for people to obey. The names of the five different "books" are transliterated from their proper

Hebrew names as follows: Genesis – Beresheet, Exodus – Shemot, Leviticus – Vayiqra, Numbers – Bemidbar, Deuteronomy – Devarim.

[19] Kepha, often referred to as Peter, stated in the book of Acts that he always ate Kosher. Eating what the Scriptures describe as food was simply part of obeying the commandments, which was simply the lifestyle that every Israelite was expected to live. There was not necessarily anything too complicated about not eating pigs, vultures, snakes or scorpions. There is often a misconception that obeying the Commandments of the Creator was somehow too difficult, which is an absurd notion. What kind of Creator would place requirements upon people which were impossible to keep. That would be cruel and unjust. Obeying the Commandments resulted in blessing to the Israelites while disobedience led to curses. It is really as simple as that.

[20] You will find that the words "Jewish," "Jews" and "Jew" are in italics because they are ambiguous and sometimes derogatory terms. At times these expressions are used to describe all of the genetic descendants of the man named Yaakov (Jacob), later named Yisrael (Israel). At other times the words are used to describe those who adhere to the religion of Judaism. The terms are commonly applied to ancient Israelites as well as modern day descendants of those tribes, whether they are atheists or Believers in YHWH. The word "Jew" originally referred to a member of the tribe of Judah (Yahudah) or a person that lived in the region of Judea. After the different exiles of the House of Yisrael and the House of Yahudah, it was the Yahudim that returned to the Land while the Northern Tribes, known as the House of Yisrael, were scattered to the ends of the earth (Yirmeyahu 9:16). Since the Yahudim represented the recognizable descendants of Yaakov (Yisrael), they came to represent Yisrael over time. With the Kingdom of Yisrael continuing to be punished in exile, the Yahudim came to represent Yisrael, and thus the term "Jew" came to represent a Yisraelite. While this label became common and customary, it is not accurate and is the cause of tremendous confusion. This subject is described in greater detail in The Walk in the Light Series book entitled "The Redeemed."

[21] Jerry Rabow in his book "50 Jewish Messiahs" Gefen Publishing House 2002 provides an interesting discussion of the varying messianic figures that have surfaced throughout history. He does not include Jesus since the Christian messiah has already been widely discussed and debated, and the goal of the book is to examine the more obscure messianic figures.

[22] The religion that we now see in existence known as Rabbinic Judaism derived from the Pharisaic sect of Yisrael. After the fall of Jerusalem in 70 C.E., a group of Pharisaic Rabbis established a religious headquarters in Yavne and developed a new religion controlled by the teachings of the Rabbis.

[23] Prior to the establishment and development of the Christian religion in the third and fourth centuries C.E., the Tanak contained all of the writings generally recognized as being Scriptures, and commonly referred to as "The Old Testament." As Christianity developed, certain letters and writings began to be accepted and agreed to be authoritative, and were eventually added to the Tanak and referred to as "The New Testament." Due to the labeling, Christianity tends to treat "The New Testament" writings as newer and more relevant than "The Old Testament." Incredibly, some in Christianity actually interpret various letters in

"The New Testament" as changing or modifying The Tanak. This is a mistake and very dangerous. As a result, I prefer not to use the labels "Old" and "New" when referring to these various texts.

24   YHWH (יהוה) is the four letter Name of the Elohim described in the Scriptures. This four letter Name has commonly been called the "Tetragrammaton" and traditionally has been considered to be ineffable or unpronounceable. As a result, despite the fact that it is found nearly 7,000 times in the Hebrew Scriptures, it has been replaced with such titles as "The Lord," "Adonai" and "HaShem." I believe that this practice is in direct violation of the First and Third Commandments. Some commonly accepted pronunciations are: Yahweh, Yahuwah and Yahowah. Since there is debate over which pronunciation is correct, I simply use the Name as it is found in the Scriptures, although I spell it in English from left to right, rather than in Hebrew from right to left. For the person who truly desires to know the nature of the Elohim described in the Scriptures, a good place to start is the Name by which He revealed Himself to all mankind.

25   Some believe that the four letter Name YHWH is ineffable or unspeakable so pronouncing the Name is not an issue. I do not believe that this opinion is compatible with the Scriptures which consistently describe the use of the Name and encourage all to know and use the Name. There is a difference of opinion concerning the pronunciation of the Name. Some pronounce the Name as "Jehovah" which is clearly not correct since there is no "J" in the Hebrew language. A very popular pronunciation is Yahweh. Some say Yahuwah or Yahowah while some simply use the short form of the Name - Yah. Because of this difference in opinion, some simply pronounce the letters "Yud - Hey - Vav - Hey" when referring to the Name. This subject is discussed in detail in the Walk in the Light book entitled "Names."

26   Wikipedia citing Cyrus H. Gordon and Gary A. Rendsburg, *The Bible and the Ancient Near East* fourth edition, 1997, Norton & Co.

27   It is a popular tradition that the fruit of the Tree of Knowledge of Good and Evil was an apple, but this could simply be tradition associated with pagan traditions involving Athena, the goddess of wisdom, with an apple. There is no mention of an apple in the Scriptures, nor is any particular fruit mentioned. According to some tradition, the forbidden fruit was the fig, and this would make sense since the man and the woman sewed fig leaves to cover themselves. It could be that they reached for the closest thing that they could find. (see Rabbi Nehemia Berachos 40a; Sanhedrin 70a. See also *The Rod of An Almond Tree in God's Master Plan*, Peter A. Michas Wine Press WP Publishing 1997).

28   Targum Pseudo-Jonathan: Genesis 3:15.

29   Hawah (חוה) means "giver of life" or "mother of all living." It is interesting to note that Adam did not name his wife until after their transgression.

30   Qayin (קין) means: "acquired" and is an accurate transliteration of the name commonly referred to as Cain.

31   Hebel (הבל) means: "breath" and is an accurate transliteration of the name commonly referred to as Abel. This name also can mean "vanity," and the Book of Yasher actually states that this was the intended meaning of the name as Hawah declared: "In vanity we came into the earth, and in vanity we shall be taken from

it." Book of Yasher 1:13.

[32] Adapted from *A Mechanical Translation of the Book of Genesis* Jeff A. Benner, Virtualbookworm.com Publishing Inc. 2007.

[33] There are some interesting omissions in the account of the birth of Qayin and Hebel which leaves room for speculation. The Targums are famous for attempting to fill in those gaps and Targum Pseudo-Jonathan provides the following account: *"¹ Adam knew his wife Hawah who had conceived from Sammael, the angel of YHWH. ² Then from Adam her husband she bore his twin sister and Abel. Abel was a keeper of sheep, and Qayin was a man tilling the earth."* Beresheet 4:1-2. According to the notes for verse 1: "This verse could also be translated as follows: "Adam knew that his wife [Hawah] . . ." Ed. Pr. Has a different version of this verse: "Adam knew [Hawah] his wife, who desired the angel, and she conceived and bore [Qayin]. And she said, 'I have acquired a man, the angel of [YHWH].'" The belief that [Qayn] was the child of Sammael . . . was derived from the fact that Gen 5:3 says that Seth was in the likeness and image of Adam. Since this is not said of [Qayin] in 4:1, the conclusion was drawn that he was not Adam's son. Ps.-J states explicitly in 5:3 that [Hawah] bore [Qayin], who was not from Adam and who did not resemble him. B. Shabb. 146a (738), Yebam. 103b(711), Abod. Zar. 22b(114) say that the serpent copulated with Eve and/or infused her with lust, but they do not say that he fathered [Qayin]. PRE 21 (150) says that he (ie. Sammael) came to her riding on the serpent, and she conceived. We conclude that the "he" in question was Sammael, since PRE 13 (92) tells us that Sammael mounted the serpent and rode on it. In effect, then, Ps.-J. is the earliest text that explicitly identifies Sammael as the father of Cain (cf. Cashdan, 1967, 33)." The Aramaic Bible Volume 1B, Targum Pseudo-Jonathan Genesis, Translated, with Introduction and Notes by Michael Maher, M.S.C., The Liturgical Press 1992.

[34] It is very interesting to view the sacrifices which were rendered by these two, because it reveals a pattern which is repeated in Scriptures, and shows us behavior which is pleasing and that which is displeasing to YHWH. We read in Beresheet that "in the process of time" they both provided an offering to YHWH. In the Hebrew we read miqetz yamiym (מקץ ימים) which literally means "in the end of days." It seems clear that this was an Appointed Time when both knew that an offering was expected of them. The Scriptures reveal that Qayin brought an offering of the fruit of the ground to YHWH, and Hebel ALSO brought the firstborn of his flock and their fat. In other words, Hebel brought an offering of the fruit of the ground to YHWH but he also brought the firstborn of his flock. The Hebrew word used for flock is tsone (צאן) which implies a goat or a lamb. I believe that this was likely the time of the Passover when all are required to offer a goat or a lamb. (Shemot 12:5). Passover is one of three times in the Torah when males are to appear before YHWH at an appointed time and place, to present an offering. The two other major feasts are Sukkot and Shabuot - during both of these feasts they would have been required to present the firstfruits of their labors which they had sown in the field. (Shemot 23:14). During the Passover and the Feast of Unleavened Bread when the Temple was operating, a lamb or a goat was offered. On the second day of Unleavened Bread – on Day 16 of Month 1, a resheet (first) omer offering of the barley harvest was offered by the priest on behalf of the

nation of Yisrael. This offering signified the lawful time from which the barley harvest could begin. For Mosheh said to count seven weeks from the time you put the sickle to standing grain. (Devarim 16:9). Now many believe that the Appointed Times first began at Sinai when the Torah was given to Yisrael through Mosheh, but this notion is not supported by the Scriptures. I believe that the Torah and the patterns found within the Appointed Times go back to the beginning. (see also Endnote 35 for a discussion of The Appointed Times). YHWH repeatedly tells us that He has declared the end from the beginning. (Yeshayahu 41:26, 46:10, 48). His patterns and His ways go all the way back to the beginning and are demonstrated through cycles – one of those cycles being harvests. Throughout the Scriptures we see the terms "in the beginning" (beresheet) referring to the beginning of a harvest or the firstfruits of a harvest and the term "in the end of days" (miqetz yamiym) referring to the end of that harvest. Many interpret this passage with Qayin and Hebel as if to show that raising animals was better than tilling the ground, but this is not the relevant point. We see that Hebel offered his firstfruits, while there was no mention of this for Qayin. Also note that the offering of Hebel involved blood, while the offering of Qayin did not. Thus the offering of Qayin was not acceptable – it did not include blood and he did not receive atonement. As a result, he was overtaken by sin and he ultimately did shed blood – the blood of his brother. This provides us with the patterns of Messiah's fulfillment of the Passover.

35 The Scriptures provided Appointed Times which are described by YHWH as "My Appointed Times." (Vayiqra 23:2). In other words, they belong to Him. The Appointed Times described in Vayiqra 23, as well as other portions of the Torah, are often erroneously referred to as the Jewish Holidays. This is a grave mistake because YHWH specifically says that these are "My appointed times." They belong to no ethnic or religious group. This topic is discussed in greater detail in the Walk in the Light series book entitled "Appointed Times."

36 Targum Pseudo-Jonathan   Genesis 6:4. The Book of Enoch also considers "the sons of God," or rather "the sons of Elohim" to be fallen angels. While neither of these texts are deemed "canonized" Scriptures, they can, at times, prove helpful in giving us insight into certain texts. From time to time I will cite from these various apocryphal and pseudepigraphal texts, not necessarily to endorse their accuracy or authenticity, but rather to show an alternate view or perspective on a particular text.

37 There is great debate about the issue of whether giants actually existed, and at the heart of this argument lies the veracity of the Scriptures. While in the past there have been certain pictures of giant remains that have been considered to be a hoax, this does not mean that all such photos and finds are untrue. For ages people have discovered giant bones. In fact, in ancient times these bones would be placed in pagan temples, believing that they belonged to the gods.

38 Michael Wise, Martin Abegg Jr., and Edward Cook, The Dead Sea Scrolls - A New Translation, Harper Collins, 2005, p. 94.

39 Shechem means "between the shoulders" and is aptly named as it sits between two mountains - Mt. Gerizim and Mt. Ebal. This is a place rich in history as it was where Abraham built the Altar to YHWH when he entered the Land. It is also one of the few places where we read about a land transaction in the Scriptures. This is

also the resting place for the bones of Joseph. To this day, in the heart of the newly named Nablus there is a tomb where Joseph's bones are kept. The Yisraelites brought them out of Egypt and this is also the place where the blessings and the curses were proclaimed. Shechem is located within the tribal Land of Manasseh

[40] Jerusalem was the place where YHWH chose to place His name only after hundreds of years at Shiloh, Gilgal and other brief stops. It was not until David became King that Jerusalem was chosen, which straddles the territory of the Tribes of Benjamin and Yahudah. Previously, YHWH had placed His Name primarily in Shiloh, the location where Joshua cast lots to determine the final division of the Land. Shiloh itself was located within the land of the tribe of Ephraim.

[41] Ziggurats are the step pyramids that can be seen around the world from Babylon to Egypt, from Mexico, Central and South America, Asia and other parts of the world. The seeds of Babylonian sun worship spread throughout the planet as a direct result of the confusion of languages and the dispersion of the peoples as described in the Scriptures.

[42] Pirke R. El. xxiv. "Sefer ha-Yashar" l.c. comp. Gen. R. lxv. 12. http://www.jewishencyclopedia.com/view.jsp?artid=295&letter=N&search=nimrod.

[43] *Nimrod and Babylon: The Birth of Idolatry*, Steve and Terri White http://koinonia-all.org/bible/nimrod.htm. The Name of YHWH and the title Elohim replaced by author for consistency.

[44] The winter solstice occurred on January 7, 2253 BCE when Nimrod began his reign as a tyrant. By the end of his life in 1972 BCE the winter solstice occurred on January 5 on the proleptic Julian calendar. By 405 BCE the winter solstice occurred on December 25, which became an important date for sun worshippers. (Contributed by Eliyahu David ben Yissachar).

[45] Syncretism is a process whereby pagan concepts, traditions and holidays were morphed and adapted into the Christian religion, thereby making conversion for heathens less traumatic, since they did not have to give up many of their pagan customs. Rather, those pagan customs were simply "Christianized" and adapted to the Christian religion. The influence that sun worship has had on the Christian religion is discussed in the Walk in the Light series book entitled "Restoration."

[46] Nelson's Illustrated Bible Dictionary, Copyright (c)1986, Thomas Nelson Publishers. (Corrected dates prvided by Eliyahu David ben Yissachar of www.torahcalendar.com).

[47] en.wikipedia.org/wiki/Sin_(mythology).

[48] Some might argue that the vowel points are different but there were no vowel points before the Masorites invented them around 1,000 C.E. Therefore, in the unadultered Hebrew manuscripts the words are identical.

[49] There is a common misconception that the Torah was not revealed to mankind until it was given to Israel through Moses on Mount Sinai. This is simply not the case. The Torah was given to Adam in the Garden and it was his disobedience to the instructions of YHWH that led to his expulsion. Noah was considered righteous because he obeyed the Torah and it is the obedience to the instructions of YHWH which sets people apart in the Scriptures. Guarding, protecting, preserving and obeying the Torah is the hallmark of those who follow YHWH.

[50] Ancient Hebrew was a visual language wherein every letter has a visual meaning

and told a story. When those letters were put together, their meanings combined to form concepts. I have made it a part of my studies to look beyond the Modern Hebrew to the Ancient Hebrew pictographs to find out the original concepts behind various words. This adds a whole new dimension to the study of the Scriptures which is both exciting and authentic. I highly recommend that you visit www.ancient-hebrew.org which has a lot of great information. There is so much that we can glean from this passage. The fact that YHWH put Abraham to sleep immediately makes us think of Adam. If YHWH did not want Abraham to see Him, He could have easily told him not to look, or even covered him like He did with Mosheh on Mount Sinai. The fact that YHWH put him to sleep seems to raise a red flag and call special attention to this incident. I believe that it reflects the fact that YHWH was in the process of making for Himself a Bride through the Seed of Abraham, and as He put Adam to sleep to take something out of him to create his bride - so He did the same with Abram. Only instead of taking something out – YHWH added something to Abram which is symbolized in the hay (ה) which was later added to his name. Rabbi Yosef Kalatsky in a Beyond Pshat article provides the following commentary: "Based on a verse in Tehillim [Psalms] which alludes to the fact that Hashem [YHWH] formed the worlds with the letters "yud" and "hay," the Gemara in Tractate Menachos states, 'The physical world was created with the spirituality of the letter "hay," and the world to come was created with the spirituality of the letter "yud." Meaning, the spiritual energy contained within the letter "hay" brought about all physical existence. G-d said to Abraham, Just as the spiritual energy in the letter "hay" was needed to bring about all physical existence, that same energy is needed to bring a change within you to be able to be the father, the Patriarch, of the Jewish people.' The additional "hay" is not merely another letter added to Abraham's name; but rather, it brought about a profound change within him; his dimension of person became the equivalent of all existence. Until the insertion of the letter "hay," Abraham had no relevance (as he was) to being the Patriarch of the Jewish people." www. torah.org. If YHWH (יהוה) did form the physical world with the (יה) which are the first two characters in His Name then one might reasonably ask – what about the last two letters of His Name. We can see the answer in the name of the first woman who is commonly called Eve, but her Hebrew name is Hawah (חוה). Her name means "life giver" and notice that it includes the last two letters of the Name of YHWH (וה). This life is not the same as the rest of creation which was already formed – this Life was the Life of YHWH which was breathed into Adam - it was what "made him in the image of YHWH." Now back to Abraham and Sarah - it is important to emphasize that there was not just one hay (ה) added - there were two. YHWH added one to the male Abraham and one to the female Sarah, and when the two were joined together, it was that Seed and that Womb which would provide the promised line from which Messiah would come forth. Those two hays are the two hays found in the Name of YHWH (יהוה).

51 The Creator's reckoning of time is discussed at length in the Walk in the Light series book entitled "Appointed Times." It is critical that anyone who claims to follow the Almighty understand His times and seasons in order to synchronize their lives with His plan.

52 The birth of Yitshaq at Passover is supported by the Targums, which were Aramaic translations of the Torah which often extrapolated facts which were implied or understood to be part of the Torah, likely through tradition.

53 The Third Day, known as Yom Shliyshiy (יום שלישי) has great significance in the Scriptures and should be the subject of much study for the serious student.

54 The Book of Yasher is not a "canonized" text, but it is referenced in "canonized" Scriptures which would appear to validate its existence and validity. See Joshua 10:13 and II Samuel 1:18. The issue of canonization is discussed in the Walk in the Light series book entitled "Scriptures."

55 The Hebrew Scriptures are the original texts and the Hebrew language was uniquely chosen by the Creator to transmit His message. There is critical information below the surface of the text which often gets lost, particularly when you start translating this ancient eastern language into a modern western language. As a result, I encourage students of the text to learn and study in the original Hebrew whenever possible.

56 Shaul of Tarsus, commonly referred to as the Apostle Paul in Christianity, recognized that the Seed of Abraham was the Messiah. In his Torah teaching to the Galatians he writes: *"Now to Abraham and his Seed were the promises made. He does not say, 'And to seeds,' as of many, but as of one, 'And to your Seed,' who is Messiah."* Galatians 3:16.

57 The Red Heifer sacrifice is intimately connected with the Lamb of Elohim because that is the one that makes people clean. Every person is tarnished from sin, which is the transgression of the Torah perpetuated from the Garden. All must be made clean before they can be reconciled to YHWH. This process of becoming clean, so that you can enter into the House of YHWH is provided through the picture of the Red Heifer, which is slaughtered "outside the camp," not on the Altar which is within the courts of the House of YHWH. The Red Heifer sacrifice provides cleansing so that one can enter the House. Only when you have entered the House do you receive atonement and offer up sacrifices on the Altar before the House. The description of the Red Heifer slaughtering can be found in Numbers (Bemidbar) 19.

58 Tehillim (תהלים) is a proper transliteration for the word Psalms. The Book of Psalms would thus be rendered Sefer Tehillim. King David repeatedly extolled the Torah throughout the Tehillim. In fact, the entire Tehillim 119, the longest of the Tehillim, is about the Torah. I would encourage every reader to read this portion of Scripture, recognizing that the entire text is about the Torah.

59 www.experiencefestival.com.

60 www.innvista.com citing Legge, Frances. *Forerunners and Rivals of Christianity* (1964) and Koster, C.J. *Come Out of Her My People* (1998).

61 www.iaushua.com.

62 From Matthew Henry's Commentary on the Whole Bible: New Modern Edition, Electronic Database. Copyright (c) 1991 by Hendrickson Publishers, Inc.

63 *50 Jewish Messiahs*, Jerry Rabow, Gefen Publishing House 2002.

64 *Rabbi Akiba's Messiah: The Origins of Rabbinic Authority*, Daniel Gruber, Elijah Publishing 1999.

65 The term "heathen" is often used in a derogatory fashion but this should not be the

case. It actually means the same as the word "gentile" or "nations." In other words, it refers to someone who lives contrary to the commands of YHWH – someone outside of the Assembly of Yisrael. Therefore, in the Scriptures, a heathen or a gentile was someone who lived outside of Yisrael, outside of the commandments, and was generally opposed to the ways of YHWH. A heathen could join with Yisrael if they decided to follow the ways of YHWH, at that point they would not longer be called a heathen or a gentile. The terms Yisrael and gentile are mutually exclusive.

66 The Christian religion was established by the sun worshipping Emperor Constantine, and was always a mixture of sun worship along with the teachings of the Nazarene Sect of Yisrael. As Christianity spread throughout pagan culture in the world, it continued to meld certain pagan elements of those cultures through a process called syncretism. As a result, the Christian religion incorporates and celebrates various pagan holidays, even though they are not mentioned or ordained in the Scriptures. This subject is discussed in greater detail in the Walk in the Light books entitled "Restoration" and "Pagan Holidays."

67 To understand this issue, one must recognize that Judaism is not the same religion that we read about in the Scriptures with an operating Temple system and a practicing priesthood. After 70 C.E. everything changed with the destruction of Jerusalem and the Second Temple. Judaism is a religion developed and controlled by Rabbis, not Levitic Priests, and it derives from the Pharisaic sect of Yisrael. It is centered around Synagogues, rather than a Temple, and has developed extensive laws and traditions which constitute what they refer to as an oral Torah. These additional rules and regulations are known as the takanot (תקנות) and ma'asim (מעשים). The word takanot means "enactments" and refers to the laws enacted by the Pharisees. Ma'asim literally means "works or deeds" and refers to the precedents of the Rabbis that provide the source for Pharisaic rulings, along with subsequent rulings based on those precedents. Over the centuries, these enactments and precedents developed into a powerful set of rules and regulations that have operated to define and control the religion now known as Judaism. These enactments and precedents established by the Rabbis, the successors of the Pharisees, were given greater weight than the Torah. Mosheh said in the Torah not to add or take away from the words which he commanded in the Torah. (Devarim 4:2, 12:32). The enactments and precedents of the Rabbis of Rabbinic Judaism do just that. One of the great Rabbis in Judaism was a Moses Maimonides, also known as Rabbi Mosheh ben Maimon. He is often referred to as "Rambam" and lived between 1135 C.E. and 1204 C.E. In his commentary on the Mishneh (tractate Sanhedrin, chapter 10), Maimonides formulated what are known as the 13 principles of faith. His principles were controversial at first, and essentially ignored for centuries. Today they are obligatory beliefs in Orthodox Judaism. So much of what we see in modern Rabbinic Judaism actually is the doctrine of men, specifically Rabbis.

68 Romans 11:33.

69 The man Aaron, whose Hebrew name is better translated as Aharon, was the brother of Mosheh. They both descended from the Tribe of a Levi, although Mosheh had been adopted into the household of Pharaoh. After the Redemption

of Yisrael, YHWH claimed the Tribe of Levi as a sort of substitute for the first born of Yisrael. *"¹³ . . . Redeem every firstborn among your sons. ¹⁴ In days to come, when your son asks you, 'What does this mean?' say to him, 'With a Mighty Hand YHWH brought us out of Egypt, out of the land of slavery. ¹⁵ When Pharaoh stubbornly refused to let us go, YHWH killed every firstborn in Egypt, both man and animal. This is why I sacrifice to YHWH the first male offspring of every womb and redeem each of my firstborn sons.' ¹⁶ And it will be like a sign on your hand and a symbol on your forehead that YHWH brought us out of Egypt with His Mighty Hand."* Shemot 13:13-16. Later on in the text YHWH declares: *"¹² . . . The Levites are mine, ¹³ for all the firstborn are mine. When I struck down all the firstborn in Egypt, I set apart for myself every firstborn in Israel, whether man or animal. They are to be mine. I am YHWH."* Bemidbar 3:12-13. This was the origination of the Levitic priesthood with Aharon and his offspring filling the position of High Priesthood.

⁷⁰   The Hebrew text refers to the brothers of Joseph selling him for "twenty silver" - basryim kaseph (בעשרים כסף). This has typically been translated as 20 pieces of silver. Some translations say "twenty shekels," but the text only says "twenty pieces." So how much Joseph was sold for is a bit of a mystery at first glance. It is likely that this amount was the same amount of silver as the price to redeem the firstborn known as "pidyon haben" (פדיון הבן). The commandment is found in Bemidbar as follows: *"¹⁴ Everything in Yisrael that is devoted to YHWH is yours. ¹⁵ The first offspring of every womb, both man and animal, that is offered to YHWH is yours. But you must redeem every firstborn son and every firstborn male of unclean animals. ¹⁶ When they are a month old, you must redeem them at the redemption price set at five shekels of silver, according to the sanctuary shekel, which weighs twenty gerahs."* Bemidbar 18:14-16. It is believed that this text shows that the "5 shekel" redemption price equals the twenty pieces of silver.

⁷¹   "Hagar is first mentioned in [Beresheet] 16:1: "Sarai, Abram's wife, had borne him no children. She had an Egyptian maidservant whose name was Hagar." The Torah does not explain how Sarah came to have an Egyptian handmaiden, nor does it specify how many years she was with her mistress before she was given to Abraham. The Rabbis connected Abraham and Sarah's stay in Egypt during the years of famine with the Egyptian handmaiden's joining their family. In the narrative in [Beresheet] 12:10–20, when Abraham and Sarah went down to Egypt, Sarah was taken to the house of Pharaoh. In response, [YHWH] afflicted Pharaoh and all of his household with mighty plagues. When, in the midrashic amplification, Pharaoh sees the miracles that were performed for Sarah in his house, he gives her his daughter Hagar as a handmaiden. He said: "It would be better for my daughter to be a handmaiden in this house [i.e., Sarah's] than a noblewoman in another [in the palace in Egypt]." The Rabbis offer an etymological explanation of Hagar's name: Pharaoh said to Sarah, "This is your reward [agrekh]," as he gave her his daughter as a handmaiden (Gen. Rabbah 45:1). In another exegetical tradition, Hagar was born to Pharaoh from one of his concubines. When Pharaoh took Sarah as a wife, in her marriage contract he wrote over to her all his property: gold, silver, slaves and lands, and Hagar also was included in Sarah's marriage contract (Pirkei de-Rabbi Eliezer [ed. Higger], chap. 26). These midrashim present Hagar as someone who was worthy to live in Abraham and Sarah's house because her

father acknowledged the existence of [YHWH]. Hagar, who would bear children to Abraham, was herself a princess, and was a fitting match for the father of the Israelite nation. She likewise was suited to be the mother of Ishmael, from whom twelve chieftains would issue (in accordance with the divine promise in Gen. 17:20). The tradition of Hagar being given to Sarah as a present from Pharaoh, king of Egypt, already appears in a Jewish composition from the first century BCE (*Genesis Apocryphon* [ed. Avigad-Yadin], p. 37), albeit without mentioning that she was the daughter of Pharaoh." jwa.org/encyclopedia/article/hagar-midrash-and-aggadah. It is also tradition that Abraham took her again as his wife after the death of Sarah.

72 *Archaeological Study Bible*, Zondervan note on Beresheet 38:11-14 at page 65.

73 Ruth 4:18-22.

74 For an in depth discussion of the Messianic patterns associated with the Chief Cup Bearer and the Chief Baker as well as the numbers associated with this event see the thematic Torah teachings of Tony Robinson at www.restorationoftorah.org.

75 *Ancient Egypt*, Lorna Oaks and Lucia Gahlin, Barnes & Noble Books 2003.

76 There are allegedly many parallels between the pagan god Horus and the Christian Jesus. Here are some of the claims made concerning the two: both were born of a virgin, both were sons of gods, both were adopted by a father named Joseph, their births were heralded by stars, and announced by angels, and witnessed by shepherds. Their birth dates are associated with the winter solstice – December 25. They both allegedly healed the sick, cast out demons, raised the dead, walked on water, died on crosses, were placed in tombs and were resurrected. There are either more or less similarities depending upon the source that you review. Because of these apparent similarities, and the fact that Horus "existed" centuries before the Christian Jesus, many sceptics claim that Jesus is simply another pagan savior god handed down through time in the tradition of Horus. The issue is not so simple though. To begin, Messianic patterns were etablished from the beginning, so it could be easy to believe that the tradition of Horus simply incorporated patterns handed down from the beginning. Second, the claimed similarities do not always exist, and a thorough search of history may show that there are not as many as some claim. Finally, there is also the factor that the one called Jesus has actually been "paganized" over the past two centuries. In other words, some of the events in the life of Horus have been added to the life of Jesus.

77 *Ancient Egypt The Light of the World*, Volume 1 Gerald Massey Elibron Classics.

78 Article *Until Shiloh Comes* by Chuck Missler taken from the book The Creator Beyond Time and Space" Chuck Missler and Mark Eastman, M.D., The Word for Today 1996, p.144-149.

79 Mosheh (משה) is the proper transliteration for the name of the Patriarch commonly called Moses.

80 *Pharaoh's and Kings – A Biblical Quest*, David Rohl, Crown Publishers, New York p. 252-256. Some believe that he was adopted by Sobekneferu, the daughter of Amenemhet III. Since Amenemhet III had two known daughters but no recorded sons it is also believed that Mosheh was destined to be Pharaoh and may have been Amenemhet IV who is recorded as disappearing. *Digging up the Past*, David Downs and *Unwrapping the Pharaohs*, John Ashton and David Downs, pp. 92 – 93, Master

Books 2006.

81   There is significant tradition, particularly in Christianity, that Mosheh was forty years old when he fled Egypt. This is not accurate according to the Book of Yasher. Some believe this because of Acts 7:30 which simply mentions the "expiration of forty years." It is highly prpbable that this forty years was the forty years that he was King of the Cushites.

82   en.wikipedia.org/wiki/Midian#cite_note-26.

83   Yithro is the proper transliteration for the name of the man commonly referred to as Jethro. He was called the Priest of Midian. The Midianites were known to worship Baal-Peor, Asherah and Hathor the Mitsrite goddess. Interestingly there is evidence that at some point in history they worshipped YHWH and circumcised their males. Could this have been the result of the influence Mosheh had on his father-in-law Yithro? We know that Yithro had a good relationship with Mosheh before and after the Exodus. It is possible that Yithro repented when he heard and saw the power of YHWH as He dwelled with Yisrael.

84   This is likened to the Commandment concerning the mezzuzah. Undoubtedly, the most significant prayer in the Torah is known as The Shema found at Devarim 6:4. The Shema proclaims: "*4 Hear, O Ysrael: YHWH our Elohim, YHWH is one. 5 Love YHWH your Elohim with all your heart and with all your soul and with all your strength. 6 These commandments that I give you today are to be upon your hearts. 7 Impress them on your children. Talk about them when you sit at home and when you walk along the road, when you lie down and when you get up. 8 Tie them as symbols on your hands and bind them on your foreheads. 9 <u>Write them on the doorframes of your houses and on your gates</u>.*" Devarim 6:4-9. The Command to write the commands on our doorposts and our gates means that YHWH is in control of that space. His Commandments are the rule of that property, which represents His Kingdom on the Earth.

85   The Scriptures speak of a future event when YHWH will gather His sheep from the four corners of the planet. (Amos 9:14; Jeremiah 23:3-8; Isaiah 11:0-16; Isaiah 35:3-10; Zekaryah 10:6-12; Ezekiel 39:28). Passover is not just a Feast, it is a "moadi" which means an appointed time which is a "rehearsal." It is not simply a remembrance of something that happened in the past, it is also a rehearsal for a future event. As a result, those who continue to celebrate the Appointed Times of YHWH should do so with joy and anticipation of future fulfillment. This subject is discussed in further detail in the Walk in the Light series books entitled "Appointed Times" and "The Final Shofar."

86   Beresheet 33:17

87   Succot, also known as the Feast of Booths or the Feast of Tabernacles is specifically mentioned as a celebration which will occur every year when the Messiah reigns from Zion. All the Nations, not just Jews, will be required to celebrate or they will be punished. This is perfectly consistent with the notion that the Appointed Times belong to YHWH and that it is the time when His Creation will meet with Him. It is commanded in Shemot 23:16; Shemot 34:22; Vayiqra 23:34; Devarim 16:16 and Devarim 31:10. We know from the Prophet Zechariah (Zekaryah) that all of the nations of the Earth will be required to celebrate this feast when Messiah reigns. "*16 Then the survivors from all the nations that have attacked Jerusalem will go up year after year to worship the King, YHWH Almighty, and to celebrate the Feast of*

Tabernacles. ¹⁷ If any of the peoples of the earth do not go up to Jerusalem to worship the King, YHWH Almighty, they will have no rain. ¹⁸ If the Egyptian people do not go up and take part, they will have no rain. YHWH will bring on them the plague He inflicts on the nations that do not go up to celebrate the Feast of Tabernacles. ¹⁹ This will be the punishment of Egypt and the punishment of all the nations that do not go up to celebrate the Feast of Tabernacles.” Zekaryah 14:16-19.

88 The mikvah is where the Christian doctrine of baptism derives, although it did not begin with Christianity and was commanded by YHWH long before Messiah came. It was a natural thing for Yisraelites to do. In fact, there were numerous mikvaote (plural form of mikvah) at the Temple and it was required that a person be immersed in a mikvah prior to presenting their sacrifice. The Hebrew word for baptize is tevila (טביל), which is a full body immersion that takes place in a mikvah (מקוה). This comes from the passage in Beresheet 1:10 when YHWH “gathered together” the waters. The mikvah is the gathering together of flowing waters. The “tevila” immersion is symbolic for a person going from a state of uncleanliness to cleanliness. The priests in the temple needed to tevila regularly to insure that they were in a state of cleanliness when they served in the Temple. Anyone going to the Temple to worship or offer sacrifices would tevila at the numerous pools outside the Temple. There are a variety of instances found in the Torah when a person was required to tevila. It is very important because it reminds us of the filth of sin, and the need to be washed clean from our sin in order to stand in the presence of a Almighty, set apart Elohim. Therefore it makes perfect sense that we be immersed in a mikvah prior to presenting the sacrifice of the perfect lamb as atonement for our sins. It also cleanses our temple which the Spirit of Elohim will enter in to tabernacle with us. The tevila is symbolic of becoming born again and is an act of going from one life to another. Being born again is not something that became popular in the seventies within the Christian religion. It is a remarkably Yisraelite concept that was understood to occur when one arose from the mikvah. In fact, people witnessing an immersion would often cry out “Born Again!” when a person came up from an immersion. It was also an integral part of the Rabbinic conversion process, which, in many ways is not Scriptural, but in this sense is correct. For a Gentile to complete their conversion, they were required to be immersed, or baptized, which meant that they were born again: born into a new life. Many people believe that immersion is a newly instituted Christian concept because of the exchange between Messiah and Nicodemus. Let us take a look at that conversation in the Gospel according to Yahanan: *“¹ Now there was a man of the Pharisees named Nicodemus, a ruler of the Yahudim. ² He came to Yahushua at night and said, ‘Rabbi, we know you are a teacher who has come from Elohim. For no one could perform the miraculous signs You are doing if Elohim were not with him.’ ³ In reply Yahushua declared, ‘I tell you the truth, no one can see the kingdom of Elohim unless he is born again.’ ⁴ ‘How can a man be born when he is old?’ Nicodemus asked. ‘Surely he cannot enter a second time into his mother’s womb to be born!’ ⁵ Yahushua answered, ‘I tell you the truth, no one can enter the kingdom of Elohim unless he is born of water and the Spirit. ⁶ Flesh gives birth to flesh, but the Spirit gives birth to spirit. ⁷ You should not be surprised at my saying, You must be born again. ⁸ The wind blows wherever it pleases. You hear its sound, but you cannot tell where it comes from or where it is going. So it is with everyone*

born of the Spirit.' ⁹ 'How can this be?' Nicodemus asked. ¹⁰ 'You are Yisrael's teacher,'
said Yahushua, 'and do you not understand these things? ¹¹ I tell you the truth, we speak
of what we know, and we testify to what we have seen, but still you people do not accept
our testimony. ¹² I have spoken to you of earthly things and you do not believe; how then
will you believe if I speak of heavenly things? ¹³ No one has ever gone into heaven except
the One who came from heaven - the Son of Man. ¹⁴ Just as Mosheh lifted up the snake in
the desert, so the Son of Man must be lifted up, ¹⁵ that everyone who believes in him may
have eternal life.'" Yahanan 3:1-15. From this exchange it seems that Nicodemus
is unfamiliar with immersion, but he was not surprised by the fact that a person
needed to be "born again." His first question: "How can a man be born when he is
old?" demonstrated he did not see how it applied to him, because he was already a
Yahudim. His second question "How can this be," only affirmed that fact. And this
is why Yahushua asked: "You are Yisrael's teacher and do you not understand these
things?" In other words, "you're supposed to be the one teaching Yisrael about these
spiritual matters and you're not. You think only the Gentiles need to be immersed
and born again, but you all need it because you are all sinners and this needs to be
taught to everyone, not just the Gentiles." So you see, being born again through
immersion was not new to Yisrael. This is why many readily were immersed by
Yahanan the Immerser - they understood their need. It was often the leaders who
failed to see their need for cleansing because they were blinded by the notion that
their Torah observance justified them. It is important to note that the tevila must
occur in "living waters" - in other words, water which is moving and ideally which
contains life. These living waters refer to the Messiah. In a Scriptural marriage,
a bride would enter the waters of purification prior to her wedding. These are the
same waters that we are to enter when we make a confession of faith and become
part of the Body of Messiah - His Bride.

⁸⁹ The union between a man and a woman is specifically provided by the Creator
as an example of the intimate relationship or "knowledge" that He desires to
have with His creation. The connection between Creator and creation was lost
after Eden, and both man and the rest of creation have suffered ever since. Sinai
was a step in the direction of restoring that connection between the Creator and
His creation. Yisrael was "chosen" as a bride to bring about the restoration of
the nations. What happened at Mt. Sinai was a marriage ceremony between
YHWH and His Bride – Yisrael. After delivering her from bondage He then
gave her the opportunity to become His Bride - if she agreed to obey the Torah.
The Torah was, in essence, a marriage contract or a ketubah. The people declared:
"All that YHWH has spoken we will do." Shemot 19:8. In other words, "I Do" or
rather "We Do." They agreed to the marriage and were commanded to prepare for
the marriage ceremony by cleansing and consecrating themselves. After hearing
the Ten Commandments they could not take it anymore, and asked Mosheh to
relay the Words of YHWH. Mosheh ascended the mountain while the people
waited. The people ultimately got impatient and decided to make up their own
celebration to YHWH and create a golden calf, just as they had seen in Egypt.
They had already been instructed not to make any images, and if they had only
waited and listened a bit further, they would have heard the instruction regarding
an altar, and the prohibition against gold and silver gods which was commanded

immediately after the 10th commandment. Regardless, they committed adultery before they even consummated the marriage. In very crude terms, it was like a bride excusing herself during the wedding feast and having relations with an old boyfriend while the groom is waiting for her to go on their honeymoon. It was understandably infuriating to YHWH. As a result, the Covenant was broken, and Mosheh literally broke the Tablets which contained the Covenant. Mosheh thereafter went up to YHWH to make atonement (Shemot 32:30). The covenant was later renewed and placed upon new tablets, this time cut by Mosheh instead of YHWH, which foreshadows the Messiah and the future Renewed Covenant, although the terms were written by YHWH and remained the same – the Torah. The desire of YHWH is for His Bride to know Him. In fact, you must "know YHWH" to be married to Him and this "knowledge" is much more than a handshake or friendly introduction. The Hebrew word for know is yada (ידע) which has a variety of meanings but in this context means intimate relations. The example which is provided through the Scriptures is the intimate "knowledge" shared between a husband and a wife. While YHWH was always a faithful Husband to His Bride, the nation of Yisrael was not always a faithful bride. She went whoring and the House of Yisrael was actually divorced from YHWH. As a result, before the restorative work of YHWH can be completed, He must renew the covenant with Yisrael, His Bride - not the Church.

90   Yisrael was to be a set apart people, a kingdom of priests so that they could be an example to the rest of the nations. YHWH spoke the following to Mosheh at Sinai: "⁵ Now if you obey Me fully and keep My Covenant, then out of all nations you will be My treasured possession. Although the whole earth is Mine, ⁶ you will be for Me a kingdom of priests and a set apart nation." Shemot 19:4-6.

91   The concept of "The Trinity" is one which derives from pagan father, mother, son worship. Examples of trinitarian worship can be traced back to Babylon. For more detail on this important subject see the Walk in the Light series book entitled "Restoration."

92   Pyramid text Utterance 485a.

93   Many people cite the Third commandment as the reason for not using the Name. Sadly, the Third Commandment was intended to regulate the proper use of the Name, not abolish the use of the Name. The Third Commandment states: "You shall not take the name of YHWH your Elohim in vain, for YHWH will not hold him guiltless who takes His name in vain." Shemot 20:7. The Hebrew word for "vain" is shav (שוא) which is used in the sense of emptiness, lying, nothingness, uselessness or misuse. Therefore, the Third Commandment is telling us to use the Name, but not to abuse the Name or bring it to naught. The Scriptures clearly reveal that the Name was properly used after the Ten Commandments were given to the Children of Yisrael, so there is absolutely no evidence to support the notion that the Name was not to be used. How incongruous to think that YHWH would go through all the trouble to reveal His Name to Yisrael only to turn around and command them not to use His Name. Another amazing truth in the Third commandment is the existence of the Aleph Taw (את) three times in this one verse. The Messiah is present in this commandment which makes perfect sense because He said: "I have come in My Father's Name . . ." John (Yahanan) 5:43 NIV.

There are other passages in the Torah regarding the use of the Name. For instance: *"you shall not swear by My Name falsely, nor shall you profane the Name of your Elohim: I am YHWH."* Vayiqra 19:12. Notice that it does not forbid people from swearing by the Name, only swearing by the Name falsely.[41] This verse contains an Aleph Taw (את) embedded within the Hebrew text as well as in the following text: *"³¹ Keep My commands and follow them. I am YHWH. ³² Do not profane My Set Apart Name. I must be acknowledged as set apart by the Yisraelites. I am YHWH, who makes you set apart ³³ and who brought you out of Mitsrayim (Egypt) to be your Elohim. I am YHWH."* Vayiqra 22:31-23:1. The Hebrew word for profane is chalal (חלל) which means to wound, to dissolve; figuratively, to profane.

⁹⁴ Two excellent documentary films have been produced which trace the Scriptural Exodus route from Egypt to Sinai. According to this new research and based upon newly discovered evidence, it appears that the real location for Mount Sinai may actually be in Saudi Arabia. See *The Exodus Revealed, Search for the Red Sea Crossing* Produced by Discovery Media Productions also *The Search for the Real Mt. Sinai* Produced by Reel Productions.

⁹⁵ The Law of Jealousy is set forth in Bemidbar Chapter 5 as follows: *"¹¹ Then YHWH said to Mosheh, ¹² Speak to the Israelites and say to them: If a man's wife goes astray and is unfaithful to him ¹³ by sleeping with another man, and this is hidden from her husband and her impurity is undetected (since there is no witness against her and she has not been caught in the act), ¹⁴ and if feelings of jealousy come over her husband and he suspects his wife and she is impure - or if he is jealous and suspects her even though she is not impure - ¹⁵ then he is to take his wife to the priest. He must also take an offering of a tenth of an ephah of barley flour on her behalf. He must not pour oil on it or put incense on it, because it is a grain offering for jealousy, a reminder offering to draw attention to guilt. ¹⁶ The priest shall bring her and have her stand before YHWH. ¹⁷ Then he shall take some holy water in a clay jar and put some dust from the tabernacle floor into the water. ¹⁸ After the priest has had the woman stand before YHWH, he shall loosen her hair and place in her hands the reminder offering, the grain offering for jealousy, while he himself holds the bitter water that brings a curse. ¹⁹ Then the priest shall put the woman under oath and say to her, If no other man has slept with you and you have not gone astray and become impure while married to your husband, may this bitter water that brings a curse not harm you. ²⁰ But if you have gone astray while married to your husband and you have defiled yourself by sleeping with a man other than your husband - ²¹ here the priest is to put the woman under this curse of the oath - may YHWH cause your people to curse and denounce you when he causes your "thigh" to waste away and your abdomen to swell. ²² May this water that brings a curse enter your body so that your abdomen swells and your "thigh" wastes away. Then the woman is to say, 'So be it. So be it.' ²³ The priest is to write these curses on a scroll and then wash them off into the bitter water. ²⁴ He shall have the woman drink the bitter water that brings a curse, and this water will enter her and cause bitter suffering. ²⁵ The priest is to take from her hands the grain offering for jealousy, wave it before YHWH and bring it to the altar. ²⁶ The priest is then to take a handful of the grain offering as a memorial offering and burn it on the altar; after that, he is to have the woman drink the water. ²⁷ If she has defiled herself and been unfaithful to her husband, then when she is made to drink the water that brings a curse, it will go into her and cause bitter suffering; her abdomen will swell and her "thigh" waste away, and she will become accursed among her people. ²⁸ If, however, the woman*

has not defiled herself and is free from impurity, she will be cleared of guilt and will be able to have children. ²⁹ This, then, is the Torah of jealousy when a woman goes astray and defiles herself while married to her husband, ³⁰ or when feelings of jealousy come over a man because he suspects his wife. The priest is to have her stand before YHWH and is to apply this entire Torah to her. ³¹ The husband will be innocent of any wrongdoing, but the woman will bear the consequences of her sin." Bemidbar 5:11-31. The text is not as explicit as the Hebrew. In essence, the woman was drinking a curse that would require her generative parts to waste away. There are around 27 instances of the Aleph Taw (את) in this passage.

96   The numbers 40 and 120 are significant as previously discussed when speaking of Noah. YHWH declared "My Spirit shall not strive with man forever, for he is indeed flesh, yet his days shall be one hundred and twenty years." The deeper meaning of this text revealed that man was given 120 Jubilee cycles. The fact that Mosheh lived to be 120 years - the entire duration given to man - is quite significant. When looking at the account of Noah we also see the number 40 repeated. We see in Beresheet 7:12 that the rain fell 40 days and 40 nights then in Beresheet 7:17 we read that *"for 40 days the flood kept coming"* and in Beresheet 8:6 *"after 40 days Noah opened the window."*

97   Traditionally, the life of Mosheh is divided into three divisions of forty (40) years – forty (40) years in Egypt, forty (40) years in Midain and then forty (40) years in the Wilderness. The Book of Yasher also has a very interesting story concerning the life of Mosheh from his departure from Egypt to his return. (See Book of Yasher 68 – 79). We also see patterns of Mosheh ascending and descending. Mosheh ascended Mount Sinai on three separate occassions for forty (40) days and forty (40) nights. Tradition holds that he descended the third time on Yom Kippur. This is the spiritual picture of the 120 Jubilee Years of Beresheet 6:3.

98   Yasher 77:42-51

99   *The Rod of an Almond Tree in God's Master Plan*, Peter A. Michas, WinePress Publishing 2001.

100   The Tabernacle is a pattern of the Garden. It is the House of YHWH and ultimately it represents our bodies, where YHWH desires to reside and become One with us. An examination of the Tabernacle is quite profound as it is covered with skin, it has a skeleton and it moves around – a vivid picture of how we are to live our lives set apart and filled with the Spirit of YHWH. The Almond Tree within the Tabernacle represents the Tree of Life, which is The Torah, but recognize that the seven branched Lampstand called the Menorah represents the seven Spirits of YHWH (Isaiah 11:2-3). It is also an Almond Tree. (Shemot 25:31-40; Shemot 37:17-24). The Ark of the Covenant is the Throne of YHWH established in our lives. This process of YHWH establishing His rulership in our lives is what the Christian Four Step prayer is looking toward, but it must be understood that His Instructions – the Torah is a vital part of that process.

101   Contrary to some popular Christian doctrines, there are no "Old" Covenants. I would challenge anyone to argue that the Covenant with Noah is "Old" and irrelevant. I regularly see the sign of the Noahic Covenant and I am assured that YHWH will continue to keep His promise not to flood the planet. Likewise, the other Covenants described in the Scriptures are still valid and have not been

replaced. The subject of the Scriptural Covenants is detailed in the Walk in the Light series book entitled "Covenants."

102 The story of Ruth is truly a story for our day - you should stop and read it now. It is not a difficult story to read and understand so I will simply point out some things to think about when you read it. Notice that the family of Naomi were from Bethlehem in the Land of Yahudah. They were from the Tribe of Yahudah, although they were in the land of Moab because Israel was under a famine. Yisrael had no king – they were in the period of the judges yet the name of Naomi's husband Elimelech means: "my Elohim is King" which gives us a hint that this story is about YHWH as King. The only reason Yisrael would be in famine is if they were being cursed, which means that they were not obeying the terms of the covenant made at Sinai and renewed at Moab. So where does Naomi and her family go - back to the Torah - they went to Moab. There Naomi's two sons marry Moabite women - who would then become part of their family. We read that not only did Naomi's husband die while they were in Moab, but so did her sons. Typically when one son would die he would take on the responsibilities of his brother's family, but in this case all of the men had died and the women, and their hope of producing seed had effectively been "cut off." The women were free to leave their connection with Yisrael and remain in Moab, but Ruth "clung" to Naomi and took Naomi's Elohim as her own. They then return to Yisrael together and the story of Ruth coming to the Land of Yisrael starts "in the beginning" (beresheet) of the barley harvest. This is highly significant because we know that the first month coincides with Abib barley and the harvest. The barley is harvested first followed by the wheat harvest as the people gather their firstfruits (bikkurim) and prepare for the Festival of Shabout (weeks). The story of Ruth takes place between these two harvests. In fact, the book of Ruth is traditionally read during the Feast of Shabuot. The Torah provides something specific concerning these times. *"When you reap the harvest of your land, you shall not wholly reap the corners of your field when you reap, nor shall you gather any gleaning from your harvest. You shall leave them for the poor and for the stranger: I am YHWH your Elohim."* Vayiqra 23:22. YHWH is specifically showing that He will make provision for the Gentiles through His Appointed Times, and this sets the stage for the process of being redeemed and grafted in like Ruth, who was previously joined to Yisrael and cut off. Ruth was gleaning the fields of Boaz and she went about the business of redemption with Boaz at the threshing floor. (Ruth 3).

103 The Scriptures provide three instances which describe the event known as the Waters of Meribah. In Bemidbar 20:8-12 we read of the incident where Mosheh and Aharon were to take "The Staff" stand before Yisrael and speak to "The Rock" which would then pour forth water. Instead of speaking to the Rock, Mosheh struck the Rock twice. Mosheh and Aharon disobeyed a specific command of YHWH. There are three instances of the Aleph Taw (את) when Mosheh was commanded to speak to the Rock. The incident is discussed two other times when we read that both Mosheh and Aharon were unable to enter into the Land because they disobeyed the Command. (Bemidbar 27:14; Devarim 32:51). Interestingly, water still poured forth from the Rock, despite the fact that Mosheh and Aharon did not do what they were told. YHWH was still glorified in the sight of Yisrael.

This is important to understand for people who claim to represent YHWH and perform miracles in His Name. Just because someone performs a miracle, does not mean he or she is in obedience to YHWH. Mosheh lost his opportunity to lead Yisrael into the Promised Land for his disobedience.

104   There is much debate concerning the exact transliteration and pronunciation of this name – especially since it is the same name as the Messiah. Some spell the name as Yeshua or Y'shua, but I believe that these are shortened versions of the Name, and fail to adequately represent the Name of YHWH which is clearly part of the Name. I believe a more accurate rendering would be Yahushua, Yahusha, Yahoshua or Yahosha. This subject is discussed in greater detail in the Walk in the Light book entitled "Names."

105   Since there is no "J" in the Hebrew language the name Joseph is more accurately rendered as Yoseph.

106   The reason that I point this out is because it is very significant and prophetic. The fact that these two sons were born in a pagan context and later adopted by Yisrael speaks to their future redemption.

107   Geikie's Hours, etc., ii., 390.

108   Shabuot is a misunderstood Feast of YHWH which involves counting from the first (resheet) barley omer offering during the feast of Unleavened Bread. The command is to count seven Sabbaths and seven sevens, and the day following the seventh seven is the day of Shabuot. (Vayiqra 23:15-16). This provides for a total of 50 days, and is based upon a count of seven sevens and seven intervening Sabbaths. This is clearly a parallel to the count involved in the Jubilee Year. (Vayiqra 25:8). This matter is discussed further in the Walk in the Light series entitled "Appointed Times."

109   W.F. Albright, *Archaeology and the Religion of Israel*, p. 92, also p. 83.

110   *The Fall of the Moon City* by Dr. David Livingston.

111   One cannot ignore the repeating pattern of sevens found in The Book of Revelation. These patterns are specifically linked to the patterns established through the Appointed Times of YHWH in the Torah. If you fail to understand the significance of the Appointed Times you will never understand the Book of Revelation. This is discussed in more detail in the Walk in the Light series book entitled "The Final Shofar."

112   The Dawning of the Day is an important time in the daily calendar. It is the time when darkness and light become divided, and I encourage the reader to examine this time closely and consider the Messianic implications that can be traced back to the First Day of Creation.

113   International Standard Bible Encyclopaedia, Electronic Database Copyright (c)1996 by Biblesoft.

114   Interestingly, the text says that the mob wanted to ravish the Levite, and he tells the story that they wanted to kill him. Also the text does not say that the concubine was dead, only that he cut her into pieces. There are details and discrepancies that should raise the eye brows of the reader. Did the Levite act appropriately in this instance? It appears that he may have done some things which were not appropriate and yet told a tale to deflect his culpability.

115   The Appointed Times described in Vayiqra 23 are held wherever YHWH chooses

to place His Name. His Name is upon the Assembly of Yisrael and particularly His Tabernacle. Historically, once the Yisraelites entered the Land they would Assemble wherever the Tabernacle was set up. Gilgal and Shiloh were two places chosen and eventually it was the City of Jerusalem. (1 Kings 8:29).

¹¹⁶ Moadim are annual Appointed Times chosen by YHWH when all males were to assemble at the specific time and place chosen by YHWH. They are outlined throughout the Torah – especially in Vayiqra 23.

¹¹⁷ The Melchizedek priesthood is one of the most mysterious aspects of the Torah. Very little information is provided except when Abraham actually paid tithes to Melchizedek – The Righteous King of Jerusalem. Abraham, a man who met and Covenanted with YHWH paid an honor to this King/Priest that should give us pause for reflection. This Priest was not a Levite because there were no Levites at that time. The Levitic Priesthood would later come from Abraham's descendants. As a result it is vital that we understand that YHWH has another priesthood that operated before Abraham and one that is in operation even now, which is separate and apart from the line of Aharon and the Levitic Priesthood established in the Torah. The Levitic Priesthood requires an earthly sacrificial system but the Melchizedek line transcends both time and space. This has great Messianic significance and it should help us understand the dual nature of the Messiah as both King and High Priest.

¹¹⁸ There are significant parallels between the Tabernacle in the Wilderness and the House which David planned to build for YHWH. The House of YHWH took a journey with Yisrael and was portable while Yisrael was moving and even during the period of the shoftim. It was only when David became King and established his throne in Jerusalem that we see the transition of the House of YHWH from a movable tent to a permanent building. This is significant and is a Messianic reference to a future time when Messiah will rebuild the House as foretold to David: "⁷ YHWH declares to you that YHWH Himself will establish a house for you: ¹² When your days are over and you rest with your fathers, I will raise up your offspring to succeed you, who will come from your own body, and I will establish His kingdom. ¹³ He is the one who will build a house for My Name, and I will establish the throne of His kingdom forever." 2 Shemuel 7:11-14. This House built by Messiah will be the New Jerusalem, only He will be the Chief Cornerstone (Capstone) (Yeshayahu 28:16; Zekaryah 10:4; Ephesians 2:20; 1 Peter 2:6) and He will build this House with Living Stones (1 Peter 2:5).

¹¹⁹ Shlomo (שלמה) is the proper English transliteration for the Hebrew name which is traditionally pronounced as Solomon.

¹²⁰ This is all that YHWH asks of His people and they continually refuse to do what He says. There are rich blessings for those who obey – like David. There are also curses for those who disobey – like Shlomo.

¹²¹ Interestingly, the actions taken by Jeroboam are exactly what Christianity has done to the true worship of YHWH. Jereboam established places of worship other than Jerusalem, he got rid of the Levite priests and set up his own priesthood, he worshipped false gods and he established new holidays. The Roman Catholic Church, from which most of modern Christianity derives, has established Rome as their headquarters, rather than Jerusalem. They have established a priesthood

separate from the Levitical priesthood. They celebrate Christmas, Easter and numerous holidays with pagan origins, all the while ignoring the Appointed Times of YHWH. They have replaced the Sabbath with Sunday and set up images which are adored and worshipped – all contrary to the Torah. As of June 29, 2008, the Congregation for Divine Worship and the Sacraments by explicit directive of Pope Benedict XVI has prohibited the use of YHWH in Catholic worship. Instead, it has been directed that the Name should be replaced by the Latin "Dominus," Greek "Kyrios," Hebrew "Adonai" or a word of "equivalent meaning" in the local language. See www.catholicnewsagency.com. I could go on, but trust that the point is abundantly clear, the Christian faith, including the Catholic Church and its' progeny in the Protestant factions have fallen into the same error as Jeroboam and the House of Yisrael.

[122] This is where it gets confusing for some due to the fact that the Northern Tribes carried the name Yisrael, rather than say – Joseph. While the united Kingdom is called Yisrael, the northern tribes are also referred to as Yisrael, the House of Yisrael, Joseph and Ephraim.

[123] www.uhcg.org

[124] These dates differ from traditional dates accepted by modern academia. They have been corrected based upon new atronomical and historical data and are graciously provided through the research of Eliyahu David ben Yissachar.

[125] Yehezqel (יחזקאל) is the proper Hebrew transliteration for the Prophet commonly called Ezekiel.

[126] Yirmeyahu (ירמיהו) is the proper transliteration for the Hebrew name of the prophet commonly called Jeremiah.

[127] Fausset's Bible Dictionary, Electronic Database Copyright © 1998, 2003, 2006 by Biblesoft, Inc. All rights reserved.

[128] jewsforjesus.org/answers/prophecy/psalm2bJ which provides support from various sources as follows: Sarachek, The Doctrine of the Messiah in Medieval Jewish Literature (New York: Hermon Press, 1968), p. 121. The interpretation of David Kimchi (13th c.), observing the validity of "son" as well as "pure". J. J. Stewart Perowne, The Book of Psalms: A New Translation with Introductions and Notes Explanatory and Critical (Grand Rapids: Zondervan, 1975), pp. 119-20. The Isaac Leeser translation of the Hebrew Bible (19th c.): "Do homage to the son" Isaac Leeser, Twenty-Four Books of the Holy Scriptures Carefully Translated After the Best Jewish Authorities (New York: Hebrew Publishing Company). Leeser's translation was the standard American Jewish translation from 1845 until the Jewish Publication Society translation of 1917. The Expositor's Bible Commentary, ed. Frank E. Gaebelein, vol. 5 (Grand Rapids: Zondervan, 1991), p. 72. Alternate literal rendering from Brad Scott, Wild Branch Ministries, Words Mean Things, Volume I, Disc 4.

[129] It is vital to understand that there are no separate numerals in the Hebrew language as there are in English. In the Hebrew Language, letters are also assigned a numerical value and the study of the numerical values and significance of letters and words in Hebrew is known as Gematria. Gematria can be fascinating as we can actually discern patterns and significance on an entirely different level that the actual meaning of the words at face value. and the fact that letters all have numeric

value in Hebrew

[130] Many times YHWH relented and showed mercy on Yahudah because of His relationship and Covenant with David. (see Yeshayahu 37:35).

[131] *The Messiah Son of Joseph* by Israel Knohl, Biblical Archaeology Review, September/ October 2008 Vol 34 No 5.

[132] Ibid, Israel Knohl.

[133] There are distinct differences between the Scriptures used in Judaism – The Hebrew Scriptures and the Bible used in Christianity. The first and most obvious difference is the division in The Bible between the Old Testamant and the New Testament. The Bible refers to all of the Hebrew Scriptures as "Old" and all of the Greek derived texts as "New." Beyond that Hebrew Scriptures are rearranged in The Bible. Some of the Hebrew texts are rearranged and ordered differently. In the case of Daniel, the Hebrew Scriptures place it with The Writings while The Bible places it with The Prophets. Daniel is clearly a unique text in many ways, including the fact that it is presented in Aramaic. It is particularly interesting that Judaism places this book with some of the most specific and compelling prophecies concerning The Messiah in The Writings. These issues are discussed further in the Walk in the Light series book entitled "The Scriptures."

[134] Pritchard, James, *Ancient Near Eastern Texts Relating to the Old Testament*, Princeton University Press, 1969, p. 309-310.

[135] Eliyahu David ben Yissachar of www.torahcalendar.com. Is it possible that Nebuchadnezzar understood the seventy (70) year prophecy given by Yirmeyahu and miscalculated his dates? Could he have actually been off by one day? Why else would he be throwing a party and using the utensils of YHWH – almost in defiance. The party may have been to celebrate the passage of the seventy (70) year prophecy and the fact that he was not punished according to that prophecy, although it appears that he started the party too early. Also maybe he did not understand that Yirmeyahu's seventy (70) year prophecies were actually two different prophecies for two different seventy (70) year periods. Thanks to Eliyahu David ben Yissachar for input on this issue.

[136] In a very vivid method of illustrating a prophetic word, Yehezqel was told to lie on his left side to illustrate the punishment upon the House of Yisrael and then to lie on his right side to illustrate the punishment upon the House of Yahudah. *"4 Then lie on your left side and put the sin of the House of Yisrael upon yourself. You are to bear their sin for the number of days you lie on your side. 5 I have assigned you the same number of days as the years of their sin. So for 390 days you will bear the sin of the House of Yisrael. 6 After you have finished this, lie down again, this time on your right side, and bear the sin of the House of Yahudah. I have assigned you 40 days, a day for each year."* Yehezqel 4:4-6. So there would be 390 years for the House of Yisrael and 40 years for the House of Yahudah. There is a mystery in the Torah about multiplying the term of punishment which needs to be applied. Yisrael was told that they would be punished if they disobeyed and they were specifically provided with their punishments. They were then warned of the time of their punishment being multiplied if they continued to disobey. *"27 If in spite of this you still do not listen to me but continue to be hostile toward me, 28 then in my anger I will be hostile toward you, and I myself will punish you for your sins seven times over."* Vayiqra 26:27-29. As a result,

the punishment for the House of Yisrael would turn out to be 390 years times 7 or 2,730 years beginning around 721 BCE.

137 The Elephantine Letters are a collection of more that twenty ancient documents written primarily in Aramaic between priests and family members who were exiles of Yahudah. They were found on an Island in the Nile in Egypt where a community of Yahudim resided. The documents provide corresponding dates between the lunar calendar and the Egyptian calendar that can be helpful in synchronizing various events which occurred during the period of time that they were written.

138 Jubilee years and Shemitah years can be viewed are using the data contained in www.torahcalendar.com.

139 The final week of the word given by Gabriel to Daniel will be discussed further in the Walk in the Light Series book entitled "The Final Shofar."

140 The Book of Maccabees is not a "canonized" text and is considered to be apocryphal and pseudepigraphal depending upon the different religions that recognize that text. The subject of "canonization" is a man-made concept and relies upon a number of factors that determine whether a particular text is "accepted" and deemed reliable. Sometimes these factors are political, sometimes they are doctrinal. Whether men and their methods of "canonizing" texts is reliable is a subject discussed in the Walk in the Light series book entitled "The Scriptures."

141 Beresheet 41 describes the interpretation of Pharaoh's dream by Joseph involving the seven cows and the seven years. Daniel was also given prophetic words concerning sevens. The Torah has some very specific times associated with sevens and these all culminate in the end of days as described in the Book of Revelation which is based upon the number seven. Interestingly, the seventh letter in the Hebrew Aleph Bet is zayin (ז) which represents a weapon or a "sword."

142 www.bdancer.com/history/BDhist2a.html

143 The Origins of Christianity and the Bible – The cultural background of early Christianity, www.religious-studies.info.

144 Backgrounds of Early Christianity, Everett Ferguson, Second Edition, William B. Eerdmans Publishing Company, 1993, p. 11.

145 Ibid, The Origins of Christianity and the Bible.

146 Ibid.

147 Ibid. (Items in brackets added by this author for clarity and consistency in the text).

148 Some information adapted and obtained from www.unrv.com

149 From the article entitled "Until Shiloh Comes" by Chuck Missler from his Book "The Creator Beyond Time and Space." (Replacement of Yahudim instead of Jews and Judah by the author for consistency sake.)

150 Aramaic texts of the Messianinc Scriptures have been available for centuries and they have been the official texts of the Eastern Orthodox church. Sadly, these texts have been neglected or ignored by the predominant Western Orthodox or Roman Catholic Church which has preferred the Latin translations. Since the Aramaic texts were written in a language that closely resembled or matched the Hebrew and Aramaic languages of the original texts it would seem natural and logical that the Aramaic would be the preferred source text, in the event that Hebrew

was unavailable. Not so, but this is just one example of the power struggles and conflicts between warring factions and denominations in the Christian religion. If history tells us anything it is that man's struggle for power is often the predominate concern and often the truth gets forgotten or lost in the struggle.

[151] This is discussed in greater detail in the Walk in the Light series book entitled "Scriptures."

[152] While it is undisputed that the Torah is an original Hebrew text, the majority view is that the Messianic writings were originally written in Greek. If you step back and examine this issue it is not such a certainty. To begin, it is clear that YHWH chose the Hebrew language to express Himself. The Greek language was primarily used by pagans and is very different from the Hebrew language. Further, there are no original Greek autographs to support the notion that the original texts were written in Greek. Rather, there are only copies of copies to a degree which is presently unknown. Since all of the original talmidim of Yahushua were Yisraelites who spoke Hebrew or Aramaic, it is very likely that all or most of the earliest texts written by these individuals were in Hebrew. There may well have been Greek texts written by other authors but that does not support the theory that the entire "New Testament" was of greek origin.

[153] A General Introduction to the Bible, Norman l. Geisler and William E. Nix, Moody Press, Chicago, 1982. Pp. 252.

[154] Ibid at 361 and 375.

[155] Relative to the original language of Matthew, there are a variety of historical sources that confirm the fact that Matthew wrote his Book in Hebrew. Eusebius provides quotes from Papias and Irenaeus to that effect. (see Papias; Hist. Eccl 3.39, Irenaeus; Adv. Haer 3.1.1). Also Epiphanius confirms that fact. (Epiphanius; Pan. 29).

[156] Relative to Shaul and his writings, being a Torah scholar, Shaul would have certainly been fluent in the Hebrew language and written in the Hebrew language. In his day, Hebrew was the language spoken by the Yahudim. (see Josephus Antiquities 20:11:2). There was clearly a distinction between Hellenistic Jews and Hebrews, such as the Sect of Pharisees. Hellenists adopted much of the Grecian culture and the language. Shaul made a specific point of claiming that he was "a Hebrew of Hebrews" (Philipians 3:5). He was born in Tarsus where Aramaic was spoken and he was likely raised in Jerusalem where he was brought up as a Pharisee, sitting at the feet of Rabbi Gamleal. As a result, there were likely many, if not most of his letters dictated or written in the Hebrew language. Shaul used a Scribe for many of his letters and it is possible that they were either remitted or translated in the Greek, but he surely operated in the Hebrew language as well. There is a strong desire in Western Christianity to refer to the "Original Greek" which is really a misnomer because there are no Original Greek manuscripts that are used as a basis for the New Testament Textus Receptus. Rather, what are used are fragments of copies, of copies of copies . . . which have been pieced together by men in an effort to reconstruct the meaning found in the original texts – whatever language they were written in. This is not to be viewed as an argument against the reliability of those texts, only to the undeserved preference toward the Greek language. This bias toward the Greek is an ongoing theme in

Christianity to separate from anything Hebrew which is likened to Judaism. This is a subject discussed in greater detail in the Walk in the Light series books entitled "Restoration" and "Scriptures."

[157]   All of the authors of the different books of the Bible were either Yisraelites or converts. As a result, there is no reason not to believe that all of those texts were written in the Hebrew or Aramaic language.

[158]   While the Hebrew offers assistance and correction, it is by no means perfect. For instance the Shem Tov Hebrew version uses a derogatory term for the Name of Yahushua which demonstrates a clear bias in the text against the Messiah. At the same time, the text was translated so that Jews could effectively debate Christians so there should have been a desire to have an accurate rendering of the text. Therefore, we use these texts cautiously.

[159]   For more information concerning the pagan origins see the Walk in the Light series books entitled "Restoration" and "Pagan Holidays."

[160]   Barnes' notes: (Note on Matthew 1:21).

[161]   The Acts of the Apostles, by Jackson and Lake.

[162]   Smith's Bible Dictionary.

[163]   A dictionary of the Bible, by James Hastings.

[164]   Alford's Greek New Testament, An Exegetical and Critical Commentary.

[165]   Encyclopedia Americana (Vol.16, p. 41).

[166]   Encyclopedia Britannica (15th ed. Vol. 10 p.149).

[167]   The Scriptures, Institute for Scripture Research, (1998) p. 1216.

[168]   http://jacksonsnyder.com

[169]   Mattityahu (מתתיהו) is the proper transliteration of the Hebrew name which is often spelled Matthew in English. The name contains the Name of YHWH and means "gift of Yah."

[170]   Fausset's Bible Dictionary, Electronic Database Copyright (c) 1998 by Biblesoft.

[171]   I am more concerned with pronunciation rather than spelling although I am not fond of spellings which hide or negate the Name "Yah."

[172]   From Chronological Study of the Life of Christ by Dennis McCallum, www.xenos. org/classes/chronc.htm.

[173]   Handbook of Biblical Chronology, Jack Finegan, Hendrickson Publishers, 1998 p. 583 and Table 169.

[174]   Paul L. Maier, In the Fullness of Time (New York: HarperCollins Publishers, 1991.

[175]   Ernest L. Martin, The Star That Astonished the World ASK Publications 1998.

[176]   Finegan at p. 243.

[177]   Eliyahu David ben Yissachar of www.torahcalendar.com.

[178]   Ibid.

[179]   Ibid.

[180]   Ibid.

[181]   Ibid, Martin quoting Thiel, The Mysterious Numbers of the Hebrew Kings.

[182]   The "Lost" Ten Tribes of Israel . . . Found! Steven M. Collins, CPA Book Publisher 1995 4th Printing p.268.

[183]   Antiquities of the Jews, 11.5.2, from The Works of Josephus, translated by Whiston, W., Hendrickson Publishers 1987 13th Printing. p 294.

[184]   Eliyahu David ben Yissachar of www.torahcalendar.com.

185   Ibid, Martin at p. 66.

186   Above information gleaned from various sources including Ernest L. Martin, *The Star That Astonished the World*.

187   Ibid Martin, home.comcast.net/~murellg/Herod.htm.

188   The age of Yahushua at the time of his immersion in the Jordan River, which marks the beginning of his ministry, is largely determined by the text in Luke 3:1-23 which gives us a strting point of "The fifteenth year of the reign of Tiberius Caesar." The fifteenth year of Tiberius has been discussed by scholars, and various dates have been proposed. Luke obviously included this information to provide and exact reference to his readers, however the issue has seemed less clear to modern readers. Tiberius was adopted by Augustus who designated him as a successor in 4 CE. Tiberius won some military victories in Germany and Pannonia. After these victories it was decided he should reign jointly with Augustus over the provinces, probably in 12 CE although arguments have been made for 11 CE and 13 CE. Augustus died on August 19, 14 CE, but the senate met and voted Tiberius Emperor on September 17, 14 CE. Tiberius reigned until he died on March 16, 37 CE. (Jack Finegan, Handbook of Biblical Chronology, Hendrickson Publushers, 1998, p. 570). In addition to these facts, the reign of Tiberius could be reckoned in factual years or regnal years in an accession or non-accession manner. There were also various calendars in use in the Roman Empire at the time, including the Julian Calendar, the Syro-Macedonian calendar, the Egyptian calendar and the calendar used by the Yahudim. So how did Luke and other historians of the day reckon the reign of Roman rulers? It is apparent that the Roman historians Tacitus and Suetonius recognized that Tiberius began to reign the day that Augustus died, but state his regnal years as having begun on January 1 of the following year. (Finegan at p. 580 and 583). It would be logical to assume that Luke would have done the same thing. Reckoning the reign of Tiberius from January 1 of the year following the death of Augustus, the first yer of Tiberius began on January 1, 15 CE. The fifteenth year of Tiberius therefore was from January 1 to December 31 in 29 CE. Luke says in Luke 3:23 that at this time, Yahushua was about 30years old, meaning he had passed his 30th birthday and was in his 31st year of life. In the last chapter we determined that Yahushua was born on September 11, 3 BCE. We also know from the way the accounts in Luke and John synchronize, and from John 2:13, that Yahushua began his public ministry shortly before Passover. As Passover in 29 CE Yahushua was about 30 years old, 7 months and 2 weeks of age. So Yahushua's age in Luke 3:23 supports the fact that the fifteenth of Tiberius in Luke 3:1 occurred between January 1 and December 31 of 29 CE.

189   For a detailed discussion of the Appointed Times described in the Scriptures see the Walk in the Light series book entitled "The Appointed Times."

190   Eliyahu David ben Yissachar of www.torahcalendar.com.

191   There is something even more profound here than the defiance of a Pharisaic Tradition. The fact that we are told the specific quantity of water which the jugs could hold (approximately 180 gallons) it is evident that these stone jugs were used for a mikvah. The fact that the scene is a wedding feast points directly to the picture of a bride becoming ritually pure to join physically with her husband. The fact that Yahushua used those pots which were supposed to provide cleansing

to the Bride and filled them with water which then became wine is an incredible picture of the work of the Messiah. At the Last Supper He declared that the wine symbolized His Blood which should take us back to the miracle of turning water into wine. It speaks of the cleansing power of His blood and as the Waters of Life cleanse a bride so the Blood of Messiah cleanses His Bride. This subject is a book in and of itself and I encourage the reader to contemplate upon this miracle which has much more significance than some "magic trick" of turning water into wine as so many simplistically perceive the event at Cana.

[192]   *Jewish New Testament Commentary*, David H. Stern, Jewish New Testament Publications, Inc. (1992) Page 25 (The use of Elohim and the spelling of Yahushua conformed for consistency by this author).

[193]   It is important to understand the difference between justice and mercy. If you are looking for justice all of the time you may get justice in return, but that may not be what you want. You see, we are all deserving of death because we have all intentionally transgressed the Torah at one time or another. Therefore if you want justice, which is something that you deserve, then you can have it – which is death. I prefer mercy – getting something which I do not deserve. Likewise, Yahushua is instructing His followers to be like YHWH - Who is patient and rich in mercy – when dealing with others.

[194]   The Essenes were one of many different Sects of Yisraelites that existed during the time of Yahushua. There is much speculation concerning whether they were a monastic group based at Qumran on the northern end of the Dead Sea or whether they were, in fact, living in and amongst the greater assembly of Yisrael. Much insight into their teachings and beliefs has been gained since the discovery of The Dead Sea Scrolls which also gives us greater insight into the teachings of Yahushua as he was probably referencing an Essene text which stated "...bear unremitting hatred towards all men of ill repute... to leave it to them to pursue wealth and mercenary gain... truckling to a depot." (Man. of Disc. Ix, 21-26).

[195]   This and other differences in readings are discussed in the Walk in the Light series book entitled "The Scriptures." See also the writings and teachings of Bart Ehrman.

[196]   www.beingjewish.com/shabbat/washing.html

[197]   A good example of the difference between the "yoke" of the Torah and the "yoke" of the Pharisees can be seen regarding the Sabbath. While the Torah only has a few specific commands concerning the Sabbath, the takanot of the Pharisees and the Rabbis consists of hundreds, if not thousands of rules and regulations. The yoke of the Torah is light and is meant to guide us in the paths of righteousness while the yoke of men becomes a burden that few, if any, can bear.

[198]   Interpreter's Bible, Exodus 12:6; also The Jewish Encyclopedia, art. Passover, page 553.

[199]   Bemidbar 9:3.

[200]   Encyclopedia Judaica, Volume 13, page 169.

[201]   *The Rod of an Almond Tree in God's Master Plan*, Peter Michas, Winepress Publishing, Appendix 3, (2001).

[202]   *The Jesus Papers*, Michael Baigent, HarperSanFrancisco, p. 118 (2006). While many of the conclusions of the book are deemed erroneous by this author, some of the

historical information is both insightful and informative.

[203] This subject is discussed further in the Walk in the Light series books entitled "Restoration" and "Pagan Holidays."

[204] Josephus, *Antiquities* 18.32f, 35, 89.

[205] Vid. Lydium de re Militari, 1.6.c.3. John Greene – "Roman Celebrations of Victory" www.tpwmi.com/jesusvictory.html

[206] Risto Santala, *The Messiah in the Old Testament - In the Light of Rabbinical Writings*, Keren Ahvah Meshihit, Jerusalem 1992.

[207] There are numerous resources that discuss the statistical probability of a person fulfilling certain numbers or prophecies. One such source looked at the probability of one person during the time of Yahushua fulfilling only 39 of the Messianic prophecies. It was calculated that the statistical probability for such a thing was 1 in 549,755,813,900. Understanding that there have probably been no more than 30 billion people on the earth since creation makes for a very powerful statement. (see brittgillette.com). There are other calculations that show an even higher degree of probability that Yahushua is the Messiah. To the skeptic this is not necessarily convincing because the mathematic assumption is basing the probability on chance. It assumes that a man has no knowledge of these predicted events and has no direct influence on their occurrence. On the contrary, any Yisraelite raised with knowledge of the Scriptures during this period of time in particular would be quite familiar with the prophecies concerning the Messiah – they were no mystery. It stands to reason that anyone who believed himself to be the Messiah would endeavor to see the fulfillment of those related prophecies. Likewise, it would stand to reason that a false messiah would also mimic the prophecies in an attempt to lay claim to the title. Therefore these calculations of chance do not apply to a person who is intentionally trying to fulfill the prophecies which tends to lessen the impact of the statistic, although it certainly does not negate it. As it turns out, neither Mosheh nor the prophets ever advised a person to use statistics to determine the identity of the Messiah. So to base your decision on the identity of the Messiah because of mathematical probability should not be the only deciding factor, but it is nevertheless quite compelling.

[208] The doctrine of Replacement Theology is one of the major problems on the Christian side of the equation which has resulted in division with those in Judaism. It has its roots in hatred and anti-Semitism and is discussed in greater detail in the Walk in the Light Series books entitled "Restoration" and "The Redeemed."

[209] Rabbinic Judaism is not the same faith practiced by the Kingdom of Yisrael that we read about in the Scriptures. Rabbinic Judaism is a religion which was developed largely because of the Great Revolt. After the siege on Jerusalem and the destruction of the Second Temple by Titus in 70 A.D., the Pharisees and possibly only surviving Sanhedrin Yochanan ben Zakkai founded an Academy at Yavneh which became the center of Rabbinic Authority. His predecessor Gamaliel II continued to solidify the power base of the Pharisaic Sect of the Hebrews who, through their cooperation with the Roman Empire, were able to survive the near annihilation which was suffered by the other Yisraelite sects such as the Sadducees, the Essenes, the Zealots, the Sicarii and the Nazoreans. There were still other sects of Yisraelites which history provides scant detail such as the

Therapeutae and those who composed the "Odes of Solomon." In any event, the Pharisees, through the enhancement of Rabbinic authority and the leadership of Rabbi Akiba developed into the leading Yisraelite sect which is now known as Rabbinic Judaism. While Rabbinic Judaism claims to stem directly from Yisrael it is not much different from the Roman Catholic church claiming a direct line of "Popes" to Shimon Kepha. These claims of authority are quite meaningless as neither religious system represents the pure faith found in the Scriptures. Rabbinic Judaism, while it may consist of mostly genetic descendents of Abraham, Yitshaq and Yaakov, is not Yisrael. In other words, you do not have to convert to Judaism to become part of the Commonwealth of Yisrael (i.e. the Kingdom of Elohim) nor do you have to accept Talmudic teaching to follow Elohim. Rabbinic Judaism does not have a Temple nor a priesthood and their Rabbinic power structure is not supported or condoned by the Scriptures. This is why the Talmud, which is not Scripture, is so important in Rabbinic Judaism, because it lends credence to their newly devised system. When the Messiah returns He will set things straight. He will find and lead His sheep and he will not need any Catholic Priests, Christian Pastors, or Jewish Rabbis to help Him.

210   en.wikipedia.org/wiki/Bar_Kokhba's_revolt. There are many problems with both Bar Kokhba and Rabbi Akiba and to properly understand the development of Judaism and Christianity it is critical to understand the essence of the Revolt. Rabbi Akiba, the father of Rabbinic Judaism supported a man who was clearly a false Messiah. He even manipulated facts to support the Messiahship of Bar Kokhba whose real name, ironically, was Bar Kosiba which can mean: "son of a liar." For a very good discussion on this subject see *Rabbi Akiba's Messiah: The Origins of Rabbinic Authority* by Daniel Gruber, Elijah Publishing (1999) ISBN: 0-9669253-1-9.

211   The term "Gentile Converts" is used simply to describe a person who was once a Gentile that repented and joined with Yisrael. It is not meant to imply that they converted to the religions of Christianity or Judaism, which did not actually exist at that time.

212   *Our Father Abraham, Jewish Roots of the Christian Faith*, Marvin R. Wilson William B. Eerdmans Publishing Company, Grand Rapids Michigan 1989 p. 65.

213   Yaakov is the proper translation for the name often refered to as James in the Messianic Scriptures. It is the same name as the patriarch often referred to as Jacob who was renamed Yisrael. This is just another example of how English translations change names which clearly distance the New Testament text from the Torah. Some hold that this was done to honor King James, but does that make it right to alter these important texts. I think not.

214   For a detailed discussion of this subject see *Messiah Conspiracy* by Dr. Philip Moore, RamsHead Press International (1996).

215   *The Islamic AntiChrist*, Joel Richardson WND Books (2009).

216   *50 Jewish Messiahs*, Jerry Rabow Gefen Publishing House 2002.

217   Sahih Muslim Book 041, Number 7015.

218   *Ibid*, Joel Richardson.

219   *Jesus The Jewish Theologian*, Brad H. Young, Hendrickson Publishers, (1995) pp. 63-64.

220   *Ibid*, Brad H. Young at p. 55.

221   Many people are confused by the modern State of Israel and the Set Apart
      Assembly of YHWH called Yisrael. The modern State of Israel is not the same
      as the Assembly of Yisrael and this subject is discussed further in the Walk in the
      Light series book entitled "The Redeemed."

222   This issue is discussed in the Walk in the Light series book entitled "The Final
      Shofar."

223   Companion Bible, Appendix 132 i & ii

224   Yirmeyahu 16:14-15, 23:7-8; Yehezqel 39:27-28; Zekaryah 10:6-12; Yeshayahu 10:20-
      23; 1 Corinthians 10:1-12.

225   For a good descripton of the timing of events and the plan of YHWH see The
      7,000 Year Plan article at torahcalendar.com.

A Note on Dates

Historical dating has long been a subject of controversy and debate in the academic
community. While certain dates involving particular aspects of a civilization
may be agreed upon, others may remain in dispute. This sometimes leads to
problems creating a complete timeline of history. Very recently some intensive
and compelling work has been completed by using astronomical data, particularly
eclipse data, which can then be used to lock together histories of various cultures,
thereby providing an accurate view of history in totality. The dates used in this
book may not always be the same as academia purports, but they are believed to
be the most accurate available. Dates provided by Eliyahu David ben Yissachar,
through the work displayed on www.torahcalendar.com, have been denoted by
placing an asterisk (*) next to them.

Appendix A

Tanak Hebrew Names

Torah - Teaching

English Name	Modern Hebrew	English Transliteration
Genesis	בראשית	Beresheet
Exodus	שמות	Shemot
Leviticus	ויקרא	Vayiqra
Numbers	במדבר	Bemidbar
Deuteronomy	דברים	Devarim

Nebi'im - Prophets

Joshua	יהושע	Yahushua
Judges	שופטים	Shoftim
Samuel	שמואל	Shemu'el
Kings	מלכים	Melakhim
Isaiah	ישעיהו	Yeshayahu
Jeremiah	ירמיהו	Yirmeyahu
Ezekiel	יחזקאל	Yehezqel
Daniel	דניאל	Daniel
Hosea	השוע	Hoshea
Joel	יואל	Yoel
Amos	עמוס	Amos
Obadiah	עבדיה	Ovadyah

Jonah	יונה	Yonah
Micah	מיכה	Mikhah
Nahum	נחום	Nachum
Habakkuk	חבקוק	Habaquq
Zephaniah	צפניה	Zepheniyah
Haggai	חגי	Chaggai
Zechariah	זכריה	Zekaryah
Malachi	מלאכי	Malachi

Kethubim – Writings

Psalms	תהלים	Tehillim
Proverbs	משלי	Mishle
Job	איוב	Iyov
Song of Songs	שיר השירים	Shir ha-Shirim
Ruth	רות	Ruth
Lamentations	איכה	Eikhah
Ecclesiastes	קהלת	Qohelet
Esther	אסתר	Ester
Ezra	עזרא	Ezra
Nehemiah	נחמיה	Nehemyah
Chronicles	דברי הימים	Divri ha-Yamim

Appendix B

Hebrew Language Study Chart

Gematria	Letter	Paleo	Modern	English	Picture/Meaning
1	Aleph	४	א	A	ox head
2	Bet	ㅁ	ב	B, Bh	tent floor plan
3	Gimel	∧	ג	G	foot, camel
4	Dalet	▽	ד	D	door
5	Hey	Ψ	ה	H	man raised arms
6	Waw	٩	ו	W, O, U	tent peg, hook
7	Zayin	⪦	ז	Z	weapon
8	Het	⧉	ח	Hh	fence, wall
9	Tet	⊕	ט	T, Th	basket,container
10	Yud	﹄	י	Y	closed hand
20	Kaph	⩊	כ	K, Kh	palm, open hand
30	Lamed	⌐	ל	L	shepherd staff
40	Mem	∾	מ	M	water
50	Nun	↖	נ	N	sprout, seed
60	Samech	⧧	ס	S	prop, support
70	Ayin	⬭	ע	A	eye
80	Pey	⟃	פ	P, Ph	open mouth
90	Tsade	✝	צ	Ts	hook
100	Quph	९	ק	Q	back of the head
200	Resh	৭	ר	R	head of a man
300	Shin	w	שׁ	Sh, S	teeth
400	Taw	✕	ת	T	mark, covenant

Note: Gematria in a very simple sense is the study of the various numerical values of the Hebrew letters and words. Since there is no separate numerical system in the Hebrew language, all Hebrew letters have a numerical value so it is a very legitimate and valuable form of study. There are many different forms of Gematria. The Gematria system used in this chart is mispar hechrachi, also known as Normative value. The Paleo font used is an attempt to blend the ancient variants into a uniform and recognizable font set that accurately depicts the original meaning of each character.

Appendix C

The Walk in the Light Series

Book 1   Restoration – A discussion of the pagan influences that have mixed with the true faith through the ages which has resulted in the need for restoration. This book also examines true Scriptural restoration.

Book 2   Names – Discusses the True Name of the Creator and the Messiah as well as the significance of names in the Scriptures.

Book 3   Scriptures – Discusses the origin of the written Scriptures as well as many translation errors which have led to false doctrines in some mainline religions.

Book 4   Covenants – Discusses the progressive covenants between the Creator and His Creation as described in the Scriptures which reveals His plan for mankind.

Book 5   The Messiah – Discusses the prophetic promises and fulfillments of the Messiah and the True identity of the Redeemer of Yisrael.

Book 6   The Redeemed – Discusses the relationship between Christianity and Judaism and reveals how the Scriptures identify True Believers. It reveals how the Christian doctrine of Replacement Theology has caused confusion as to how the Creator views the Children of Yisrael.

Book 7   The Law and Grace – Discusses in depth the false doctrine that Grace has done away with the Law and demonstrates the vital importance of obeying the commandments.

Book 8   The Sabbath – Discusses the importance of the Seventh Day Sabbath as well as the origins of the tradition concerning Sunday worship.

Book 9	Kosher – Discusses the importance of eating food prescribed by the Scriptures as a aspect of righteous living.
Book 10	Appointed Times – Discusses the appointed times established by the Creator, often erroneously considered to be "Jewish" holidays, and critical to the understanding of prophetic fulfillment of the Scriptural promises.
Book 11	Pagan Holidays – Discusses the pagan origins of some popular Christian holidays which have replaced the Appointed Times.
Book 12	The Final Shofar – Discusses the walk required by the Scriptures and prepares the Believer for the deceptions coming in the End of Days.

The series began as a simple Power point presentation which was intended to develop into a book with twelve different chapters but ended up being twelve different books. Each book is intended to stand alone although the series was originally intended to build from one section to another. Due to the urgency of certain topics, the books have not been published in sequential order.

For anticipated release dates, announcements and additional teachings go to:
www.shemayisrael.net

Appendix D

The Shema
Deuteronomy (Devarim) 6:4-5

<u>Traditional English Translation</u>

Hear, O Israel: The LORD our God, the LORD is one!
You shall love the LORD your God with all your heart, with all
your soul, and with all your strength.

<u>Corrected English Translation</u>

Hear, O Yisrael: YHWH our Elohim, YHWH is one (unified)!
You shall love YHWH your Elohim with all your heart, with
all your soul, and with all your strength.

<u>Modern Hebrew Text</u>

שְׁמַע יִשְׂרָאֵל יהוה אֱלֹהֵינוּ יהוה אֶחָד
וְאָהַבְתָּ אֵת יהוה אֱלֹהֶיךָ בְּכָל־ לְבָבְךָ וּבְכָל־ נַפְשְׁךָ וּבְכָל־ מְאֹדֶךָ

<u>Ancient Hebrew Text</u>

Ⴈⴼⴳ ⴅⴿⴼⴰ ⴌⴰⴰⴿⴰⴳ ⴅⴿⴼⴰ ⴰⴳⴷⴱⴰ ◎ⴹⴹ
Ⴇⴹⴌ ⴀⴲⴹⴷ ⴇⴲⴳ ⴰⴹⴹ ⴳⴼⴳⴳⴰ ⴅⴿⴼⴰ ⴶⴰ ⴶⴷⴼⴰⴰ
Ⴇ◎ⴳⴹ Ⴇⴲⴷⴷⴰ

<u>Hebrew Text Transliterated</u>

Shema, Yisra'el: YHWH Elohenu, YHWH echad!
V-ahavta et YHWH Elohecha b-chol l'vavcha u-v-chol
naf'sh'cha u-v-chol m'odecha.

The Shema has traditionally been one of the most important prayers in
Judaism and has been declared the first (resheet) of all the Commandments.
(Mark 12:29-30).

Appendix E

Shema Yisrael

Shema Yisrael was originally established with two primary goals: 1) The production and distribution of sound, Scripturally based educational materials which would assist individuals to see the light of Truth and "Walk in the Light" of that Truth. This first objective was, and is, accomplished through Shema Yisrael Publications; and 2) The free distribution of those materials to the spiritually hungry throughout the world, along with Scriptures, food, clothing and money to the poor, the needy, the sick, the dying and those in prison. This second objective was accomplished through the Shema Yisrael Foundation and through the Foundation people were able to receive a tax deduction for their contributions.

Sadly, through the passage of the Pension Reform Act of 2006, the US Congress severely restricted the operation of donor advised funds which, in essence, crippled the Shema Yisrael Foundation by requiring that funds either be channeled through another Foundation or to a 501(c)(3) organization approved by the Internal Revenue Service. Since the Shema Yisrael Foundation was a relatively small and operated very "hands on" by placing the funds and materials directly into the hands of the needy in Third World Countries, it was unable to effectively continue operating as a Foundation with the tax advantages associated therewith.

As a result, Shema Yisrael Publications has effectively functioned in a dual capacity to insure that both objectives continue to be promoted, although contributions are no longer tax deductible. To review some of the work being accomplished you can visit www.shemayisrael.net and go to the "Missions" section.

We gladly accept donations, although they will not be tax deductible. To donate, please make checks payable to: Shema Yisrael Publications and mail to:

Shema Yisrael
123 Court Street • Herkimer, New York 13350

You may also call (315) 939-7940 to make a donation
or receive more information.